Paramahansa Yogananda
January 5, 1893–March 7, 1952

SOLVING THE MYSTERY OF LIFE

COLLECTED TALKS AND ESSAYS ON REALIZING GOD IN DAILY LIFE, VOLUME IV

by

Paramahansa Yogananda

ABOUT THIS BOOK: *Solving the Mystery of Life* is the fourth in the "Collected Talks and Essays Series" of Paramahansa Yogananda's lectures, informal classes, and inspirational writings. Most of these selections are talks that Sri Yogananda gave either at the Self-Realization Fellowship International Headquarters in Los Angeles or at one of the Self-Realization Fellowship temples that he founded. Sri Daya Mata, one of Sri Yogananda's earliest and closest disciples (and president of Self-Realization Fellowship for many years until her passing in 2010), originally recorded many of these talks in shorthand, thus preserving them for the benefit of future generations. First published in Self-Realization Fellowship's magazine, *Self-Realization,* the talks were later compiled by Self-Realization Fellowship and published in a multi-volume series of anthologies, which, in addition to *Solving the Mystery of Life,* includes the books *Man's Eternal Quest, The Divine Romance,* and *Journey to Self-realization.*

Authorized by the International Publications Council of
SELF-REALIZATION FELLOWSHIP
3880 San Rafael Avenue • Los Angeles, CA 90065-3219

The Self-Realization Fellowship name and emblem (shown above) appears on all SRF books, recordings, and other publications, assuring the reader that a work originates with the society established by Paramahansa Yogananda and faithfully conveys his teachings.

First edition, 2025. This printing, 2025.

Library of Congress Control Number: 2024952503

ISBN: 978-1-68568-225-5 (hardcover)
ISBN: 978-1-68568-226-2 (paperback)

Printed in Italy
1530-J8598

Dedicated by Self-Realization Fellowship
to our beloved third president,

SRI DAYA MATA

whose faithful devotion to recording the
words of her guru for posterity has
preserved for us and for the ages the
liberating wisdom and God-love
of Paramahansa Yogananda

THE SPIRITUAL LEGACY OF PARAMAHANSA YOGANANDA

His Complete Writings, Lectures, and Informal Talks

Paramahansa Yogananda founded Self-Realization Fellowship in 1920 to disseminate his teachings worldwide and to preserve their purity and integrity for generations to come. A prolific writer and lecturer from his earliest years in America, he created a renowned and voluminous body of works on the yoga science of meditation, the art of balanced living, and the underlying unity of all great religions. Today this unique and far-reaching spiritual legacy lives on, inspiring millions of truth-seekers all over the world.

In accord with the express wishes of the great master, Self-Realization Fellowship has continued the ongoing task of publishing and keeping permanently in print *The Complete Works of Paramahansa Yogananda*. These include not only the final editions of all the books he published during his lifetime, but also many new titles—works that had remained unpublished at the time of his passing in 1952, or which had been serialized over the years in incomplete form in Self-Realization Fellowship's magazine, as well as hundreds of profoundly inspiring lectures and informal talks recorded but not printed before his passing.

Paramahansa Yogananda personally chose and trained those close disciples who have headed the Self-Realization Fellowship Publications Council since his passing, and gave them specific guidelines for the preparation and publishing of his teachings. The members of the SRF Publications Council (monks and nuns who have taken lifelong vows of renunciation and selfless service) honor these guidelines as a sacred trust, in order that the universal message of this beloved world teacher will live on in its original power and authenticity.

The Self-Realization Fellowship emblem (shown above) was designated by Paramahansa Yogananda to identify the nonprofit society he founded as the authorized source of his teachings. The SRF name and emblem appear on all Self-Realization Fellowship publications and recordings, assuring the reader that a work originates with the organization founded by Paramahansa Yogananda and conveys his teachings as he himself intended they be given.

—*Self-Realization Fellowship*

CONTENTS

ILLUSTRATIONS

Cover: Paramahansa Yogananda, Los Angeles, 1950

PREFACE

The following words were written by Sri Daya Mata (1914–2010), third president and spiritual head of Self-Realization Fellowship/ Yogoda Satsanga Society of India, to introduce Man's Eternal Quest, *Volume I of Paramahansa Yogananda's* Collected Talks and Essays.

The first time I beheld Paramahansa Yogananda, he was speaking before a vast, enraptured audience in Salt Lake City. The year was 1931. As I stood at the back of the crowded auditorium, I became transfixed, unaware of anything around me except the speaker and his words. My whole being was absorbed in the wisdom and divine love that were pouring into my soul and flooding my heart and mind. I could only think, "This man loves God as I have always longed to love Him. He *knows* God. Him I shall follow." And from that moment, I did.

As I felt the transfiguring power of his words on my own life during those early days with Paramahansaji, there arose within me a feeling of the urgent need to preserve his words for all the world, for all time. It became my sacred and joyous privilege, during the many years I was with Paramahansa Yogananda, to record his lectures and classes, and also many informal talks and words of personal counsel—truly a vast treasure-house of wondrous wisdom and God-love. As Gurudeva spoke, the rush of his inspiration was often reflected in the swiftness of his speech; he might speak without pause for minutes at a time, and continue for an hour. While his hearers sat enthralled, my pen was flying! As I took down his words in shorthand, it was as though a special grace had descended, instantly translating the Guru's voice into the shorthand characters on the page. Their transcription has been a blessed task that continues to this day. Even after such a long time—some of my notes are more than forty years old—when I start to transcribe them, they are miraculously fresh in my mind, as though they had been recorded yesterday. I can even hear inwardly the inflections of Gurudeva's voice in each particular phrase.

The Master seldom made even the slightest preparation for his lectures; if he prepared anything at all, it might consist of a factual note or two, hastily jotted down. Very often, while riding in the car on the way to the temple, he would casually ask one of us: "What is my subject today?" He would put his mind on it, and then give the lecture extemporaneously from an inner reservoir of divine inspiration.

The subjects for Gurudeva's sermons at the temples were set and announced in advance. But sometimes his mind was working in an entirely different vein when he began to speak. Regardless of the "subject for today," the Master would voice the truths engrossing his consciousness at that moment, pouring forth priceless wisdom in a steady stream from the abundance of his own spiritual experience and intuitive perception. Nearly always, at the close of such a service, a number of people would come forward to thank him for having enlightened them on a problem that had been troubling them, or perhaps for having explained some philosophical concept in which they were particularly interested.

Sometimes, while he was lecturing, the Guru's consciousness would be so uplifted that he would momentarily forget the audience and converse directly with God; his whole being would be overflowing with divine joy and intoxicating love. In these high states of consciousness, his mind completely at one with the Divine Consciousness, he inwardly perceived Truth, and described what he saw. On occasion, God appeared to him as the Divine Mother, or in some other aspect; or one of our great Gurus, or other saints, would manifest in vision before him. At such times, even the audience would feel deeply the special blessing bestowed on all present. During such a visitation of Saint Francis of Assisi, whom Gurudeva deeply loved, the Master was inspired to compose the beautiful poem, "God! God! God!"

The Bhagavad Gita describes an enlightened master in these words: "The Self shines forth like a sun in those who have banished ignorance by wisdom" (V:16). One might have been overawed by Paramahansa Yogananda's spiritual radiance, were it not for his warmth and naturalness, and a quiet humility, which put everyone instantly at ease. Each person in the audience felt that Gurudeva's talk was addressed to him personally. Not the least of the Master's endearing qualities was his understanding sense of humor. By some choice phrase, gesture, or facial expression he would bring forth an appreciative response of hearty laughter at just the right moment to drive home a point, or to relax his listeners after long and intense concentration on a particularly deep subject.

One cannot convey in the pages of a book the uniqueness and universality of Paramahansa Yogananda's vivid, loving personality. But it is my humble hope, in giving this brief background, to afford a personal glimpse that will enrich the reader's enjoyment and appreciation of the talks presented in this book.

To have seen my Gurudeva in divine communion; to have heard the profound truths and devotional outpourings of his soul; to have recorded them for the ages; and now to share them with all—what joy is mine! May the Master's sublime words open wider the doors to unshakable faith in God, to deeper love for that One who is our beloved Father, Mother, and Eternal Friend.

DAYA MATA

Los Angeles, California
May 1975

INTRODUCTION

Ask yourself what is the purpose of your life. You have been made in the image of God; that is your real Self. Realizing the image of God within you is the ultimate success—infinite joy, fulfillment of every desire, victory over all difficulties of the body and incursions of the world.

—Paramahansa Yogananda

This is the fourth anthology of talks and essays by Paramahansa Yogananda—a sequel to *Man's Eternal Quest* (1975), *The Divine Romance* (1986), and *Journey to Self-realization* (1997). The wisdom in these volumes is not the studied learning of a scholar; it is the empirical testimony of a dynamic spiritual personage whose life was filled with inner joy and outer accomplishment, a world teacher who lived what he taught, a *Premavatar* whose sole desire was to share God's wisdom and love with all.

Meditation has entered the mainstream in the years since the publication of *Journey to Self-realization,* the previous volume in this series of Paramahansa Yogananda's *Collected Talks and Essays.* According to the National Institutes for Health (the primary federal agency for medical research in the United States), the percentage of U.S. adults who practice meditation has more than doubled since the beginning of the 21st century; and in 2024 the United Nations General Assembly unanimously adopted a resolution to declare December 21 as World Meditation Day. Many of course come to meditation for its health benefits, but Paramahansa Yogananda points out that meditation can do much more for us than help to alleviate anxiety and stress. More importantly, he says, it can reveal to us our true nature as immortal souls, made in the image of God. And he explains why experiencing this for ourselves—in reality, not as a merely inspiring thought—is the ultimate purpose of life.

This great purpose of life does not minimize the importance of and the joy that can be found in our everyday lives. Indeed, in this volume Paramahansaji shows how all our daily activities—whether relating to family, career, personal growth, or relationships with others—can be infused with a greater meaningfulness and sense of achievement when we understand our lives in the context of this overarching purpose.

Even as meditation has become more popular, the perception lingers among some that meditation is a way to avoid or escape one's responsibilities to society. On the contrary, Sri Yogananda explains that to seek God within is to simultaneously come to the understanding that God is within *everyone*—all those we encounter in our daily life—friend and "enemy" alike. And with that we realize what we can do to help build a better world, one based on the true source of our common humanity. It is this combination of ideals—to seek God inwardly in meditation, and outwardly in our daily life and in our fellow world citizens—that inspired Paramahansa Yogananda to name his organization *Self-Realization Fellowship.*

"We are all part of the One Spirit," Paramahansaji said. "When you experience the true meaning of religion, which is to know God, you will realize that He is your Self, and that He exists equally and impartially in all beings....Do not settle for intellectual satisfaction about truth. Convert truth into experience, and you will know God through your own Self-realization."

A Unifying Spirituality for the Global Family

Today the world is in a pivotal place. People are faced with countless outer challenges related to rapidly proliferating change and complexity in the fabric of daily life. There is also a rise in the inner challenges related to loneliness, mental illness, and family instability. Many are seeking new ways to amplify healing and find direction through meditation, yoga, positive psychology for personal growth, spirituality that unites rather than divides—and through a more purposeful life of compassion, empathy, and service to causes that contribute to a better world.

In countless awakening souls, there is growing recognition of the need for a more balanced way of living, both individually and as a world civilization. Increasing world interdependencies are revealing the critical need to learn to live as one global family.

Recently there has been tremendous growth in the number of people drawn to the Kriya Yoga teachings of Paramahansa Yogananda from all parts of the world—of all ages, religious affiliations, and cultural backgrounds. This is one sign of the authentic spiritual awakening taking place today around the globe, an awakening that is crucially vital for our world so often in a state of struggle, turmoil, and uncertainty.

All around us, in every department of life, we see how powerfully the nonsectarian "how-to-live" teachings brought by Paramahansaji are resonating with the spiritual needs of the 21st-century global family.

About the Teachings in This Book

Paramahansa Yogananda came from his native India to the United States in 1920.* For the next thirty years he taught the spiritual science of Kriya Yoga meditation and the art of balanced spiritual living to hundreds of thousands, not only in America but in India (during a return visit in 1935–36) and around the globe. He founded Self-Realization Fellowship, with headquarters in Los Angeles, to publish and disseminate his teachings worldwide—and to perpetuate, through disciples trained by him, the spiritual legacy entrusted to him by his lineage of enlightened masters. He described his life's work in his renowned *Autobiography of a Yogi,* which was published in 1946 and remains a best-selling spiritual classic to this day.

The Guru's talks in the earliest years of his ministry were recorded only spasmodically. But when Sri Daya Mata became a disciple of Paramahansa Yogananda in 1931, she undertook the sacred task, faithfully recording, for the generations to come, all of her Guru's talks and classes. This volume is but a sampling: under the direction of Paramahansa Yogananda, many transcriptions—particularly those containing private instruction and meditation techniques and principles given to Self-Realization class students—were compiled along with some of his writings into a series of *Self-Realization Fellowship Lessons;* other talks appear as a regular feature in *Self-Realization* magazine.

Most of the selections in this volume are lectures or classes given at Self-Realization Fellowship temple services or at the international headquarters in Los Angeles. A few of the talks were given at informal gatherings or *satsangas* with small groups of disciples; or at meditation services in which the Guru experienced ecstatic communion with God, affording all present a glimpse of that blissful consciousness.

Glossary and Notes for the Reader

As most of the talks set forth in this book were presented before audiences familiar with Self-Realization teachings, some clarification

* See "About the Author," page 371.

of terminology and philosophical concepts may be helpful to the general reader. To this end, many footnotes have been included; also a glossary explaining certain Sanskrit words, and other philosophical terms, and giving information about events, persons, and places associated with the life and work of Paramahansa Yogananda.

It may be noted here that unless otherwise indicated the quotations from the Bhagavad Gita in this volume are from Paramahansa Yogananda's own translations, which he rendered from the Sanskrit sometimes literally and sometimes in paraphrase, depending on the context of his talk. For most Gita quotations we have used the definitive version given by Paramahansaji for his comprehensive translation and commentary: *God Talks With Arjuna: The Bhagavad Gita—Royal Science of God-Realization* (published by Self-Realization Fellowship in 1995). In talks where he was rendering a Gita passage more freely in order to emphasize a specific point, the paraphrase has been retained and noted as such in the footnote citation.

Revealing the Mystery of Life and the Essence of All Religions

Paramahansa Yogananda honored all the great religions and their founders, and held in respect all sincere seekers of God. Part of his world mission was to reveal the complete harmony and basic oneness of original Christianity as taught by Jesus Christ and original Yoga as taught by Bhagavan Krishna (see *Aims and Ideals of Self-Realization Fellowship,* page 376). This goal saw significant progress with the publication in 2004 of his monumental 1,600 page commentary on the Gospels, *The Second Coming of Christ: The Resurrection of the Christ Within You*. In his writings on the teachings of Jesus, as well as his commentary on the Bhagavad Gita mentioned above, he showed that the practice of yoga establishes an inner attunement with God that constitutes the universal basis of all religions. Abstractions of theoretical religion pale before actual experience of God. Truth cannot be wholly proved to any seeker by another; but by the practice of yoga meditation all of us can prove truth for ourselves through the irrefutable assurance of our own direct experience.

"What is the use of life's difficult journey if we have to go to the grave with still unanswered questions?" Paramahansa Yogananda asks in the title talk for this volume, "Solving the Mystery of Life." "We must find out what life is all about. If we concentrate on God, we find that He had a definite purpose in creating us. We ought to understand that purpose, and it can be understood by meditating on our souls. Right within us is the key to the mystery of everything."

May this volume help you in your search for the Truth that lies within you.

Self-Realization Fellowship

January 2025

SOLVING THE MYSTERY OF LIFE

Expanding Your Consciousness for All-Round Success

Compilation from talks on this subject given in October–November 1939, Self-Realization Fellowship Golden Lotus Temple, Encinitas, California

The door to the kingdom of heaven is in the subtle center of transcendent consciousness at the point between the two eyebrows. If you focus your attention on that seat of concentration, you will find tremendous spiritual strength and help from within. Feel that your consciousness is expanding in divine consciousness. Feel that there are no barriers, no attachments to the body, but that you are moving on and on into the kingdom of God, which can be entered through the spiritual eye.*

Pray with me: "Heavenly Father, open my spiritual eye so that I can enter into Thy kingdom of omnipresence. Father, do not leave me behind in this mortal world of misery; lead me from darkness to light, from death to immortality, from ignorance to endless wisdom, from sorrow to eternal joy."

The Limitless Spiritual Power Within Us

As you march along the twisting and branching pathways of life, seek foremost to discover the path that leads to God. In the time-tested methods of India's illumined *rishis,* the universal way has been shown how to conquer uncertainty and ignorance by following the trail of light divine they have blazed, straight to the Supreme Goal. The teachings of Self-Realization Fellowship are the voice of India's masters, the voice of truth, the voice of scientific

* The single eye of intuition and omnipresent perception at the Christ (*Kutastha*) center (*ajna chakra*) between the eyebrows. The spiritual eye is the entryway into the ultimate states of divine consciousness. By awakening and penetrating the spiritual eye, the devotee experiences successively higher states: superconsciousness, Christ Consciousness, and Cosmic Consciousness. The methods of doing so are part of the Kriya Yoga science of meditation, whose techniques are taught to students of Paramahansa Yogananda's *Self-Realization Fellowship Lessons* (see glossary). *(Publisher's Note)*

God-realization, through which the new world will find understanding, emancipation, and salvation.

It is only in God-consciousness that we attain ultimate freedom, complete redemption. As such, we must try our utmost until we receive from the hands of heaven the certificate of our Heavenly Father's acknowledgment, with which He gives us victory over all things. This world is only a testing place of God wherein He is trying us to see whether we will develop the limitless spiritual power within us or limit ourselves to material attractions. He has remained silent, and it is up to us to choose. I think we will not make a mistake if we follow the teachings that India has given, and in which her masters have specialized. Her supreme gift to the world is the knowledge of how to find God, through step-by-step methods. If you follow the Self-Realization teachings I have brought to you from the Masters of India, you can find God in this life. This I declare unto you. Begin now, before the opportunity is lost and you are whisked away from this earth.

Each word that is coming to you through me is coming from God. And what I tell you, I have experienced. If you practice these truths you will see for yourself that what I am saying is real. I am giving you golden nuggets of truth; they will make you rich in Spirit if you use them to their fullest potential. While the world rushes along, knowing not where, waste not your time in shortsighted pursuits. Why chase after a little money or a little health? These are blind alleys. We appear to be so weak: something goes wrong and we collapse. But behind every bone and fiber, behind our every thought and volition, is the infinite spirit of God. Seek Him, and you shall attain complete victory. You will smile at the world with a smile from within, showing that you have found something far greater than material treasures.

True Success: To Make Your Life a Glory and a Happiness to Yourself and Others

Very few persons understand the expansion of consciousness that constitutes true success. You have come into this world without knowing what marvelous faculties you possess, and most of you live without trying scientifically to develop their potential. As a result, your life on this planet is more or less uncertain. But instead of living an uncontrolled existence, blown about by the winds of seemingly capricious fate, you can live a controlled existence by which you can schedule your life and make it yield what it should yield: an expansion of consciousness that unfolds in all-round development of the divine potentials within you.

Success is when you have so expanded your consciousness that your life is a glory and happiness to yourself and to others. Success is not something achieved at the expense of others. You have seen, when traveling by car, invariably there are some "road hogs"—those who drive too slowly and won't let anyone pass them. On the highway of life, some people are road hogs. They are stubborn in their selfish ways; they neither progress themselves nor give others a chance to go ahead. Miserly persons are one such example, hoarding their wealth instead of using it to create opportunities and well-being for others. Of all the weaknesses of man,* selfishness is one of the meanest demons. By the magnanimous spirit of one's soul it should be conquered.

Real success, rather than being a contraction into self-interest, extends itself in serviceful expansion. The flower, though bound to a stem, by its fragrance and beauty expands its sphere of usefulness. Some blossoms waft their perfume a little distance; others lack fragrance, but still reach out with their beauty to bring us happiness. Trees give of their expansion by providing cool shade and luscious fruits, and converting the waste of carbon dioxide into oxygen for us to breathe. The faraway sun, seemingly small in the sky, radiates beyond its sphere to give us light and warmth. The stars share with us the joy of their jewel-like luster. All of God's expressions in nature send out a vibration that in some way serves the world. You are His highest creation; what are you doing to reach out beyond yourself? Your soul is a beacon of infinite power. You can expand that power from within and give light and health and understanding to others.

Some persons I have met, through the years have not changed at all. They remain always the same, like fossils. The difference between a fossil and a plant is that the fossil is the same now as it was millions of years ago, but the plant keeps on growing. You want to be a living seed. As soon as it is put in the ground, it begins

* In his talks and lectures, Paramahansa Yogananda generally used the masculine gender, as was the custom of his time. His usage, however, was rooted not in the narrowly exclusive sense of the word man, denoting only half of the human race, but in its broader original meaning; the word is derived from the same root as Sanskrit *manas,* mind—the uniquely human capacity for rational thought. The science of yoga deals with human consciousness from the point of view of the essentially androgynous Self (*atman*). As there is no other terminology in English that would convey these psychological and spiritual truths without excessive literary awkwardness, the use of man and related terms has been retained herein.

pushing up and drawing sunlight and air, and then it throws out branches and eventually it becomes a sturdy tree and covers itself with flowers. That is what man is intended to be: an expanding spiritual plant, not petrified wood.

You have the capacity to throw flowering branches of power and success all around you, that the inspiration of your life may waft its influence over the entire cosmos. Henry Ford was only one little man who started his work in a small garage, but by his creative initiative he made himself felt all over the world. The same with George Eastman, who invented the Kodak. There is a place in heaven for successful people—and they enjoy that heaven. I am speaking of what I know from my own experience. Every great man who has made something of himself in this world by exercise of the God-like powers in the soul has recognition in heaven.

Activate the Divine Law for Progress and Success

This creation is not run by blind forces. It operates according to an intelligent plan. If God created hunger but didn't think of creating food to satisfy that hunger, where would we be? It is unreasonable to suppose that this world is just a chance result of different combinations of atoms, with no guiding intelligence behind those atoms. On the contrary, it is evident that there is law and order in the universe. Your life, and all life, is governed with mathematical precision by God's intelligently framed cosmic laws. So by the divine law of action or karma, cause and effect, everything that you do is recorded in your soul. Thus, according to the measure of your work, whatever you accomplish through will power and creativity will be your passport after death to the heavenly regions earned by dutiful souls. And when you reincarnate in this world, you will be born with those mental powers developed by your previous efforts.

Suppose one is born in this life with a sickly body and a paucity of material goods and advantages, but still tries unto death to do everything to the best of his ability. His refusal to acknowledge failure creates a dynamic magnetism that will attract health, helpful friends, prosperity, and so on in his next incarnation. Or suppose one makes the determination: "I will do something magnanimous to serve humanity," but he dies before he has a chance to see through to completion his noble undertaking. When he comes back again, that determined resolution will carry over into his new life, along with those mental powers necessary to accomplish that goal. All so-called "hereditary" advantages and "lucky" opportunities in life are not the whims of chance but the lawful result of causes set in motion by one's own actions, sometime in the past. That is why you must start to achieve something now to insure your future success.

To activate that law of action you must be active. Exercise your powers, rather than ossifying in inertia. So many people are lazy and lacking in ambition—doing the bare minimum of work to somehow live and eat until they die. Such a slothful existence is hardly worthy of being called life. To be alive is to be on fire with purpose, to move forward with undaunted determination toward a goal. You must be enthusiastically active, make something of yourself, and give something worthwhile to the world. It is because my Master [Swami Sri Yukteswar] strengthened in me the conviction that I could be something that I made the effort to achieve, in spite of all the forces that tried to stop me.

Many individuals think great things, but do not act on them. However, it is the activity that creates the greatness. Unless you actually accomplish, you are not successful. It is not enough just to think success or think ideas; they must be demonstrated. To think you are virtuous does not make you virtuous. So thinking success does not make you successful. You may say, "I am an admirable spiritual person"; but only if you behave spiritually are you spiritual. All action begins with thought, which is action on the plane of consciousness. To be manifested, thoughts must be charged with dynamic will by concentration and perseverance to rouse the indomitable power of the mind. Thus, to think greatness is a first step, but then you must empower the idea with will and set in motion the corresponding laws of action. "Understanding this, wise men who have sought after salvation, since pristine times, have performed dutiful actions. Therefore, do thou also act dutifully, even as did the ancients of bygone ages."*

Overcoming Obstructions Around You and Within You

It is inevitable in this world of relativity—light and darkness, good and evil—that whenever you try to expand, you will meet enemies. This holds true in all endeavor: The minute you try to accomplish anything, there is resistance. As soon as a plant tries to emerge from its seed, first there is resistance from the earth, and then the bugs go after it, and then it has to struggle against the weeds that compete for its food and water. The plant needs help from the

* Bhagavad Gita IV:15.

gardener. And the same is true for human beings. If because of adverse circumstances or inner weaknesses you haven't the strength to put forth branches of success on the tree of your life, you need the assistance of a teacher, or guru, who can help you cultivate the power of your mind. The guru teaches you the art of meditation, of cauterizing the weeds of limiting habits and bad karma that are trying to choke your ground. You must resist these enemies; you must go on trying. Without battle you cannot achieve anything. But neither do you willfully hurt anybody with ruthless tactics to get your way. You use the spiritual powers of mind and will to conquer the obstructing forces and circumstances around you and the self-engendered limitations within you. Then you can be what you want to be, and accomplish what you want to accomplish.

Remember, you have the power to be strong. Right behind your consciousness is the omnipotence of God. But instead of utilizing that divine strength, you have built up a solid wall between yourself and His power. Your concentration is always focused outside, dependent on the material body and world, instead of inside on the Divine Indweller.* That is why you think you have limitations.

Strengthening the Success-Producing Power of the Mind

Then what is the way of expansion, the way of progress? It is to look within, to release your inner powers. Each one of you can do so. Start today. Mind is the principal thing; it is the instrument of God by which everything is created. It is most flexible; it will create according to any pattern of thought. Mind makes health and spirituality, disease and ignorance. What is disease but the thought of disease? What is ignorance but the thought of ignorance? What is failure but the thought of failure? I have studied all walks of life, and I see those who do not succeed are those who do not cultivate the power of the mind.

To try for success in any worthwhile endeavor is to increase the power of your mind. As your mind power develops, so does your magnetism, the attractive force generated within you that draws conditions and persons that promote success. Worthwhile relationships are important to you. You do not want the advantages of success without friends (be they family loved ones or supportive acquaintances) who will appreciate and help you, and with whom

* "Ye are the temple of the living God; as God hath said, I will dwell in them, and walk in them; and I will be their God, and they shall be my people" (II Corinthians 6:16).

you can share your happiness. The high quality of your mind power and magnetism will attract those friends who contribute to the meaningfulness of your life. Do your part to make lasting friendships by being a true friend. Try to improve your own personality. The Lord has made you something unique. Nobody has anything quite like what you have. You have a face and a mind that no one else has. You should be proud of yourself and not indulge in envy and self-pity. Be a straight shooter, be fearless, be honest, be kind, compassionate, understanding, interested in others without being intrusively curious. The silent vibrations of your mind power and magnetism will speak to others of your sterling qualities.

Break Out of the Cubicle of Your Limitations

The tendency is to think, "I am what I am. I cannot be different." Believe that, and you are doomed to stay that way! If you reason, "I have this much ability, and I can do no more," you are certain to remain just where you are. You forget that in your youth you were filled with ambition, afire with conviction that you could "conquer the world." But gradually the world closed in on you; you were captured by enemies of pessimism, inertia, and naysaying preconceptions that pigeonholed you and your capacities to achieve. Do not remain in that cubicle for the rest of your life.

There is a way to break free. For a small nation, surrounded by enemies, it is difficult to achieve independence or expand its territory; but that is because the barriers are outside. In achieving mental and spiritual independence, it is not a question of external obstructions. The confining barrier is yourself and the bad habits that you have created. You concentrate on your limitations and the mental hedges you have cultivated. By your own decree you have imprisoned yourself and precluded your development. But whatever boundaries you have created you can undo and destroy, provided you go about it in the right way.

The ordinary man's consciousness is like a small house; that is his kingdom. Perhaps he looks a little beyond, but he has no wish to expand. And some people mentally and spiritually are locked up in a tiny room, their aspirations closeted by a dogmatic conviction of ordinariness. These "walking dead" lack belief in any possibility of conquering new ground.

Do you realize that each one of you is potentially a spiritual giant, a spiritual counterpart to the powerful Genghis Khan, who was one of the most successful conquerors in history. Of course, earthly conquest is not so laudable if it brings in its wake bloodshed and suffering. One may conquer worldly dominions and reign over an opulent kingdom, but still be a slave to misery and fears. To be a conqueror of self is to be truly victorious—to conquer your circumscribed consciousness and expand your spiritual powers without limit. You can go as far as you want to go, past all limitations, and live a supremely victorious existence.

Break out of the mental cell of ignorance that has you confined. Think differently. Refuse to be limited by thoughts of weakness or age. Who told you that you are old? You are not old. You, the soul, are eternally young. Impress that thought on your consciousness: "I am the soul, a reflection of ever-youthful Spirit. I am vibrant with youth, with ambition, with power to succeed." Your thoughts can limit you or they can free you. You are your worst enemy, and you are your best friend. You have all the power to accomplish what you want, if you motivate yourself, if you remove the mental kinks that are blocking the flow of conviction.

The Antidote for "Can't Consciousness"

I have seen persons who, despite ill health, have made up their minds to achieve something. Their ailing body was always trying to divert their attention, but they overcame that physical barrier and undeterred went on and on, realizing their goal by sheer strength of mind. And I have seen others with wonderful health, but peanut brains. No matter how you try to convince them, they say, "I can't do it." They are stopped by the mental barrier of feeling inadequate. And some people have both health and intelligence, but they do not succeed because they have spiritual barriers of bad habits. Whether from physical, mental, or spiritual causes, failure starts with the avowal, "I can't do it." Such is the force of the mind and the vibratory power of words. When you say to yourself, "I can't do it," no one else in the whole world can change that decree. You must destroy that paralyzing enemy: "I can't."

There is an antidote for "can't consciousness": the affirmation "I can!" Create that antidote with your mind and administer it with your will.

The companionate impediment must also be vanquished: "I can do it, but I *won't* do it." Many people have this mindset, because it is much easier to sit and do nothing. The worst sin against your progress and success is to be mentally lazy. Physical laziness is sometimes forgivable because you have worked hard and the body wants to rest. But mental laziness is absolutely inexcusable; it petrifies your mind. If you forsake "won't" laziness, if you make up your mind that "I have got to do it, and I must do it, and I will do it," success will surely materialize.

Throw out all negative thoughts. Overcome the idea that you cannot do a thing by simply starting to do it. And then continuously keep on doing it. Circumstances will try to slap you down, to make you become discouraged and again say, "I can't do it." If there is a devil, that devil is "I can't do it." That is the satan that has disconnected your dynamo of eternal power; it is the main reason you do not succeed in life. Throw that demon out of your consciousness by your indomitable conviction: "I *can* do it." Mean it, and affirm it as often as you can. Mentally believe it, and energize that belief by acting on it with will power. Work! And while you work, never give up the thought, "I can do it." Even if there are a thousand obstacles, do not relent. If you have that determination, then what you go after must inevitably come to pass; and when it does, you will say, "Well, it was so easy!"

So why should you surrender to inertia and live in a crust of ignorance? Isn't it better to burst that shell of "can't" into the free air of "I can"? Then you will know that mind is all-powerful; anything your mind can think can be materialized. There is no obstruction but your "can't" consciousness. See how wonderful is the way of expansion I am showing you. The words, "I can, I must, and I will"—that is the way to change yourself and achieve absolute victory.

God Has Given You Mental Dynamite

You will never win unless you make the effort. God has given you mental dynamite sufficient to destroy all your difficulties. Remember that. It is the most effective force you can use to be victorious in life, to break free of limiting weaknesses and habits into an all-accomplishing expansion of your consciousness. Are you going to remain a walking dead person, ready to be buried in the grave beneath the debris of your errors? No! Do something in this world—do something wonderful! Whatever you do will be recognized by God. And even if the world fails to recognize you, if you have done everything you can, that infused mental power will remain with your soul. Wherever you go—in this life or beyond—you will have with you that invincible spirit. As the Lord Krishna exhorted the warrior-prince Arjuna: "O Scorcher of Foes, forsake this small weakheartedness! Arise!"*

I have used that power of mind throughout my life, and I have seen it work. You, also, when confronted by ill health and failure, should meditate deeply and mentally affirm: "Almighty Father, I am Thy child. I shall use my inherited divine powers of mind and will to shatter the causes of failure." Rally those mental forces at night, when the distractions of the world recede and your mind is highly focused and recharged in meditation, prayer, and God-communion.

What more shall I say to you? These thoughts are practical; they work. And if you make up your mind to use them, and get busy, they *will* work. You can demolish your difficulties; you can break down the ramparts of ignorance that have enclosed you for incarnations. You will know that as an immortal child of God, death cannot kill you, nor can birth in this fleshly cage completely inhibit the transcendent power within you.† By the soul you must redeem the soul, that no matter where you are, you have at your command the irresistible divine powers of mind and will to vanquish every obstacle in your path!

Material Achievements Do Not Constitute Real Success

Ask yourself what is the purpose of your life. You have been made in the image of God; that is your real Self. Realizing the image of God within you is the ultimate success—infinite joy, fulfillment of every desire, victory over all difficulties of the body and incursions of the world.

Human life is a constant confrontation with problems. Everyone has a different problem to face: fifteen hundred million people, and fifteen hundred million different problems to be coped with every day. Some have heart trouble, some have colds; some have too much money, some have none; some have anger, some have a bland indifference; but who has happiness? The real measure of success is happiness: Whatever your position in life, are you happy?

The common idea of success means having wealth and friends and beautiful possessions—the so-called "good life." But material

* Bhagavad Gita II:3.

† "No weapon can pierce the soul; no fire can burn it; no water can moisten it; nor can any wind wither it. The soul is uncleavable; it cannot be burnt or wetted or dried. The soul is immutable, all-permeating, ever calm, and immovable—eternally the same" (Bhagavad Gita II:23–24).

achievements do not necessarily constitute real success, because things and conditions are subject to change. Today you may have; tomorrow you may not have. So do not think that just by becoming a millionaire you can consider yourself successful.

You may work hard to reap success in business, but before you realize it your life becomes unbalanced, leaving you no freedom to enjoy the things you want to do, and giving you such worry and nervousness that your health breaks down. Suddenly all your success means nothing and you feel that you have wasted your life. Or by concerted effort you may develop a healthy body, and yet find yourself so poor that you are miserable in being unable to satisfy its needs. You may even have both health and money, but still feel that inner fulfillment has eluded you; catering only to the body and ego will never satisfy the soul. You may have everything, and yet find that ultimately it amounts to nothing at all, because you have no happiness. Unless there is happiness in the heart, you have no success.

However, very few can be happy without possessing at least an adequate quantum of money and health. Most persons must have something to be happy about; their happiness is conditional on outer circumstances, because the mind has not been trained to be unconditionally happy from within. You think you would be happy if only you could acquire all the things you feel you need in order to be happy. But desire begets desires; and satisfaction will never come if you go on multiplying your wants. Before you buy something, you think you cannot do without it; but once you have it, you think little of it as you begin to wish for something better. No matter how often you experience this, when you are in the grip of an impulse to buy something new, again you feel you must have it and will not be happy until you do. Success lies in learning the art of inner contentment: Acquire what you need, and then be satisfied with what you have.

Don't Be Enslaved by Temptation to Live Beyond Your Means

Some people are habitual impulse buyers of things they don't need. They fritter away their funds. Get in the habit of shopping carefully and buying wisely. If you have some extra money, save it; don't "hark to the shark" who is always tempting you to hand over your earnings for some new "must-have" gadget or "guaranteed" investment. Whenever someone lures you with silver-tongued propositions, remember the story about the fox and the crow. The crow had a sweetmeat in its mouth and the fox wanted that tidbit. The fox, being foxy, said: "Please sing for me, Mr. Crow; you have such a beautiful voice." The crow was flattered and started to sing; but as soon as it opened its mouth, it dropped the sweetmeat. The crafty fox picked it up and ran away. Beware of anyone who psychologizes you; he wants something from you. Never be cajoled by anybody's attempt to manipulate you to desire something unnecessary to your real happiness and success.

Simplify your life, so that you are not dependent upon too many possessions. To feed your every desire automatically creates unhappiness. I compare the American civilization with the Indian civilization: All the progressive advantages I wanted for India, to alleviate her poverty and physical suffering, I see here. But I find that most of the so-called successful persons here are just as miserable with their wealth as are the less fortunate in India without it.

Western life is so full of complexities; you have no time to enjoy anything. But if you examine your life, you will find there are lots of ways that you can simplify without feeling deprived. Realize the folly of desiring more and more luxuries bought on installment plans. Save up for what you need and pay for those needs outright—no installment plans with high interest to worry about. Of course, there is value in giving business to others who must sell their goods to make a living. But don't be enslaved by temptation to live beyond your means; for when you come to a tight corner, everything will be gone.

Save something out of each paycheck. To live without capital is a weakness courting disaster. Better to have a smaller car and home and some savings in the bank for emergencies, which are bound to come. It is a great mistake to spend all you receive just to get something new or luxurious. I think both husbands and wives independently should have a little nest egg in the bank, as well as a joint savings, on which they can rely when an unexpected need arises.

Saving is an art, and it requires sacrifice. But if you buy frugally, and live simply, you will be able to save something every week or month. I see so many workers who spend on unnecessary things, and consequently they are always in debt. I remember a couple who had a beautiful home in Florida. Whenever they saw something they liked they immediately bought it on the installment plan. But the time came when that home was only a terror in their minds. I said, "These are not your things. You don't own them. You have just borrowed them on installments. Why are you afraid to lose them? Why not live more simply without this constant worry that is destroying all your peace and enjoyment?" Because of their indebtedness, they did finally lose everything. They had to go back to the simple life and start all over again.

It is possible to enjoy vicariously so many of the good and beautiful things in life without the terrible nervous depression of worry about how to pay for owning them. Lots of desires can be satisfied that way.

Analyze Your Desires Before Acting on Them

A worthwhile desire is like a divine steed which, instead of leading you to the valley of darkness, will lead you toward the kingdom of God. Analyze each desire as to whether it will contribute to your spiritual welfare and betterment. Anything that leads you away from material enslavement to the kingdom of true happiness is the right kind of desire. Every motivation is good that brings forth a flower of God's manifest qualities and understanding. If anyone hurts you and you forgive him, you are leading yourself to the kingdom of God. If anyone is quarrelsome and you give understanding, you are taking yourself to the kingdom of God. If someone is suffering and you reach out with aid and compassion, you are moving into the presence of God.

True success is dependent on attainment of a proper desire—not when you are bent on acquisition at the cost of others' welfare. Riches achieved through reprehensible means may appear outwardly to be success; but inwardly your soul will not be at rest. Your conscience is like a shoe: When it doesn't fit, it may look nice outwardly; but no matter how carefully you walk, you know exactly where that shoe pinches. One who is good before his conscience is good before God as well. Do not stand convicted before your conscience. If your conscience is clear you can stand against the opinion of the world; no matter how dense the darkness around you, you shall pierce the gloom. Materially ambitious people pursue their passion for success and do not care if it comes by wrong means. Regardless of what they may achieve, they are never really successful, for they are never happy. If you want to succeed, do it in an honorable way.

True success achieves those things and fulfills those desires that are wholesome—beneficial to one's physical, mental, and spiritual welfare. As soon as you are confronted with some inner urge, ask whether that desire is wholesome or not. Know the difference between motivations that are good for you and those that are not. Use reason and discrimination when going after success in fulfilling your desires.

The Successful Person Is Characterized by Self-Control

Harmless pleasures are all right; but those that hurt your mind and body are bad. Anything that enslaves you is not good. The power for our well-being and lasting happiness lies in self-control, in being able to do what we ought to do when we ought to do it, and in totally avoiding what we should not do. The successful person is characterized by self-control; he is unbound by whims and habits. To have complete mastery is to eat when and what you should eat; and when you shouldn't eat, you don't eat. When you want to mix with people, you mix wholeheartedly; and when you need time to be alone, you don't mix. If you use your time wisely in worthwhile activities, you and your life, as an extension of yourself, will be worthwhile. Worldly people want to sponge your time; they want to pull you to their level. Why settle for uselessness? Use your time in introspection for self-development, and in creative thinking and deep contemplation, and you will have great power over yourself.

If people persist in bothering you during your quiet times, or if you need respite from inharmonies at home, go to some peaceful place and stay alone for a while, listening to the soft sounds of nature and of God within. All the happiness you seek lies within you, in the image of God within you. Why settle for spurious imitations of happiness in drink, movies, and sensual gratifications? That is the way of the world. True happiness needs no supports. As a poet wisely philosophized: "Having nothing, yet having all."

Remain Unconquered in Spirit Through All Challenges and Trials

You can learn to be happy at will and to hold on to that happiness within, no matter what happens. Some people are absolutely crushed by their tests; others smile on in spite of their difficulties. Those who are unconquered in spirit are the real successes in life. If you can so train or condition your mind that you are content regardless of what you have or do not have, and if you can stand the challenge of all your trials and remain calm—that is true happiness. Suppose you are suffering from a terrible disease; when you are asleep you are happily rid of it. Resolve to have that mental aboveness at all times; make up your mind to be happy at all costs.

Jesus had such success in controlling his mind that he could willingly endure crucifixion and even resurrect his body after death. That was a demonstration of supreme success. His unconditional joy in God is the kind of success everyone is ultimately to achieve. It lies in owning yourself; when you, the soul, are able to be the boss of your life.

Say to your mind, "I am the boss; I am happy now, not tomorrow—when all the 'if' conditions are fulfilled." If you can command yourself to be happy at will, God will be with you, for He is the Fountainhead of all rivulets of joy. You don't know the power of the mind. If you are happy, it creates a positive vibratory attitude that can attract health and money and friends—everything you seek. Contrarily, when you are not happy, when you have a negative attitude, your will is paralyzed. Success in anything is dependent on being able to attract what you need by a strong, positive, happy will.

Analyze whether you have made a success of yourself. If you are habitually depressed, it is because you haven't made a success of your life. Things you have been wishing for years since childhood remain unfulfilled, and your morose mind has adopted a what's-the-use attitude. Revive your worthwhile goals with an energized will.

Success Means Creative Power to Attain What You Need

Success is not to be measured by how much material wealth is possessed, but whether you are able to create at will what you need. Think of that power; it comes from the superconscious mind, the infinite capacity of the soul. If you use that power to infuse your creative ability, you can overcome any difficulty that obstructs your path.

Suppose you need a car and you have the power to get it (by right means)—that is success. Suppose you need a house and you have the power to acquire it—you are successful. Suppose you want to have the right companion to share your life, and you pray to God to guide you and you meet that person—that is success. But how to go about achieving the power that makes for that kind of success at will? How to control the conditions that promote success instead of being controlled by your self-created cause-effect destiny? Very few in the world put forth enough determination and will to control their destiny.

Consider your immediate needs and always pray to God that you might have the creative power and will to meet them. Remember that man has not invented anything; he only discovers what God had already created in His ideations and made manifest in the causal world of thought from which all things in heaven and earth come into being. Therefore, the secret of success is to get more and more in tune with God.

Three Creative Powers: The Conscious, Subconscious, and Superconscious Minds

You have three tremendous powers given to you by your Creator—your conscious mind, subconscious mind, and superconscious mind. You mostly use your conscious mind with its sensory input and its ability to reason. You are not that much acquainted with the other two minds, so their potential remains largely undeveloped.

Environment influences conscious effort. In a community someone creates a successful business and suddenly others see the area as holding a fertile opportunity to start similar rival businesses. As a result, some are bound to fail. One needs to employ all the power of discriminative reason at his command in considering the potential effects of environment in his field of endeavor. Ill-conceived hasty determinations are a sure formula for failure, and an insult to the willing-to-help abilities of the conscious mind.

There is always opportunity for success. Condition your conscious mind power to watch for opportunities—to recognize the little openings that take you where you want to go, and to seize those opportunities that are consistent with your goals.

By every honest effort, use your conscious mind to succeed. There is so much capacity in that mind—reason, discrimination, creative thought, will power, concentration. Search out opportunities by being more aware, and then apply yourself with concentration to your tasks. First, find out your abilities and then apply yourself. Whatever you are interested in, go after that; the seeds of success are best nurtured by an enthusiastic interest.

Do not get lost in wrong influences. The conscious mind is easily discouraged by the limitations imposed on it by environment and the suggestions of people. In the beginning I was considered useless by my family because I did not seek the offerings of the world. But I resisted their disparaging thoughts. As soon as you accept the limitations of external conditions and naysayers, your creativity and will to succeed become paralyzed. That is the analysis applicable to everyone who has failed in life.

Using the Instrument of the Subconscious Mind

Next, in controlling destiny, is to employ the instrumentality of your subconscious mind; the mental faculty behind the conscious mind. That mind is the memory and habit mind. It stores all of your experiences and solidifies your thoughts and actions into habit patterns. Anything that you do with conscious attention, your subconscious mind saves in a blueprint in your brain. If you think you are a failure, a blueprint of failure is set in your subconscious mind. That preset conclusion is disastrous to the processes of success, a major reason for which people fail. No matter what your conditions in life, or the outcome of your efforts, you have no right to think failure, to hypnotize your mind with that belief.

Whatever you want to accomplish, affirm and believe in its attainment, in spite of contrary evidence. Create the pattern of success in your subconscious mind and make it work for you. Sit quietly and think deeply about your goal; concentrate on how to attain it. When you are still, when your restless and "can't do it" thoughts quiet down, the new convictions in your subconscious mind can help you. As you go deep into thought and begin to think a problem through, you go beyond the limits of the conscious mind and can feed into the conscious processes of reason valuable information from the memories and from the imaginative creativity of the subconscious mind.

The All-Knowing Power of the Superconscious Mind

Behind the subconscious mind is the superconscious mind. The power of God within you, the power of limitless control, lies in the superconscious mind. That mind cannot be suggested with failure, but it can be eclipsed by the suggestion of failure. The superconscious mind is the all-knowing intuitive consciousness of the soul. That mind can be tapped in deep concentration and in soul-contact in meditation.

Remind yourself always, no matter what comes, "I have the power to succeed. And though the conscious mind is conditioned to my environment, the Lord has given me unlimited power in the superconscious mind and the subconscious mind. As I begin to control them, I shall be able to control my destiny." There is no jinx in your destiny except in lack of application of the powers of your conscious mind, and in the bad habits ingrained in your subconscious mind. You must never be discouraged; to be discouraged is to admit failure, to trademark yourself with failure. If your conscious mind says, "I can't do it," the subconscious mind records that failure thought; and the more you think negatively, the deeper you drive that failure idea into the library of your subconscious mind. Then you are done for—unless you again make the conscious effort to do away with the persistent conviction of failure by taking positive steps to think and act with a confident will.

When you think, "I can succeed," think it so deeply that you drive out any notion of failure. If nine times you try to succeed, but you fail, still you can try the tenth time! Do not give up; never admit failure.

Practical Application of Intuition

Begin every venture by asking for God's help: "Lord, I shall try my utmost, but guide me to do the right thing and to avoid mistakes." Then you must use your intelligence and reason to determine how to accomplish what you want to achieve. At every step, pray to God for guidance; feel His assurance in the intuition of inner calmness. That is what I do. After I use the intelligence of my conscious mind, I use my intuitive power as well as the other powers of my subconscious and superconscious minds; and I see that the creative divine light comes to guide me, without fail.

There is always uncertainty in depending only on the material ways of success. But the intuitive way of success is different. Intuitive perception can never be wrong. It comes by an inner sensitivity, a feeling by which you know in advance whether or not you are going to succeed by following your determined course.

The testimony of the senses and the rational mind may tell you one thing while the testimony of the intuition tells you otherwise. You should follow the testimony of the senses first—learn all you can about your goal and the practical steps needed to achieve it. Whether you are investing your money, starting a business, changing your occupation, after you have investigated, compared, and applied your intelligence to the limit, don't rush headlong into it. When your reason and investigation points to one thing, then meditate and pray to God. In inner silence, ask the Lord if it is all right to go ahead. If you pray deeply and earnestly and find that something is turning you from it, don't do it. But if you have an irresistible positive impulse, and you pray and pray and go on praying and this impulse still persists, then go ahead. Your prayer for guidance must be sincere, so that whatever impulse you feel will be from God and not mere reinforcement of your own flawed desire.

That is the way I developed the practical application of my intuition. Before starting any endeavor, I sit in meditative silence in my room and go on expanding that power in my mind. Then I throw the concentrated light of my mind on what I want to accomplish. I know my thoughts have worked; what I perceive in that state must come to pass.

After all, we are the most powerful of receiving and broadcasting stations. The little barrier of flesh means nothing. Our thoughts are powerful creative forces floating in the ether ready to accomplish their purpose when they are concentrated and consciously directed. But most persons do not know how to make their thoughts work for them. Their minds are full of static. Concentration and meditation tunes those thoughts and focuses them on manifesting success.

Enlarge Your Success by Helping Others to Help Themselves

A selfish agenda limits success. You should express the universal consciousness of your soul. You don't have to work only through the hands and brain of your own body. You can make your influence so widely felt that your goodness works through thousands of hands and brains. You think of your little body, how to feed, clothe, and give it comfort. I think of how to better the lives of thousands of souls, of being successful in giving people their own power of strength and wisdom. The satisfaction this gives is beyond words.

The success I have found in helping people to help themselves is a success that no one can destroy. It has been fun to do things for God. I have no ambition for myself, but I have much ambition for God, and for sharing Him with all. Unless you sacrifice some of your desires for the welfare of others, you can never be a real success. If you include the welfare of others in your efforts to succeed, you have a greater chance to be successful than if you think only of yourself. And above all else think of God and ask Him to guide you. I would have had a lot more trouble with the building of this society if I had not received inner divine direction, because each one who came wanted me to do it his way. This organization will succeed because I have followed God's way. Satan always tries to obstruct good works, but God shows the way to overcome all evils.

The Ultimate Success: To Be With God All the Time

Our purpose in life is to know the meaning of this universe. It is only a dream of God, just like a motion picture, which reveals great drama or comedy and then is over and forgotten. So is life. It seems so real and so permanent, but it will be over with shortly. All your problems and struggles will be forgotten when you leave this world for the better world of the afterlife. So do not take this life too seriously; look behind this drama to the Master of this universe, the Author of this dream play.

Many people say, "I will never be able to realize God." That is the hardest thought to remove. But as you pray and pray and never mind how many times God does not answer, if still you pray, still you love Him, then only will you succeed. Even eons of seeking God are nothing compared to eternity with Him. When you continuously pour out your heart in demanding God-realization, you will surely find His answer.

Do not waste your time. The way to true success is to be with God all the time. Seek Him first. Do not remain stagnant; laziness is not happiness. At night be with Him. And awaken in the morning ready to battle with the world, with Him by your side. With faith in your power to succeed say, "Come along, world. I am ready!" You will control your destiny; one by one your shackles will fall away. You will know that you are no longer a prodigal wanderer on earth, but that you have reclaimed your heritage as a son of God.

The only reason I am here with you is to declare what God has given to me. Finding the Supreme Power, I found the thirst of all my desires quenched forever. Don't delay; follow these teachings, that you may feel the wonderful things I have felt on this path. It has not only given me complete harmony in body and mind, but also contentment and happiness indescribable, and His constant guidance. You shall feel His presence in the caressing breeze; you shall see His bursting ever new joy in the ocean; He will warm you in the sunshine. He will watch you through the over-arching sky; and the heavenly bodies of stars and moon and sun will be windows to His presence. From His everywhereness you will see His benign eyes peering at you with love.

Every morning when you begin your day, think not only of serving your own welfare, but of how many others you can help. For their own betterment, interest them in the cause of Self-Realization Fellowship. If you are all interested in truth as much as I am, how great shall be our power to banish ignorance from the world. Everything that you do to help others in the way of this spiritual path will be remembered by the Father.

Feel the Power of Spirit Moving Through You

Now, close your eyes and concentrate within. Feel great peace within you. Feel peace all around you. Feel the power of Spirit moving through the calm portals of your mind; feel the peaceful glow of the Father within. He is hiding in every thought, in every cell, in everything within you. Feel Him.

Let us pray: "Heavenly Father, I am no longer surrounded by barriers of 'I can't.' I have within me Thy great explosive power of 'I can!' Lord, bless me that I develop that power, so that I may destroy all my barriers and expand my territory beyond the limitations of my existence until I conquer the forces of this earth and of Thy cosmos by being one with Thee."

Solving the Mystery of Life

Compilation of talks on the same subject, given at Self-Realization Fellowship Golden Lotus Temple, Encinitas, California, December 29, 1940, and three weeks later at Self-Realization Fellowship International Headquarters, Los Angeles, January 19, 1941

The only purpose of life is to find God. Until you remember that, all the pathways of earthly life—all efforts to attain fulfillment—lead to blind alleys. When you find a little happiness, and then comes sudden disease or sorrow; when the hopefulness of youth gives way to the sobering realities of adulthood; when you earn perhaps millions of dollars and yet find yourself bored with all the things money can buy; when you see all your loved ones die, one by one—then the mystery of life begins to thicken, and you ask: "What is it all about?"

The Self-Realization Approach to Life's Essential Questions

Science is marching on; and religion, instead of lagging behind or heaping more darkness on others, should adopt a scientific attitude. It is time for you to cut your cords of superstitions and make yourself free, for you are a child of God. Unless you acknowledge that, and find the image of God within you, you shall not be free. No one can free you from ignorance and suffering until you open your own eyes of wisdom. If you follow the principles that we teach, you will free your self by yourself.

So follow the *Lessons* that are sent out from Self-Realization Fellowship. You will find in them the study of a lifetime. Through them you will find freedom from the prison of mortal life—and from the millions of questions that lie unanswered in your brain. Why are we here? What is our destiny, and how can we control it? What is God and why did He make this earth? And if God is good, why is there evil in this world? What must we do in order to have joy? These are the questions that constantly pound on the doors of our souls.

Answers will be found in the *Lessons:* the mystery of karma and reincarnation, which explains the causes of what befalls us in life;

the reasons we are made to love, only to have our loved ones taken away by death, and where they go when they leave us; the latent powers of soul, mind, and will by which we can make life divine. But you must be earnest about practicing what you learn—for your own sake, not mine. I am here only to interest you in the truths that have given me emancipation; I have no other interest. I am here to tell you how to find that freedom.

And if you follow these teachings, you will realize that this work has given you not mere sermons or words, but something by which you can prove to yourself—beyond any doubt—the truth that will make you free.

Never Be Afraid to Question

First of all you must understand this one point: God is never afraid of questions. I have always asked God, "Why do you keep us suffering here on earth in ignorance, disease, and trouble, while You are sitting in heaven with all the joy and strength and power of the universe?"

We must not expect to understand all at once the plot of this book of life written by God. When you are reading a novel, it is considered most fascinating when you are kept in suspense about what the end will reveal. It leads you through endless mazes of intrigue and experiences, until on the last page, suddenly you find out how the hero wins. And you think, "What a fine novel that was!" In the same way you cannot understand God's novel until the end, for He is the Master Novelist.

To those who know God, He unravels the mystery. When I received the answer, it was so wonderful, so beautiful and satisfying. But the mystery of life is very, very difficult to understand unless you know the Maker of this universe. For His law is different from any law that man has conceived.

The Mystery of Good and Evil

In human beings you see that some people enjoy marvelous health, and some people have been sick and ailing from the very beginning of their lives. You will reason, "Well, that is the law of karma." And yet karma alone doesn't seem sufficient to explain everything. Yes, individuals reap the results of the evil actions they sow. But who created the impulses that tempt human beings to wrongdoing in the first place? If we are made in the image of God, our innate being must be good. We didn't create anger and greed, jealousy and revengefulness, but they are there.

And why is there mass destruction and death from floods and other natural disasters, which don't discriminate between the just and the wicked? Who created the deadly bacteria and viruses that periodically decimate the population—both the good and the bad—during times of plague and epidemic? Our karma may make us susceptible to these misfortunes, but we didn't create them.

Why are these evils created? Who is responsible for them? Well, God is responsible for all things—including the existence of Cosmic Delusion (Satan or *Maya*), which is the source of evil in the cosmos and in our lives.* But that makes Him also responsible to redeem us. In His greatness and goodness, God must have some purpose for this world. Remember, no matter what you have to go through in this life, you will one day have complete understanding of this mystery when you come to the last page of the book of this life. But it is fruitless to try to understand that book all at once.

Genghis Khan took millions of prisoners. When he was asked what should be done with them, he said, "Cut off their heads." There seems to be no interpretation of the law of karma that would justify that action for each one of the millions affected. And yet there is a law that is secretly moving through everything—through all the seemingly contrary dualities of the cosmic delusion (*maya*) by which God has created the universe.

It is very difficult to understand God's operation of that law. All the laws of ordinary ethics will not explain it. The only way you can solve the conundrum of good and evil is by acknowledging the division between ignorance (born of cosmic delusion) and wisdom. God—the Lover behind all love, the Joy behind all joys, the Power behind all nature, the Intelligence behind all things—has hidden Himself behind the veil of cosmic delusion. And we have complete freedom to shut Him away from our lives or to accept Him.

God is not a vengeful judge, punishing us with the law of karma. That is why the teaching of the Gita is so sweet. "The All-Pervading takes no account of anyone's virtue or sin," Lord Krishna assured

* An in-depth explanation of this concept may be found in Paramahansa Yogananda's commentary on the New Testament: *The Second Coming of Christ: The Resurrection of the Christ Within You*, Discourse 7, section titled "The Nature and Origin of Evil." *(Publisher's Note)*

Arjuna, pointing out that we punish ourselves when we allow the wisdom of the soul to remain covered by the veil of ignorance.*

Pain, disease, sorrow, suffering, death—these have all been created by metaphysical Satan as a veil of ignorance that covers the truth. God is truth; He is present in us as the pain-proof, blissful, immortal soul. And He has given us intelligence and free will, that perhaps we might seek to unveil this truth and thereby solve the mystery of life.

Do Not Dislodge Your Mind From Divine Consciousness

All great saints have told us that we are made in the image of God, and we must not desecrate that image by fear, anger, hatred, impatience, and other negative emotions. All these dislodge your mind from the divine state. Learning the art of living in this world without giving up the divine image of calmness and joy in which God has created you—that is the mystery of life you have to solve. And that is what yoga teaches.

Although the Lord has surrounded us with limitations everywhere, still the mind can be free. There are martyrs who have accepted death by fire, smilingly. That is the state of mind that is really free—when no sorrow or pleasure, no ups or downs in life, can disturb you.

The masters have said, try to remedy the cause of suffering, and yet be undaunted by it. Don't be disturbed or touched by life. When there is some outer cause of disturbance, and you try to remedy it yet do not become affected inside, then you have mastered the yogic virtue of *titiksha,* divine patience.

By unceasing mental aboveness, or evenmindedness, you neutralize and ultimately defeat the effects of cosmic delusion. Strengthen your mind so that you cannot be hurt. You don't realize what beauty and freedom is veiled behind the surface of life. Meditate! And make your mind so strong that you can rise above everything—so that no pain of the body or circumstance of life can really touch you. To be the ruler of your own consciousness is true kingship.

* "The All-Pervading takes no account of anyone's virtue or sin. Wisdom is eclipsed by cosmic delusion; mankind is thereby bewildered. But in those who have banished ignorance by Self-knowledge, their wisdom, like the illuminating sun, makes manifest the Supreme Self (Spirit)" (Bhagavad Gita V:15–16). An illuminating explanation of how Cosmic Delusion, rather than God, entangles man in karmic suffering is given in Paramahansa Yogananda's commentary on verses 14–16. *(Publisher's Note)*

It is the greatest ignorance to think that you are the body, because you are not. You might just as well think you are your coat. The pain that you suffer when you think you are the body is nothing but your delusive attachment to the body, which you have cultivated since you were born. On the Self-Realization path we receive definite techniques that help us to withdraw the mind from consciousness of the body. We are taught that if you can so retire from the consciousness of the body that you can perceive yourself separate from the body—that is, as a soul—then you will see the mystery of life solved.

The Mystery of Life Is Solved by Right Attitude and Detachment

If you are not seeking God, what is the use of this life? For every little taste of honey, you get ten doses of bitterness. Life in this world gives you more slaps than caresses. That is why more people are unhappy than happy. Very few people can truly say they are happy. In their hearts they are not happy. Unless and until they have learned self-control of the mind, something always comes along that makes them unhappy.

Though tests in this life are many, if you concentrate on your misfortunes you will find that they are increasingly harder to endure. But if you concentrate on the good in the experiences that come to you, you will find that your good fortune more than outweighs your tests. We so easily allow our minds to be poisoned by our experiences and our difficulties. By the conscious expression of right attitude, learn instead to master your mind.

For instance, last night until three o'clock, I was thinking of many things as to the future of this institution, and again and again the Lord said, "I am testing you." I replied, "That is all right, Lord. I am not at all disturbed." This morning I find that more landslides have taken place, and much work has been undone. The damage that has been done everywhere is as bad as ours. Why did it come, this test? I exactly know the cause.*

* Here Paramahansaji is speaking of the work undertaken to combat erosion of the clifftop site of the Self-Realization Fellowship Golden Lotus Temple at Encinitas, California. According to historical weather data, a few days before he gave this talk in December 1940, the area experienced the greatest 24-hour rainfall ever recorded up to that time. "Heavy rains loosened soil in Del Mar [a few miles south of Encinitas] that led to a landslide along a train track, derailing the train and killing three," according to a contemporary report. After several years of preventive efforts, the Golden Lotus

This is the attitude I have: It is like when there are some children playing, and a naughty boy comes along and breaks their toys. The children cry and scream: "You have destroyed my doll house!" Well, that is the way it is with me. I have built a little doll house [the Golden Lotus Temple], and Satan comes along and kicks it and breaks it. Why should I react like an angry child? These are the little tests of life. They are nothing compared to what some others may be going through. It gives me greater calmness, greater joy, greater peace, to do things with complete determination that the Spirit within us can be tested, but it can never be suppressed. That consciousness has given me the greatest calmness and joy, which nothing can take away.

I am enjoying kingship now. These tests are nothing. The peace of my life is apart from anything going on around me. That is the way I have solved the mysteries of life.

We must always remember at every turn of life that this is God's drama. This is God's *lila* or play—creation, preservation, and destruction. Play your part in this cosmic show, but be apart from it. As soon as you give credence to it, you are finished.

Never think that your failures make *you* a failure. All our faults and errors, and the outer difficulties they may cause, are temporary; we are eternal. It is the attitude of victory or failure that we have in our minds that determines whether or not we have been truly victorious in life.

Victory over life's tests and trials is achieved by an attitude of complete inner detachment from the world—identification not with the body or outer environment but with your eternal Self, the soul. For this world is not a place for building your dreams of perfection. Here you are to preserve the image of God within you so that you don't lose yourself in the slums of matter.

Now, as you strive for that detachment, what should be your state of mind? Should it be all the time grave? Not at all. Just mentally remember and affirm: "As a wave from the ocean I have come, and back to the bosom of the ocean I will go. I came from joy, I live in joy, and in that joy I shall one day melt again." That is the example the great masters have shown of how to behave toward life.

Temple was lost in a major landslide in July 1942. A few weeks later, Paramahansaji publically stated: "A long time ago God showed me this landslide that was to come, so I knew it would happen....It is all a part of the world disaster about which God told me [in the years immediately preceding World War II]. The Evil Force, through the karma of the people, is going to cause much destruction." *(Publisher's Note)*

Where Are the Souls Who Are Sincere in Their Search for God?

The method of religious services and worship in America is very different than the spiritual training given by the masters in India. Here in America people love to listen to lectures. These are helpful in order to create the enthusiasm and desire to seek God, but most religionists have listened to more than enough sermons about God already. What is really necessary is to live the truth in your lives that you hear about on Sundays, to meditate and practice His presence every day.

When you go to a restaurant, you are not satisfied with reading the menu that describes the food. You want to taste the food yourself. Yet how many persons remain satisfied with mere words about God! How many of you can stand up and say, "I know God. I know the Supreme Being. I know that He is with me. He talks with me and He guides me as I move through life." I urge you: Don't be satisfied unless and until you can truthfully say that you have God in your heart.

He is very difficult to find; yet He is the easiest to find if you mean business with Him. He is the one Power behind all our existence. We must find Him.

I have lectured all over the country, to thousands of people, but I saw that out of the crowds of superficial seekers in each place, perhaps only one or two souls were really interested in seeking God in earnest. As a result I have more or less deliberately run away from congregations who come only to hear a lecture. I am looking only for those who are deeply sincere in their wish to know God. I am seeking those who are becoming more conscious of their souls and are using their discrimination—those who think; those who understand that this life is something more than merely eating, sleeping, and drinking; those who don't act like animals, but are beginning to realize they are made in the image of God.

Understanding the Purpose in Tests and Crises

It is because that kind of training is lacking that this world has become a veritable lunatic asylum! It is God's big zoo, and I think the angels and God look at our crazy behavior with amazement through the fence of ether that separates the heavenly realms from the physical world. Here we are fighting and carrying on like animals. The trouble is that though God gave us the power to be godly, we carry on like savages. Why does such great barbarism persist? Because man is using his intelligence wrongly. The power and freedom that God has given us has been misused.

Every twenty years or so war has come, because people are filled with hate and jealousy and the other expressions of ungoverned material desire. Then for a little while they have peace, and then war starts up again. And we see that while mankind is suffering, God in heaven with all His power seems to remain neutral. But that is not true. God gave us full power, even as He has. He would never have sent us out into delusion without first endowing us with His divinity. Beneath the wave of every human consciousness is the ocean of His power. The purpose of all tests is to prod us to bring out that hidden, unlimited power of God within us to solve those problems. Until we realize that, we only know this life as a great mystery. The whole game is to realize that our power is greater than our tests.

We all think that if we were God, we would create a much better world—at least a world free from suffering and a body that is stronger and not subject to pain and sickness. Well, God *wants* us to use the power He has given us to make the body better and to make the world better. We have already made the world better in some respects; but when we don't understand the reason for the tragic experiences in life, naturally we don't see the justice of God.

We are not animals, who are held to no code of morality but do not accrue karma for their actions, having no power of free will. As human beings made in the image of God, we must guide our behavior by moral laws or face karmic consequences—individually as well as en masse.

Hate and trouble begin in the mind and germinate in the heart. And they vibrate electrical energy in the heart. The radiation of that electrical energy is tremendous; and when hate and other Satan-inspired emotions are widespread in the consciousness of the masses, great disturbing currents go all over the world. And sometimes they disturb or awaken the Satan-created germ- and disease potentials hidden away in the ether, and they drop down on the earth. And then we have terrible diseases. I predicted that this influenza would come, and it is a result of man's hatred and warring nature.*

* Paramahansa Yogananda made this statement on December 29, 1940 (after the start of World War II in Europe and Asia). Research published in the Archive of Internal Medicine in 1942 confirms: "During the late fall and early winter of 1940–1941 an epidemic of influenza involved most sections of the United States, as well as the Hawaiian Islands, Puerto Rico and probably many other areas." *(Publisher's Note)*

I have told you before about this war—and how good or evil behavior on a mass level affects the fate of nations and the harmony of nature.* You see, there are three factors behind man's sufferings: first is the influence of cosmic delusion, as I already explained; then there is individual karma—wrong actions affecting one's personal circumstances; and third is the effect of mass karma.

My Master used to say, "Learn to behave." One must realize how great is the meaning of that phrase. To behave rightly despite all satanic temptation is the most difficult thing to do, but the most necessary for happiness. Life on earth seems so mysterious, but still we can see that the principles of virtue are the only way to lasting happiness and peace. An accumulation of good mass karma resulting from a populace living in harmony with divine laws could make the earth a veritable heaven of divine harmony, health, prosperity.

God's Mysterious Purpose Will Be Accomplished Without Fail

The way of virtue is very subtle. And that power of God is going on in spite of the dance of destruction that is taking place during this war. It may seem that the law of God is losing, but ultimately it will win. God's power is being resisted by the ignorance of man, but man is too weak to destroy that power. Even so, the results of his wrong or evil actions can make this earth into a torture chamber for millions of people—as is seen during times of war or other disasters.

But the world is not going backward. And I predict that out of this war good will come, according to the mysterious law of God. God made this schoolhouse of the world so that we would learn to evolve ourselves. He is not in a hurry.† Like naughty schoolchildren who are all the time getting into fights until they grow up, the world

* In several talks given within a few years before this one, Paramahansaji explained how social, economic, and natural calamities—including floods, storms, and earthquakes—result from the mass karma created by war and widespread wrongdoing on earth. See, for example, the following: "The End of the World," in *The Divine Romance*; "Nations Beware," in *Journey to Self-realization*; "The Ten Commandments: Eternal Rules of Happiness," in *Man's Eternal Quest*. *(Publisher's Note)*

† Hindu philosophy teaches that dharma, the mental virtue governing the progress of civilization, gradually increases through four yugas, world ages, over the course of a 12,000-year planetary cycle; and then declines in reverse order for another 12,000 years. Our present age is in the second stage (Dwapara Yuga) of the ascending arc. Humanity has left behind the barbarism of the lowest or Dark Age (Kali Yuga) of this cycle, but still has a long way to go before reaching the apex of spiritual development in the fourth or Golden Age (Satya Yuga). These cycles are described by Swami Sri Yukteswar in his book, *The Holy Science*. *(Publisher's Note)*

also has to grow up. Before the First World War, war was considered chivalrous. But now those who wage aggressive war are considered international gangsters. So humanity has evolved somewhat, but not yet enough: people don't want war, but still the countries are fighting. The world must become more and more spiritual for wars to diminish.

As long as the world uses the methods of Satan in the conduct of life and pursuit of desires—for money, sex, and power—there will continue to be much suffering. It is only the methods of Christ that will save the world. Love, international brotherhood, peace, joy, sharing—these alone can bring peace to the world.

You will see that after this war, Europe and other countries will be so battered that the idea of war will be an object of terror, and anyone who advocates wars of aggression will be considered a candidate for prison—or a psychopathic ward! We may not see this in our lifetime, but it will come.

So you see, my dears, the world is progressing. God's powers are immutable, and they will go on winning without fail. And remember: You can do much to alleviate the suffering of the world. For every soul is a part of God, as every wave is a part of the ocean.

If we were like the stones, we couldn't do anything but be what we are. But we are different; we have the power to reason and to think and to govern our actions by soul discrimination—and most of all, to seek and find God. In that freedom lies the solution to this mystery of life.

Concentrate on Knowing God

The mystery of life has been solved by various saints and masters who have experienced God. But they inevitably find words inadequate when they try to talk about Him. As one great saint said, "All I can say about God is that He is." And yet there are some things we can say about what God is. God is the joy that you are seeking in everything. God is the sound of all vibrations in the universe—the holy *Aum* or Word by which all things are created and sustained. God is all wisdom. God is all peace and all calmness. God is all love. God is everything, in everything; thus there is a living relationship, a living communion, linking all animate and inanimate creatures in this world—an immanent intelligence which is trying to bring out the God-essence that is everywhere veiled.

Through self-effort in the moral and disciplinary techniques and meditation methods practiced by illumined saints, we can tear away the veil of ignorance and remember that we are made in the image of the Lord. Then we begin to see the link between God and man and all living things. Then we are hastening the approach toward unity, and bringing more balance in the world. That is why the Masters sent me to the West to give this teaching.

What is the use of life's difficult journey if we have to go to the grave with still unanswered questions? We must find out what life is all about. If we concentrate on God, we find that He had a definite purpose in creating us. We ought to understand that purpose, and it can be understood by meditating on our souls. Right within us is the key to the mystery of everything. But the person who does not meditate and calm the restlessness that veils the soul will not find it, or God.

Keep God Always in Your Heart

Devotion plus knowledge of the law of meditation makes it much easier to contact Him. The yogi seeks God methodically, using definite techniques in order to contact God. To be successful, devotion as well as determination is necessary. A yogi with real devotion doesn't become discouraged; but goes on practicing meditation and steadily progresses.

You may be the most materialistic type of person, but if you have love for God and if you go after Him persistently in daily, deep meditation, with all the sincerity of your heart, you will surely know Him. When you love your child, no matter where you go your child is always there in your heart. You must love God in the same way. He must always be there in your heart.

That is why Christ said, "Love the Lord thy God with all thy heart, with all thy mind, and with all thy soul, and with all thy strength." That means your whole attention must be on Him when you are meditating, and then He will respond to you. And love God with all your strength. That means to relax—to withdraw all the life force from the external activities of the body and put that energy on God.*

And last is the most difficult: love God with all your soul. Unless you know your soul, you cannot fulfill this divine commandment. That is the purpose of meditation techniques: to calm all

* Here Paramahansaji is referring to the techniques of *pranayama* (life energy control) taught in the science of yoga and imparted through the *Self-Realization Fellowship Lessons. (Publisher's Note)*

restlessness of body and mind so that you can see the clear reflection of the soul mirrored in the unruffled lake of your consciousness. As soon as you are calm, you will feel that clarity within, and you will say, "The Spirit is mirrored in me as my soul." Then as your perception deepens, you will experience that Spirit spreading over the whole universe as Joy, as Light, and as the thrilling, energizing, and peace-bestowing Cosmic Sound.

When you sit for meditation, practice the techniques I have given you. And I promise you this, that if you follow these teachings and get busy meditating, you can go as far as you want to go in your own awareness of God. Everything that your heart has been panting for, you will find fulfilled in Him.

So start the new year with a new understanding and a greater joy, by making the effort to know Him. Meditate, meditate, meditate! And then you will see that no matter what your faults are, you will find Him. For remember: He created you and He can never forsake you. And if you call to Him in the secret silence of your soul, and if you are determined that He must come to you, then He will come—and the mystery of life will be solved.

The Art of Right Action

A talk given to residents at Self-Realization Fellowship International Headquarters in 1934. Passages from this talk were used in several different SRF Lessons, which were being compiled according to Paramahansaji's instructions during that period. The entire talk, never before printed in complete form, is presented here for the first time.

The ordinary person is a motor being—an object constantly in motion. The inner environment of such individuals is never really at peace. A calm human being is poised—controlling all his emotions instead of allowing emotions to control him. Throughout the day, have a controlled existence. Until you do, your peace of mind will be victimized by fluctuating emotions, impulsive movements of the muscles, activity and reactivity of the senses, continual restlessness of the thoughts. Let none of these in any way disturb your peace. You must be able to control your mind, and thus your body, by self-mastery.

Are You Governed by Calmness or Restless Impulses?

A calm person reflects restfulness in his eyes, keen intelligence in his face, and proper receptivity in his mind. He is a person of decisive and prompt action, but is not moved by impulses and desires that suddenly occur to him. A restless person is like a puppet that dances at the instigation of emotional desires arising in response to the temptation offered by others.

Be sure to work, slowly or fast, from a center of calmness. Under no circumstances work or act from a center of restlessness, with your concentration centralized on your restless state of mind. All actions should be performed with peace, calmness, self-possession, intelligence, and keen concentration.

When you can combine in yourself the placidity of the crocodile and the eager activity of the beaver, then you will be a balanced human being.

Pay Mindful Attention to Every Situation You Are In

Always reflect your balanced attitude in your interaction with others. A calm person has his senses fully and clearly cognizant of the environment in which he places himself. A restless person does not notice what is happening around him, consequently he misunderstands everything and gets into trouble with himself and others. A calm person, by virtue of his self-possession, is filled with understanding and consequently is always at peace with others, and is always happy. Never change the center of your concentration from calmness to restlessness. Perform all activities with concentration centered in calmness.

Many persons think that their actions have to be either restless or slow. That is not true. If you keep calm, with intense concentration, you will perform all duties quickly and efficiently. The true art of right action is to be able to act efficiently at both slow or rapid speeds without losing your inner peace. The proper method is to establish a controlled attitude, wherein you can work with peace without losing your inner balance.

This does not mean that you should be calm for a while and then let your mind run riot. It is not the person who meditates a long time for one day and then does not meditate again for several days who becomes successful on the spiritual path. The person who meditates regularly and always holds to the aftereffects of meditation throughout the day is the one who quickly approaches to godliness and Cosmic Consciousness.

Transforming Yourself From a Material Being to a Spiritual Being

Thousands of persons are wholly material beings. Their thoughts and their very movements reflect materiality. They are nothing more than matter in motion. Do not be like them. Cultivate inner calmness and poise by keeping your consciousness always disciplined by concentration and meditation.

A man once came to me preaching the superiority of the mind; but when I analyzed him I found that his mind was concentrated on his body. His mind was concentrated on his hat, shoes, and dress; and that was all there was to him. The vulture soars high but its mind is on the creatures in the canyon below. Similarly an intelligent person's mind may be roaming in the realm of ideas and yet be centered on the body and the attachments to which the body is subject. He whose concentration is on his person—on the exertions of the body, the muscular activity produced by the nervous system—is a material being.

Rising above body consciousness does not mean neglect of the body nor of one's work. One should care for the body and perform one's work with his mind on the divine purpose to be fulfilled by attending to these duties. He who can keep his concentration centered on his inner Self even while he is busy with his work is a spiritual being.

It is extremely important to find out whether or not you can keep the continuity of your calmness throughout the day. Your muscles, your senses, your desires, and the misunderstandings of others, all come to disturb the quietude of your soul. To be controlled by moods is to be a part of matter. If you keep your mind on the resolve never to lose your peace, you can attain godliness. Keep a secret chamber of silence within yourself, where you will not let moods, trials, battles, or inharmony enter. Keep out all hatred, revengefulness, and desires. In this chamber of peace, God will visit you.

Be in the World but Not of the World

Though you must remain in the world, be not of the world. Real yogis can talk and mingle with people, but all the while their minds are rapt in God.

The spiritual man works with the consciousness that God is the Doer. The material man works too, but he works and acts with the consciousness that *he* is the doer, and as such he makes himself miserable through his likes and dislikes. Man's egoistic feelings, expressing as likes and dislikes, are entirely responsible for the bondage of the soul to the body and earthly environment. Material desires take control of the consciousness of one who is not watchful enough in governing the reaction of his feelings to his various experiences in the world. Desires and their resultant attachments and aversions destroy the equilibrium of the inner nature, like stones pelted into the calm lake of consciousness. Watch yourself with eagle eyes of concentration to find out whether your mind is concentrated on the inner Self or on desires that are the outcome of contact with matter.

Above all, be true to yourself. If you are true to yourself, God will be true to you. Very few people *wish* to be good, and fewer still *try* to be good. Those who constantly try to be good are the ones who are going to find God.

The minutes are more important than the years. If you do not fill in the minutes of your life with thoughts of God, the years will slip by and when you need Him most you will not be able to feel His presence. But if you do fill in the minutes of your life with the thoughts of God, you will find that the years of your life automatically will be saturated with the consciousness of God. Never think of tomorrow. Take care of today and all the tomorrows will take care of themselves. Do not wait until tomorrow to meditate. Do not wait until tomorrow to be good. Be good now! Be calm now! It will be the turning point of your life.

Live More Within Your Self

No matter what you are doing, keep your concentration on the peace of meditation. That is the way of intimate contact with God. Ordinary souls live useful, active lives; but they do not know the art of living within themselves. They are living identified with matter, and therefore misery. The calm person is happy, for the cultivation of calmness and self-control is the only way to real happiness. Constantly be aware within. Make the inner effort of will continually, that you may always remain on the throne of calmness.

Most people dilute the steadiness of their minds with the constant fluctuations of their environments; therefore they lose control over themselves. If you let a bagful of mustard seed be scattered on the ground, it is hard to collect them again in the bag. The mind is a bag of consciousness filled with mustard seeds of thoughts, and if you recklessly slash the bag with the dagger of restlessness, then all the thoughts, like mustard seeds, will scatter, and it will be hard to get them together again. As the oil is unseen within the mustard seeds but can be extracted by grinding them, so by recollecting your scattered thoughts of God and grinding them with the power of concentration you can bring out the oil of Self-realization.

The Power to Shape Your Own Life

Under all circumstances you should be calm and self-possessed. No one should be able to excite you. No matter what happens, even if storms of trials come, you must be able to steer the ship of concentration calmly to the shores of blessedness.

The ordinary person is influenced by his worldly environment. The man of concentration shapes his own life. He plans his day and finds at the end of the day that his plans are carried out; he finds himself nearer to God and his goal. A weak man plans many wonderful things, but finds at the end of the day that he has been a victim of circumstances and bad habits. Such a person usually blames everyone but himself.

Remember, you should blame no one but yourself for your troubles. If you make up your mind that you are going to control your circumstances by living according to spiritual laws, then by the power of those laws your circumstances will adjust themselves accordingly. Eventually you must learn to lead a controlled existence.

Every morning make up your mind that you are going to be better, you are going to be kind to your friends and enemies alike, you are going to meditate more deeply than you did the day before, you are going to know something about good books, and so forth. In other words, you are going to go on improving. Analyze yourself and find out whether you are the same person that you were a few years ago or not, and whether you have overcome any of your past bad habits. This will tell you whether you have been progressing or not. You must not lead a stagnant existence. Every day spur yourself on to greater achievements.

Your body is like an obstinate dog. Leash your mind and body with will power, and hold them to the direction in which you want them to move. Do not allow them to pull you in the wrong direction and thereby fall into the ditch of misery; whip them when they disobey, for the more you whip them the better they will respond to your commands. Your mind and body have become rebels, constantly protesting to you about the impossibilities in your path; but if you whip them hard, they will hurdle those barriers.

Use Self-Analysis to Gauge Your Progress

If you know that you are progressing spiritually, mentally, and physically every day, you can be happy; but if you find that you are becoming touchy, finicky, or gossipy, you may know that you are going backward. The best test is to analyze yourself and find out whether you are happier today than you were yesterday. If you feel that you are happier today, then you are progressing; and this feeling of happiness must continue.

You only grow by deep meditation and intelligent, controlled activity. The deeper you meditate and the more willingly you serve, the happier you will be. And remember, every wrong that you do to others, you do to yourself first in thought and deed. Let your mind and soul be cleansed. Every day happier than yesterday; that is the standard of spiritual life; and if you find that you are not growing happier and happier, you are going backwards.

This is the easiest way of determining your own spiritual progress. If you find yourself floating down the current of custom and opinions of others, the first step is to make time to get away from everybody. You don't have to retire into the jungle; nor do you have to be rude to others. Just sit quietly and think. Have it out with yourself. Tell yourself that you are going to allow no one to hurt you or take away your happiness and peace.

You Can Be One With God in This Life

Cling to the consciousness of peace, which is the aftereffect of meditation, and go on increasing that peace by increasing the length and depth of your meditations and by performing actions that bring you true happiness, and you will find that you are fast approaching God. If you do not make a conscious effort in this life, several incarnations may slip by without your reaching the goal. But if you make the effort from now on, from this minute, and try to keep your concentration on the inward peace of meditation continuously, then you can be one with God in this life.

Keep your concentration on the blissful aftereffects of meditation every minute of your existence, and do not neutralize that peace with disturbing thoughts. If you gather concentration in the pail of meditation and have a leak of restlessness, your concentration will run out. You must not have any mental leaks.

In meditation and in activity, let this be your constant prayer:

"Father, Mother, Friend, Beloved God, may Thy love shine forever on the sanctuary of my devotion, and may I be able to awaken Thy love in all hearts."

From Selfishness to Self-realization

Finding Happiness and Freedom by Serving Your Greater Self in All

Self-Realization Fellowship Golden Lotus Temple, Encinitas, California, August 31, 1939

As the spirit of God brings words that are suitable to express what I feel for Him and the way I feel Him, I shall speak to you tonight. And if even a little spark of that perception ignites the vast dark forest of your mortal ignorance and God-indifference in which your soul has been wandering, you shall find a blaze of life, a divine flame, in which all shadows of delusion are no more. You shall bask in the light of His glory, the Light that never fails, the Light that "shineth in darkness."

There are many pathways in life through which we may move toward God. In fact, all constructive pursuits we undertake—any activities performed with the desire to do good either to self or to others—ultimately lead us from the limitations of the little self, or ego, to realization of our divine Self, one with God.

Two Kinds of Selfishness

There are various definitions of selfishness and unselfishness. Many persons think of selfishness as bad. But actually there is no action we can perform that is not selfish. Take the example of Jesus on the cross: That was a supremely unselfish act; but still, Jesus knew the effect of that sacrifice would bring joy in fulfilling God's will and freeing his incarnate spirit. When we do good, it is because we want to feel the peace and happiness that results from acting rightly. And when we do wrong, it is because we think—erroneously—that it will bring us satisfaction.

Selfishness is that by which every effect of your actions reaches yourself. As long as we retain the consciousness of individuality—the body-identified ego or the pure soul consciousness, an individualized spark of God—there is nothing we do without a reference to the self.* That is why there is no unselfish act in the whole world, because we do not do anything without knowing that the effect of our action will reach us. You may object: "Well, I had $50 and gave it to someone who was in need. Was not that unselfish?" No. You felt the pain of that person, and so you gave that money to him to relieve your pain. You got a satisfaction out of giving.

The word "selfishness" has been poisoned by being associated only with actions that advance one's own interests regardless of others' well-being. But spiritual selfishness is wonderful. When you say, "I want the happiness of making someone else happy," there is nothing wrong in that. I do not find happiness unless I can make others happy; it gives me great joy to give to others and to do good for others. That is a good selfishness. The idea is to avoid mean selfishness—thinking of self and nobody else. As soon as you say, "I am interested only in what I can get for me," you are showing wrong selfishness. Everyone would begin to dislike you.

Selfishness that destroys somebody else's selfishness is not selfishness. My master, Sri Yukteswarji, was given a silver field glass, and a man asked if he could borrow that glass. Master said, "Yes, but when will you return it?" The man said, "In a fortnight."

When he didn't return the telescope as promised, my Guru asked him about it. The man remonstrated: "You, a holy man, are so worried about getting back your field glass!"

Then Sri Yukteswarji said, "All right, next time you come for the glass you won't get it—because you have deprived me of using it for others' enjoyment, as I used it for yours."

To be "half-baked" in spiritual understanding will not do. Such individuals do not want to be common worldly persons, yet neither will they make the effort to be truly great. All words and little substance, they are like a colorful balloon—attracting attention, but full of hot air. It is in spiritual actions, not in philosophical pronouncements, that you show real advancement in Self-realization.

* The Sanskrit word for the ego-principle, *ahamkara,* literally means "I do." Paramahansa Yogananda has explained: "When by yoga the ego is united to the soul, and the soul to the Spirit, the ego loses its delusion of being a mortal whose actions are governed by the law of karma"—the cosmic law whereby all actions cause effects that return to the doer, for good or for ill.

Discriminating Between Spiritual Selfishness and Mean Selfishness for Soul Progress

Discriminating between spiritual selfishness and mean selfishness requires that you hone your power of good judgment and keep it always keenly attentive. Selfishness is all right if it does not hurt anyone else. If you say to someone, "I want to build a road to develop my property and it will require demolition of your home," that is wrong. On the other hand, if this road is not primarily for your personal benefit but needed by many, many people, then it is a good selfishness and some fair settlement with the one homeowner should be mutually agreed on. You see, everything is relative. Only through discriminative good judgment will you be able to recognize the face of error and choose the ways of wisdom.

Mean selfishness is bad for you because it is blind. It makes you think you are going to be the winner, but often causes you to do the very things that destroy your well-being. The person you want to hurt out of mean selfishness is going to be all the more determined to get back at you. You think acting against that person is somehow in your best interest; but as I often say, very few people know in what lies their own good. The devil is commonly painted with a big body and no brain; likewise, those who do evil are acting brainlessly, because evil eventually destroys the evildoer. Most people are thus engaged in self-destruction—I find that so amazing. I have given opportunity for self-improvement and spiritual progress to thousands, yet so many of them continue to destroy themselves by greed and the blindness of misguided self-gratification.

Humility and Love Reveals the Truth About Others

No matter what your trials, you must not allow them to bring bitterness. Keep your wisdom awake and love in your heart. Without love you shall never have right understanding. As long as the ego rules your consciousness, you are blinded by narrow self-interest. You cannot clearly perceive the truth about persons or situations, and therefore respond wrongly. Even the smartest man is often fooled by a smarter man. But humbleness sees through everything—humbleness and love. Those who open their eyes of humbleness and love know truth, and the truth makes them free.

It is quite common to think you know better than anybody else, but it is foolish to treat others as if they are wrong. There is always someone who knows more than you—and there is always another who knows still more than that person, and so on. Truly great persons never think they know it all. They analyze and compare their judgment with that of others.

If you always think you are the smartest, you will continually misunderstand others. But if you free your understanding from the emotional reactions of the ego, you will be able to see people for what they are. Test them by love. Try giving love to anyone with whom you have difficulties; and if love doesn't work, you know impartially the limitations of that person.

The best way to keep your understanding clear is to see no evil, hear no evil, speak no evil. Some persons are always negative and gossiping about others' faults; by doing so they maintain the comfortable self-deception that they themselves are free from those evils. But those who are great have nothing but kindness for others; if they offer positive criticism it is only to help others. The cure for those who are blinded by meanness and hatred is introspection to find out the faults within themselves before they presume to see the faults in others.

Love your enemies. Hate no one. As Gandhi says, "I am the friend of all, but I cannot say I have no enemies. If some consider themselves my enemies, I cannot help it; but I am not their enemy." Go on doing good. Some will praise you, some will blame you. You cannot please all. Even Jesus paid with his life for his good works in the name of God. Just go on doing good before your own conscience, separating your soul from mean selfishness.

National Selfishness Is a Cause of War

It is blind selfishness that makes you exaggerate your own position and disregard the position of others. There is so much misunderstanding and conflict in this world because man gives little or no consideration to others involved. What caused this last war?* Selfishness—industrial selfishness, each country thinking only of itself: "My nation is the best and mightiest; and our people should take whatever we please, regardless of others."

Thinking of war is making it a reality. Militarists in Europe and Asia are thinking of it very strongly. God is trying to make them unthink it, because thought is a very potent force. Warlike mentalities are dangerous, for those who play with guns like to see them go off! Politicians should work harder to achieve national goals through

* I.e., reference to World War I.

peaceful means. (I am not speaking of defensive war, of course, when necessary to protect one's homeland against aggressors.)

Differences between nations and individuals should be resolved through mediation. If contentious parties do not learn to feel for each others' needs, and use aggression as a means to assert their own goals, in the long run they will lose more than what they thought to gain. Look at Napoleon and Kaiser Wilhelm. They had all, but when national selfishness led them to become aggressors, they got the worst of it. Selfish ambition does not pay.

Blind, mean selfishness is the root cause of all trouble. The common attitude is, "I just want to live my own life," forgetting that everyone else says, "I want to do the same." I, I, I—the big ego! It is the perpetrator of trouble. Ego must be controlled. Everybody wants to put his or her comfort first; each wants the best seat. Rather than fighting about what in the end is trivial, it is better to give in—not as a matter of weakness, but as a matter of discretion. If somebody fights for my seat I will gladly say, "Please, sit down." But if somebody told me not to meditate or I will forfeit my life, I would use discretion—not making a confrontation, but privately continuing on meditating just the same. It is wisdom to compromise when by doing so you can promote understanding; but never be shaken from following what your conscience knows is right.

Selfishness Disappears as God Is Realized

Ego is born as the result of ignorance. All great masters tell you to forget the I, because it blinds you. Because who is great? Dare you think of yourself as great, when God alone is the sole Reality? Before Him, what are you? You can't survive a tiny pinprick on the vital center of your brain. Still you think I, I, I. It is very destructive, causing you to believe your power is more than it is. While a superiority complex is bad, so is an inferiority complex. Both are forms of egotism. When you are one with God, naturally you have all the power God has. But until you have attained that realization, do not emphasize the I. Your consciousness must be: "God is. God is. Not I." As you begin to feel and realize this, egotistical selfishness cannot remain. Rather, you find expansion of your consciousness in His consciousness. The right kind of selfishness is the joy you find when you mingle yourself with God, the Supreme Self.

By practicing the meditation techniques I have given, you will realize God. And as you deal with people, wherever you are, give first consideration to the needs of others. Let your comfort be in thinking of the comfort of somebody else. There is no need to speak of it. When you do good to yourself, you never announce it; but as soon as you help others, you want everyone to know how noble you are. It is most admirable when you do for others as naturally—and as inconspicuously—as you do for yourself. Then you are not developing the I, but manifesting God within you—God who has been eclipsed by the I. That is a most wonderful way to expand your consciousness. You will no longer feel you are bound by your body. You will begin to feel your identity with people, becoming sensitive to what others are feeling.

Each individual has a different set of sensations. All of us here tonight are in the same room, but some of you feel the chapel is warm and for others it seems cooler. Some feel comfortable and calm, others are trying to still their worries. Each one of you feels differently because of the sum total of all the feelings of hurts and happinesses you have gathered through many lifetimes. Those personal *samskaras* (karmic tendencies) are lodged like seeds in the brain, sprouting when stimulated by the right conditions. That past-life accumulation of sensations and habits creates a general feeling in your body and mind, and identifying with that condition is what creates your "second nature"—your subjective, egoistic sense of limitation to a particular body and personality: "This is what I am."

Every one of you has particular idiosyncrasies. Ego is the nucleus around which all your sensations and characteristic habits are clustered. You identify yourself as that cluster of sensations experienced by that indwelling consciousness. When you will have expanded that consciousness by meditation and thinking of others, you will no longer be a limited human being, identified with the selfish ego-centered perspective of your one body. You will feel your greater Self in everyone.

Wisdom Is the Fuse That Destroys the Bomb of Ego

It is very hard to put a fuse to that bomb of ego. Wisdom is the fuse to destroy it. The Bhagavad Gita says: "The Supreme Spirit, transcendent and existing in the body, is the detached Beholder, the Consenter, the Sustainer, the Experiencer, the Great Lord, and also the Highest Self."* One saint of India was placing flower-offerings on the altar during his daily worship, when his mind became so deeply concentrated within that he perceived that Ultimate Truth.

* Bhagavad Gita XIII:22.

He started putting the flowers on his own head, saying: "I bow to my Self. My little I has died; unbound by the body, I am Spirit, the Sustainer of the Universe." What a release comes with that liberating realization—what inconceivable bliss!

From childhood you have hypnotized yourself by your egotistical habits into forgetfulness of your divine nature, your true Self or soul. You are neither a man nor a woman. If you live in a barn house do you call yourself a barn? Yet that is exactly what you have done to your Self by succumbing to the hypnosis of the body-identified ego. You are not what your bodily house defines you to be. You are pure Spirit—naught else but That. When you close your eyes so you do not see the body anymore, you can feel you are the invisible life and consciousness that dwells in that form. But as soon as you open your eyes and again put on the consciousness of the body, you are identified with all your moods and limitations, and you forget your greater Self.

In our hearts and souls we are all naturally unselfish. We like to be good, to love others; and we like to have their love and appreciation in return. No one wants to be bad. Even an evil person thinks he is all right. He doesn't want to be evil. But his habits of blind selfishness, indulgence in self-gratifications, are very, very strong until that ignorance is finally overcome by wisdom.

To progress toward Self-realization, analyze yourself every day to determine whether you are making sufficient effort to get out of the clutches of your habits. Again and again I emphasize to you the necessity of having wisdom and wakefulness, so that you do not let yourself be swept along with the stream of humanity toward oblivion. You are not an animal or an insentient stone; you are the living God within. You must conquer. God has given you the power you need to do so. "O Arjuna! By the practice of yoga, the *muni* ('he whose mind is absorbed in God') quickly attains the Infinite. No taint (karmic involvement) touches the sanctified man of action who is engaged in divine communion (yoga), who has conquered ego consciousness (by attaining soul perception), who is victorious over his senses, and who feels his self as the Self existing in all beings."*

* Bhagavad Gita V:6–7.

The Virtue of Won't Power

Self-Realization Fellowship Golden Lotus Temple, Encinitas, California, April 26, 1942

In meditation and ecstasy, God's power and bliss pour over us like a flood; but we must realize that the divine flood does not come until we pray deeply and continuously. When we do, then His infinite grace bursts upon us. Although God is silent and invisible to most people, still, when in meditation we again and again knock at the gates of heaven, gradually we coax His silent Presence to pierce the clouds of our unknowing. A little mercy-rain begins to shower upon us, increasing until it becomes a deluge of grace that destroys in its wake all our frailties. In order to be saved, we must be baptized not merely in water but in this flood of God's blessing. Spirit is everywhere present, but we do not avail ourselves of this Spirit-baptism because in mortal ignorance we isolate ourselves from that subtle flow of Divine Grace. We must become strong in our prayer-demands for God's response, and refine our knowing-power by meditation, until we are consciously immersed in the salvation-bestowing flood of His grace.

What Is "Won't Power"? Why Is It Necessary?

Our subject today about the virtue of won't power is a unique and very practical one. If we survey our inner selves, the majority will find that mostly their lives have been full of *yeses,* with very few *nos*. Because most persons follow their impulse to yield to what is immediately pleasant, rather than saying no to what is not for their highest good, they are frequently led unresisting into wrong pursuits that create trouble for them. But all great men and women are full of *nos*—they have said many more *nos* than *yeses* in life. That discrimination is what sets them apart from everyone else. It often seems difficult to exercise will power, but it is easy to develop won't power. It doesn't cost anything to say no. "You can lead a horse to water, but you can't make it drink." That is won't power.

I remember the story of a little boy who lived with his doting grandmother. She pitied him because his parents had died, and liked to indulge him in every way. One day he brought home from school a pen belonging to another boy and showed it to his grandmother, asking her: "May I keep the pen?" She thoughtlessly said, "Yes, it is all right." The next time the boy stole some books. She didn't scold him for it. Gradually he began to steal money, and in ten years he became a full-fledged thief. He was caught and convicted, and when he was being sent off to prison, he asked to see his grandmother. She came, and he asked her to draw near so he could tell her a secret. And instead of whispering to her, he bit her ear very painfully. She cried out and asked him why he did it. He replied: "That first day I brought home a pen that didn't belong to me, you said it was all right for me to keep it. If you had stopped me then from taking that pen, I would not be here today."

It requires will power to teach your children won't power. That is wonderful training to give them, that they must always be able to say no, for temptation is everywhere.

Discrimination and Won't Power Go Together

In order to develop won't power, the prime factor is discrimination. It should constantly guide our conduct. We should always think first before we act. This does not mean rationalization, which will always find reasons to justify what we want to do. We should exercise the wisdom of pure discrimination to supply the mind with reasons for the good things we should do and for avoiding the bad ones we should not do. That is how to protect the mind from the influence of automatic impulses and habits and the lure of temptation. Temptation is temptation because we don't know, or don't keep in mind, the reasons why we shouldn't do certain things. Temptation then becomes more active and discrimination is overclouded, passive—and thus easily overpowered. That is when temptation gets hold of us.

How many are the temptations that we are subject to! According to India's masters, it is desire that foments our bad habits—anger, greed, attachment, egotism, avarice, and so on. Now, "desire" covers a lot of territory. Not all desires are harmful. Desires that bring hurt to us or someone else are bad; but there are also desires whose fulfillment will give us true and lasting happiness. The point is, just as soon as you have a desire, you should inwardly ask yourself whether you should accede to that desire or use won't power against it.

Discrimination and won't power must go together. If you have discrimination without won't power to implement it, you will not succeed in life. How often you make up your mind not to do a certain thing, and right away you find yourself doing it, compelled by habit. The best antidote for bad habits is won't power. When you say *no*, and immediately engage your mind in cultivating the opposite good habit, bad habits lose their power to bother you. But you must mean *no*!

The world conditions us differently. As soon as any desire comes, we think its fulfillment is a necessary part of our existence. That is an insidious delusive error that creeps into our consciousness. One difference between East and West is that in India we are trained to have more *nos* in our life. We are taught not to destroy our will power or won't power by following our desires without discrimination. Most of you in the West have not learned to develop that kind of discrimination. Whatever your mind has suggested as necessary, you have followed through on. But it has not brought you happiness. That is one reason I am grateful to have been born and raised in India. My mother always tried to teach me to discriminate between my good and wrong desires. Sometimes she would explain why she said no, and sometimes not.

The Importance of Childhood Training

You do great injury to your children by granting all their desires. I remember there was a rich man's son my mother knew. His mother used to give in to anything he wanted. One night he wanted to do something that was very improper; and she told him, "Go ahead, it's all right." My mother heard about it and said to that boy's mother, "You are spoiling your child for good. You are tolerating his bad behavior; but the world will not tolerate it. When he grows up into an unpopular adult, he will not appreciate you; he will blame you." One of the habits of this undisciplined child was refusing to eat what he was served. Despite his mother's cajoling, he wouldn't touch his meal until given his preferred foods. She talked it over with my mother. Mother said, "That is very simple. I can make him eat, but you must not get softhearted. The next time he says that he won't eat, just say, 'That's all right. You don't have to eat if you don't want to.' And then call me."

So the next time the boy threw a fit about his food, his mother placated him just as my mother had suggested. The son was taken aback at this turn of events. He expected that his mother would coax him to eat. Mother went over, and she and the other lady sat down and began to visit. The lunch was put away. Two o'clock came, and the mother became very restless and said, "I ought to fix him something he likes. He must be starving." But Mother advised her not to do it. Three o'clock came, and the child began writing on a placard against the wall, "If you call me just once, I will go to eat." But my mother advised, "Pay no attention. Just ignore it." And they went on talking. Unsuccessful in his attempts to interrupt them, the boy finally came right near the mother and stood there silently with his placard: "If you call me just once, I will go to eat." The mother turned to the child and said, "Of course you may eat now." He gladly ate the food she put before him. But he never forgot that lesson, and never tried that ploy again. He had learned that he had to eat what was put before him or go without. Hopefully, for his sake, a more disciplined life continued thereafter.

Your love for your children must not be misused. Do not cater to what they want; give what is good for them. Real love teaches them to know the difference between good and bad desires. When your child says, "Mother, I won't eat spinach, I want cake" and you give in to him, you are foregoing the training that will bring the happiness of good health habits. Why is it so easy in life to do things that are wrong and harmful? It seems there is something in this world that always lures us to do what we should not do. That is the setup of this world—the things that cause us trouble are made to seem the most attractive to the senses. You fail to help the child learn won't power by allowing him to cater indiscriminately to his likes and dislikes. Instill good health habits in children from the beginning. Teach them to eat those things that will benefit them. If they become habituated to crave meat and to develop greed for too much candy and pastries, they will fill themselves up with these things and drop the nutrition that promotes health in the body. The more one eats meat, the less appealing he finds salads. Too much meat-eating leaves residue that is converted into acids that harm the body. How silently the body is sabotaged when it is overloaded with unhealthful foods and deprived of ample fresh fruits and vegetables. Evil is so skillfully camouflaged! Often you do not know that you have trouble until it is too late.

Wisdom is the best antidote for temptation. But people often do not take wise advice seriously—about diet or anything else—until they begin to have problems. They do not apply wisdom in a practical way in their everyday life. But wisdom means applied theory. Wisdom means converting the truths you know into practice. My success in life came because whatever I have learned that was beneficial and in accord with truth I have tried to apply in my life. I did not keep it merely as a theory. If I found that something was right, I went after it. And if I was shown that something was wrong, I forsook it.

How few have had the training in childhood that helps us as we grow older. Though many persons may have been taught the divine laws from Scripture, such as the Ten Commandments, those edicts were not brought down to the pale of human existence and practical utility in daily life. As a result, they are either not followed or applied only when expedient. But the saints analyze the reasons behind God's laws. They don't command you to follow them. They tell you it is your privilege to do right or to do wrong, but that if you do wrong you will suffer the consequences.

Once I observed in a missionary school in India that during the Bible class there was disruptive noise and unruliness because the teacher was trying to force his view of Christian dogma on the children, and they made fun of it among themselves. Years later in my own school,* I had made up my mind that I would not force anything on the students. Part of the curriculum was to discuss different qualities mentioned in the Bible—for instance, the study of why shouldn't we be greedy. When I taught those classes on the Bible, the students found them so interesting that they purposely never rang the bell on time to dismiss the class. I would ask such questions as, "What is it called when you disregard the fact that your body doesn't want nutrition and you don't need more food, and yet you go on eating?" The answer is greed. And what is the result of greed? The answer is indigestion. And when you keep on overloading the body, what happens? The answer is chronic indigestion. And what does that bring? The answer is sickness and maybe even death. So summing it up, should we be greedy? All of the children responded, "No!"

When the boys of my school went back to their homes for vacation, the parents didn't have to force rules on them. They had learned how to behave. I didn't tell them, "Do this and don't do that." I knew that when boys are told not to do something, they all the more want to do it! I said to them when they came to the school, "This is your home. I am not going to police you, because I want you to learn to govern yourselves. My duty is to explain to you why it is in your own best interest to behave in a certain way—to point

* See *Ranchi School* in glossary.

out why you should not lie, why you should not be greedy, why you should not fight, why you should not steal, and so on." Once these things were explained to them, and they understood the whys, the boys themselves made rules according to those principles—and they were even stricter than mine! They elected a leader who by consensus of opinion was the best of the lot. He had to live up to those rules that were given, and they all tried to follow his example. As a result I had a most successful school.

Training Your Power of Discrimination

You should train yourself in the same way. Consider yourself a child in the school of cosmic training. When your mind and senses suggest doing a certain thing, use discrimination and ask whether that action will bring peace or happiness or sorrow. Unless you clearly explain to yourself why a certain course of action is the correct one, you will not succeed in doing the right thing. Seek that explanation within yourself, in the cosmic school lessons of your discriminative consciousness.

Suppose you are trying to decide about something. On one side you feel inclined to do it, and another part of you says, "Better not." Now then, ask your discrimination: "Why shouldn't I do this?" You may not get an answer at first, but if you wait a bit and analyze calmly and objectively, something inside tells you: "If you do this, you might get hurt." If you do not heed that voice and do it anyway, you find later that action has caused you trouble. In time, you find that as soon as you ask the inner mind, the right answer will come. Most of the time, persons without the clarity of discrimination will get a wrong answer, because they are used to following their desires and habits, and the only voice they can hear is that of the rationalizing sense-inclinations of the lower mind. But as the discriminative faculty of the higher mind is gradually developed, the wisdom of the soul's all-knowing intuitive power begins to guide one's determinations in everything.

By our use or nonuse of discrimination between right and wrong, either we please God or displease Him. Suppose you wake up in the morning and tell yourself, "Today I will make time for deep meditation." Then, the next thing you know, your desires get in the way—you fill your day with material busyness—and you have forgotten all about meditation. Years pass in this way, and you find you have made no progress toward knowing God and your real Self. You have wasted your time, for the most important part of life is to commune with God. He has given you the power to seek Him or to forget Him. The trouble is that in the face of tempting distractions you have no won't power. Your mind says, "What is the use of meditating right now? I need to get up and do such-and-so." But I know what the little-by-little that I meditated every day has meant to me, what answers it has given to me. Now as soon as I pray, I find that God's Light comes over me, and I smile. He tells me, "This world is all a nightmare, My son; it is not real. The only thing that is real is the Light Eternal. That is what you are; and that is what everyone is. You must teach them that they are not mortal beings in the darkness of this human life; they are immortal rays of My spirit, one with My eternal life within." "The light shineth in darkness, and the darkness comprehended it not."*

Discrimination aids the unfoldment of your divine nature. As soon as a desire comes, don't think, "It is my desire"; it doesn't belong to you. You are not the little body-identified ego; therefore do not think of its wants and "necessities" as your own. You are the soul, having everything that the Father has. That is my consciousness all the time. Any desire that comes, I take care to discern whether that desire is from God or from my mortal self. And I make up my mind to use my won't power to reject anything that is not beneficial.

In this way I have been able to follow religiously all the rules that I make for myself. There is not a day, morning and night, that I have missed the Energization Exercises and meditation. That is the secret of success—to give priority to your important desires, not to the multitude of your lesser desires. Most people never progress because they neglect their highest duties. That is why they are dissatisfied with life. Millions are led by their same old wrong habits every day. They have become like psychological furniture. Furniture remains always the same, becoming antique with time. Anyone who cannot say no to bad habits does not grow and improve in life; they are psychological antiques. I refuse to be like that; and so must you all. Develop your won't power—it will be a changing power within you. When temptation of wrong desires comes, resolutely say no to them and they will go away. Each time you do this, you change. With won't power, you no longer remain the same.

Perhaps as a child you were ill-tempered and angry, and now decades later you are still a slave to the anger habit—destroying

* John 1:5.

your peace and making everyone around you uncomfortable. Why remain attached to harmful habits? Take, for instance, the habit of greed. It is common to eat a little more than we should. But to be greedy to the point that you make yourself sick is unwise. Most of mankind's heart disease is due not only to wrong eating but to overeating. When people have consumed their too-heavy meal, they not only finish up with ice cream but put nuts on top of it! Eating for your health and enjoyment of food is fine, but to enjoy food at the cost of your health is sinful. It is not in the enjoyment of your senses that sin lies; it is when you are not able to curb enjoyment—that is, when you have no control over yourself.

Be Understanding and Compassionate Toward Others

Another time to use won't power is to refrain from gossip. Gossip means you love to revel in others' mistakes or moral misery. When you do that, you show that you do not know how to be a friend, and you could never be looked upon as an example or teacher of others. Jesus said, "He that is without sin, let him cast the first stone." When a person does wrong, he easily excuses himself; but when anyone else does wrong, his immediate reaction is to judge and condemn the wrongdoer. Instead, be frank with yourself; put yourself in that person's place and see how you love to forgive yourself. Why shouldn't you as readily be able to forgive others? People make mistakes not because they are essentially evil, but because they do not discriminate; they rather move by the impulses of their ignorance.

I remember one boy in my school was accused of some wrong act. The teachers felt it was sufficiently serious that they wanted me to expel him. That would have meant that for four years he could not get into any other school. I said, "I won't do that to him; I cannot sponsor such an idea. He may have done wrong, but I shall reason with him and forgive him." There was a big commotion of disagreement. So I said to the teachers: "Remember all the things that you have done during and since your childhood. Can you tell me you have never done anything reprehensibly wrong?" They all hung their heads. "If that boy were your son, would you send him out?" No one spoke. I said, "He is my son, and I will hear him."

So I called this boy to me; he came in very defiant: "Go ahead, I know you are going to throw me out."

"What makes you think so?" I replied. Again he challenged me rebelliously: "Go ahead." I replied, "How childish of you. You have done wrong, and you are proud of it. What is the matter with you? Suppose you did do wrong. That doesn't mean you have to do wrong again."

He hung his head. "Don't do it again," I said. He looked at me like the little child that he was. "You mean you won't send me away?"

"You know that what you did was wrong, don't you?"

He said, "Yes."

"Isn't that enough?" I said. "Don't repeat it."

Tears came in his eyes and he told me, "You know, I had made up my mind that if you sent me away, I would use my life to do all the evil things that I could." Then he went on, "I am sorry for what I have done, and promise you that I will never do it again."

Years later when I went back to India, I learned that he had gone to England to further his education and opportunities. He now had a successful career, was very spiritual, and had a wonderful family. He came to me in tears and said, "Do you remember me?" I greeted him lovingly. He said, "That day that you forgave me made me what I am today. It is all due to your faith in me." He embraced me and cried like a child.

If I had sent that young boy away from my school, he would not have become the remarkable man he is. He would have been nothing today. So remember, love changes people; their part is to repent of their wrongdoing and cultivate discrimination and won't power to guide their future behavior.

Exercise Your Won't Power With a Spirit of Humility

Now, just because I have said you should develop won't power, it doesn't mean that you should belittle people with your noble nos. When confronted with a wrong choice, just inwardly say, "I won't" and outwardly be silent. Someone may suggest, "Let's go out and have a drink together." Do not make yourself repugnant before others or try to impress them by how high above such things you are. There are many ways that you can graciously decline without making others feel uneasy. Those who drink always want others to drink with them. Suppose you have to transact business with such people. There is no need to offend them when offered a drink. You can very graciously say, "Thank you, not today," or "Thank you, let me have a ginger ale."

You will be on the way toward becoming a master of yourself if you silently develop your won't power without being discourteous to anybody. You need not do as others ask in order to avoid hurting their feelings. Just be silently firm. There is no need to advertise it to everyone. Inwardly use that won't power and say to yourself, "I will do only what is good, but I will refuse gracefully so as not to offend others." Do you see my point? If you learn to exercise won't power in the right way and at the right time, you will find out that you are becoming a dynamo of power within. You will be loved by God, for He wants you to resist the harmful temptations that His creation has placed here on earth. Only sissies succumb to temptation; it is a master who is strong. When your conscience and God believe in you, you do not care what the world thinks about you according to its standards.

Last of all, self-mastery requires that you use won't power to restrain the impulses of the ungoverned ego. Egotism is either an inferiority complex or a superiority complex—both are evil, both originate through egomania. Egotists think first of themselves, "I, I, I," all the time. The very sight of such an individual makes others shrink. Is it not the person who is humble and considerate that you love most? He who advertises himself all the time nobody cares for. The humble person is like the attractive silent fragrance of a flower. Banish the bad habit of egotism. As soon as you catch yourself asserting "I, I, I," inwardly command yourself, "I won't think of myself so much." Eventually, through that willfully directed won't power, you will overcome egotism. Do not be so forceful in your opinions. Is it not much better to say to your friend not, "I know so," but "Don't you think so?" You may think that forcefulness persuades people to think your way, but it will do just the opposite. All great men are wonderful; they are very easy to talk with because they are humble.

If you develop won't power, you will not find it difficult to awaken the will and power to be a master of yourself. You will have the inner strength to follow through on your discriminative resolutions: "When my mind says *I can't,* my wisdom says *I will.*"

Different Forms of Love for God

Self-Realization Fellowship International Headquarters, Los Angeles, April 30, 1934

My spiritual duty is to impress on you the importance of the harmonious development of body, mind, and soul. Your duty is to follow these teachings regularly, by which you will nurture that development physically, mentally, and spiritually.

The completeness of life, which expresses itself as happiness, is founded on man's relationship with his Creator, the soul's awakening realization of its essential connection with God. Ignorance of this truth is the root cause of all misery; nothing material can permanently assuage it. Thus Jesus said, "Seek God first, and all things will be added unto you."* Those who forget God do not find real happiness. So when God takes possessions away from you, He is telling you not to become entangled in matter. He wants only to remind you to seek Him; because if you forget the Creator, everything will forsake you—all happiness and peace will fly away. The fulfillment of life's purpose really begins when the search for Him begins.

The Devotee Can Enjoy Various Relationships With God

There are various relationships that can be developed between the devotee and God that characterize the divine search. This is not a generally accepted concept in the West. But God has appeared to His devotees in numerous forms.

You can look upon God as the Master and yourself as the servant—yet the inherent defect in this is that you are made in His image and are thus His divine son. One may even accept God as the Servant, for He is serving the devotee in everything. He is the supreme Servant, tending to all needs of the universe. He showed the greatness of His humble servitude when He, in Jesus, washed the feet of the disciples.

* Matthew 6:33.

Another form of relationship with God is that of Father and son. Jesus had that relationship with God. But again, that relationship can be transposed with God as the Son and yourself as the father or mother. A sainted devotee in India found God by looking upon Him as her son. One day the infant Lord Krishna, an avatar (divine incarnation of the Infinite), prankishly stole some milk-curd cheese, filling his mouth with it. His mother Yasoda came running, scolding, "You will choke! Come here." At last she caught him and put her finger in Krishna's mouth to make him open it. When he opened his mouth, Yasoda saw the whole universe within him. Quickly she turned away from the vision, desiring to know the Lord only in the form of her adorable baby.

Then there is the love of the son for the Mother. That has been my principal relationship. We are devoted to the father, but we love mother because her compassion forgives us when the stern reasoning of the father will not. Mother's love is always forgiving. That is the unconditional love of God, the love of God incarnated in the mother's heart. The Divine Mother-child relationship is so wonderful because no matter what you are, She always loves you. Never call yourself a sinner, for you are a child of God, a child of the Divine Mother. And the Mother never forsakes you when you make mistakes, for She knows that then you need Her even more. She will help the repentant child to reform and to rectify its errors.

There is another relationship—God as the Beloved, you as the loved one. That is a very difficult conception, but some pure souls have succeeded. It is not a path for those who have not mastered body consciousness, because that relationship with God is nullified by any taint of carnal thought. To find God by that relationship is thus difficult, because it demands only the purest love.

When you think of God as your Friend, that relationship expresses the grandest form of love and devotion. Friendship is the touchstone by which we may know the purity of any relationship, human or divine. It has the sweetness of all forms of love without their contamination. In parental love there is a compulsion of nature; and in all other forms of human love there is some selfish compulsion—but not in true friendship. When you speak of a sibling and say, "He is my brother," that means he is born of the same parents and you have to love him as such. But when you say of another, "He is my friend," that means you offer to him your love that is pure and unconditional—that you have freely chosen to give your love to him.

A friend may be like a father or a mother to us, or a faithful confidant and supporter. In all human relations God has tried to express His love for us. So look to Him as your Divine Friend, the one you freely choose to love unconditionally and who loves you eternally. Such was the relationship between the devotee Arjuna and his intimate Divine Friend Lord Krishna, the avatar in whom Arjuna saw the Infinite incarnate. Through his devout, worshipful friendship, he received enlightenment and liberation from the Universal Spirit as his Divine Friend Krishna.

In the friendship relationship with God, there is both devotion and love: the reverence of worship and the consummation of union. Love is complete surrender. Devotion says "I adore Thee"; love says "Thou and I are One."

Devotion and Love Combined Is the Supreme Form of Expression Toward God

Devotion is a deeply reverential admiration for God. It is characterized by an element of separation between the soul and Spirit. In love, there is a merging of the two into One. In devotion, your desire is not to establish oneness with God, but to keep your separate identity for the joy of standing apart and worshiping the Object of your adoration. The attitude of devotion is, "I am Thy son, and Thou art my Father"; or, "I am Thy lover, and Thou art my Beloved"; or, "I am Thy devotee, and Thou art my Lord." In this state, the devotee doesn't want to say or feel, "Thou and I are One," but rather, "I adore Thee." Even though liberation has been attained, the devotee is free to retain his individuality in order to enjoy, throughout this life and all eternity, the bliss of beholding God and worshiping Him with the offering of devotion.

When love and devotion are combined, that is the supreme form of expression toward God.

Divine Law Is Very Exacting Without Love and Devotion

Along with the reverence of devotion and the surrender of love, there must also be knowledge and application of the law by which He can be known. If you follow the law of scientific yoga concentration and meditation, you learn how to rise above your flesh consciousness; then you will realize God and can go back to the Infinite. However, without love and devotion, the law alone is very exacting. But when with the faithful practice of the guru-given yoga techniques of God-realization, you can say with the fervor of your heart and soul, "God, You are my Divine Friend—my Divine Mother, my Divine Father"—His heart melts. These things that I am telling you are not from any text. These are truths that I receive in my communion with God.

God Has Already Given Himself to Us

Love and devotion for God is something I can talk about day and night and never end. It is something very intoxicating, very solacing. The Lord says, I can give you salvation if you make the effort; but I cannot give My love and devotion, for if I give that away I become poor.* This is the treasure of God, His very essence. It is so all-fulfilling; He has naught else of worth, in comparison, to give. He has, veritably, given Himself.

God has given to you the blessedness of belonging to Him always. You have only to realize that. He feels insulted when you base your relationship with Him on prayers for money or fulfillment of material desires. Why make prosperity your utmost goal, for it will seek you when you seek God. There is not a need or wish that God hasn't satisfied for me. And I do not have to ask. You should pray only for one thing: that you may be with Him always. When you have prayed for that, you have prayed for everything else.

One great saint said, "He who seeks God is the cleverest of all persons," because others seek God a little bit and then lapse into dependence on material things for their happiness, and instead they get sorrow and trouble. In God you will find everything that will make you lastingly happy.

In seeking God, remember, there is one thing He lacks, one thing He is seeking from you: your love and devotion freely given to Him from your heart. When you are engaged in outer rituals and vocal prayer your mind cannot go deeper within, and your feelings will be restless. To reach God, your prayers must be interiorized with concentration and permeated with devotion. No matter how you try, without devotion you are a poor, poor marksman.† But with devotion, you have touched God; He will surely come to you.

* From an old Bengali chant, "Divine Mother's Song to the Devotee," translated and set to music by Paramahansa Yogananda in his *Cosmic Chants* (published by Self-Realization Fellowship).

† Reference to Paramahansaji's prayer "Heavenly Hart, I hunted Thee in the forest of consciousness," in *Whispers from Eternity* (published by Self-Realization Fellowship).

God is not a respecter of persons as to their worldly merits. Those who make the real effort within their hearts, they alone can find Him. Your highest duty is to seek God and to spread this message. For to give food to the hungry is good, to give strength to the weak is better, but to give God is the highest good. Every day, bring the word of Self-Realization to hungry souls. By your example, bring devotion for God to the hearts of those that you love.

Talk With God After Meditation

Meditate at home regularly in the way you have been taught. Before you begin meditation, prepare your consciousness with devotion, with the thought that God has expressed Himself through all loves. His love is the reservoir, and all these forms of love are openings in that reservoir. So invoke the Divine Presence as "Heavenly Father, Mother, Friend, Beloved God."

After you have meditated, talk with God. Take any aspect of love you want and give devotion to God in that form. Again and again pray to Him and demand, "Never leave me, Father. Be with me always and always and always." That is how my time is passed in great joy. In devotion is the conjunction of your feeling with intellectual and intuitional perception of God.

Meditate at night; don't go to bed until your heart is aflame with devotion. And every day be fishers of men, to establish His temple in the hearts of others. Life will be just a dream of happiness if you do this.

"God; God; God; God. Be with us always."

The Devotional Way to God

Self-Realization Fellowship Golden Lotus Temple, Encinitas, California, March 2, 1941

Who has created the cosmic cornucopia with its surfeit of forms tumbling into place to decorate the universe and people the earth? When we look at the workings of a watch, we understand that it is man who has made the intricate parts and put them together. But when we look at the lawn, we must ask, "Who created the power in the seed that dressed the soil with verdant grass?" And who made us to behold the wondrous mysteries of creation? The Creator is hiding Himself, that perchance someday we may seek and find Him. The divine man has succeeded in that search; he is conscious of the One who is secreted within us and who is hiding everywhere. He is conscious of the Power behind all powers, the Maker of wisdom and love, the Source of our ability to produce the thoughts we think, the Fountain of all life that flows within us and all beings.

I see Him everywhere. It is His tears that are weeping in the rain: tears of mercy that plants may live and bring forth their blossoms and fruits; tears of His love for the world. Our loved ones love us because the Lord loves us. We separate ourselves from God, and that is why we do not feel Him. But it is He whose love comes to us through our father, mother, friends. He is the love within our family love; the love behind our love for our country; the love that embraces all races; the love in our hearts we give to everything we love. If we expand that love, we will find Him at last.

Because God is, therefore all things are. Without Him, naught exists. The moon, the stars, the lightning are but the borrowed beauties of the Most Beautiful. Without Him they cease to be. Can the waves play on without the ocean? No. But the existence of the ocean is unconditioned by the presence of the waves. So is the surge of our life dependent on the Infinite Sea of Life. The dance of vitality and play of passion in the body exist only because of the power of God, which comes continuously percolating through our consciousness. But all these things will disappear if He withdraws Himself.

How Devotion Reveals the Hidden Presence of God

To discover the hidden presence of God, you must love Him; but it came to my mind, how can you love God without knowing Him? You cannot love anything that is unknown to you. Can you love a flower you have never seen? Can you love the ocean if it is just a word to you? Could you love someone you had never known or heard about? Could you love someone as a friend whom you never met? Could you love anything that you knew nothing about? How, then, is it possible to love God, having never seen Him? I cannot say that anymore. I see Him all the time. Every thought you are thinking right now, I see as coming from that Light. When you see from a hilltop how beautiful are the twinkling lights of a city, you forget that it is the dynamo that is providing the electricity to illumine the bulbs. So when you see the sparkling vitality of human beings, but you do not know what is enlivening them, then you are spiritually blind. That Power, even though unseen, is very evident. It is all the time playing hide-and-seek behind our thoughts. Because God chooses to remain hidden, that is why it is difficult to think of Him and to love Him.

The paradox is that the simplest way to know God is the way of love. There is a way of knowledge (*Jnana Yoga*) by which He can be known: the path of analytical discrimination, eliminating all that is not God— *"Neti, neti,"* not this; not that. Another way is to purify oneself by performing nothing but good actions and renouncing the fruits thereof (*Karma Yoga*). And then there is the path of devotion (*Bhakti Yoga*), continuously thinking of God until one sees Him in everything. He is so evident if we look for Him with the eyes of devotion. We must make Him know that we are wanting Him, that He cannot continue to elude us. If we press Him with our thoughts, with our longing for Him, He is bound to express Himself; He is bound to respond.

God's presence is so close; it is just as though somebody is playing hide-and-seek with you in a dark room. Though you do not see the person, you feel that he is there. That is how God is, just behind the darkness of your unseeing eyes. He is talking to us through the wise man. And He is inspiring us through the great ones, such as Christ, Krishna, and the Masters. He is, but where is He? That is what devotion answers: You do not have to see Him in order to become devoted to Him. Devotion means that you know He is omnipresent around you in the dark conundrum of cosmos, playing a divine game of hide-and-seek with you. Behind the leaves, behind the wind, behind the warm rays of the sun—He is hiding, but He is there. He is not far away; that is why it becomes easy to love Him.

God is the greatest lover our hearts can know. He loves to be pursued, because the only thing He hopes for is the love of His children. To receive their love is the sole purpose for which He sent forth creation. He has everything within Himself, except our love. He gave us free will to love Him or to love Him not. He wants us very much. That is why He sends His saints to show us the way back to Him.

Attitudes for Victory Over Your Obstacles

God has created passions and temptations; but such barriers were not meant to block completely the way to realizing the presence of God. All of life's struggles are like an obstacle course, hurdles to be overcome in the race to God. You may not be first to finish the race, but you will succeed if you try hard enough. Though it is difficult when life presses you down, still if you make the effort with strong determination, you will triumph over every challenge. When the final lap of this obstacle race is finished, He will garland your victory with His everlasting love. But most people are too lazy even to try!

God wants us to get through His race of life. You will be receptive to His help if you show Him that you love Him. Have the love of God always in your heart, that you may know He is hiding, but is ever near. You cannot escape having to go through obstacles and troubles. That is the way of life; it is painful. The greatest saints have suffered, and suffered with a smile for God. There are many persons who have never suffered sickness and at the time of death have just fallen asleep without any difficulty. But that does not mean they are yogis, united to God. Lots of animals have also lived and died without suffering. The equanimity of yoga is when your love rises above all obstacles that God has put before you. In that transcendence you find Him. As one great saint of India used to pray: "Come to me as a touch of pain, for in pain I urgently remember Thee. If I should ever forget Thee, in the thickets of joyous tears touch me with the finger of pain to wake me from that forgetfulness." So pain was given not as a cruelty or to destroy us, but as an awakening, a reminder that we must reach the Immutable One where all pain ceases.

Anything that causes pain and suffering should be avoided if possible. But when it does come, unless you are able to endure without embitterment and despair, you cannot reach the kingdom of God. Look at Jesus Christ on the cross. Consciously he had to go through the dreadful sensations of pain until he had overcome the flesh. When he lifted his consciousness to God-awareness, he realized instantly that it is all a delusion; and then the arms of the Father enfolded him. This whole drama is between pain and love. Your love must be greater than your pain.

To be unfailing, love must be unconditional. Conditional love is selfish love. Selfishness is that trait by which you want everything to be to your advantage and in which you give little or nothing in return. Conditional love says, "I love him because he loves me; he does so much for me." Similarly, some persons love God because He has given them life, and health, and other gifts of being. Conditional love of God reasons: "I don't know what life is all about, or what may happen to me. I don't know how this body is sustained, how it digests food, how it maintains its health. Unless I pray to God He might neglect me." Now that is a very poor way to think of God. It is a sort of barter between God and human beings: "You look after me, Lord, and I will love You."

Receiving God's Freely Offered Abundance

The relationship between God and human beings is not a conditional contract between a boss and his employees. It is a relationship of love, and that is where I want to take you today. We, as children of God, have a claim on God as our Father. We do not have to grovel to show our gratefulness to Him for anything He gives. It is natural for a father to look after his child; that is his responsibility. Therefore why pray to God for this or that material thing? If you realize your loving Father-child relationship with God, you will receive what you need without asking. Never doubt that. It is because you doubt that you do not receive. Your doubt, your lack of faith, holds you back from entering into God's freely offered abundance. You should rather say to Him: "Father, I am Your child. You know when I have a pain in this body. You know my every need. Why should I ask for these things?" Didn't Jesus say, "Are not two sparrows sold for a farthing? and one of them shall not fall on the ground without [the sight of] your Father."*

* Matthew 10:29.

The Lord knows every thought moving through etheric space throughout the cosmos. The perception of an ant is only conscious of the little bit of space around it; by comparison, man's vision is vast. Likewise, man's perception is infinitesimal compared to God's conscious awareness of everything in this universe. He doesn't have to be reminded of your needs; rather you need to remind yourself to reestablish your divine relationship with Him as your loving Father and the Source of all.

As the electric lights of a city are connected with a dynamo, so all life is connected with God. Some persons see and comment on the beauty and usefulness of the light in the bulb. Other mentalities reason where that light comes from, and that reason leads them to the dynamo. If you are conscious of the Source of this life, you will know how to draw continuously on its sustaining power. And even when the radiance of life is taken out of your body at death, you follow it consciously into the Eternal Light—that Great Life which lights the little bulb of flesh.

This Essence of life is unknown to millions, and yet they are always using that power of God. Why not be conscious of that Power?

The devotee whose love for God is unconditional says: "I didn't ask You, O Lord, to create this body. Why should I have to ask You to care for it? I will not thank You for creating me, for this body is a nest of pain and limitations." This may sound sacrilegious, but it leads to something wonderful. It is your duty and privilege as His child to lovingly demand of Him His attention, not by weak supplication, but by affirmation of your divine status and rightful endowments—above all, your right to know your Heavenly Father. Your part is to love Him, unconditionally. The devotee thinks, "I am much more than the animals who are bound by instinct. I have the ultimate freedom to receive You, or to cast You away, Lord. You have not imposed Yourself on me, nor made it a necessary condition to my life that I must love You. Because of that freedom, I love You, Lord. I love You, not because You have given me life, not because You look after this life, but freely do I love You, without any condition."

We may not realize it, but in effect God parted with everything when He created human beings and endowed them with free will. Having set in motion His self-perpetuating cosmic laws that maintain the universe for the benefit of His children, He became not the Owner but the Observer of the drama—how human beings would use their freedom. Would they embrace or reject His omnipresence amongst them? Instantly He could reclaim all manifestation except the love of His children, to whom He gave the freedom of will to cast Him aside or to accept Him. That is the greatness of God. We should choose to love Him, or we miss the whole magic and joy of His creation. Love gives and doesn't ask for anything in return. "You have given me love, my Lord, and I know by the happiness love gives that it is a joy to love You. In the love You have placed in my heart You have given me something of my own that I can give to You without seeking anything from You." God gave us life, He gave us the power to love, He gave us everything, along with the freedom to cast Him aside. In other words, He has given to us, asking nothing from us. His greatest blessing is His unconditional love, given silently, without reservation or expectation. We, being His children endowed with the power of His unconditional love, should use that power to find Him: "O Lord, I do not want anything from Thee but Thy love alone; and without condition I give my love to Thee."

Yoga Uncovers the Inner Dimension of Outer Worship

There are various modes of expression of devotion to God. Sage Vyasa, writer of the Bhagavad Gita, says: "Devotion is worship of God." Worship implies a reverential separation between the devotee and God—the worshiper and the Object of worship. Several verses in the Gita define various forms of ceremonial worship, the ultimate of which is to make one's whole life a ceremonial offering to God; that is, all the time to be busy with expressions of devotion to attain realization of God.*

Acts of devotion are much better than merely reading spiritual books and scripture. Reading takes you inward and gives some inspiration, but in itself it does not give you the contact of God. Intellectual knowledge of God does not mean that you know God. A great mistake in the modern world is reading about God or listening to sermons about Him without trying to commune with Him, thinking that actual communion with God is impossible. How, then, can one presume even to talk about Him who is impossible to know? But the saints I have met, who have communed with God, say, "Don't just read about God. First taste Him; and then you will

* See Bhagavad Gita IX:13–34, as well as Paramahansa Yogananda's commentary on these verses in his *God Talks With Arjuna: The Bhagavad Gita* (published by Self-Realization Fellowship).

be able to speak thousands of words about Him, as with a thousand mouths. But if you don't taste Him, everything you say will be mere surmises." Perception of God is what is necessary. Then even if you have no grace of language, if your heart is filled with Him, others will feel the power and conviction of your direct perception.

For the average worshiper, some ceremony is good. The ceremonies in India are most wonderful in rousing devotion if performed with an understanding of their symbology. The altars are adorned with garlands of flowers, joss sticks (incense), and oil lamps. You sit, or stand, or kneel before the altar and chant as symbolic offerings are made. These rituals were discarded by the yogis, however, because they hold the attention outward. When the conch shell is blown and the gong is beat and the tinkling of bells are sounded—all of which are depictions of astral sounds—very few can think deeply about God. The mind is kept engaged in the ceremony. Nevertheless, most people prefer ceremony, for, unlike the yogis, they do not like to turn inward because initially they experience only darkness and silence. So some ceremony is helpful in the beginning to awaken devotion.

Whatever you do sincerely, God appreciates. But ceremony without love for God is misleading; it becomes mechanical. If the mind can remain deeply focused on God, and the ritual is done with devotion, however, then the response of God is there. I have performed those rites for hours at a time, and become completely absorbed in God. But through my guru, Swami Sri Yukteswar, I found something that roused my devotion even more, without any outward ceremony, and that was the practice of Kriya Yoga—the supreme *yajna* or ceremonial rite of inner worship.*

In the West there has been nonunderstanding of the images in the temples of India. If imaginary concepts are fashioned into statues and worshiped for themselves as possessing some spiritual power, that is idol worship. But when you enshrine the figure of Krishna and worship him, thinking of the Divinity within all his qualities, that is not idol worship. You like to have the picture of your father or your mother or your children around you, because it makes you think of the qualities of those you love. So it is when one places respectfully on the altar the figure of the Lord Krishna or Christ or some other symbolic depiction of an aspect of God's divine attributes.

* See *Autobiography of a Yogi*, chapter 26, and *God Talks With Arjuna: The Bhagavad Gita*, Chapter IV (both published by Self-Realization Fellowship).

It may also seem strange to the Western mind how devotees in India look after the form of God represented in the temples. The image is dressed and variously adorned. Devotees take to the temple in the morning a little food to be offered to the Deity. The devotee's first thought of the day is of God. They know God is not troubled by cold and hunger, but still, out of devotion, the devotee makes symbolic offerings while all the time he is inwardly worshiping God as Spirit. By his external acts, the devotee merely personalizes God to include Him in his daily life.

There is the story of one great saint in India, Sri Ramakrishna. He used to worship and pray in the Dakshineswar Temple before an image of the Divine Mother as Kali. So intense was his longing and unceasing prayer for some response from Her, so great was his outpouring of devotion, that the stone image on the altar became the most beautiful, living form of the Mother, who spoke to him, saying, "My devotee, I am here with you." This was a true miracle, a true demonstration of response from the Divine. So devotion is not blind emotionalism, but the opening of divine sight through which the hidden God is revealed.

Chanting is another way of awakening devotion. The great devotee Ramprasad realized God through his devotional songs; as did Sri Chaitanya, who danced in ecstasy as he sang the name of God.

But now I say, "O Divine Mother, I don't have to use flowers and incense and these other external offerings to arouse my love for Thee. When I say Thy name, that is all that is necessary. My heart is locked in love for Thee. My body cannot move; my breath cannot flow without Thee." The devotee who feels God as the only reality existing within him, and himself existing in God, is united with God, one with God in unconditional union. That devotee inwardly perceives: "When I eat, I am eating for Him. When I serve, my hands are His. When I speak, my voice is His. It is God who is feeling and loving through me." Such a devotee looks after the body as the temple of God. He realizes that it is God who has incarnated in the body.

There is no longer Yogananda. It is He who is living in this body. If He says for me to do something, I do it. If He tells me not to do something, I will not do it; and even if the whole world urges, I will not go against His will. The ego stands a little apart to hold on to the consciousness that He is there. And sometimes the ego loses itself by merging in Him. If an idol made of salt bathes in the sea, it will melt in the sea. So sometimes the devotee says: "I was diving in the Ocean of Nectar. But as I myself was made of honey, I felt myself merging in that nectarean Sea. So I withdrew a little, for I wanted to remain separate enough to enjoy worshiping and tasting that Incredible Sweetness." So the devotee employs his ego habit to keep himself just a little apart from complete dissolution in God. But he lives for God alone: "I am happy doing only God's will; serving Him who is residing for a time in this body, and who is in the forms of all." So this is a different aspect of devotion: To do everything completely detached, while striving and enjoying only to do the will of God. Even if anything untoward happens to the body, the devotee is anxious to make it right only because God is in that bodily temple.

Commune With God Enthroned in the Depths of the Heart

When you are worshiping in external ways, your mind is outside, and God is hidden variously behind the dense barriers of material objects. But when you are worshiping God in the temple of silence within the body, you are right there with Him—your consciousness touching His Consciousness. Self-Realization Fellowship shows you the way to this inner communion with God, who is veritably enthroned in the depths of the heart. Yogis concentrate here at the Christ or *Kutastha* center in the middle of the forehead, the seat of concentration for the practice of scientific techniques of God-communion. Those who call to Him only with devotion concentrate at the heart center, the center of feeling. On this point there is always a controversy between the *bhaktas* and the yogis. When you are perceiving God, there is both love and wisdom. Love and wisdom become one and the same. When you have wisdom, you have love. When you have love, you have wisdom. There is no separate pole. So by concentrating initially at either the heart center, as do the *bhaktas,* or the Christ center, as do the yogis, God can separately be felt. Then in that actual communion with Him, these two poles come together; there is no separateness anymore of the two centers; heart and mind are as one.

When you are absorbed in love for God, His response is there at the heart center, a tremendous feeling of calmness and divine joy welling up in the heart that draws your attention or concentration to that center. That feeling in the heart is like a great comet of light; and in that light is the love of God. It is that feeling which you should concentrate on in the heart. Those who are in earnest about God are aware of these subtle spiritual experiences. As soon

Paramahansa Yogananda in Los Angeles, January 26, 1950, at a banquet in celebration of India's becoming a republic

During the years 1920 through 1935, Paramahansa Yogananda conducted extensive lectures and classes to capacity audiences in major cities across the United States. The Guru is photographed above with students who attended his class in Los Angeles on the science of Kriya Yoga, January 30, 1925. A newspaper account of his public lectures earlier that week in Los Angeles' Philharmonic Auditorium reported: "The Philharmonic lobby looked like the New York subway Times Square station in the evening rush. By six-thirty every seat within the huge auditorium had been taken....Outside the total number drawn by the event was swelled to an easy 6,000. And the occasion? Not the coming of Christ but of another oriental, Swami Yogananda."

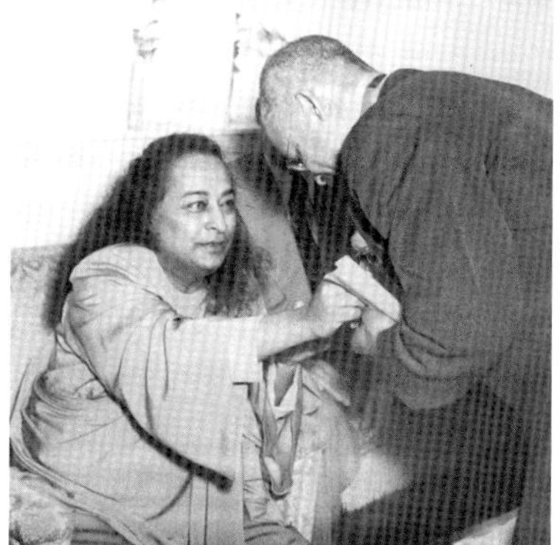

(Left) Governor Alvan T. Fuller of Massachusetts greets Paramahansa Yogananda at the State House in Boston, September 19, 1928. *(Right)* Paramahansa Yogananda presents special award on behalf of Self-Realization Fellowship to Los Angeles Police Commissioner Dr. John A. Somerville for his outstanding work in social service and race relations. The occasion was the dedication of SRF India Center, Hollywood, California, April 8, 1950.

as I concentrate on the heart, I feel that light, that glow of God's all-consuming love.

If you have that love for God which brings actual perception of Him, you do not require the formal discipline of renunciation. It becomes automatic; all lesser desires and attachments fall away. The selfish man is not a man of God, because he is always thinking of the desires of the ego apart from God. Renunciation is the means by which God can be known, but it is not the end in itself. Love is much greater than mere renunciation. Love is a joyous giving. When that is in the heart, there is no pain in parting with anything. When renunciation for its own sake is uppermost, the devotee rationalizes, "Why should I part with this or that?" He discriminates in giving. Renunciation is made to seem so terrible that few want to follow it. But when love for God is there, then even the renunciant has no feeling of renunciation. You gladly do without anything or everything for love of God. The most enjoyable way of life, whether as a monastic or a householder, is to be in love with Him.

"The Most Wonderful Existence You Can Imagine"

The devotee who is in love with God says, "Even though I don't see You, Lord, I know You are right behind my thoughts. I could not think or reason without You. I could not will without You. I could not walk or speak without You. So, Lord, I know You are here with me all the time, behind my brain, behind my love, behind my whole existence; and that is why I love You." When you are conscious of His presence within you and that your whole being is solely dependent on Him, that is the devotional way to God. If you have this awareness of His immanence, how could you be selfish when you see Him in everyone? He who loves God, loves God in everyone.

There is a story that two persons had loved each other as friends for a long time. To prove their friendship they decided to pool a substantial amount of their resources—the one who had more contributed more. They bought two equal pieces of gold, one for each. After some time, the larger contributor demanded of his erstwhile friend, "Give your gold piece to me. It is rightfully mine." The other friend said, "All right, take it. It is yours"—thus relinquishing even his share of the investment. His friendship was unconditional. He could not feel enmity toward his friend. He fulfilled their pact to give to each other freely, while the selfish friend had a flaw of greed in his love.

Jesus had that perfect, unselfish love of God, and that is why he could give his life for all. "Greater love hath no man than this, that a man lay down his life for his friends."* When I love someone, I gladly suffer pain for that person. With God's permission I have taken on the karma of others to lessen their suffering. Pure unselfish love in God's love is a most wonderful state of consciousness. It is an ecstasy day and night.

God richly rewards His devotees. But the word "reward" is obnoxious to me, because I do not seek a reward from God. Since He has given me unconditional love to possess as my own, I want to give that love to Him. Even if for a thousand years He does not reply, what of it? Give your love to God just the same, without even asking, "Come to me." Give to Him without condition.

In the devotional way to God, the devotee says, "Lord, I will be happy in the giving of my love to You, even though my offering may be inadequate. I am not seeking for Your response; I am not asking You to receive my love. Whether or not You receive it, whether or not You respond, I am glad just to give my unconditional love to You; that is all. It is my greatest happiness. Unceasingly I give that love to You, and to Your manifested Presence in the temple of flowers and all nature, in the temple of friends and loved ones, in the temple of devotees, in the temple of my soul. I know that as You have made me in Your image, I am one with You always. Even if You never reply to me, I give my love to You, my Lord, and shall keep on giving unto eternity. That is all I know."

He who is a true lover of God stands by Him equally during sunny days of joy and dark days of trials. Why not? Those who are in love are day and night thinking only of their beloved one. So is this romance with God. It is the most wonderful existence you can ever imagine.

* John 15:13.

Divine Devotion

The Love for God That Sets You Free

*Self-Realization Fellowship Golden Lotus Temple, Encinitas, California, August 31, 1939**

Two things are necessary to find God: knowledge of divine law, and devotion. Ignorance of God's laws causes man to convert what God has created into engines of destruction. Could you think of getting up right now and killing the others in this room? You couldn't; none of you would act outside of the divine law in that way, no matter what the incitement was. But when the drugs of ignorance, selfishness, and false patriotism are instilled, knowledge of divine law is overpowered by man's base emotions; a person in that state is even ready to kill. Emotional ignorance—feelings ruled by material desires and attachments—is the death of knowledge and right action.†

Attachment to Materiality Takes Us Away From God

Devotion is not emotion. Devotion is one's steady love of God. I find that no matter what I am doing there is no desire in me that can divert my mind from God. Why? Not because contrary desires have been suppressed, but because I have something infinitely greater—that which God has given to me. I saw that all the material comforts and satisfactions that desires promised me could not give unconditional happiness. But in the desire for God, in communion with God, I found the supreme happiness. Finding that, I did not want anything else. Money, cars, friends, houses—nothing else gave me that happiness which He gave me.

* This talk was given just prior to the outbreak of World War II.

† "Brooding on sense objects causes attachment to them. Attachment breeds craving; craving breeds anger. Anger breeds delusion; delusion breeds loss of memory (of the Self). Loss of right memory causes decay of the discriminating faculty. From decay of discrimination, annihilation (of spiritual life) follows" (Bhagavad Gita II:62–63).

I remember how great was my joy on the day my father bought me a motorcycle. Soon my friends began referring to me as "the motorcycle swami," as daily I rode from Calcutta to see my guru [Swami Sri Yukteswarji] at his ashram in Serampore. But I could never feel quite as much happiness in possessing that motorcycle as in the initial pleasure I had in receiving it. Every day I wanted to feel that first joy again, but I could never do so. That is the way of desires; they always promise lasting happiness, but are powerless to deliver that fulfillment.

But I did enjoy the sense of freedom this mode of conveyance gave to me. So one day I asked my guru, "Master, am I attached to that motorcycle?" (He was aware of my every thought.) He said, "Certainly not! What is the use of taking a car or tying yourself to a train schedule when you have your motorcycle?" But one day an acquaintance of mine expressed a desire for it, and I gave it away to him. I never missed it.

The valiant enjoy all good things, but they are never attached. They know God is with them, and whatever they say and feel reveals the glories of God. "O Arjuna! when a man completely relinquishes all desires of the mind, and is entirely contented in the Self, by the Self, he is then considered to be one settled in wisdom....He who is free from worldly loves, fears, and angers...who is everywhere nonattached, neither joyously excited by encountering good nor disturbed by evil, has an established wisdom."*

Attachment gives mental torture. That is why the body-identified individual fears death. Death is not painful, physically speaking. That is what every person will find when he leaves the body. The pain is only in the mind, when the imagination of the consciousness lingers on trying to cling to the physical experiences that must be left behind. The attached individual laments, "I cannot hear the music I love; where has it gone? Where are all the beautiful things I used to see, the foods I savored, the touch of my loved ones?" Well, one doesn't miss them when one goes to sleep! Why create desires for this and that which are pleasing only to the body and senses, so that when you die you miss them? Those mental attachments are far more painful than death is. Death itself is a most pleasant experience. You suddenly find yourself in an angelic body of astral light and energy; you realize you have no bones to break, no head to bump, no stomach

* Bhagavad Gita II:55–57.

to ache. Many times I have experienced in *samadhi* that wondrous freedom from the body prison.

Once I was coming into my room and suddenly I saw myself lying on the bed, dead. I was so shocked! And the Lord said to me through the voice of Lahiri Mahasaya, "How do you like being dead?" At first I was shaken; then I replied, "Lord, it is all right. How can I be dead when I am fully aware and talking to you?" The voice laughed and the experience was over; and I saw again that there is no reason to be attached to the body. My body had been dead to me, but still I was conscious and talking.

You do not have to use your vocal cords in the spiritual method of talking. You think what you want to communicate, and the other person receives it. God not only feels our thoughts, He can hear the sound of our thoughts. Thoughts are vibrations of consciousness, and all vibrations produce sound. That is how the thoughts of others can be known by those with an intuitive sensitivity. Even when you say something only mentally you are producing a sound that conveys your thoughts, though that subtle vibration is beyond the range of the physical senses. All the time thoughts of others come to me, but I do not speak of what I perceive. When you speak about the private lives of others, it cheapens your consciousness.

Each human being represents a great problem—a complexity of adopted habits of thinking and acting from the consciousness of mortal limitations. The conundrum for each person is how to get free of those habits that bind him, how to regain the soul's native, unconditioned divinity. What is the way? The masters tell us to perform the habitual activities that are necessary for life in this world without attachment to them. Attachment limits the soul to the egoistic delusion of dependence on outer conditions. Do not be attached to anything. It is just as binding to be attached to vegetarianism as to be attached to a diet of meats. To think, "I eat healthful foods because God has given me a body to look after, but I am not attached to any food"—that is best.

Devotion and Adherence to Divine Law Free Us From Attachments

Above all, to untie the mortal ties that bind the soul, you must have devotion for God. He loves the devotion of His children—not as the dedication of the slave to the master, which is tainted with fear of Him; but the heart's devotion of willing surrender that springs from love of Him. In fear there is always an element of begging, a prayer for some desire to be fulfilled. But the devotion of surrender has no fear in it. "Thou art my Father. I am Thy child. It is my privilege to love Thee, to express my love for Thee, to know Thee as my Father." We should seek God not because He is powerful, or the source of all riches, or the master of life and death, but because He is our Father. We have an eternal relationship with Him. He has given us the power of choice to reject Him or to accept Him, that perchance we would use that free will to seek Him instead of His gifts.

Devotion transcends law; but remember, if in addition to devotion you follow the divine law as shown in the ways of the Masters, it will be so much easier and quicker to find Him.

When I found the glory of communion with God, then the one great desire possessed me to give that love to all. That is why I urge you: From this day on, every day, pray unceasingly, "Lord, reveal Thyself; Lord, I love You." You do not need to go anywhere to have that relationship; find your communion wherever the Lord has placed you. It is such a wonderful way to live. That joy and glory no one can take away. And the proof of it is to go on giving that love to all. Some will give you garlands and some will give you hate. But remember that it is God you must always strive to please. When He is pleased, everybody is pleased. God will speak through your conscience and guide you to what is right in all things.

Most of you are being used in some way by others. Everywhere it is the same; most persons are always thinking first of themselves and never minding the effect they have on others. Why shouldn't I think of God first? Why shouldn't I think of saving my soul? That gives me a supreme treasure to use for the benefit of all. To lead an impartial existence in service to God and others is to express the highest wisdom. If you don't, you yourself cannot be free from the enslaving influence of others.

We are great imitators, just like monkeys. Sometimes it seems as if Darwin was right about our ancestry! We are always trying to keep up with the Joneses. The Joneses do something, therefore we feel compelled to do it. Do not be an imitator. You are a wildflower, a beauty unsurpassed. In each soul is the unique imprint of the grace of God. Nowhere in the world is there another exactly like you. Of that you can justly be proud!

Be strong, unafraid of anything, always doing what is right. And remember, the company you keep determines the moods and habits you develop. Company changes your thoughts. Until you are established in wisdom, you are helplessly vulnerable; you have no protection from the vibrations of wrong companions. Therefore, always choose your company wisely. And no matter who you are with outwardly, within yourself always keep the fire of devotion to God burning. Just like the Zoroastrians: They always keep a sacred fire kindled in their temple. The flame of your devotion must be perpetual. When you awaken in the morning, arouse that flame; when you are working or associating with others, whatever you are doing, God-devotion must be supreme in your heart. Hear no evil, see no evil, speak no evil. And when wrong vibrations try to encroach on your consciousness, pray: "Lord, in this temple many demons have danced, but there is a secret sanctuary within me where there is ever burning the taper of devotion for Thee. Wilt Thou come into this temple of mine? Thou and I, Lord, in unending communion! Wilt Thou come?"

Seek God Until He Comes

Never expect Him to come simply because you have meditated a certain number of years. Just say, "I know I am poor, Lord. Before You I am very little. Still, You made me Your child. I am following Your law of meditation and right action; but I know You are above the law, and it is for You to reveal Yourself when You wish to do so." He does not grant that final revelation until the time is right and He is sure of your love, but He does give measure for measure. If you eat chilies, they will give you a certain sensation of heat. So it is with devotion. The joy that you find in devotion is the responding presence of God. Behind every thought you think of God, there is the call of God. And if you constantly fan the flickers of that desire for Him until it becomes ever-burning devotion, He will come. Never be discouraged, for He will come. Do not care how long it takes. Delay will only heighten the joy of your ultimate meeting with Him. When at last the saints conquer, the pain and suffering they went through as necessary for purification are forever forgotten the instant they make contact with God.

Ever-burning inner devotion for the Lord is the light by which you behold God. In every nook of life try to behold Him there. When you watch the flowers, see Him in their beauty and fragrance. See Him in the glorious colors in the dawn and sunset and moonlit heavens. It is His invisible hand that is painting scenery on the sky and in the faces of those who love Him. In this world there are faces of lust, faces of craftiness, faces of evil and sarcasm; but there are also faces that reflect the face of God. Those are the faces that inspire more devotion than all the scenery of nature's beauty—those who express the pure love of God, who are ready to sacrifice for Him, who say: "There is only one I want to please and that is my Father."

If ever you have a desire for God, it can never be crushed. I want you to know that. This is a message of hope to you: If you have had the desire to be redeemed, you will find salvation. You may delay your development, but sooner or later that desire will lead you to Him. Why wait? Why let anyone shake your determination? You must find Him. Let no one dilute that desire.

You do not have to wait for the Lord. Day and night I used to cry and wonder when I would know Him, when I would see Him. But He came when I was least expecting Him. He said, "Where are you looking for Me? In the stars? I am there, but you don't see Me. In the sunshine? I am there, but you don't see Me. Look for Me and feel My presence where I am most easily to be found.*

"Him whom you are looking for in the stars and the wind and the ocean and in books and temples of the world, I am He within you in your love. I am with you always there. In every tear of longing for Me that you shed, I am with you. In your every whisper of devotion, I am there. I love the secret honeycomb of your heart where you store love for Me. Every day, like a bee, you brought devotion there; and secretly I came to drink the nectar of your devotion."

The Joy of Communing With God Through Devotion

God loves devotion. If you have devotion, nothing can destroy your spiritual life; for in devotion you have the response of the Lord. There is such joy, such happiness. You do not have to run away from your duties. No matter how busy you are, still you have the time to say, "Lord, I love You." Sometimes when I am in the car, or in the thick of the crowds, everything will disappear and the light of the Lord will come; and He says: "I am here. I am everywhere; but most of all I am here within you." The ocean is immeasurably huge, but to each drop the ocean is intimate. The vast ocean encircles the globe, but the most important thing to each wave is the presence of the ocean right within it and behind it.

As soon as I close my eyes, I leave the world and find the Lord is with me, and I say: "Thou art my life, Thou art my love, Thou

* "He is within and without all that exists, the animate and the inanimate; near He is, and far; imperceptible because of His subtlety....The Light of All Lights, beyond darkness; Knowledge itself...He is seated in the hearts of all" (Bhagavad Gita XIII:15–17).

art my health, Thou art my power. I seek no other health, no other wealth, no other love or power, but Thee." Jesus said, "Seek ye the kingdom of God first, and all these things shall be added unto you." That is the real teaching. God has proved that in my life. Every desire I have had, every little wish I have thought of, He has granted—sometimes in the strangest and most unpredictable ways. Behind each gift I see the hand of the Lord.

There can be no excuse for omitting Him from your life. You will find Him if you make up your mind. Some will call you fanatic; it doesn't matter. What you are in the eyes of the Lord, that is what you are. Do not be influenced by the delusion of the world's opinion. Care about what the Lord thinks of you. It is the greatest romance there is. That love shall never grow old nor fade nor die. It is eternal satisfaction, eternal fulfillment.

Only those who love God can love forever. God is the Immortal Lover and you are His beloved. If you pursue Him with your soul's longing of incarnations, with all the unrequited yearning of centuries, you will find that eternal romance. For He alone can truly fulfill the promise of love everlasting; no one else can. Human love is an enticement to what is behind that love—God. But if you try to find in human love the satisfaction that only He can give, you will be deceived. Your happiness will be smashed and your heart will be broken. So I learned from my love for my mother when she was snatched away by death. I cried to God, "Why did You take the diamond from the ring of my heart?" But from that most tragic cruelty of my life, seeking to assuage the loss of my earthly mother's love, I found the eternal love of my Mother Divine.*

The Purpose of Life Is to Teach Us to Seek God Willingly

Do not pay undue attention to this drama of life. Seek romance with God. He is the greatest Lover because He loves us more than Himself. The one who loves you truly will always seek your highest good. The one who loves himself will always be angry when you cross his wish. We cross God's wishes all the time, day after

* In his *Autobiography of a Yogi* Paramahansaji writes: "I loved Mother as my dearest friend on earth. Her solacing black eyes had been my refuge in the trifling tragedies of childhood....Years passed before any reconciliation entered my heart. Storming the very gates of heaven, my cries at last summoned the Divine Mother. Her words brought final healing to my suppurating wounds: 'It is I who have watched over thee, life after life, in the tenderness of many mothers. See in My gaze the two black eyes, the lost beautiful eyes, thou seekest!'"

day. When I first read that Jesus told us to forgive our enemies "not seven times, but seventy times seven," I thought that much forgiveness was beyond what should be reasonably expected. But when I prayed for understanding, God replied: "For 365 days a year, through countless incarnations, I have forgiven each of you." Then I said, "Lord, such is Thy love—unconditional, without measure."

When you meditate, you know it is the Beloved who teaches you in so many ways. I had always thought that God must be a revengeful being—life seems very cruel because there is so much suffering. But I found the Lord to be supremely kind. He tolerates our ignorance and all the workings of our ignorant habits. Though He is so powerful, He doesn't say, "Why bother with these little people! I will take their life away." Despite all the wrongs we have done, still He loves us and is waiting for us. He is so much worried about us. He will never be happy until all of us go back to Him. Why do we suffer? It is we who bring pain on ourselves, because we act against the harmony of the Lord's universal laws. Those laws work for good or ill according to our behavior, to teach us right from wrong. So it is not that God hurts us or rewards us; but when we love Him, we reach Him above law and He surrenders Himself.

The hearts of most persons are like stones to God, never deeply moistened by the water of His love. Do not be indifferent toward God; for on a heart of stone, the seeds of devotion can never take root and grow. Love Him and forget Him not. Live in that love.

Of your own free choice you must seek God. He will not awe you with miracles to attract you to Him; but if you find Him you will be spared the tragedies of many incarnations. Life is a never-ending mess. Get out of it! Free yourself! I found my way out of it long ago, because I resolved that nothing is as important to me as He is. Each of you can do likewise. Do not give all your time to the world; save some time every day for God alone. The world can get along without you. Why do you think you are indispensable? Forget that. It is the hardest thing to please God—and the easiest if you love Him, if every night you do not go to bed until you have communed with Him. Stay in that communion; cry for Him and practice the techniques of meditation. Do not be worried about what troubles you may be facing in your life. When the Lord is with you, there is no fear.

I have found Him. He is with me day and night. I never thought there could be so much love. It is so great—indescribable joy. In His love is all fulfillment. You want nothing else. I speak of the love of

God; and all those that shall feel and receive it shall be redeemed in this life and shall realize the glory of the Infinite. "Father, I thank Thee for all the love Thou givest me. It is all Thine. And I pray that all of us behold Thy face in the light of our devotion. Thou art everywhere hidden, but we behold Thee in the light of devotion.

"O Divine Beloved, change our hearts of stone into the soil of devotion, that the seed of love may grow into a mighty tree where Thou wouldst come to rest. Beneath the shady boughs of the tree of devotion, there Thou and I will find eternal union. 'A flask of wine, a book of verse, and Thou beside me singing in the wilderness'—in the pristine solitude of the heart wherein the crowds of material desires and restless thoughts are absent.* Intoxicated with the wine of wisdom, in meditation and in activity I shall ever sing to Thee. Even in sleep, the muffled cry of my devotion shall call to Thee.

"Father, Mother, Friend, Beloved God, give us the joy of devotion and the intoxication of craving for Thy Presence as ever-existing, ever-conscious, ever-new Bliss. Thou alone art sufficient to quench the thirst of our desires. Give us devotion, that we may feel Thee unceasingly and work only for Thee. The instruments of our hands, our eyes, our ears are Thine; our every thought we dedicate unto Thee. Our own Beloved, lift us from the dream of delusion. Make us one with Thee. We bow to Thee."

Self-Realization Fellowship Has Been Sent to Help You Find God

I wish I could express to you the millions of truths I felt here tonight. Many people think that this body would be tired after lecturing. Never! I am not even conscious of lecturing to an audience. What I feel, what I enjoy in communion with my Beloved, I share with you. That privilege makes me supremely happy.

For countless years to come this light shall travel over the earth—not a message of belief but a system of techniques by which you can redeem yourself. Follow these teachings; practice the techniques. Every day you will feel you are advancing. You will feel actual development. Most religions try to hold followers by rousing their emotions or intellect, or insisting on blind belief in theological dogma. But the Masters of India hold you by your own realization.

* Paraphrasing from *The Rubaiyat of Omar Khayyam,* translated by Edward FitzGerald. See quatrain XI of *Wine of the Mystic,* Paramahansa Yogananda's spiritual interpretation of this beloved masterpiece of Sufi mystical poetry (published by Self-Realization Fellowship).

Never forget that. This path of Self-Realization Fellowship is the way to know Truth yourself through step-by-step realization. When I found that, I dedicated my life to serving all with what my Master gave to me.

What the great Masters of this path have done for me! I met many charlatans when I was young. I pity them. I was blessed that I didn't follow them; they would have ruined my life. But those who love God give you His love; and once you have that, you are free.

So get busy. Do not waste your time. Day and night have unceasing devotion for God. You are bound to reach the Goal. Your own experience will hold you to this path. That is the only kind of seeker we want on this path. I could teach in a way that would stimulate your emotions or your intellectual curiosity, but I want to hold you only by your awakening Self-realization. Let your own realization of God be your loyalty to this cause. If it doesn't give you that, good-bye.

I am coming here for a few wonderful souls I find here. Those that have been in tune, I know. I have killed the ego long ago. My desire is the desire of the Spirit, and whoever has tuned in with my desire has found Him. That is the truth. I know it. It is not emotionalism; they live in that constant communion with God.

I used to wonder what will happen to the devotees when I will leave this body. But now I know that those who are in tune with me, no matter whether I am in this world or beyond, they are ever with me. For to be with the Lord is to be with those who are with Him also. Many times I have remembered those disciples who have gone on. Because of the love of the Lord I remembered them; and all those I have remembered, through incarnations, I bless whenever I think of them. And with the same love that I give to them, I love all; because all are the children of God. To me there is no America, no India, no Germany, no Italy. Everyone is my brother or sister, born of the same Father, my Beloved.

Spread God's love; never foster hate. Racial prejudice, color prejudice, all prejudices, must go. Let us become saturated with the consciousness of the universal love of God. That love tells you to love your country; to love the world as your country; and to love all souls as your own family. When every soul shall realize this, the earth shall truly be a heaven.

Cultivate Friendship With God

An informal talk at Self-Realization Fellowship International Headquarters, Los Angeles, August 19, 1926, just after Paramahansaji had returned for an interim stay amidst lecture series he was giving continuously throughout the United States

I am very happy to see you all and to be here with you again. I have been so busy that it didn't seem I would ever be able to come. When we think of God and try to find Him within, no matter where we are we always feel at home. But I am glad that this night there is the opportunity to come to you and be with you and with God. This I can say: You have a great opportunity in this calmness, in this stillness, to make an honest effort to know Him.

I offer a prayer as it comes to me from within—a prayer of my renewed love to my Father, and to my fellow beings, my own:

"Father Divine, I thank Thee for the privilege of offering another prayer to Thee. With the combined devotion of Thy children, I thank Thee. In this house the atmosphere is vibrant with Thy bliss, Thy Spirit Divine; our minds are rejuvenated with Thy strength. Father Divine, may Thy limitless power flow within us and around us. May the mortal cup of our lives be filled with Thy nectar of immortality.

"Thy glory shines through darkness and light; Thou art everywhere! We feel Thee in the twinkling stars; we feel Thy greatness in the majestic mountains; we feel Thy vastness in the overspreading expanse of sky; but we feel Thee most within the temple of our souls. Great Being, in Thine omnipresence we stand face to face with Thee in unity with Thine infinite love, Thy boundless might. We, Thy little flock, are gathered here to manifest Thy glory. Teach us to be faithful; teach us to feel Thee again and again. Divine Being! our own Father, come to us; be with us this night. Renew us with Thy love. Reawaken us in Thee."

Constantly Bring Your Thoughts Back to God

Always remember: Whenever you have a little leisure time, use it to cultivate your friendship with God. This is my humble suggestion to you, garnered from my own experience. It is very easy to get an answer from Him if with deepest concentration you demand His response; but it is the most difficult accomplishment I know of if the mind wanders. The best way to get in touch with the Divine Spirit, I have found in my life of ceaseless activity, is to bring the thoughts back to Him constantly, especially in the gaps of time between activities. I never excuse myself if I am in any way inattentive to Him. In this way, I find that I have lots of time for the Great Being; in the midst of activity I often speak to Him. How I am speaking to Him? The old idea of God sitting in a distant heaven somewhere on a throne does not engage my mind—if He is there, all right, I don't mind; but I like Him to be with me. To make Him "nearest of the near, dearest of the dear"—that is my business in life. You also can have that personal relationship, by giving to Him your soul in prayer.

God Is Found in Stillness and Calmness

In order to cultivate friendship with God, in order to love Him, we must get acquainted with Him. In stillness and calmness, give your soul to Him. In the space of a few months, perhaps, I could teach you about the Divine from the words of wisdom in the Vedas and the other scriptures; but it would do you little good unless you realized those truths within your Self. Realization is found only in inner calmness. Calmness is loved by God. Calmness is the altar and sanctuary of the Father. Practice seeking Him in calmness. Meditation is the way. That is the best advice I can give to you. Books and classes and philosophical explanations you can have, but this do not forget: Use all your free moments to meditate and cultivate a friendship with God.

For the first few minutes in meditation your mind will wander, but persevere longer until the thoughts become still. You will think: "Oh, I have this work to do today; I will meditate sometime later tonight." So long as you do not feel the supreme importance of knowing Him, that "tonight" will never come to you; diverting engagements will fill your mornings, noons, and evenings, until when night comes you helplessly surrender to sleep.

So when you sit to meditate, keep the mind concentrated. Drive away stray thoughts and insist, "Father, be with me. I want an answer; I want to feel Thy blessing within me." Again and again tell Him that, each time in a deeper way. To pray absentmindedly is of little use—"Father in Heaven, I love Thee"—all the while thinking of a nice cake you want to eat. Say the first word "Father," that is enough; but say it until you feel it. Then go on to the next phrase of your prayer.

That is one difference between East and West. For instance, Western music did not appeal to me when I first arrived in America; but now I understand it, how it progresses like a story to a climactic conclusion. In the East we don't use music in this way; we take one phrase and repeat it over and over until we are lost in the feeling it expresses.*

What is the use of reciting a whole book of prayers without feeling any love for God? Real prayer is not intellectual; it is feeling what you say to God. That feeling has to be cultured: In the beginning you do not feel love for God because you do not know Him.

Those who are near and dear to us we love. To them automatically we express what we feel; it wells up spontaneously from our hearts. Why? Because they are real to us, we can see them right before us or in our mind's eye. But God we do not behold because we have not tried to know Him. We might infer His presence in flowers and other beauties of nature; but to have direct contact with Him requires deep meditation.

A Guided Meditation to Experience God

We will have a few minutes of meditation:

Let us this night make the effort to know Him: "Father, come to us, make us feel Thee within." Close your eyes, and mentally pray that, again and again, deeper and deeper, until you feel you are saying it with your whole soul. "Father, be with us, make Thyself real to us this night." Concentrate on the region of the heart and feel great love coming into it. Visualize that love—north, east, south, west—all space is filled with love. The Great Reservoir of Love is right here, within your soul and surrounding you in every

* In his *Autobiography of a Yogi* Paramahansaji writes: "[In Indian music] a musician has creative scope for endless improvisation around the fixed traditional melody or *raga;* he concentrates on the sentiment or definitive mood of the structural theme and embroiders it to the limits of his own originality....At each playing he clothes anew the bare skeleton of the *raga,* often confining himself to a single melodic sequence, stressing by repetition all its subtle microtonal and rhythmic variations.

"Bach, among Western composers, understood the charm and power of repetitious sound slightly differentiated in a hundred complex ways....

"Hindu music is a subjective, spiritual, and individualistic art, aiming not at symphonic brilliance but at personal harmony with the Over-Soul. All the celebrated songs of India have been composed by devotees of the Divine. The Sanskrit word for 'musician' is *bhagavathar,* 'he who sings the praises of God.'"

direction; but you have never tasted of its silent depths. The heart is the door through which that Love will flow. Concentrate there and say: "Father, open the door of my heart; pour Thy love through that door!" Feel the great love of God is flowing through you, consciously filling your body, mind, and soul, and flooding all humanity and all creatures.

Concentrate on this thought: "Father, be with us as Love; Father, be with us as Love." Tune your soul; go on directing all your thoughts and feelings into that prayer, just as the conductor of the symphony orchestra leads the musicians in playing and playing until the music reaches a climax. Let not your mind wander; feel yourself in the midst of the joy of that infinite love. "Father, Father, Father, be with us!"

Deepen your concentration; pray again and again: "Father, Father, manifest to us as love, Almighty Love. Open the door of our hearts; open the door of our hearts; open the door of our hearts. Let Thy love flow through; let Thy love flow through; let Thy Christ love flow through. Reveal Thyself to us as Love; flood our consciousness with Thy love, O Glory Divine!"

Now feel you are relaxed, floating on an ocean of love; your body and mind, thoughts and feelings, are all buoyed in Spirit, wafting toward the farthest shores of the universe. Feel that every being is receiving the vibrations of that Infinite Love that bathes all creation. "Love to all nations and races; love to all creatures; love to all living things. The love that we feel for all, Father, we lay at Thy feet. Almighty Father, the love of friends, the love of those we love, comes from Thee and belongs to Thee, our Father. Teach us to break the boundaries of our human love and feel Thine infinite love."

Persevere Until God Is Found

My work is fulfilled when I have awakened in you even the tiniest spark of the love I feel for my Father. It took a great deal of time to get acquainted with Him; it seemed in this life I would never be able to succeed, for the mind was so restless. But as often as the mind tried to trick me into abandoning my meditation, I would trick the mind: "I will sit here, no matter what noises or distractions come. I care not if I have to die trying; I will keep on to the end." As I persevered in this way, once in a while a glimpse of the Divine Spirit would come; like a spark, so near and yet so far, appearing and then flitting away. But I stayed resolute. How I waited! with infinite determination in the invisible silence. The deeper the concentration became, the clearer and stronger became His assurance. Now He is with me always.

Blessed you are that you are hearing the message divine, the message of Spirit, the message that solves the mystery of the universe. What fear have you? Cast out all fear! There is nothing to be afraid of anymore when you have touched the Great Power of Spirit, which controls the very forces of creation, all the machinery of this universe. What greater hope could you have, what greater security could you seek, than the contact of the Infinite Being that is the essence of all that exists?

Those who are wandering solely in the wasteland of material consciousness, astray in a desert of suffering, we don't blame them. We only say, "Why do you forget the essence of your being, and your soul's claim on the Father? The earth upon which you stand was planted with life by God; why forget Him who is the Source of everything?" We don't condemn anyone who is temporarily bewildered by delusion, for we know that everyone who makes the effort can find their way to God, right here amidst daily life, with all its activity and responsibilities.

Often it is two o'clock in the morning when I am finished with my interviews; those around me will say, "You should go to bed now." I tell them, "If I lower my gaze, the subconsciousness of sleep will come. But when I lift my eyes I am in superconsciousness, and something comes that is more wonderful than a million sleeps! I lose myself in the wonderment of the Divine Father."

God Is the Joy and Happiness We Seek

The bliss of contact with God never grows stale; He is Eternal Joy. Is there any person in the whole world who does not want joy? I see all kinds of people; I look at their faces, not to judge them, but to see if in their countenance I behold what I have found. In my early days, if in the remotest corner of my heart I had a desire for some material possession, I made it a point to observe persons who had those things, to see if they were happy. Never did I find one! So I gained a lot of experience through the experiences of others. There is no need to live the experience of putting the hand in fire to see if it burns. If you touch a high-voltage wire even lightly to see how it feels, it will electrocute you. Look at those who pursue worldly goals: How many are really happy? But God has made me very, very happy. He is the only harbor of safety from the storms of this world. "Take shelter in Him with all the eagerness of thy heart.

By His grace thou shalt obtain the utmost peace and the Eternal Shelter."* In Him I have found the joy of my life, the indescribable blessedness of my existence, the wonderful realization of His everywhereness right within me.

I want you all to have that. You cannot know Him by mechanical prayer, nor by reading or intellectual study, but by devotion. Cultivate that. What you feel for those you love, give of that to God. Say to Him: "The great love I feel for my dear ones, God, I give the first of that love, the essence of that love, to Thee. Receive my love!" This is the way to get acquainted with Him. But few souls give even this simple measure of love to God. Whoever truly loves God, knows Him, feels Him. You should all thank Him for the great opportunity He has given to you to know Him. When I am with those who have pursued this line of thinking, those who love God more and more, I feel a great harmony. God says of those souls: "Their thoughts fully on Me, their beings surrendered to Me, enlightening one another, proclaiming Me always, My devotees are contented and joyful."† All I want to culture within you is that relationship with Him wherein each time you say "I love you, God," every cell, every feeling, every thought will awaken in the endlessness of His joy.

* Bhagavad Gita XVIII:62.

† *Ibid.* X:9.

Establishing the God of Bliss in the Temple of Your Soul

A talk to early Self-Realization Fellowship students, Los Angeles, March 8, 1925

This teaching should be preserved to be given to humanity for redeeming humanity. Buildings and centers and temples of stone are necessary, but they are only material. My greater wish is to create a temple in your souls, wherein God can be established forever. By your practice of meditation on *Aum*—the great Amen or Cosmic Vibration of God's omnipresence—and the awakening of the higher centers of consciousness in the brain and spine, so that you can contact God, you will find a temple within you that time shall never disintegrate. That spiritual temple in which you will worship God—your spiritualized consciousness in which you shall house God—that will never be broken. Practice the techniques I have given you; then I will establish within your souls an immortal temple of God-realization.

Strive Always to Help Others

Serve one another. Try to be more tolerant toward others; their intolerance cannot be overcome by your own intolerance. Cleanse your heart of jealousy. Avoid criticism of others. It will make you extremely happy if you will concentrate upon your own constructive effort in regard to your spiritual affairs. Think of the Christ-love; that will give solace to your heart. Establish in your hearts permanently only kindness and peace. Always help others with love; help them by your example. Your right, spiritual behavior will have far greater force than anything you say. Try to be an ideal example. Seeing you, thousands will be reformed. Let this sink deep in your consciousness.

This is just the beginning of your spiritual realization. And whether I am here or not, remember, there is no barrier of space for souls. As you improve yourself and awaken your soul, you will be conscious of eternal connection with me; and above all, you will always be in touch with God. In Him we shall always be united. He who can bring to us all those whom we love, establish Him in your soul.

Commune With God in the Temple of Meditation

Meditate each morning and night; and in order to improve still further, have a longer meditation of at least two hours on Sunday—or any day of the week. Practice the techniques of concentration and meditation to calm the breath and still the mind and feel the sacred vibration of God's presence within you. Withdraw the life energy into the spine and brain and magnify it with Cosmic Energy. After the techniques, pray to God with all your religious fervor and devotion: "I want to talk to You; answer me! The cry of my soul goes forth. Father, teach me; lead me. Show me how to help others, my universal family of brothers and sisters. Teach me to establish peace, to bring heaven to earth."

By your practice of meditation and exemplary behavior, all your bad habits will be spiritually conquered. Cultivate love in your heart. Give of your harmony. You will be like a flower. Look at the flowers—they know nothing of criticism. They just attract you by their beauty and fragrance, and you love them. Each one of you is a psychological flower; people will like you if you exude the perfume of soul qualities. Wherever you go, be a beautiful soul-flower, attractive to all humanity.

In breathlessness of deep meditative stillness, feel the presence of Deity: the God of love, the God of our souls, of our hearts and minds, the powerful God, the tangible God. Pray with me:

"Come Thou, O Spirit, into our temple of silence! Possess us, invigorate us, renew us. The temple is cleansed and purified; the incense of devotion is burning. Give us realization! Let our understanding, our vision, our feelings and thoughts ignite, making a sacred ritual fire to glorify and celebrate Thy coming. Our hearts are pure. Our minds are pure, and with the purity of our soul's offering we shall worship Thee. A token of love this night we offer to Thee. Our souls burst with love and sincerity and sympathy. We are Thy children, suffering, yearning for Thy caress. We are Thy little children; forgive us our frail failings, forgive us our mistakes. Make us feel Thee in every tremor of creative vibration; in Thine immanence is our joy. Come Thou, Divine Father, Divine Mother! Possess us. Possess us. Possess us. In tears, in unexpressed longing, in the language of prayer, with our deepest feelings and thoughts, with everything that we have, we want to worship Thee. We want to love Thee, for Thou art our own. Renew us! O Divine Fire, set us ablaze with Thy glory. O Celestial Fire, Love Celestial, immerse us in Bliss. Make us feel Thine immortality within us.

"Divine Father, teach us to love one another. Teach us to serve our greater family of the world, even to be willing to die for them. Make us feel the expansive joy that lies in serving. Teach us how to culture harmony, to see the good in everything, to establish on earth Thy goodness which is in heaven. Come! Come! Come! Spirit, come! We have prayed with our awakened souls. Keep us within Thy vision; show us that Thou art within us. Thou art the Home of Worship, calling us back to our true home in Thee. Bless us to feel Thy love within us, within every nook of the mind, in every fiber of our being.

"Aummmm, Aummmm, Aummmm. Divine Mother, Divine Father, come! Divine Master, teach us. Divine Father, possess us! Come! Come! Possess us! Possess us!"

Practice the Techniques of Meditation Religiously

Learn to love God. Love Him as the sacred vibration of *Aum,* the "Great Comforter," that comes to you, that brings God's love and bliss to you. Through practice of the techniques, that divine Presence comes over you, spiritually possessing you. Always approach God with supreme devotion. By love and devotion, He can very easily be moved to respond. And remember: Just as there are physical laws that govern our material well-being, so there are spiritual laws that control our progress toward God. These laws, embodied in the science and techniques of yoga, are important. They are inevitably a condition of realization. So along with the development of devotion, follow the spiritual methods, with unwavering faith. They are necessary—for they bring actual experience of God as *Aum,* as the Light of God, and as He manifests Himself in His varied aspects that come in deep meditation.

Have that faith which knows no doubt, but which walks straight ahead, intent on the spiritual light, trampling on karma and destiny—trampling on fear, failure, and obstacles. Go forth in spite of all difficulties, with infinite faith that He who is within you, He who is the life of every body cell, is supporting you. Without Him, not a drop of blood can flow nor any tissue live; upon Him you are dependent every minute of your existence. No power equals His. He, the most powerful, nevertheless does not impose Himself upon us.

Materiality vies for our attention; but the great God, whose dominion is infinite, is the ultimate silent, humble One in the universe. If you want to be in tune with the Omnipotent Infinite, be humble, be strong in perseverance, and have infinite confidence in Him. Love Him. Put your whole faith in Him. With the power of faith, march on, march on!

By daily meditation, never forget Him. Every day new vistas, new revelations of His presence will come to you. Strength will come; for His power is there. Acknowledge it firmly, let it sink calmly into the depths of your being. When by the science of controlling the life energy [Kriya Yoga] you master the subtle forces through which He creates and sustains all things, you will share in His dominion over all creation.

The great God is within you; acknowledge Him by your convictions. Awaken your soul with this message; and once awakened, sleep no more! With that power awakened, manifest strength and peace; transcend the inglorious, the inharmony, the contradictions. Mistakes and error are in your mind. Let your soul force drive them from your consciousness, and everywhere you will see and experience harmony. Those whose thoughts are inharmonious will always find inharmony. It is largely a perception from within, more than conditions without. Culture harmony within you, and you will spread it to others. They will be saved from dissension, harmony will reign. Everywhere you go, into the most incongruous circumstances, you will be able to find and nurture an underlying harmony. You will cooperate with and preserve the acting, the manifestation, of Divine Law.

When you are going to the Father's house, do not be sidetracked by the beautiful gardens of spiritual phenomena along the way. Mental powers distract many from the Goal when they come in the course of meditation. Pay them no attention, nor use them to impress others. Just practice meditation day after day. Then when you are in need, your accumulated spiritual power goes out automatically to help you—or to help others—even without your conscious awareness.

Practice the techniques religiously. Joy such as you never dreamed of will come into your life. When God comes to you, everything is joy. Then you can no longer bear to be selfish. When you stand in the midst of a crowd—some sick, some weak—and you are vibrating with joy, your mind says: "How can I give this to them?" But you cannot give it until the other person is able and willing to receive it. Even God cannot help one who shuts Him out. Those who are not receptive, you can help only by giving your love and spiritual example.

Everyone Can Attain Cosmic Consciousness

Do not judge anyone, and never feel that you are better than others. When you realize that everyone is a miniature God, you have reverence for all, for you behold that it is God who is sleeping and suffering in each unawakened soul. How can you ignore Him there? Your soul is seized by one thing: a heartfelt cry of compassion for the other person. You want to share your joy with all, even if you have to die for it, as did Jesus. It would be extremely selfish to have this joy of God and see that others can have it and that you can give it, and not do so. I wake up each day with the thought of how these teachings will be immortalized. That thought is a divine obsession.

Every minute there is joy in Cosmic Consciousness. It is everlasting. Nothing can take it away. It is firmly fixed—and it is all that can be firmly fixed. Worldly gain and accomplishments and fame end with pain of unfulfillment in the heart. Lasting joy will be found in God and in giving His joy to others.

Everyone can reach out to the world and give people their blessing. Fields and fields of work are calling. Disease and bacteria fill the hospitals with suffering souls; and psychological bacteria of evil habits and desires fill the jails. Help to do away with the root cause of such misery: man's ignorance of God. Souls are crying for help everywhere. If you want to help them, you must be able to be an example; you must follow the way of perfecting yourself.

A pang of fear seizes the selfish heart at the thought of self-sacrifice. However, giving up of self is not a negative passivity; but positive attainment. The Bliss-consciousness of your true Self expands as you detach the binding desires of your ego-self. Your gain will be infinite.

No matter what happens, never give up your contact with Bliss. The only way to get it is by regular meditation. Your Bliss is your God. Sacrifice for others, but hold onto that Bliss; then God will be real to you.

All of you can have that state of Bliss. Listen to this teaching and practice it; do not indolently fall asleep spiritually. You will see a wondrous change in yourself—in your life. Without regularity in meditation, you may follow this teaching for a little while, then become negligent, then forget all about it. But if you regularly touch the depths of meditation even briefly, even for ten minutes, your zeal will never wane and die.

Practice the Hong-Sau Technique with deep concentration.* You will have the blissful realization: "I am the Self of all." Great illumination will come. It is the way to develop pure God-concentration. God's attention is concentrated everywhere in the cosmos; your attention is concentrated mostly on the little body. But when you teach yourself to concentrate on your real Self, and thereby rise above body- and breath-consciousness, the whole world becomes your expanded Self.

If there is a little pain anywhere in your body, you know it and say "Ow." God's body is the universe; He knows every little thing that happens everywhere. Great yogis likewise know all things, through contact with *Aum*—the vibratory presence of God pervading all creation. They do not have to use telepathy; they know because they are in tune with the omnipresence of that Cosmic Vibration. So long as your consciousness is exclusively body-bound, you cannot feel the expansion of *Aum*. You have to rise above the body by superconsciousness, by the transcendence of *samadhi.*

The scientific way of entering the superconscious state is by the methods of life-force control I am giving to you. If you faithfully practice these techniques and meditate deeply, I prophesy you will never give it up. Lord Buddha sat under the bodhi tree in meditation with the firm resolve:

Beneath this banyan bough,
I take this solemn vow:
Let derma, bones, and body dissolve;
Until the mystery of life I solve,
From beneath this tree,
I shall never, never be free.

So should all of you feel resolute when you sit in meditation: "I am unshakably determined to know God." With perseverance, a new awakening will come, a new inspiration. Every fear will fly away from you, even the fear of death. Death will come for this body only once; but some people die repeatedly in their thoughts of fear of death. Be fearless in the consciousness, "In life and death I am ever living in God."

Day by day this consciousness will impinge on you when you practice the techniques. When you enter the deep interiorized calmness in meditation, you are free from the bondage of the body.

* See *Concentration Technique* in glossary.

Then what is death to you? Where is fear? Nothing has the power to make you afraid. That is the state you are seeking. Concentrate on *Aum,* merge with *Aum* in deep meditation; through realization of God's immanence in Cosmic Vibration, you will "come unto the Father"—the Bliss-Consciousness of the infinite transcendent Absolute.* You will say: "I and my Bliss-God are One. I have everything in this universe. Death, disease, doomsday, fires, nothing can take that Bliss away!"

* Here Paramahansaji is quoting and interpreting the words of Jesus in John 14:6: "No man cometh unto the Father (Cosmic Consciousness) but by me (through the Son, or Christ Consciousness)." In the *Self-Realization Fellowship Lessons* he explains: "The underlying import is: He who contacts *Aum* finds entry into the immanent Christ Consciousness; and, through the portals of Christ Consciousness, he 'cometh unto the Father.'"

Connecting Your Life With the Astral World

Self-Realization Fellowship Golden Lotus Temple, Encinitas, California, November 15, 1940

Go deep into the inner sanctum of meditation, mentally praying with utmost sincerity: "Father, reveal Thyself!" Keep on until you feel that your heart is bursting with longing for God and you are crying inside, without crying outwardly. With undying devotion, mentally affirm: "Father, reveal Thyself unto me! Thou hast created me; therefore, Thou must redeem me. I did not ask to be created; but since Thou hast put me here in human life, Thou must reveal Thyself unto me. As Thy children, it is our privilege to love Thee, for Thou art ours. We pray and ask Thee as our Father: Reveal Thyself. It is not Thy pity that we want, but Thy love—for Thou art our Father and we are Thy children. Heavenly Father, as Thy true devotees, we know we can never perish, but will find eternal life in Thee. With all the earnestness of our hearts we pray, reveal Thyself!"

Great is the grace and bounty of God; this we discover if we know Him. But I reject the concept of God as the Almighty from whom we must beg special favors of His bounty and grace. Love must be the supreme motivation in our hearts when seeking God—not a whining attitude of soliciting mercy from Him. God is not a vengeful deity who is always poised to smite us with His power. He is our own Father; He belongs to us; therefore we should love Him. A father loves his children and is duty-bound to be gracious to them. So there is nothing surprising about God looking after us—it is His fatherly obligation. You keep Him at a mental distance by fearing Him. The word *fear* in connection with God must be absolutely abolished. Even when we make mistakes, the Father loves us. God has nothing to do with our punishment. Though He has created us and sent us to sojourn for a time in mortal existence, He is extremely anxious to redeem us. We punish ourselves by remaining ignorant of our relationship with Him, of our own immortality and divinity as His children.

The Father cannot free us unless we wish freedom; and the Father cannot bind us if we don't want to be bound. God has given us the privilege to cast Him away or accept Him, with the hope that we would use our free will to seek Him and to find Him at last. I think that is the greatest of all greatness in God. Otherwise He would be a dictator who forces His will on His subjects. God never imposes Himself. He says nothing about Himself, even though He is everywhere, and everything in the universe depends utterly upon Him. He is silent and yet He is audible—unheard by those who are attuned only to material sensations, but knowable by devotees who seek Him in meditation as the Infinite Presence behind gross vibrations and hear His cosmic voice of *Aum*, Amen, informing and sustaining all creation.*

Until you know your spiritual nature as connected with that divine Creative Force, what a mystery this life is! Today you are here and tomorrow you are gone. When you pass over to the life after death, this whole world will become as a dream to you. You don't grieve when you have to change a worn-out coat you have been wearing. How foolish it is to think that this body—the "overcoat" worn by your soul—will be permanent. It seems real now, but it will disappear. Then where will your soul go? To the astral world—the "heavenly" realm of light and indestructible life, the realm of vibratory life energy hidden behind the veil of the gross material universe.

Why Should We Try to Connect With the Astral World?

From the astral world we come at birth, and there we shall return at death. Someone asked me why we should try to connect with the astral world now. To this I reply, "Because that is where you will realize the freedom of your true nature. You were there as a soul cloaked in an astral form to start with; and because you are not there now and have lost that memory is why all your misery persists." By entering that other world, we learn the causes and healing of all suffering and diseases. We discover the secret of our existence—what happens after death, and where we were before

* The references to meditation throughout this talk refer to the techniques of the Kriya Yoga science taught by Paramahansa Yogananda in the *Self-Realization Fellowship Lessons. (Publisher's Note)*

birth, and how to live in the material world without losing our divine connection.

This world has a lot of limitations and the astral world has none. When a soul leaves the expansiveness of the astral world to be born on earth, that human baby finds himself restricted and confined in the mother's womb and wants to get out of it but can't. For nine months he has to wait. Then he is subjected to the helplessness of infancy. As he grows into adolescence he must fight his way through passions and emotions, which if he doesn't control will get him into all kinds of misery. Then he marries, struggles to support a family, and perhaps is happy for a little while—but as he gets older everything starts to go wrong with his body-machine and eventually he dies. Every day this drama of mortal limitations, whatever be its minor variations, is playing itself out in your life; and still you cling to this world as most desirable. It is not.

If you could perceive the astral world, you would know that it is infinitely more real than the earth-plane, which is just inert matter without the enlivening powers of the upholding astral world. Material existence is only a shadow of that higher, finer dimension of reality. This world is the result of the astral world. The blueprints of everything in the physical universe have been astrally conceived—all the forms and forces in nature, including the complex human body, have been first produced in that realm where God's causal ideations are made visible in forms of heavenly light and vibratory energy. Then they are materialized in physical form out of the ether. But the astral body of man and the astral counterparts of everything in nature are vastly more beautiful, more vibrant, more expressive of the harmony and perfection of the Divine Creator than what we perceive when our consciousness is limited to matter.

The astral world is not the ultimate liberating experience; the soul attains complete ascension only through realization of its oneness with the Creator Himself. Nevertheless, soul progress begins with the effort to disengage from the delusion of material bondage into the higher awareness of one's finer astral existence. Learn to be more transcendent now; identify with the life of your astral self and its connection with the astral world.

How to get to that higher plane? In thought you are always there; but because you are so identified with the physical perceptions of your thoughts, the underlying astral world that powers those thoughts and perceptions is not as real to you. Your soul sojourns there every night when you are asleep, only you are not conscious of it. For just a little while during wakefulness the soul is in the material environment. The rest of the time it is in the astral. Whenever you are using the subconscious mind—dreaming or employing its creative power of visions and visualization—you are to some degree in the astral world. So it isn't that you do not get there. You are always there, unknowingly linked with the astral source from which the life and intelligence and sensory powers of your physical body are constantly flowing. You are working from that astral plane. Even though you think you are a material being dependent on the material world, you are not. You should learn to get acquainted with your real base of operations.

Suppose you have two houses—one in the slums where there is constantly turmoil and fighting going on, and another in the beautiful section of town where there is order and harmony. When you go to your better home, you find peace and contentment. That is what I urge you: Live in the consciousness of your finer astral body rather than "slumming" in the physical.

Meditation Frees Us From the Limitations of Material Existence

As long as you enslave yourself to the demands and desires of the physical body, so long you are in for trouble—much trouble! Why are you so attached to the body? Only because you have chosen to be. Meditation is nothing magical; it is the natural process of doing away with attachment to the flesh and transferring your consciousness to the spiritual side of your nature. We meditate not only for the peace and joy and happiness it brings, but also to free ourselves from the limitations of material existence.

The body is a remarkable machine; normally it keeps on running for decades. Yet it is still a nest of troubles. Heat and cold, disease and weakness and pain, are always assailing it. The doctor, like the mechanic who repairs automobiles, can often repair the body. But the real control of the physical body is in the astral world. With many chronic diseases no doctor knows what to do to effect a cure, because any trouble of karmic origin deeply imprinted in the astral body cannot be healed by purely physical means. The cure lies in employing the proper flow of subtle life energy and consciousness from the astral body and astral plane. Just as when the lights in your house go out, you have to check the wiring back to the dynamo. If there is something wrong there, the whole electrical system of the house will be out of order. So with chronic disorders of the physical body, you have to repair your flawed connection with the astral-body dynamo of power.

When modern science will discover how to go deep into the subtle electromagnetic constitution of man, it will be able to correct most any medical condition in ways that would seem almost miraculous today. In the future, healing will be effected more and more by use of various types of light rays. Light is what we are made of—not gross physical light, but the finer spiritualized light of *prana,* intelligent life energy. That light is the real essence of everything. This earth is not "earth" as you see it; it is light. But you cannot perceive that until you know the underlying astral world.

The Nature of Delusion in the Material World

Everything in the material world is a copy of its counterpart in the astral world; but the material manifestation is a gross one, limited and distorted by the law of relativity. The principle of duality or relativity is inherent in creation; shadow as well as light is necessary to apprehend a universe of separate forms and creatures. Relativity operates in the astral world too; but on that plane there are no fixed limitations—everything is perceived as different vibrations of light, naught else. In the material world delusion is deeply embedded in that law of relativity, preventing the physical consciousness from understanding things as they really are. You don't perceive things in their essence as light because the instrumentality of your physical senses is too gross. You instead experience the relative difference between solids, liquids, and gases as so radical that if you leave the solid shore and try to walk across the liquid ocean, you drown. In the astral world, even though you can cognize the shore as solid and the ocean as liquid, there is no drowning in the astral liquid. You differentiate the solids from the liquids only as varying vibrations of light, which do not clash with each other. You can glide just as easily through "solid" light and "liquid" light. Or you can walk on liquid light in your solid body of light, as Jesus showed when he walked on the water. To him, both his body and the sea were naught but relativities of astral light, which he could alter at will by the power of mind. He demonstrated that a fully God-realized master can control the astral light underlying material creation. That is how he performed his miracles, such as healing the sick and raising the dead, feeding multitudes with a few loaves and fishes, and resurrecting his own body.

There is not one human experience you can think of for which the astral world has not an exact duplicate. You can experience birth and death and marriage and disease and everything that you see in the physical world. Relativities of light can create sensations and perceptions experienced as real. In the material world, because the law of relativity is so heavily laden with delusive power, man is constrained by those "realities." In the astral world, everything is changeable at the command of the mind.

How important it is to live in that finer realm! I am all the time there—even now as I am talking to you. Such happiness comes; there are no words I can use to describe it to you. In this gross world, you get tired of everything; even the most enjoyable things eventually become tedious or boring. But in the astral world the creations of your will are ever new. You will never tire of that world. If you want to be young you can be so. If you want to appear as a man or as a woman or in any form you wish, you can do so. You do not have to worry about money for your needs; a mere command of your will provides whatever you want. Wouldn't it be wonderful to be able to do that here? This earth is so limited; some persons have plenty while others starve. But in the heavenly astral world there are no such inequities; every being has according to his desire. If you want an opulent palace, it is there for you. If you want snow or heat or light or rain, you can have it just by the power of thought. With astral light the mind can create anything. You are free from all limitations when you know the kingdom of heaven, the kingdom of God, which is behind this world.

The Astral Heaven

Is God a hoary man sitting on a throne at some point in space, surrounded by winged harp-playing angels? That is a limited concept held by some dogmatists whose understanding cannot conceive the real nature of God as Spirit, the Infinite Absolute. "Men without wisdom consider Me, the Unmanifest, as assuming embodiment (like a mortal being taking a form)—not understanding My unsurpassable state, My unchangeable unutterable nature....I, the Unchanging and Everlasting, sustain and permeate the entire cosmos with but one fragment of My Being!"*

The invisible God, however, can also become visible. Saints who by *samadhi* meditation have gone into the astral heaven (higher

* Bhagavad Gita VII:24 and X:42.

than the ordinary astral world where most souls go after death) tell us that God is not only formless but that He takes form also.* In fact, it is that One Spirit who has become everything in this universe. He is not only the impersonal Absolute. He can also be very personal, manifesting as the Heavenly Father or the Divine Mother or in any deity-form that His devotees want to see. But He cannot be limited to a form.

In Spirit, God and all His angels are absolutely one. Likewise, no delusion of separation or finitude is imposed on those souls who have found their final liberation. But because souls retain their individuality they can reappear from the light of Spirit as separate forms. At the time when a soul is liberated and returns to God, the Lord and His ascended saints take individualized forms, and there is great rejoicing and festivity—a wondrous celebration in the supernal astral heaven of celestial beauty and bliss. In that Paradise, if there were only the One Light of undifferentiated Spirit, there would be no guests, no food, and therefore no festivity. Just as the one beam of light from a movie projector, passing through a film of individualized images, can show a grand festivity of interacting characters on the screen, so in the heavenly celebrations everything is made of light. God (in a deity-form), the angels, the devotees—all are made of the inconceivably subtle light of pure consciousness, differentiated by their own will into individualized forms. When the celebration concludes, they dissolve themselves again into the ecstatic bliss of undifferentiated Oneness—merging into the One Light, One Spirit.

There are no limitations, no forced routine, in heaven. Advanced astral beings can order their environment and actions just as they please. It is freedom eternal. If you want to go to the farthest star, traveling through the ether faster than light, you are allowed to do so. You can be a star, a human being, an angel—anything you want to be—all at will.

These are some of the advantages of the ultimate realms of the astral world. Of course, most souls after death do not ascend straightway to the kingdom of God. They go to one of the higher

* The astral world consists of graduated levels of greater or lesser spiritual refinement. "In my Father's house there are many mansions" (John 14:2). Higher than the ordinary astral world are the various levels of the astral heaven reached by very advanced souls. These are discussed in detail in Paramahansa Yogananda's *Autobiography of a Yogi*, chapter 43, and *The Second Coming of Christ: The Resurrection of the Christ Within You*, Discourse 10. *(Publisher's Note)*

Paramahansa Yogananda, Encinitas, California, 1937

(Above) Paramahansa Yogananda in front of the SRF Golden Lotus Temple, Encinitas, California, 1937. *(Below)* The Guru leading an Easter sunrise service on the Hermitage lawn in Encinitas, 1938. The Golden Lotus Temple (lost to cliff erosion in 1942) is partially visible in the background.

or lower regions of the ordinary astral universe, as determined by their good or bad karma, and after a time reincarnate on earth. Souls who have been evil, or who have strong material desires and attachments, must come back soon to work out their materialistic karmic burden. Souls who were fairly virtuous on earth have the chance to stay longer in the better astral regions; and when they reincarnate on earth again they have an inborn impetus toward self-improvement and spiritual progress.

Live in Astral Freedom Now

We go to the astral world automatically after death, but why wait for death when you can have that greater freedom now, even while living in the physical body? Unless you are somewhat advanced, your astral sojourn in the after-death state may be more like a rejuvenating sleep with astral dreams interspersed with short periods of conscious astral wakefulness until you wake up in your next earthly reincarnation. But if you can consciously get into the astral world now, you will be able to go there consciously after death; and you will be able to come back again to earth consciously when the time is right for you to continue your lessons in the school of earth life. And when your earthly karma is burned up, you will enter the astral heaven and never have to take another forced earthly incarnation.

What is the use of giving so much of your attention to this world? I am not wasting my time here. Because I made the necessary effort in meditation to find God, even when I am working in the fields or mixing with people I behold that great Light. Such joy! Every minute, every second—no matter what I am doing. Once in a while I feel I am in this world, and once in a while the Lord withdraws my spirit in ecstasy, and my body is lifeless. There is no wind, there is no body, there is no sunlight, there is no ocean, there is no breath, there is no temple. There is just One Light—that Light eternal. And then as my consciousness comes down I see that Light change itself into the temple, into the wind, the ocean, and into my body. It is like the movies. The one beam of light is throwing all those different scenes on the screen. How pure is this Light, how powerful—and how terrible is the movie which it throws on the screen. That is how life is. When we keep our minds on the Light, it is wonderful. But when we concentrate on the world, we are caught up in the terrible drama of delusion.

Until you realize this through meditation, the world is a prison—all trouble and disease and disappointment. Most of the people are poor. Most of the people are sick. Most of the people are unhappy. You may think you are all right now; but you don't know what might happen to you the next minute. Why don't you seek to know your real Self, cloaked in light in the astral world, instead of being subject to a thousand sufferings in this gross world? Body is not well; eyesight is going; stomach is weak—why should we tolerate these things? We have subjected our souls to such delusion. Everyone looks for the latest diet or vitamin to be a little stronger, a little healthier. But all these things you make such a fuss about will sooner or later fail you. That is why Jesus said, "Take no thought for your life, what ye shall eat; neither for the body, what ye shall put on." Now do you understand why he said that? He wanted us to concentrate on the unlimited Divine Source of life, not on matter.

Think of those in Europe whose lives and homes are being destroyed by the bombs of war.* This earth is perpetually a place of war—the battle of good and evil inherent in physical creation. Bombs of suffering are falling everywhere. The animals fight and eat one another—and supposedly superior man behaves no better. If you were animals, you would say: "This is my cave, and if any other animal comes near me I will kill it." That is how territorial nations are fighting today. But where will the instigators be one hundred years hence? They will be gone from this earth, and it will have no more importance to them than a forgotten dream. Man should rather use his brief span here to achieve something lasting: to find freedom in God.

The only purpose of life is to get away from the delusion of this material world. Wait no longer. How dare you forget God! I testify to you of the existence of God's astral kingdom; now why don't you seek it? You are always trying to create that picture of perfection here on earth, but it is fruitless. You will never succeed, for this world is a place of too many limitations. That utopian dream is but the lost forgotten memory of your experience of the astral world. "Methinks that sometime, somewhere beyond the sky, in a little kingdom all my own, I built a castle of my dreams—a beautiful garden-paradise all my own. Methinks I lived there long in perfect happiness." These kinds of dream-imaginings are subconsciously present in the minds of everyone. And there is a way to realize those

* World War II.

dreams. Imagination is not unreal; it is the borderland of what is yet to be real. Everything you imagine can be created by a will that is guided by wisdom.

Jules Verne wrote wonderful books of "science fiction," but today those imaginings are real. Think of all the wonders that once were considered fantasy but have now come true. Somebody imagined the automobile and someone else imagined electric lights and another imagined the airplane and so on—and now these marvelous inventions are commonplace.

How to Materialize Your Cherished Dreams and Goals

Imagination is a portal through which you can transcend the imposed limitations of this world. All creative persons use this power. With wisdom and will, whatever you can imagine, and continue to imagine, can become real. I tell you, that things which do not exist now in this world will be created for you. Imagination can be materialized. When you develop spiritually, you can materialize your thoughts. When you sit still and let your imagination go as far as you can into the realm of your cherished dreams and goals, and if you can hold your mind to one-pointed concentration on the image of what you want to achieve, it will be shown to you in a true-to-life vision. And if you apply strong will power to realizing that vision, ultimately it will manifest—healings can be effected, successes attained, disasters in your environment lessened or avoided, seemingly impossible needs or worthy wishes fulfilled. Your mind united with your soul is such a powerful dynamo of spiritual existence! And yet you don't utilize that power. Why shouldn't you? By increasing the intensity of your concentration and calmness, you can consciously realize your connection with the unlimited realm of the astral world. In meditation, when you think you are the calmest you can be, try to be even more calm; gradually your consciousness will become attuned to that higher dimension. Get out of limiting material consciousness and you will see your mind's imaginings working to manifest all your wisdom-guided dreams through the universal underlying creative astral powers.

To develop mental imaging, I used to sit in a room and concentrate on visualizing everything in another unseen room, until my immediate surroundings disappeared and I was seeing in exact detail everything in the other room. By practice, develop proficiency in visualization (concentrating the mind's eye on what you wish to achieve) and devisualization (banishing any images that distract from what you are concentrating on). These powers of imagination—used together with the power of will, power of inner silence, power of concentration and opening of the spiritual eye—will lead you to the astral realm and increased ability to manifest your thoughts in material form. Such is the power of thought, the Lord's creative principle that brought everything in the universe into manifestation—first as causal ideas of consciousness, then as subtle light-forms in the astral world, and then by materialization of those "blueprints" in the physical world.

The Spiritual Eye: Portal to the Higher Realms

As Self-Realization students know, when your spiritual eye is open in meditation, you see the astral light of the spiritual eye as a ring of golden radiance encircling a sphere of opalescent blue, and at the center, a five-pointed silvery-white star. If you can penetrate that star, you are immediately in God's kingdom in the astral world. So learn to concentrate and meditate deeply. Though the spiritual man experiences the physical world and works through the instruments of the physical body, he does not identify himself with any sensation of the body; he is always centered in the spiritual eye. I never take my mind away from there, no matter what I am doing.

If you keep your mind there, the calming and spiritualizing influences flowing from the astral world will make you a different person than you are now. Don't have restless, shifty eyes. If your eyes are always distractedly looking everywhere, your mind is likewise wandering. Eyes that are constantly blinking reflect the consciousness of a nervous individual. Keep your mind calm and centered at this point between the eyebrows, not flitting restlessly in matter. Even when you are sleeping your mind should be at that spiritual center. If your body and mind are still in meditation and you keep your gaze and attention turned upward to that point, you will experience the blessings of the astral world consciously. That is why saints in ecstatic communion are depicted with upturned gaze—looking up into heaven. By concentrating on the spiritual eye in deep meditation, one can penetrate into that higher dimension. Your astral body is there now, though your mind and physical body are here. You depend on what you can see with your two physical eyes and that keeps you continually deluded. If you look into the spiritual eye, you will know the true nature of everything and can receive the right answers in business and all other matters. You can use this power all the time; it is unlimited within you. When you live at will in that astral world you will be guided by the Supreme.

Spirituality Does Not Mean to Be Otherworldly

I am not giving you this lecture to make you mystical, or to stir in you a desire for the entertainment of phenomenal experiences and powers. The point is to awaken you from the delusion that you are a limited mortal, helplessly subject to the whims of physical existence. You live, move, breathe, act, because of your innate astral self and its powers flowing from God. This true incarnate nature is what I want you to realize and utilize. Know your Self as connected with the Omnipotent Source of your being. Imagine, affirm, will, meditate to realize your true Self as the soul cloaked in a wonderful astral form of light and power. That thought alone, far from making you "otherworldly," energizes your life and accomplishments in the here and now.

Those persons who acquire some understanding and then assume the attitude that they are too "spiritual" to undertake constructive activity in the world remain in delusion. Lazy persons who take refuge in their meager spiritual development and look down on constructively active people, mentally criticizing them, "O yes, I am spiritual and you are materialistic," will never get very far. You have to work hard on the spiritual path. Laziness is a major curse of mankind. It not only destroys your prosperity and material accomplishments, but it is destructive to the divine expression of your soul. If there is anything that makes you forget the soul, it is laziness. If from the very start of your life you always want things "easy" then you are done for. The spiritual man who is working hard is the happy man. And how well he sleeps! His life is balanced.

I like the American people because they are actively industrious. Activity is wonderful if you do not let it make you nervous. It is spiritually fulfilling to act with calmness and with your mind always centered on God. When I work, I concentrate on what needs to be done at that moment; I do it, then forget it until it needs my attention again. And if I can't do it, I don't let it distress me. Some people with their little home and little job are all the time worrying and nervous. Any person who is nervous is in the physical world. If you are calm and happy, you are in the astral world. Always work from the astral world; and as soon as the physical world starts to eat at your peace of mind, get away and retire into inner silence. If you develop the ability to live in interior quietness, you can remain in the calm state even in the midst of noise and discord. That ability shows the astral influence upon you. I can go to sleep at will, even if cannonballs were flying around me.

That is why it is necessary to meditate and live more in the consciousness of the astral world. In the physical world there are so many difficulties that come along. You will "go crazy" trying to cope with your problems unless you can draw strength and guidance from the astral heaven within you. Just think when you were a child and had no worries! You were in heaven. But when you had to start out on your own, what troubles you had. The way to fly away from your material troubles is to have recourse to that astral world. Money does not make happiness. Having reasonable financial resources no doubt helps, but your first necessity is to have God.

I could make myself "crazy" this minute thinking of all I have to do for this work. But there is a time for everything. My time with God comes first. "I am ready to do everything for You, Lord, working day and night; but my happiness lies in my contact with You." I remain in His astral kingdom. That is my home. I am living on the earth just as a servant lives and works in the house of his employer: I know my home is elsewhere.

So must you live. Do not form attachments to this world. If you do, you are in for trouble; you are going to be sadly disappointed. This is not your home. The heavenly kingdom of God is your home. Live there now. No matter what you are doing, concentrate on your inner peace and calmness. Keep your mind at the spiritual eye, and keep your thoughts busy with God's thoughts. Meditate more, churn the ether with your prayers, until out of the silence the light of God appears. If you want to know God in this life, never go to bed at night until you have made contact with Him. If for one whole day and night you would pray and meditate, remaining in your room and not seeing anyone, intensely praying that God will come to you, He would definitely respond. But who is willing to give even that much time and effort? Such is delusion. The consciousness of outer duties and habitual restlessness takes precedence, and you remain attached and limited to the physical body and its world.

Dear ones, do not forget the message you have received today; use it. Meditate deeply and regularly, until the spiritual eye is opened and you can fly through it to the astral kingdom. Remain always in the sphere of happiness born of meditation, no matter what happens. Live in the consciousness of astral freedom. Without fail you will be able to do this by devoted practice of the techniques of the Kriya Yoga science I have given to you.

I remember long ago I went back to Cincinnati after several years' absence and met with the Self-Realization Fellowship students there. A number of them told me: "When we took your classes years ago we found them wonderful. But just the same, because you didn't return, we went to another teacher. However, we have come back to you, for you have given not only inspiration, but actual techniques. And whenever we practice them we get results." I gave my life to this SRF path of our great Gurus because these teachings give to the world a practical methodology whereby all devotees can know by tangible experience that they are progressing toward God.

This world is a terrible dream. I hope you all realize this. To the last breath of my dream existence I shall tell you how to get out of this dream as soon as you can. Do not wait. For one evil thought may lead you to the valley of death, and one good thought may lead you to the kingdom of God. So get busy with yourself. Then, at the end of the trail of life, you will find the wonderful harmony, peace, and beauty of God. He is waiting for you; He is very much worried about you because He cannot free you without your cooperation. Concentrate on that great peace within you, and you will see all shadows of world limitations melt away—and that behind this motion picture of delusion, there is a heavenly astral world eternal.

Every night in meditation, throw yourself at the feet of the Lord. From the depths of your heart, cry to Him. Cry for Him until your head and your heart seem to burst with longing for Him: "You must come. Reveal Thyself to me!" If you do not give up, the Lord will come unto you. He will awaken you from this dream world and lift you to His bosom of eternal light, immortality, and freedom.

Harmonizing Your Life With Spiritual Vibrations

Compilation of talks given at SRF International Headquarters, Los Angeles, January 6–10, 1935. Excerpts from one of the talks were printed in an early issue of Self-Realization *magazine and later in the* SRF Lessons. *Paramahansaji's complete presentation from these talks, plus some additional material, is published here for the first time in book form.*

As you stand on the shores of matter, remember that your real home is the Kingdom of Peace; and that is where your mind should be. Don't be attached to this earth. At any moment an accident or disease may carry you away without notice. This is only a temporary home. Your real home is with God. Meditation forms the rainbow bridge by which you can reach God.

During deep meditation, perception of body consciousness ceases to exist. Realize that you are not caged in the body. The Heavenly Father embraces you within and without. Realize the Infinite Presence.

[A period of meditation followed, after which Paramahansaji continued:]

In deep communion, God comes as ever new Bliss. The God of the clouds, the God of the moon and the sun, the God who is templed in all creation is within you and manifests as peace. Learn to love Him as the peace and bliss of meditation.

May the *Aum* vibration, conjoined with the music of the spheres, dispel all your darkness and bring joy and understanding in your heart.

Heavenly Father, Guru and *Paramgurus,* saints of all religions, and the Spirit in our body temples, I bow to you all.

[Sings:] O-o-ommm, O-omm, O-om.

Make yourself sensitive to the vibrations here; tune in with the vibration I send forth. You must understand why these vibrations are modulated and divided into three tonal qualities, from loud to soft. All creation consists of three vibrations—the creative, the preservative, and the destructive vibrations. So, when we chant the first *Aum,* that represents creation; then the second represents preservation of creation, the force that holds the universe and all lives within it in balance according to the intelligent plan of the Creator; and the third, sung softly, symbolizes the destructive or dissolving vibration, by which all manifestations in creation go back to God again when their part in the cosmic drama is over.

The Sound of the Universe

Every vibration produces a sound. The whole universe is vibrating at a terrific speed; and that vibration can be heard when your higher faculties are awakened by meditation. The Hindus call it *Aum,* the Christians call it *Amen,* and the Muslims call it *Amin.* The cosmic sound is "the faithful and true witness" of God's creation.* When a motor is running, you know that it is doing so by the sound. The same is true of creation. The Cosmic Motor is working, and *Aum* is its sound. Wherever there is activity, there is sound, but the highest and the lowest sounds are not audible to the human ear.

Spirit's first vibration is the *Aum* sound, and if you tune in with this sound, you will be in continuous contact with the Intelligent Force in all creation, and with God. This sound can be heard in meditation, and if you are constantly listening to this sound, you will feel the presence of God within it as the Christ Consciousness.

The deeper students on this path will hear that great *Aum* in the ether when chanting *Aum* as we have just done. That sound has healing potency. It is pure. It harmonizes all individual manifestations in creation that otherwise would clash and conflict and war with each other. When that harmony comes, it brings healing of body, mind, and soul. Those mind-radios that are in tune through faith will receive that healing vibration.

Tuning Your Mind-Radio to Receive Divine Vibrations

When you scientifically try to understand the human body, you will find that it is a very powerful super-physical radio. It has broadcasting and receiving mechanisms in the heart and brain. By concentrating at the Christ center at the point between the eyebrows, you can tune in with God's vibration; and you can also broadcast to

* "These things saith the Amen, the faithful and true witness, the beginning of the creation of God" (Revelation 3:14). "In the beginning was the Word, and the Word was with God, and the Word was God....All things were made by Him; and without Him was not any thing made that was made" (John 1:1–3).

Him from there. You can also broadcast and receive from the heart center. But the point between the eyebrows is more of a broadcasting station; and the heart, the center of feeling, is the most sensitive receiver.* Just as different stations have different wavelengths, so different minds are attuned to different qualities of vibration. And according to the degree of your contact with God, you can send out into the ether a stronger vibration than that of a mortal mind circumscribed by physical limitations. Every thought you send forth that is propelled by the power of your soul-experience will produce tangible results in the ether. But your mind must be in tune through faith before you can send or receive those healing vibrations.

Faith is more than mere belief; it is the knowing power of the soul, by which you can intuit the unseen high-vibrational realms beyond the material world. Wrong habits of thought create static of disbelief or doubt in your heart. But if you keep on striving to cultivate faith, which develops through contact of God in meditation, you will receive the vibratory broadcast of healing and blessings I send to you when I pray and chant *Aum*.

So many people write to me for prayers, and I put that list of names on my breast and I pray: "Father, don't turn a deaf ear to the wailings of these souls. If anyone can help them, Lord, it is You. But give them the faith by which they can receive Your everlasting help, and the power by which they can correct themselves. Father, do not close Your ears to their prayers. Help them!"†

As your faith increases, the power of your mind-radio increases. You can "tune in" God and the saints on your mind-radio, but you must have a very powerful radio of devotion and faith. Ceaselessly tell the Lord: "One day I will catch Thee on the devotion-tuned radio of my heart!" His program is omnipresent in the ether; but He is very far away if you have no faith.

You must learn to think of God as nearer and dearer than your father or mother or most beloved friend. That is why He has given you all forms of love, that you may practice love in those relationships and then give that love to Him. You don't know why you feel

* This subject is explained in SRF Lesson 89, "How to Develop Your Mental Radio." *(Publisher's Note)*

† Paramahansa Yogananda founded the Self-Realization Fellowship Prayer Council at the Mother Center and the SRF Worldwide Prayer Circle to serve as a similar channel for God's healing vibrations to be broadcast to all who request prayers for body, mind, and soul; and for world peace and harmony. Information about how to request prayers, and to participate in this divine service, can be found on the SRF website.

attracted to your child or to your spouse or your parents as you do. Whence did that love come? From God. Just say to Him, "Lord, I love You more than anything and anyone in this world, because You gave me the love I feel for my father, for my mother, for my child, for my wife, for my husband. Lord, I give my love to You!"

Saying it just once or twice will not do. Every day pour out your love to Him. You must try to feel what you are saying to the Lord. When you are sincere—when you "talk straight" with the Infinite, you will receive His response. You will see His magic presence playing hide-and-seek with you behind all the screens of material life. You will intuit His invisible power and beauty behind everything.

Understand and Apply the Law of Vibration

God's creative Word—Cosmic Vibration or *Aum*—is the sustaining power behind all that exists. His intelligent vibration creates and guides the universe. To perceive and know that is the absolute Truth about the universe. But there is also a relative truth, because there are other intelligences in creation, given free will by the Creator; and their individual choices are the source of inharmony, disease, and the chaos perceived by our mortal eyes all around.

We live in a vast ocean of vibrations—physical, mental, and spiritual—which affect our bodies, minds, and souls. If you know the laws of vibration, you can choose which kinds of vibration you allow yourself to be sensitive to. You can learn to absorb only good harmonious vibrations, and protect yourself from contrary or harmful or degrading vibrations.

Vibration means motion—any kind of motion. Unless vibration has rhythmic intelligence to guide it, it becomes disturbing. Intelligence itself is vibration, and consists of various forms of thought. Thoughts are separated from each other by their different rates of vibration; without this relativity of vibration it would not be possible to cognize any vibration in the universe.

Different rates of vibration, balanced in the cosmic rhythm, produce before us the majestic cosmos. As the sun holds the planets and their moons around it by its great magnetic force, so in the miniature cosmos of the body our ego binds our thoughts and cells together. If this ego has left the body (as in death), or is inactive during prolonged unconsciousness, all the thoughts will vanish from the body, the strings of vibratory life forces will be burst asunder, and the cells will begin to decay.

What Kind of Vibratory Environment Are You Creating?

Ask yourself each day what sort of thoughts and vibratory energies your ego is drawing around itself, thus creating the kind of life you are living. Different people are characterized by different qualities of vibration—both in what they draw unto themselves and in what they broadcast out to others. By understanding and applying the laws of spiritual vibration, you can bring divine harmony and healing into your body, mind, and soul.

Thought is only intelligent vibration. Our thoughts and moods have vibrational qualities. We identify with those qualities and think, "This is the way I am." That is a very limiting way to live. By applying the science of vibration, you can change your inner and outer environment in order to live in peace, harmony, and happiness.

Everything in creation has its own particular rate of vibration. If two waves move side by side, there is harmony, but if one wave strikes another, there is a conflict of forces. In your life you should avoid contradictory vibrations in order to live harmoniously. The vibrations of one's physical surroundings should harmonize with the vibrations of the physical being. If you want to be a harmonious individual, you should have harmonious vibrations of color, form, and so forth around you.

People, nations, places, all have characteristic vibrations that affect our consciousness. Colors and sounds have vibrations that affect our consciousness. Each of the cerebrospinal centers also has a characteristic vibratory quality, and by tuning our consciousness to those centers in the yogic way we can partake of and express the vibrational intelligence and powers within each one.

Yoga has deeply explored the scientific properties of vibration, and how to use idea vibrations, energy vibrations, and material vibrations to make life as it should be. For example, *mantra* is an idea vibration of creative power and intelligence, expressed mentally or verbally. The science of *mantra,* affirmation, and chants can be used to consciously change the vibratory environment within yourself.*

* Paramahansaji taught that one application of this is found in the Hong-Sau Technique of Concentration given in the *SRF Lessons,* whose successful practice calms the breath and vibrations of restlessness in the mind and makes it easier to perceive the divine vibration of *Aum.* See also *affirmation* in the glossary. *(Publisher's Note)*

Develop the Ability to Discern the Vibrations of Other People

In relation to people, how do you know when you get good vibrations or bad vibrations from them? First of all, there is a "feeling." Some people do not distinguish between real vibrational differences and the judgmental attitude of their sense-identified mind and its egotistical likes and dislikes. You must keep a very kind feeling within your heart at all times—a feeling that is absolutely unprejudiced. That feeling can judge better than all the intellectual reasoning in the world.

The best way to know what kind of vibrations people radiate is to pay attention to the radio receiver of your feelings, right in your heart. The heart, the center of feeling, is the most sensitive instrument of all. For accurate results, however, you must be free from any attraction to the opposite sex, from prejudices, and from any emotional feelings of attraction or repulsion toward others. A neutral state of consciousness is necessary. When your heart-radio can receive the vibrations of others with the antenna of pure feeling, which does not judge from prejudice and emotion, then you have developed spiritual sensitivity.

The spiritually sensitive person loves everyone. You naturally love those who are dear to you, and you must learn to give that kind of love to the whole world. In the soil of your heart the seeds of love are growing; cultivate those seeds with the water of universal love and universal sympathy.

As soon as you love all people with the intensity of the love that you have for your family, then you are expressing divine love. The whole purpose of loving is to develop that kind of love. Universal love is trying to vibrate through you, but attachment, limitations, and concentration on the senses hinder the free expression of that universal love.

Conquer Wrong Vibrations in Your Environment

You can always sense the general vibratory rate of other persons' health, mind, feelings, and soul. Ill persons have negative, inharmonious, body vibrations, and they should reject them. And if you live with sick people all the time, they tend to make you sickness-conscious as well.

Some people vibrate nervousness; some, temper; and some, cruelty. Other people have no will; the minute you meet them you feel their spinelessness. Some people vibrate kindness and you love them immediately. Always keep your heart in tune with positive high vibrations. If those around you are negative, you must create a countering positive vibration in your own heart. You must be stronger than the thoughts and suggestions constantly vibrating from other people. That is the way to conquer wrong vibrations that come into your environment.

Vibrations of thought are so powerful that if you live in the same house with persons who have wrong thoughts, their wrong vibrations will affect you unless you are powerful enough to protect yourself. If you have a very powerful good vibration of your own, you do not need to be concerned about being unduly influenced by people who have wrong vibrations.

Even in foods God creates harmony of color, and when you cook foods too much, you destroy these colors. In this way you contradict the harmonious vibrations of foods, so that they become inharmonious.* In eating, in arranging furniture, and so on, you must have harmony. Cheerful colors always create happiness in the mind. Some colors and combinations of colors are soothing, while others are irritating.

Harmonizing Vibrations of Reason and Feeling

Then there are vibrations of reason and feeling (emotion). You should have a balance of feeling and reason if you want to be happy. That can come only by surrounding yourself with vibrations of kindness plus vibrations of intelligence. And you get vibrations not only from outside; you can and must create the right kind within yourself.

What you need is a complete balance between the vibrations of reason and feeling. You must be ready to feel everything that is around you, and yet use clear-sighted reason to estimate everything according to its real value at the same time. That is why the combination of man and woman in a relationship on a spiritual plane is very good, for then they help each other to express pure feeling and pure reason. As one meditates deeply and unites soul with Spirit, this balance of pure reason and pure feeling is expressed in the highest degree.

Another point about reason and feeling: If you want to absorb the vibration of a devotional chant, you should tune in the heart by concentrating there while repeating it; and if you want to absorb

* Yoga provides a profound science on the vibrational properties of various foods. Paramahansa Yogananda discusses this subject in the *Self-Realization Fellowship Lessons* on diet and spiritual food. *(Publisher's Note)*

the vibration of a wisdom chant you should tune in at the point between the eyebrows. If you want God, the best way is to concentrate deeply and continuously at the eyebrow point. Then your heart will automatically be in tune.

Become a Person of Strong Soul Vibration

A strong soul vibration is evident when a person is always conscious of being with God; and when you are with such a person, you feel the presence of God. That is the vibration to carry with you wherever you go, so that whoever comes in contact with you may forget all but the power and love of God. Try to be the clear crystal through which the sunlight of God's presence may reflect to all mankind. This kind of vibration gives joy to you and at the same time it burns away all evil.

The vibration of God is the most intelligent of all and produces perfect harmony. When you let that vibration pass through you, all other vibrations become harmonious within you. As Jesus said: "Seek ye first the kingdom of God, and all else shall be added unto you." To "seek ye first the kingdom of God, and His righteousness"* is to make attunement with the Eternal Source of life, beauty, power, and truth the first and foremost priority of your earthly existence.

Any hindrances to the expression of this divine harmony through you are limitations you have created, or allowed to accumulate: attachment, prejudice, habit, concentration on the senses, and so forth. Find out what your own hindrances are by becoming aware of them, and then eliminate them.

Charge Your Mind-Radio for Higher Perception

The senses are tuned only to the vibrations of matter. If you use all your time and energy working through the five senses of sight, hearing, taste, touch, and smell, you will lack sufficient force to operate the higher radio of intuitional perception. You can't tune in with the supernal harmony of the Divine Plan unless you recharge your brain. Songs cannot come into a radio without the help of electricity. Is not that so? The radio in an automobile is connected with the battery in the car; and when the battery goes dead, then the radio won't work.

Likewise, if you want to convert your body and mind scientifically into a super-radio you must conserve your life force. Too

* Matthew 6:33.

much greed, too much living on the sex plane, and too many desires deplete your vital energy. Have more self-control; then your body will remain highly charged. Your whole being will tingle with that tremendous power.

Always remember that there is enough energy in your body, and in the ether all around your body, to keep you always strong and divinely vitalized. Only you must learn to contact it by will power, through techniques such as I have given you in the *Lessons*. By mastering them, you will be able to feel that every cell of the brain and every fiber of the heart, charged by God's energy, has become an instrument of perception and feeling; you will know things without being told.

In meditation, rightly practiced, you charge your body and mind with infinite power; you charge your heart and brain with devotion and deepest concentration. Thus you convert your body, mind, and soul into a super-sensitive radio. When you feel that tremendous current in your body, and your mind has become very powerful through constant meditation, then you can tune in with God and the angels. You will hear or feel their song of truth-vibrations; and by further advancement you will also be able to see them. You will have "spiritual television." This is not a simple matter. First, you have to electrify your body-battery fully by long and deep meditation.

See and Feel the Divine Templed Everywhere

The God that I perceive is as real—more real—than all this human panorama. By constantly desiring that my eyes should be opened, I received Him. I had closed my eyes to Him, but through unswerving determination and constantly trying to surround myself with harmonious vibrations within and without, through regular meditation, my eyes were opened and I saw Him templed everywhere.

Do you see what a marvelous mind-radio you have? There will be no other instrument invented by science that can detect the presence of God; it can be done only by this human radio of yours. Use it to feel the eternal vibrations of God.

So remember this: develop a fine sensitivity. After you meditate deeply, then use that perception and the sum total of the feeling that you have after meditation, and concentrate that feeling in the heart. Then it will give you power to radiate good vibrations and to absorb good vibrations, and it will also give you wisdom.

Radiate Peace and Harmony Wherever You Go

Wherever you go, carry the consciousness of God's peace within you, and pray: "Let that peace vibration flow through my hands and eyes and through my speech, and through every tube of my thought." When that vibration flows from within you, you do not have to worry. If you are in a hades, you will make a heaven there; and if you are in heaven, you will make it better!

Let that vibration flow through your hands, eyes, and feet; and whoever comes in contact with you will feel its blessing. Just say: "God flows through me. What am I afraid of?" And wherever you are, that vibration will correct wrong surroundings. You will absorb only good vibrations when in that state of spiritual attunement.

Suppose you come with kindness in your heart to a divine person who radiates that vibration; then your kindness increases and the giver receives more kindness too. That is the vibration you want to emanate from you, instead of being rude or discordant with people.

Remember: Unless there is a relativity of vibration there cannot be cognizance of any vibration in the universe. Do you realize how much that statement explains? *Anything* of which you are cognizant has a relative vibration within yourself. One who is quick to see and judge evil in other persons has the seed of that evil within himself. The Godlike person of pure and high vibrational tone is always aware of the God-spark in all he contacts, and his magnetic soul vibration draws to greater intensity that vibrational force in those who come within his vibrational range.

When your eyes become spiritually opened, then you see the eyes of the Infinite looking at you through the eyes of everyone you meet. Behind the voice of everyone, you will hear the voice of the Infinite. Behind the will of everyone you behold the will of God; and behind all human love you feel only the love of God. That is a wonderful sort of existence, when all veils of matter are lifted and you find the Infinite and yourself in continuous communion. He will play hide-and-seek with you in the blossoms and all things beautiful; the stars will shine with a stronger light and the sky will be smiling on you with the smile of the Infinite. And every person you meet will see something of that Spirit throbbing behind your eyes, and will feel uplifted.

Every day try, by your own example, to bring others to the spiritual path. Do you realize that every good thought you have for others will determine your future life, according to the law of karma? And that the greatest good you can do is to bring God into the lives of others? My duty, given by my Master and *Paramgurus,* is to set ablaze a fire of wisdom and God-love here; and yours is to bring to that light other souls who are in darkness.

Spirituality Has Never Been More Important Than Now

Never in world history was it more necessary than now to follow the path of spirituality. From the frightful specter of world war, we see that technology and inventions must not outpace spiritual development. But the world is marching on, progressing and evolving, no matter what happens. We are living in strange times and we have great opportunities, if we would but take them.

All over the world, different nations have contributed to different phases of civilization. India's contribution to the world is spiritual knowledge. Truth is universal, and can be found in the esoteric traditions of all great religions; but India, more than any other nation, has kept alive the highest truths and methods of God-realization that were lost to humanity at large during the Dark Ages. Those truths and techniques are being given worldwide for the first time in this modern era in the *Self-Realization Fellowship Lessons*.

In the *Lessons* you are taught the method of attuning your consciousness with the Divine Force that sustains and gives life to all creation. By awakening your latent instruments of intuitive knowledge, you can feel that Force flowing through you and through all that exists and can know the truth about everything.

All spiritual truth has to be experienced within yourself in order to be real; otherwise it is merely intellectual knowledge. And if you would make the effort to have that realization, you would know that truth is more than belief or speculation. It must come as unshakable intuitive perception to every individual. In the secret niche of your heart you can find God's presence. India shows you how. It is not easy to find God, but it is simple if you pursue the right way. You can't find the door if you look for it in the ceiling; you must look where the door is. So, the door to the soul is within. Learn to find and open it by the scientific techniques of yoga meditation.

We are living in a new age, in which long-hidden techniques of knowing God can be learned by all. Use them to tune your life to the Divine. The song of God is in the air; the song of the angels is in the air. Every saint that ever lived has a program in the air. St. Francis, Babaji, and a few other saints have vibrations which I know directly, as well as the constantly broadcast help from my own guru Sri Yukteswarji. Each of the saints and masters vibrates a particular type of consciousness and energy. By tuning in with them we can help ourselves develop the particular quality that is necessary in our makeup or in any circumstances we encounter.

I have my favorite saints with whom I tune in. Right here in this chapel one day St. Francis came to me. I beheld him with open eyes. So, these saints are not mythical. But this cosmos is so vast, with many planes of existence higher than this earth plane, that it is very hard for an ordinary person to recognize souls who have changed their bodily garments for a finer angelic garb.* If you want to see the masters, saints, and angels, you must develop your body, mind, and soul into a super all-wave radio or television. Every one of you must feel that the masters are with you, so that you make your life a conclave of divine understanding.

Every Minute Is a Link Between You and God

So do not waste your time. Some bacteria experience in two hours what it takes us years to feel. They are born, give birth, and die within two hours. Scientists also are studying life in the electron and the atom. This short span of life that we have is but a wink of eternity, and from that standpoint we are just like the bacteria. With every wink of God, a lifespan of one hundred years passes away.

Every minute is a link between you and God. So you should not waste your time here on earth, but learn now to be master of yourself. Do not be controlled by your desires. Do not allow yourself to do anything that you should not do. Be the master of yourself. If you know that you are master within yourself, nothing else matters.

Every morning, concentrate on the heart and make your resolution to simplify life and meditate more. Plan a definite program for yourself to follow, so that you keep on improving day by day. And pursue that program relentlessly. You are a child of God! But you can only prove it by some definite accomplishments. Live each day to its fullest. Most people live too much in the future or in the past. Live today fully, and laugh at the future. Tell yourself: "The future waits for me—I am not waiting for the future!"

And don't dwell on errors of the past. That is dead and gone; it doesn't belong to you. Don't bring the dead ghosts of your past

* On other occasions, Paramahansaji explained that liberated saints and masters, though no longer bound to the phenomenal worlds, can nevertheless manifest themselves in astral or causal form at will. Those whose intuitive powers are developed can thus behold them. *(Publisher's Note)*

with you on your forward journey; disclaim them and their power to limit what you are striving to become. Dispel all inharmonious vibrations from your life by meditating regularly.

Prayer and Technique for Receiving God's Vibrations

Before the rhythmic vibrations of God's perfect harmony, all wrong vibrations are consumed; all discordance is destroyed. Establish God's vibration on the altar of your heart. Meditate, calm the heart, and pray:

"Through every feeling and every pore of my heart, O Purifying Light, O Incandescent Flood Divine, flow through me, that I may create in myself and my environment vibrations of health, power, wisdom, and love; and at the same time burn away all inharmonious and wrong vibrations.

"Infinite Father, let that heavenly vibration of Thy presence descend through my medulla into my brain, my body, my hands." Visualize and feel His power as you pray.

Now raise your hands over your head. Concentrate and you will feel that vibration trickling through the sensitive antennae of the fingers and hands. Say, "Father, I receive Thy divine energy, blessing me, through my hands. Roast and electrocute all latent seeds of wrong vibrations within me. Charge my brain, my mind, and my soul with Thy power.

"Heavenly Father, manifest Thyself on the altar of my being. I shall behold the good in everything. Give me the determination to contact the great Holy Ghost *Aum* Vibration in meditation and to radiate the harmony of that vibration to all.

"Even as I do what brings happiness and well-being to myself, so will I do for others. Each day, I shall try to relieve somebody from physical suffering, from mental suffering, and from the spiritual suffering of ignorance. As I have been uplifted by the teachings of Self-Realization Fellowship, so shall I try each day to bring some spiritually thirsty soul to the cause of truth.

"Peace! Joy! Peace!"

How to Guide Your Life With Correct Thinking

Using Reason, Discrimination, and Intuition to Reach Life's Goal

Compilation of two talks on this subject, given in 1940 and 1941, Self-Realization Fellowship Golden Lotus Temple, Encinitas, California

"Heavenly Father, bless us that we make Thee the only king on the throne of all our ambitions—the supreme ambition of our lives.

"Heavenly Father, may we make Thee the polestar of all our shipwrecked thoughts, to guide us surely to our safe harbor in Thy kingdom.

"Heavenly Father, may we think correctly to find Thee as the true Goal we are seeking in the pursuit of all our desires. Bless us that all the rivers of our desires ultimately converge in the ocean of Thy Spirit.

"*Aum*. Peace. *Aum*."

Look for the Hidden Spirit in All Creation

God resides in a higher realm than we do not because He wants to keep away from us, but so that we may stimulate the desire to lift our consciousness to where He is. If you give up that desire, you can never find Him. You must make Him more important than everything else. And when you try unceasingly to find Him, you *will* find Him. Look for His hidden Spirit even in this physical world. Whenever you feel the leaves moving and swaying, feel the gentle whisper of God. It is God's breath that has touched the leaves which whisper to us of the gentleness of His presence.

After I had sought for years, the One whom I looked for through the mist of tears—the One I had sought in the vacant sky, the unanswering stars, and the boisterous blue brine—that Mighty One suddenly talked to me. Nature is very beautiful; but still, in one sense, it is very silent: it tells us of the beauty of everything without revealing the Beauty that is behind everything. But when we find God within, His presence becomes so evident without. When in deep meditation I felt His presence, no longer was God hiding from me. All of Nature's veils were lifted and I was face-to-face with the Deity.

Just as everything seems so real when you are beholding a motion picture, and then suddenly you remember that it is only a movie, and you see the tree and the ocean and the action on the screen all converging into dancing electricity as you look up at the great beam of light that throws the pictures on the screen—in this same way, everything around me was dancing in that eternal light. Everything was thrumming with His presence. There was no longer the material earth; all was one Light—a stupendous motion picture of cosmic creation.

That is what you can realize also, provided you overcome the tests of earthly existence. You must realize that greater than everything else in life is the pursuit of God. Greater than all other desires is the desire for God. Greater than all other ambitions is the ambition to know that Eternal Power. God seems remote when you spend so much time on lesser things; but when you continuously cultivate that greatest desire, nothing can prevent you from having a living, personal relationship with God. It isn't that you always have to sit down and think of God in meditation. It is dwelling in the constant thought of Him, no matter what you are doing. But that constant thought will be cut off unless there is meditation and mixing with spiritual people.

This world is full of material things whose surface appearances hide the underlying Spirit-essence. The light that you see with your physical eyes is not the true light. Beholding only that lesser light, you live in darkness, because you don't see God. The sunlight that illumines the world of nature and the electrical light devised by man both hide God. They are far grosser than the astral and causal light of the higher realms.

Your mind is like a radio receiver that can be tuned to various ranges of vibration. It picks up from this world what you concentrate on. When you concentrate on the world through the senses, it will only have value and meaning to you in terms of what you can see, touch, taste, hear, or smell. When you concentrate on business, the world will only have one value and use to you: the amount of success you can achieve. Concentrate on science and only what science can prove in this world will have value to you. Only that is real to you on which you concentrate.

In waking consciousness, our faculties of knowing are mostly concentrated (either actively or passively) on the body and the world. But as you read the many pages of the book of nature, when you try to find who is the Author of that mystery novel, and what is the science behind all sciences, and what is the Power behind all creative will and intelligence, you find God alone. Spirit is the ultimate Reality; naught else. When you connect with that Power, all your desires become fulfilled; all your thirst for knowledge becomes quenched; all your hunger for truth becomes satisfied.

Learn to Distinguish Between Truth and Fallacy

How to think correctly in order to find truth: That is today's subject. To many people, it may seem a rather stale subject. But correct thinking is the cue to the right conduct of life. It is the door to all forms of success. Every individual should be interested in learning how to think correctly. This should be the theme of education.

So many people go through life without learning to distinguish between the correctness of thought and the fallacy of thought. As a result, life looks to them like a deep, dark forest, and they easily become lost in confusion. They have no searchlight of correct thinking in hand.

What is correct thinking? It is apprehending the truth about ourselves, and about the world around us and its real character; and deciding correctly about the right course of action in any given situation. Incorrect thinking, on the other hand, beclouds our understanding with all manner of delusions, and leads us to choose paths that lead to unhappiness.

As we move along in life without the searchlight of correct thinking, what happens? We get caught in the brambles of worry, which hold us back. We fear the uncertainties of life, because we do not know what to do about them—the tigers of sickness and poverty that may be lurking in the darkness; the wolves of unscrupulous business competitors who try to take away what you have by unfair means; and so on. Many are the fears that pervade the mind and cloud your sense of direction as you travel in this dark forest of life without the searchlight of right thinking. But if you learn to think correctly, you will be able to find the way to your goal no matter how dark it is around you.

In the dark jungle of life there are many pitfalls. What are they? Your moods and bad habits. You get into them and you can't easily get out. Moods and bad habits are your greatest enemies. You are going along and suddenly a bad mood comes; you cannot then see things clearly and are apt to behave badly. You make yourself and others uncomfortable.

The evenminded person has no difficulty with anyone. The one who is angry is always going after everybody, always misunderstanding. When you are not evenminded, you cannot think correctly. As I will explain to you, correct thinking, once you learn to use it, is the searchlight that leads you past pitfalls of habits and moods.*

You also meet snakes in this jungle of life. These are your unfulfilled desires. They are venomous; they are always striking you. Your happiness, if not safeguarded by right thinking, dies because of unfulfilled desires.

Of course, there are certain desires, like the desire to know God, that are all right. Even as a child, the thought that the desire to know God should be uppermost was very strong in my mind. As I grew, I realized everything else was impermanent. And when I observed the cruelties that life imposed on those deluded by this world, I felt a terrible sting of helplessness. That is why I dedicated my life to finding God. In His hands lies the solution to the intractable mysteries of life and death. You must pray to Him as I did: "Father, You have created me, so You must take care of me. I want to be released from the darkness of Your *maya*-delusion, and I want to show others the way to freedom as well."

Most of humanity is traveling through the dark forest of life without the searchlight of right thinking. Here and there we find people who carry a little flashlight of correct thinking to guide them; but for most their "batteries" have weakened or completely burned out. But walking blindly through the dark while merely hoping you are on the right track won't get you where you want to go.

Using Reason and Discrimination to Advance Consciously Toward Life's Goal

So how are you going to develop correct thinking? By using reason, discrimination, and intuition.

What is the definition of reason? Reason means thinking connected, purposeful thoughts—thoughts that are connected in a

* Decades after Paramahansa Yogananda gave this talk, a branch of modern psychology called cognitive behavioral therapy clinically proved the effectiveness of correcting wrong thinking in order to get rid of unwanted moods and heal the psychological diseases of depression, low self-esteem, and related disorders. See, for example, *Feeling Good: The New Mood Therapy* by David D. Burns, M.D. (1980). *(Publisher's Note)*

logical sequence and that lead to one objective or conclusion. Intelligent persons govern their lives by connected thought or reason, and achieve their goals much quicker than the haphazard thinker.

Now ask yourself this question: Does everything you do have a reason? No. That is why your life is as it is—why your progress and happiness are a matter of happenstance, conditional on outer circumstances rather than on conscious self-determination. Life has become a sort of zig-zag walking along the path of life because you haven't guided yourself by reason. You know, there is a punishment for jaywalkers, who are heedless of traffic laws when crossing a busy street; and likewise, those who won't follow the "crosswalk" or guidelines of reason are naturally punished by the laws of life. Learn to reason, learn to think more deeply, about where you are going and the best way to get there.

In your material life you must take reason as your guiding light. Use your reason in selecting how you will use your time. Most people sleepwalk through life and wake up at the end to find that they have spent their lives in uselessness. Those who direct their lives methodically, using their God-given reason, are blessed by God. And those who live a disorderly life have wasted their time completely.

Incorrect thinking is the bane of our lives—incorrect thinking about leading a balanced life, in choosing friends, in business, in making those decisions that set the course of our life's journey. Worldly persons spend their lives chasing after life's gifts and cannot spare any time for the Giver. Is not it reason that tells you to love the Giver more than His gifts? You should give more time to the Giver of all gifts, and less time getting His gifts.

When you use law in material life for progress or success, that is called reason. And when you use reason for spiritual progress and knowing God, it is called discrimination.

Reason must always have one aim, wisdom. It must not be used merely to wander in the blind alleys of matter, or to lose yourself in the jungle of intellectuality. It is when you seek God that you are on the right highway to ultimate wisdom. All lesser aspirations are roadblocks in your path. If you love any aspiration more than wisdom, then you stop there at that point. For example, you may have a desire to be a great artist, or a great success in business; but don't take that as your supreme goal, for your reason is blind if you use it only to seek material objectives. Your reason must always tell you that though you have to do something to get along in the world, the greatest purpose for which you came on earth is to find God. That is the correct use of reason.

You have to live within your body, therefore you must keep your body healthy; and you have to perform your duties in this world; but the greatest accomplishment is to correctly fulfill your duties to the world while all the time thinking of God.

Spiritual individuals don't care much what outer role they play in life, but they strive always to be with God. They think, "Why waste time unnecessarily on the temporary things of this world, when all will be taken away one day? Let me use my reason to seek and persevere on a path that will take me to God." That is supreme reason, and highest wisdom.

If you keep your light of reason and wisdom awake, ever burning, you cannot stumble on the pathway of life. People who go into the forest in the dark without light to show them the way stumble and fall. But if you go through life with the light of correct thinking, you will not stumble in the jungle of material existence. You will see the pitfalls of delusion and avoid them. It is the light of correct thinking that can defeat all enemies of lasting happiness.

Recognizing the Limitations of Reason

Correct thinking is born of reason, discrimination, and intuition. Together, these shed a guiding light of truth and wisdom on the path we must follow through life to reach our divine goal.

The conclusions we reach through reason alone are not always right. Consider the two processes of reasoning, inductive and deductive. We see one crow that is black; then two crows that are black; and when millions of crows have been found to be black, it is concluded that therefore all crows are black. That is inductive reasoning.

Deductive reasoning depends on accepting the premises derived through inductive reasoning. We say, "All crows are black; this is a crow; therefore it is black." But that reasoning is fallacious; you cannot say that all crows are black just because most crows are black, because in Australia they have discovered white crows too.

Based on such reasoning, most persons accept as a proven fact that all human beings are mortal, because the testimony of observation says that every person born on earth so far has eventually died. Reasoning that way, you would have to say, "All men are mortal; Jesus was a man; therefore Jesus was mortal." But that is not so. After his death, he came back again. My Master, after his bodily death, resurrected himself before my eyes; and Mahavatar Babaji has been living for centuries.* Therefore, that deductive reasoning is wrong in this instance.

To think correctly, to use reason rightly, first you must find out whether your deductions are based on a proper premise. If the data on which you base your premise is wrong, your conclusion will be wrong also.

Both inductive and deductive reasoning are subject to fallacies, because they depend upon the data furnished by the senses. For instance, perhaps you see in the dark a piece of rope on the floor in your home, and you panic, thinking it is a snake. Your senses deceived you, so your conclusion was wrong. We often make such mistakes, the masters say, because our senses cannot represent things to us correctly.

From the data of the senses you see this earth as a solid mass. That is wrong. Nothing is solid. Analyze the most solid stones and metals, and you will find they are nothing but a dance of electrons and protons. And underneath are subtler forces of life force and consciousness. Jesus could walk on the water because he saw water and earth and his body as they really are. Miracles can be explained when you realize that ultimately everything consists of vibrations of life electricity organized by intelligence flowing from the creative thought of God. Jesus could heal the bodies of others, and perform his other miracles, because he could control that intelligent force behind all atomic matter by the power of will.

Don't Base Your Thinking on Faulty Premises

How different your life would be if you saw things as the masters do! On this dark path of life, think how many people fear accidents and death. But as soon as you have correct thinking, there is no fear. Why should you fear sickness? The body is not you. So many of the fears and worries that beset you are based on faulty premises, because you cannot see what you really are. You have accepted the delusion that you are a body, subject to harm and eventual annihilation; and that is why you fear. If you know that you are Spirit nothing can hurt you. This understanding comes through meditation; and when it does, cessation of fear is instantaneous.

The impressions of the body must not be ascribed to the immortal soul; this is the essential lesson we are to learn on this plane

* See *Autobiography of a Yogi*, chapters 43 and 33.

of human existence. Be cautious but never afraid. Fear is born of wrong thinking; caution is the sense-to-avert-danger consciousness born either of right reason or of intuitive feeling. Fear is the only thing to be feared, for it paralyzes will power and clouds the good judgment by which we steer clear of hazards on the path of life.

Some persons don't like to acknowledge danger; they admonish themselves and others: "Don't think negatively!" But you cannot conquer anything by running away from it. Face your fears, and the other forms of wrong thinking lurking consciously or subconsciously, so that you can destroy them from your mind.

Your thoughts have power to make you fearful or wisely cautious, weak or courageous, happy or unhappy. The victorious yogi, having mastered the instruments of body and mind, is never unhappy. Isn't it better to face the trials of life with unshakable inner happiness, rather than to have health, riches, everything else the outer world can offer, and yet be unhappy within yourself? It is incorrect thinking that makes you unhappy.

Why unquestioningly accept the premise that you must have this or that from the world in order to be happy? Such thinking is fallacious, for all joy lies within your soul. By making your happiness conditional on outer circumstances, you fall prey to moods, anger, and other emotional upheavals when your desires are contradicted. And such emotions quickly extinguish the guiding light of clear and correct thinking.*

Correct Thinking Is Guided by the Soul

Correctness of thinking means you must be guided by your soul and by discriminative intellect, and then you will find that all your good desires and habits will cooperate to guide you to happiness. But as soon as you allow the senses to guide you, you are thinking incorrectly.

The greatest masters of India say there is a great tug of war going on between the senses and the soul. Each is trying to control the mind and intelligence. The senses pull the mind toward material gratifications, while the soul prompts the intelligence to direct the course of life wisely to achievement of higher goals.

* "Brooding on sense objects causes attachment to them. Attachment breeds craving; craving breeds anger. Anger breeds delusion; delusion breeds loss of memory (of the Self). Loss of right memory causes decay of the discriminating faculty. From decay of discrimination, annihilation (of spiritual life) follows" (Bhagavad Gita II:62–63).

India's scriptures describe the body as a chariot, with the senses as the horses, guided by the discriminative intelligence of the soul through the reins of the mind. Spiritually ignorant persons, living in self-exile from the soul, let go of the reins of the mind and allow the senses to run according to their own impulses. Their thought process is a prisoner of the impulses and desires of the senses, no matter how "free" they proclaim their thinking to be.

As soon as you become sense-bound, incorrect thinking begins. You are thereby led into bad habits. Some people, for instance, think they have to eat lots in order to live. It is not true, but the senses make it seem so. No matter how sick it makes them, they still overeat. And after a time they become a slave to that tyrannical habit of greed. The person of self-control will eat only what he or she needs for health and vitality of the body and its instruments. The same principle applies to all the senses. Incorrect thinking comes due to adhering to the senses and not guiding their impulses by reason.

Therefore, how are you going to think correctly? Is there no escape? Yes, there is; but you must take control of the reins of your mind. In order to think correctly you must harness your thoughts with will power to the discriminative wisdom of the soul. You must not be addicted to any sense. Anything that you do against your will, cut it out. Just cut it out. Refuse to give in.

In my early years in America, I used to like to drink the Canada Dry ginger ale; it reminded me of the lemonade we had as children in India. My students here noticed that I enjoyed it; and soon, everywhere I went, boxes of it were given to me from all sides! One day, traveling by train during hot weather, there wasn't any available, and I missed it. I realized that it had become a habit with me, and I cut it out. I said, "So, Mr. Ginger Ale! I see that I am not drinking you; you are drinking me! Goodbye!" I impressed the thought on my mind: "I won't touch it again. I no longer like it; I cannot stand that flavor!" And the next day, to test myself, I took a little sip in my mouth and it almost made me throw up. I had burned up that habit from my consciousness so that it no longer existed in my brain. Many years later, when someone offered ginger ale to me, still there was no desire for it.

(Very few people know how the different foods really taste, because they give their own tastes to them through habits of liking and disliking cultivated in their thoughts. But when you are not attached, you taste everything as it is. That is true. Don't be overpowered by attachment or aversion to anything without reason. Things that taste repugnant to you may taste palatable to someone else.)

Thoughts become all-powerful when an intuitive conviction of truth is impinged on matter by concentrated will power. You can change your body and accomplish many things in the world by application of that intuitive concentration. The science of affirmation that I have taught you makes use of this principle. That gives you correctness of thinking, provided you have no particular sense governing you. As soon as you are slavishly tied to any one of the senses, all your processes of thought revolve around gratifying that sense.

So remember: You can only gain that power of correct thinking provided you don't become addicted to any sense, and provided you meditate. The sense addict has incorrect thinking and is always putting sense pleasures first. But wisdom consists in giving first importance to God.

Don't let your habits run away with you. Don't let the world run you. You must run the world. I could find so many excuses to forget God—there have been so many duties since I came to America. If I had not had my Master's training, I would have absolutely lost myself.

Let God be first. No matter how late it is, meditate. Last night I didn't sleep until 4:00 a.m. My mind said, "You must go to bed," but I sat and meditated and in a little while the whole room was alive with God's light. That is what I want you to achieve. While you have your body, make the effort for that divine contact. Everything material that you acquire through this body will pass away. Do not wait to realize this until death removes you from this world. Money you cannot take. Health you cannot take. What can you take? The things of the soul.

Developing the Power of Intuition

Most people have desires, but not the ability to reason or to think clearly about them. So they end up doing the wrong things in order to achieve those desires. They are made so restless by their desires that they lose their self-possession and misuse their reason in an attempt to achieve those goals. And their actions seem completely reasonable to themselves!

Reason must be rightly developed so it won't be misused. The important thing is to refine the power of reason until it becomes intuitive. Whenever you need correct thinking about a situation, calm yourself first. By meditation, go deep into the calm region of the soul; and as soon as you are aligned with your soul, inner vision and illumined understanding will come and you will be able to think correctly and find the right course in everything you do. Soul intuition is the light that can never make mistakes.

Don't let the mind run constantly after your problem. Let it rest at times, for intuitive guidance often makes itself known through the loopholes between thoughts and emotions when the mind is calm. But see that you don't rest so long that the opportunity to take effective action passes you by.

God doesn't have a brain through which He reasons out what to do. Do you think God has to think millions of thoughts before He can do anything? No. He knows everything and does everything instantly. He moves by the power of intuition, the power of omniscience. And He has given us the power to live that way also. To remain on that plane of intuition is the supreme way of developing correct thinking.

Intuition sees all, whereas reason sees only one thing at a time. Reason is a sort of ray that comes out of the light of intuition. Reason will show a correct path one step at a time, providing you keep your reason calmly focused on what is before you. But suppose someone brings a light that sheds its radiance over the entire jungle or forest. Isn't that better than a little flashlight that shows only one thing at a time? So it is with intuition. The spherical light of intuition sheds its brilliance over the entire forest of life. When you look at any object or circumstance in that light, you first *feel* the truth about it. You don't reason; you know by intuitive feeling, which then tells you what you are going to do. That is how I guide my life. It is far superior to reason, for after you reason you can still make mistakes.

As rays of light shoot out of the massive sun, so reason shoots out of the sun of intuition. Soul-intuition is the progenitor of reason, and reason is ultimately dependent on that power. It is intuition that lights all the reasonable thoughts of your life. Therefore, to have conscious contact with intuition is the best way of ensuring that you reason rightly. This can be done by learning the yoga way of keeping your faculties of discrimination and understanding fully charged with life and intelligence from the soul.*

* Here Paramahansaji is referring to the methods of Kriya Yoga meditation taught in the *Self-Realization Fellowship Lessons,* which bring conscious contact with the soul and with God. *(Publisher's Note)*

Some people reason all the time and still come to wrong determinations. And some people are full of common sense, and they do things rightly even without much reasoning. That is their intuition at work, even if not fully developed.

March Confidently Through Life With the Light of Intuition

Why not develop and use that power by which you can see and reason correctly? When in touch with intuition, you may say something that may have no meaning at the moment, and people will ask why you said it. And you may reply, "I don't know why, but I know I am right." And later it is shown that you are right. God has given you that intuitive power by which you can feel and know when you are right. It is your divine heritage, because you are made in His image and you have the power to see behind the obscuring veil of matter—to know the truth about anything without inferential processes of reason.

Because we have gotten away from that power, therefore we have to blunder along through this forest of life. But if you develop that intuitive power, you will never have to blunder anymore. You become full of life; all your faculties are energized from within. You don't wander in the blind alleys of life guided only by reason.

Those who are equipped only with the small flashlight of reason will not always avoid the pitfalls on the pathway, and will fear the uncertainties and dangers in the surrounding darkness. But if you walk with the spherical light of intuition wherever you go, you give light that illumines all things around you. And from no dark corners can troubles jump upon you. You are able to march on confidently through the jungle of life, and emerge victorious. Isn't that a wonderful life that you can lead?

So, dear ones, meditate more and develop the power of intuition, until you can feel that power always guiding your thinking, directing you in everything. And that light will illumine all the dark corners of life and lead you to His kingdom.

Reason is a wonderful power, and you must develop it, you must use it. But even it is limited. But when you are calm and silent and cultivate the superior power of intuition, then you can use that power in your everyday life.

Always remember: As you move on in this dark path of life, the greatest thing is to develop that intuitive faculty. That can only come through meditation; there is no other way. When I use intuition it always shows me the right decision to make. It never fails.

I am afraid of nothing. I am not looking for anything. I have finished all desires. It is not a negative state—the positive presence of God is so sufficient that nothing disappoints me. And my greatest pleasure in meeting people is in giving this truth to them. But it can't be transmitted to you unless you meditate. Never forget that. Never. Meditate! Where there is a will there is a way. When you make up your mind and will to do a thing, you can do it. That is correct thinking.

Pray with me: "Heavenly Father, Thou art first in my consciousness. Bless me that I learn to so concentrate that I can find Thee and commune with Thee in everything. Heavenly Father, I resign myself to Thy presence. Work through my soul, through my body, through my mind, through my reason and intuition, for when You are with me I shall think everything correctly. *Aum.* Peace. Amen."

Mastering Your Moods With the Thought-Sword of Wisdom

Self-Realization Fellowship Hermitage, Encinitas, California, June 27, 1943

Millions of people are walking the earth thinking they are free. But are they truly free? They imagine they are doing what they want to do, but in truth their actions are compelled mostly by their moods. Freedom to do exactly what one wants to do, arising naturally from what one ought to do, comes only when the ego's moods are mastered.

No one really wants to go through life in gloomy moods. It is so much better to be peaceful than to be angry. Yet despite good resolutions to the contrary, as soon as somebody does a little thing that the ill-tempered person doesn't like, his face becomes flushed with anger and he is wholly subject to that ugly mood. From morning until evening most everyone indulges in their different moods. Analyze yourself: Sometimes you are happy, sometimes you are peevish, sometimes you are sad or discouraged, and so forth. Day after day, you go on living with these ups and downs because you don't know how to control them.

Moods Cloak the Soul

Moods are commonly thought of as a mental attitude or emotional disposition predominating in the consciousness at any given time. But yoga philosophy goes deeper. The Sanskrit word *bhava* is a broad term for mood, or more specifically, one's state of being, ranging from emotions to divine absorption in meditation. Generalized, it is the particular manner of being—the nature, character, temperament, way of thinking or feeling, the state of mind or consciousness—that is an individualized expression cloaking the soul. Thus, there are various kinds of moods, some good and some bad. All good moods should be nurtured; they are those that do not distort the clear expression of your innate divinity. Bad moods are those that destroy divine moods. Restless moods destroy the mood of soul calmness. Anger moods destroy the native peace of the soul. Anything that disturbs the soul's mood of calm happiness is destructive. As soon as disturbing moods come, slay them with the thought-sword of wisdom.

This world is a spiritual hospital, and until you are cured of the delusion relative to the body-bound ego, you won't be discharged. You will be reborn on earth repeatedly until you free yourself from mortal ignorance. Indulgence in harmful moods is the gravest slavery we have created in our delusion. He who is bound by anger and greed and their companionate inclinations cannot pass the gates of delusion into freedom. The yoga of the Bhagavad Gita and sage Patanjali cites the discipline of mind required to attain mastery.*

The Wisdom-Realization That God Has Become Your Self

The highest wisdom is Self-realization—knowing the Self, the soul, as eternally inseparable from God. The most pernicious evil is not to see that God has manifested Himself in this world and in yourself. In truth, every unit of finite matter is the expression of God. You don't know it is God, and that is your mistake.

God who is infinite has become the finite. Why couldn't He become one form? He is everything. If you could see into the essence of flowers and gems and every other manifestation in creation—including your own self—you would see that the One Being is at the innermost core of all that exists. "O Arjuna! I am the Self in the heart of all creatures: I am their Origin, Existence, and Finality."†

It is said, "The tree came from the seed, but the seed came from the tree. Which was first?" Such questions lead to an infinite regress, because the limited human intellect cannot apprehend a First Cause. With our mortal mind we see only one link in the eternal chain of life. The beginning and end of all created things are hidden in the depths of the Infinite; only the middle is visible. In the grand panorama of creation, the invisible Infinite becomes visible in the finite; and those with eyes to see can discern in every finite thing the marks of the Infinite.

To the seer of ultimate Truth, the startling contrasts of good and evil, light and darkness, the demon and the divine man, are *in essence* the same, because he beholds behind those outer manifestations the

* "A calm and contented mental clarity, kindliness, silence, self-control, and purity of character (*bhava-samshuddhi*) constitute the austerity of the mind." — Bhagavad Gita XVII:16

"By cultivating attitudes of friendliness, compassion, gladness, and dispassion, respectively, toward happiness, misery, virtue, and vice, the consciousness (*chitta*) retains the unruffled calmness (of the soul)." —Patanjali's *Yoga Sutras* 1:33

† Bhagavad Gita X:20.

one God. Just as a moviegoer sees that both the evil villain and the hero are the results of the one beam of light thrown on the screen, so the sage of divine wisdom sees the Infinite Light in all things, and works to bring out that Light hidden beneath the shroud of evil moods in ignorant persons.

Those who follow the devotional approach of worshiping a personal God (Bhakti Yoga) know that even the formless Infinite can be realized in a finite form. As the Divine Mother, or Heavenly Father, or one of the Deity personifications known to devotees down the ages, it is the impersonal and invisible Infinite who has become very personal and finite. Yet when God manifests in a finite aspect, the entire Infinite is throbbing therein. Just as the radio vibration which is spread over millions of miles of space vibrates through one radio, so the Infinite can vibrate through one finite form.

It is easier to approach God through devotion to a personal concept of Divinity, for the minds of most persons cannot begin to relate to the formless Impersonal Absolute. For a long time I have enjoyed that personal relationship with God as my Divine Mother and Father and Friend. But at other times I have not been devotional at all; for in personal worship you think of yourself as separate from God. Worship is imperfect union with God; it keeps the devotee apart from the object of devotion. In perfect oneness with God you cannot say you worship Him. You only know, "Thou and I are one. I cannot have any existence separate from You."

That wisdom-conception of the Infinite is very beautiful too, because in it there is complete unity with God. You do not stand as a slave before Him—a mere created being subject to creation's constraining laws—but know yourself as the unconditioned, infinite Self. You merge in the Absolute Bliss, Absolute Existence, Absolute Consciousness. As long as you remain in that state, everything that is of your confining ego-personality is gone.

"Mind nor intellect, nor ego, chitta;
Sky nor earth nor metals am I.
I am He; I am He; Blessed Spirit, I am He.
Beyond the flights of fancy, formless am I,
Permeating the limbs of all life;
Bondage I do not fear; I am free, ever free,
*I am He, I am He, Blessed Spirit, I am He."**

* Paramahansa Yogananda translated these lines from a longer Sanskrit chant composed by Swami Shankara; a musical rendition ("No Birth, No Death") appears in Paramahansaji's *Cosmic Chants* (published by Self-Realization Fellowship).

That conception is so marvelous! Whenever the idea of sin or trouble tries to ensnare you, anchor yourself in the Divine—do not think yourself separate from God. Drown your personality, your ego, your moods and habits, in oneness with that Infinite Perfection. Affirm and realize: "God is all. I am His manifestation. He is I."

It is wrong to say, "I am God"; but it is all right to say, "God is myself." The wave cannot claim to be the ocean; for the ocean can exist with or without the wave. But the ocean has become the wave. So when you affirm the truth that God has become yourself, you can feel the formless Oceanic Spirit that has become the finite wave of your little self. Egotists cannot realize that. When you *think* you are with Him and continue to behave in wicked and selfish ways, know that you are yet in delusion. When you merge in the Infinite, when your consciousness becomes anchored in Him, nothing remains that is of the ego. All thoughts, feelings, actions become pure.

Remember, if you hold on to the truth, "God has become me," and accordingly behave divinely, you will be liberated from the delusive imperfections of body and mind. No matter if your body is afflicted or diseased—even when death is at your door—if still you do not give up and you can retain that consciousness that you are free, you will be free. Such is the power of thought and consciousness that God has given us.

The Power of Thought Can Create Miraculous Changes

There was a saint who noticed that one of his students was silently critical because the saint once in a while ate meat, even though enjoining on the students a strict vegetarianism. So the master said to this critic, "Can you digest everything I can digest?" The student replied, "Certainly," thinking he would then be invited to share his teacher's savory meal. Instead, the saint scooped up a handful of hot nails from the blacksmith's fire and began to swallow them. The disciple was stunned. The saint had merely changed his thought; to his consciousness, meat or hot metal were identically of the One Spirit. All miracles performed by masters in this world have been done by the power of thought, the underlying matrix of creation.

Thought is everything. To illustrate, close your eyes and visualize a black horse on the left side and a white horse on the right side. Now change the white horse to the left side and the black horse to the right side. See them clearly in your mind. The transposition is easy and instant, just by changing the thought. The black horse is your bad habit, and you change it into a white horse of good habit. See how simply it is done by the power of your own thought.

A repetition of thought becomes a habit. And moods are nothing but crystalized habits from the past. Way back in some forgotten incarnation you allowed yourself to harbor the ego-born thoughts of being peevish or angry or sad, instead of quickly evicting those harmful attitudes from your consciousness each time they arose. So today those past-life tendencies or habits burst forth as moods—with or without some outer stimulus of present circumstances. Often you don't know why you are in the mood you are in; you just are. Because it has become "second nature" to you, that is why you think you can't get out of it. But you need only remember that your seemingly intractable mood is nothing but a thought that was strengthened by repetition sometime in the past.

Why should you let your moody thoughts enslave you? With the thought-sword of wisdom, destroy the thought-cords that bind you. Life is a battle and you must fight to win it. Do not let moods rule you. You have been carrying those tendencies through perhaps hundreds of incarnations. Why allow them to remain with you? Conquer them right now. Determine to do so and it will be done. Do not put it off. If you say, "Tomorrow I will conquer," that tomorrow will never come. Instead affirm, "Today it is gone," and it will be gone, because mind is all-powerful.

Moods hypnotize your soul and there begins your downfall. There is no excuse for you to say *I can't.* Whenever I hear a person say that, something rebels in me. "I can't do this and I can't do that!" Who has given you that verdict but your own mood? When you say *can,* who can make it *can't*? These are just two aspects of thought. In creating this world of duality, thought was split into good and evil. So it is as easy as thinking to be good, and it is just as easy to be bad.

In a paradise you can be miserable and in hades you can be a god. That is all done by your consciousness. There is no hades worse than the hades of anger and moods. The devil of moods is inside. As soon as you feel a mood coming on, trample it.

The anger mood is a terrible bondage that must be conquered. The irate person harms himself first—and then he tries to hurt others. They then retaliate and try to hurt him even more! The only cure is to destroy anger from within. It can be done just by one thought: "I *will* be free from anger." Say to yourself, "I am the calm imperturbable soul; I can never be angry." But if you say *can't,* you have given the verdict to yourself that you are a prisoner of anger. And it is the same with greed and with everything else that binds you.

Another mood to be conquered is blasé indifference. Some persons are bored with everything. Why not cultivate an interest in the wonders of life? When interest is gone you are as good as dead. Be fully alive by enthusiasm for noble achievements and divine happiness.

Who can stop you from thinking you are a god? No one. You are your only obstruction. "The self that befriends the Self is its own friend, and the self that is inimical to the Self is its own enemy."* When you say to yourself that you are a sinner you are finished. Never let anyone tell you you are a sinner. Always affirm the truth: You are good, you are divine, you are free. And then get busy harmonizing your behavior with that truth.

Freedom From Moods Is Found in Inner Calmness

While affirming your goodness as a child of God, do not be blind to the flawed attitudes of your second nature, or your moods will be very hard to get rid of. If you have a blot of ink on your face, everyone sees that blemish—everyone but yourself! You do not see your psychological face. Hence the necessity to be guided by discrimination in order to recognize wherein you must change. If you haven't developed that pure discernment, adopt the discrimination of your guru. The guru says, "I am your mirror. There is the ink." Analyze yourself impartially according to the wisdom in his teachings.

I see people who remain imprisoned all the time in their moods. Some cling so tenaciously to their wrong attitudes; and to support themselves they say, "I feel God is guiding me." When delusion is strong, that is when the help of a true guru is so important. His wisdom is the voice of truth; he will never cater to weaknesses nor offer flattery when change is in the disciple's own best interest. He tells you plainly what is wrong, and if you try to correct yourself you will be free from those moods. To be free from moods is to be able to live divinely. I found that by remaining calm inside, in the calmness of my soul, I was a free man. I wouldn't give that up for anything in the world, for without that calmness I can't do good to anybody. It is my most preciously guarded possession.

No cannons of moods can reach you if you remain in the fortress of inner spiritual calmness. Your only sanctuary of freedom is that haven within yourself. But people make it very hard for themselves by not trying to remain in that state. Instead, they have the habit

* Paraphrase of Bhagavad Gita VI:5.

of restlessness. They think they cannot sit still and cultivate the peace of the soul in meditation. They would rather be on the go. That is their mood.

The hypnosis of moods keeps people bound more than anything else. Some persons can sit and read shelves full of books, but to sit still and meditate seems terrible to them! To me, reading is a most tedious way to spend time. It feels like an ocean is trying to inundate me as I read somebody else's thoughts. Meditation comes easier to me; and is far more fulfilling. Two or three hours I sit immersed in one divine thought, and know no time at all. If you make the effort to realize how interesting your soul is, you won't know time when you immerse yourself in that consciousness. Your soul will pour out to you infinite wisdom; you will find that all knowledge is written in that image of God within you.

In the beginning of my efforts to meditate long, I kept reminding myself: "It is not so many hours. For incarnations you were away from your Self; now you must get back there." Just as soon as I strongly impressed that thought on my mind, my consciousness became lost to the body—absorbed in the inner bliss of soul-contact.

You think meditation is so difficult because you have developed the mood of being with the body. This body itself is a mood. It is a delusion God has put over our souls. "Why think we must go into *samadhi*?" the mind asks. "How nice is the body!" your mood says. But in stark contrast to the soul, I feel the body is most repugnant. It is anything but perfect—all the time giving some trouble and clamoring for attention. It coughs and sneezes and is never all right. Why do you want to love the body? Why do you want to put a garland of adoration on it?

The mood of restlessness is a graft onto your real nature. Your real nature is calmness and freedom. Establish yourself in that consciousness; make it so natural that you feel the Self all the time. I am the Self. I no longer have to meditate to feel my identity with the Self. That realization is always there. Most of the time I don't feel the body because I am in the Self. The yogi breathes or doesn't breathe, eats or doesn't eat—no matter what he is doing, he is always cognizant of the Self. He has changed his mood from the mood of ignorance to the mood of wisdom.

Be Free of Moods and You Will Get Along With Everyone

When you see people behaving according to their indifferent or bad moods, finding fault with everybody and everything but themselves, don't add to their difficulty by being intolerant. Rather, help to heal them by the kindness of your right example. I do not ask anybody to conquer anger if I do not conquer it myself. If I were to get angry over someone's misbehavior toward me, I would be lowering myself to that person's level. Find no fault with anyone but yourself. If your behavior is correct, you will also see a change in others.

It is your own fault if you get into trouble with others. Analyze yourself. You will be surprised to see that when troubles come, most of the time it is because you are not acting or thinking rightly. If you control your own attitude, you will get along with anyone. I have purposely mixed with those who have opposite views from mine. I made it a point to win over their feelings of enmity.

To conquer human hearts is a wonderful art; it consists of sincerity and living the spiritual life. Many persons, as soon as they find out someone's weakness, want to rub salt in that wound. But if instead you keep your calmness, saying and feeling in your heart, "I don't want to mistreat you," that person will feel your sincerity. Always treat others sincerely in spite of how others treat you. When you cannot come to an agreement with them, remain silent. You do not go along with their error; you are silent, that is all. Remain centered in your Self, in the good qualities of your soul, and continuously give understanding to people. Then you will be a conqueror of hearts.

The only way you can remain impervious to the moods of others is not to be moody yourself. If you feel insulted, everyone will seem to insult you. If you feel no one can insult you, no one can. I never saw anybody who could offend my Master [Swami Sri Yukteswar]. He was above hatred and insult. He conquered by the spiritual power of his wisdom.

It is important to know how to deal with the moods of people, especially in the business world. If you are going to discuss some business deal and you find the person is in a mood, it might be necessary to change the subject and wait for a better time. Worldly persons are mostly moody because they have never tried to control their tempers. Very few are calm. They say anything according to their mood.

When possible, avoid people when they are in bad moods. Get out of their way. Then, when they are all right, mix with them. And if the situation is such that you cannot leave their presence, still you can be inwardly away from their moods—not in disdain but in mental withdrawal. For example, simply refrain from acknowledging a person's anger. If you recognize and respond to it, then begins the trouble. If you refuse to be touched by it, that anger will be spent to no avail. Anger toward you cannot work unless you accept it.

Most persons know they dare not fight in the office or workplace lest they be fired, so they save their moods until they come home—then they let loose. What inane foolishness it is to indulge in fractious moods and inflict them on others. Your emotions give you a false sense of mastery over others, but actually you are a slave. It is a form of temporary insanity; you should be in a padded cell. When you feel yourself in a perverse mood, lock yourself away from others and get rid of it. This isn't permission to hide away and take your time wallowing in your mood. It is just better not to show yourself to others while you summon the will and positive thoughts to quickly control your bad mood.

People are such victims of their moods, suffering from them all the time, like a ravaging disease. Even if their bodies are healthy, their character is mutilated by the smallpox of moods.

The healthy mind is immune to disfiguring moods. That state is so grand. When you are completely free from the dictates of your second nature, the flaws of the ego, you anchor in the Truth of your real nature. In that state it does not take any effort of will to be good. Say you are angerless and you are. Say you are peaceful and you are. Your divine soul qualities are at your command. There is nothing to it.

Keep this vow: "I am going to behave perfectly no matter how others behave toward me." It can be done. When you remain in the calmness of the soul, you will know God. And when you know God, you will see in every human being a temple of God.

He who claims authority to be a spiritual teacher is not necessarily so; but he who sees God in all, whose hands remain folded in humble adoration of all, he is a Christ. Regard others' comfort and others' happiness, and behave rightly and sincerely—then you will have the world with you. And even if the world is not with you, God will be with you. Jesus was a king because he made his throne in every heart.

God is the bliss of meditation. Feel that He is the boundless Joy in your heart. Use the heart to find God. The brain and the heart are the doors to God-realization. Instead of using their instrumentalities to entangle yourself in passions and moods, use them to find God and attain your everlasting freedom.

Destroying the Consciousness of Fear

Self-Realization Fellowship Golden Lotus Temple, Encinitas, California, June 30, 1940

Fear is the psychophysical manifestation of man's expectation of physical, mental, or spiritual harm. It is associated with the desire to avoid pain; if there were no pain in human life, we wouldn't fear anything. If we analyze it, we see that fear actually increases pain. It can double a person's suffering. That is why one should learn to lessen fear and ultimately conquer it completely.

Do you know that if you had no fear consciousness you would never suffer? If you had absolutely removed all fear, even if you broke a bone in some part of the body, you wouldn't feel pain. You would feel some sensitivity, a recognition that you had been injured; but you would not suffer. Fear emphasizes that sensitivity into pain. The fear attitude says what a terrible thing it is that has happened to you, that you should be afraid—and immediately there starts the pain.

God never intended us to have pain. Sensations were given to protect the body from harm; but pain developed when man allowed his mind to become the slave rather than the master of sensations. Many years from now, when you will read my talks, you will find in scientific books research supporting these truths.*

Pain is nothing but a mental construct. If you see a stranger cut his finger, you don't feel pain; but if a mother sees her child injured, she suffers too. Pain is caused by a sympathetic reaction, a mental attachment. If the mind recognizes and strongly asserts that it is

* Summing up a recent study done by Dr. Robert Coghill of Wake Forest University, published in Proceedings of the National Academy of Sciences, the British Broadcasting Company reported in September 2005: "U.S. experts say they have strong scientific proof that mind over matter works for relieving pain. Positive thinking was as powerful as a shot of morphine for relieving pain, and reduced activity in parts of the brain that process pain information." Dr. Coghill explained: "Pain is not solely the result of signals coming from an injured body region. Pain needs to be treated with more than just pills. The brain can powerfully shape pain, and we need to exploit its power."

separate from the body, how then can bodily injury inflict pain on the mind? Just as under a local anesthetic you may undergo a surgical procedure but not feel pain because the mind is disconnected from that part of the body, so pain can be transcended at will by persons who have self-control and a mind that is nonattached and impersonal toward the body.

Though the bodies of even great masters may suffer disease or injury due to metaphysical causes of taking on the karma of others, they know themselves as the indestructible life and consciousness within the body, separate from the innate fears of the physical form. Why should you enslave your mind to the body through the delusion of fear that makes you suffer? In deep meditation, you too will realize your Self as the transcendent soul.

Train Your Children and Yourself to Be Fearless

Psychological studies show that if from early childhood we were trained not to fear, most of the pains of the body would disappear or be greatly lessened. That is a fact. A doctor in the orthopedic ward of a hospital told me that children vie with each other to be the first to get their deformed limbs operated upon; whereas adults have to be coaxed for weeks, and at the time of their operation they are usually beset with emotion and fear. Because children's minds are still pure—their brains having yet to record life's tragedies—they are less subject to pain. Having just come from the astral plane, where they dwelt in impervious bodies of light, they are less attached to the vulnerable physical body than are adults, and are therefore not as afraid of hurting it.

Of course, even in small children you will see some who are very fearful, because they have brought from a past incarnation a subconscious fear complex; but usually, the brain of a newborn gives the child a fresh start in life. Although children are not really children—they are aged souls of many past lives—still their former habits and attachments are pretty well covered up when they are reborn so that they have a chance to begin anew in the infant life. But if a child has a latent phobia from the past, some present experience may rouse the dread that is buried in the subconscious mind, and in a moment the child may become chronically fearful for seemingly no reason. If such a fear complex is there, it must be transmuted by gradually teaching the child fearlessness. If a child is brought up in fearlessness, even the apprehensions that are lodged in his consciousness from past incarnations can be cleared out.

Parents should never nurture fear in their children. The threat of ghosts and scary stories are not the impetus you should use to correct a child's behavior. You may be impairing the child's outlook on life. Intimidation is harmful, such as, "If you don't behave, the boogeyman will get you," or to threaten shutting the child in a dark closet. Fear of darkness and of scary ghosts go together. To rouse such fright in a child is terrible; it creates a nervousness that paralyzes the natural progress of the soul.

Whenever anxiety or apprehension comes, the best recipe is to drive it forcibly from the mind. Do not wait, because fear quickly increases the impulse of fear. Under no circumstances let fear take control of your mind and will. Whenever there is a fear, look at it squarely in the face: Try to remove the outer cause and take steps to embolden the mind to overcome that trepidation. If you are afraid of the dark, put on the light until calmness returns. And then turn it off and practice remaining and moving about in the dark for longer and longer periods, until that dread no longer exists.

Fear Attracts the Very Thing of Which You Are Afraid

Instead of fear, implant a sense of caution. Caution means simply, "I must not do this, because it portends a harmful result. God has given me this body; I am expected to take care of it." To learn from each mistake not to make that same blunder again—that is being cautious. Say there is a certain possession that you like. You take logical care of it, and it never breaks because you have been cautious. But then say you have another treasure, one that you are always afraid will break. It is not unlikely that it will be broken, because of your obsessive fear.

People think fearfulness will help them avoid what they are afraid of, but fear is not a bulwark of protection. Fear actually tends to engender the very thing you are dreading. When you are afraid of something, it captivates your thinking with deep feeling and attention. Thoughts are powerful vibratory creators. Whatever you think of intensely and continuously tends to come to pass in your life. Many financial failures and much suffering of disease are brought about that way: You undergo a little trouble with your health or your business, and the anxiety this rouses becomes lodged in the brain. You begin to dwell on that fear so much that your mental image bursts into manifestation, bringing about the very thing you are afraid of!

Take the fear of accidents. If you continually harbor such apprehensions in your consciousness, you are making mishaps all the more likely. Why? Because that fear will be paralyzing the brain and nerves—the mind will be busy with unreasonable worry instead of with caution and calm effort to do things right. As a result you bring about the very misfortune you fear.

Healing the Body Through Fearlessness

Fear also does immense harm to your physical well-being. In severe cases, it may stop the heart or brain action.* In the present war [World War II], many have died of fright. And there have been known cases of individuals whose hair has suddenly turned white out of dire fear.

Numerous ailments are worsened and also caused by nervousness and fear. Chronic indigestion is one of them. The supreme factor in the health of the body is the life force; and when the flow of that energy is obstructed or impeded by tension and worry, the nerves do not function properly to transmit the impulses by which the food you ingest is digested, or by which the body's immunity and other vital activities are regulated. You see, life energy in the flesh is controlled by mind; and if your mind is filled with fears and anxieties, that energy becomes paralyzed; and then your health suffers. I have healed many people just by removing fear from their minds. You would be surprised to know how many diseases can be cured this way.

In treating disease there is a mental approach as well as a physical or chemical approach. Most people rely on the latter, using surgery or drugs; but often find that there are many ailments for which medical science has no cure. The mental approach works

* *Newsweek* magazine reported in its October 3, 2005, issue: "You can call it the Northridge Effect, after the powerful earthquake that struck near Los Angeles at 4:30 on a January morning in 1994. Within an hour, and for the rest of the day, medics... faced a second wave of deaths from heart attacks among people who had survived the tremor unscathed. In the months that followed, researchers at two universities examined coroners' records from Los Angeles County and found an astonishing jump in cardiovascular deaths, from 15.6 on an average day to 51 on the day of the quake itself. Most of these people turned out to have a history of coronary disease, or risk factors such as high blood pressure. But those who died were not involved in rescue efforts or trying to dig themselves out of the rubble. Why did they die? In the understated language of *The New England Journal of Medicine*, 'emotional stress may precipitate cardiac events in people who are predisposed to such events.' To put it simply, they were scared to death."

much more effectively—if the mind is convinced that it has all power over the body.

The mental method of healing was extolled by Jesus when he said, "Thy faith hath made thee whole." I have used mental methods in almost all departments of healing, and I know mind power works. But it will not work if you do not follow the right laws; you must know how to use the mind. In most cases, attempts to heal by mind power fail because the mind continues to entertain fear. While mentally affirming that you are well, in the background of your mind you are doubting. When you affirm, "I am well; I have no cold," do not hold the fear thought that the cold is persisting. Go on affirming positively, continuously, until the thought of the cold is completely driven out from your conscious and subconscious minds and the thought of health is irrevocably installed there.

Mental healing is not a simple matter. That is why I advise those who haven't mastered the laws of mind that it is all right to take physical aid. But at the same time keep on conditioning your consciousness to make your mind work for you. Remove the paramount impediment of fear, which chloroforms the mind. Suppose you have been suffering from a disease for five years; fear makes you think you will never get well! It is necessary to keep reminding yourself, "Throughout my life I was all right, except for these five years. Why should I not think I can regain good health?" Doubt must be completely removed from your thought. Mind is everything; cultivate its power by practicing fearlessness.

Fear subconsciously pictures the disease you are dreading and thereby creates a favorable environment in the body to keep those disease germs alive. For example, if you are afraid of colds, you will succumb to them much more easily than if you have a strong, positive mind. Fear is a powerful element in the spread of tuberculosis and other dangerous maladies—and in allowing the increase of germs in the body once disease is contracted. Patients who are filled with fear often succumb quickly to their ailment. Persons who live fearlessly are certainly less susceptible to disease. Presence of germs is not the only factor. Millions of germs are always all around you—hidden under your fingernails, for example. If you could see them all, you would be worried sick! Lots of diseases come and go in the body without your knowledge. Do not give them strength to cause perceptible illness by fearing you will get sick. Once in a while it is good to have the body examined by a doctor, but do not dwell all the time on the body's potential frailties. Since the body is controlled by mind, if the mind is well, the body will be well. Hold strongly to the thought, "I am all right." That attitude and mental affirmation releases an abundant flow of life energy, removing all kinds of difficulties.

I will tell you a true story that has a practical moral. When my boys' school in India quickly outgrew its first location, our benefactor, the Maharaja of Kasimbazar, transferred us to a larger property. But the place was infested with malaria, and soon the young children and all the teachers were sick—except myself. I had strongly made up my mind to stay well despite the unhealthy environment. They used to boil the water before drinking it; I would drink it untreated and was never affected. But of course we could not stay there; I went to the Maharaja and said, "I told you not to send the students there, that they would get sick." He countered, "Then what good is the training you are giving them?"

In response, I told him the story about the mother who took some homemade soup to her son in the hospital to help him get well. After the first spoonful, she asked, "Son, are you feeling better?" And the sick boy protested, "Mother, the soup hasn't even reached my stomach yet!" So I said to the Maharaja, "You see, these boys have come straight from the comforts of their homes, and they haven't had sufficient time to assimilate their training in mind power. The 'soup' of fearlessness had not yet reached their stomachs, and it was too soon to test them." Then he understood, and gave us the use of his summer palace in the healthy climate of Ranchi.

Yoga Overcomes the Fear of Death

The strongest of all fears that we bring from childhood is the fear of death, because we have experienced that fear through so many incarnations. But death is not the end of life; it is nothing more than a transition from one plane of life to another. It is just like moving from one house to a different house. When the body-house is broken down with injury or disease or worn out from old age, God says, "Come out. I will give you a nice new home to live in." There is nothing to fear. It happens to everybody—saint or sinner—so it must be good. Why live with apprehensions? As long as you are not dead you are alive; and when you are dead it is all over and there is nothing to worry about!

Many persons fear death because they think it will be painful. But death itself is absolutely devoid of pain. It is felt only as a mental pain by those who dread losing the physical body, and cling to it in panic when life is being pulled from the body and they struggle unsuccessfully to breathe. But if you have no fear, there is no such mental experience, rather a peaceful sense of relief at being freed from the troublesome fleshly cage.

You are not afraid when you fall asleep and have no consciousness of breathing. So why should cessation of breath at death cause you fear? That fear is a great enemy created by a wrong understanding that death is something terrible. Long practice of yoga meditation neutralizes that delusion; it teaches you the peace of the breathless state while living. In the complete calmness of body and breath brought by deep *pranayama* meditation, you find yourself directly sustained by God's cosmic energy, and realize: "Man shall not live by bread—or breath—alone." You know that you are much more than this physical body; your immortal Self is above the need for food and sunshine and breath. So when death comes, you have no fear; for its freedom from body consciousness is already familiar to you.

Death is the cessation of life's sorrows. It doesn't come as a punishment, but as a necessary end to our fleshly confinement, that we may leave this earth and travel in a freer state to higher realms. The body may be interred or consigned to ashes, but the soul is freed—it cannot anymore be subjected to the tortures of the body. Your spirit will say, "Well, for a long time I have had to worry about getting hurt and paying bills and all the other troubles of material life. Now that burdensome body under my care is gone, and I am free in the peace of this astral land and body of light." When you have earned freedom from the travails of this earth, be glad. But never seek death; when you do that, it shows you are afraid of life and are not learning its lessons. You will have to come back again and again until you do.

Replacing Fearfulness With Contentment and Security in All Situations

Fear of poverty is another phobia to be overcome. Of course, it is our duty to care for the less fortunate; millions lack basic material necessities. But poverty consciousness brought about by fear is the cause of suffering in millions more. Contentment with what you have is a much richer source of happiness than being chronically afraid because you haven't got this or that. The person who is happy doing everything he can to better his lot, without wasting his energy on fear and apprehension, is much happier than the millionaire who is always worrying about his money. If you are fearful, you will never be happy; and you will make yourself a failure. Remind yourself as often as necessary that you are not going to allow fear to create mental suffering or paralyze your efforts. Even if you fail temporarily, do not lose courage—pick yourself up and try again. Refuse to accept the fear that you cannot ultimately succeed.

Constantly cultivate the soul's immortal power, by meditation and God-contact, and use that power in all difficulties. The soldier goes where bullets are flying like mosquitoes, despite his fear of being shot and dying. But the spiritual soldier is even greater: he conditions himself not to be afraid of death or anything else. He knows that many times, through many lives, he has fallen into the bosom of God at death; and just as often he has come out of the bosom of God at birth. There is nothing to fear about the cycles of life and death. If you fear what these experiences hold for you, you will have to reincarnate repeatedly until you learn to overcome that delusion. All imperfections must be worked out, until the soul is disentangled from the chains of fear and regains its native immortal freedom.

Some persons think they will never get salvation because they are afraid they are unworthy of God's favor. They think He is partial to certain souls. But if you study the lives of the many saints who had been egregious sinners, you will see that God totally forgave their erroneous ways. For saints are those who faced their errors, analyzed them, and then tried to eradicate them. The most heroic conquerors in the spiritual life are those who have conquered fear of failure and have persevered until they were victorious over their weaker self.

Many years ago when meditating I used to think, "Will I ever get ecstasy?" I was afraid that *samadhi* would never come to me. But as soon as I gave up those fear thoughts, it was there. I said to myself: "How strange! I was afraid my mind was too restless to find God." When I lost the fear that I would never have God, I found Him.

Remember: You are a most fortunate child of God. "As many as received him, to them gave he power to become the sons of God."* Do away with the fear that you will never know Him. Mentally say, "Lord, I am Thine immortal child. I am made in Thy same divine image as are the exalted ones of Your children." You have a claim on God as valid as that of the greatest saint. So be proud of yourself. You are free to seek Him and by meditation to realize your

* John 1:12.

divinity. You can rise beyond the highest ideal of man; your mind can encompass infinite galaxies of stars, for you are a child of God. You have no cause to be afraid. Identify with your soul each day in meditation, and you will know: "I was never born; I was never dead; though my births and deaths have been as many as the waves of the sea. The wave comes out of the ocean and goes back into the sea again. I come from God. I am Life Eternal. I live and move and have my being in that Power evermore."

Never accept the limitations of your environment. Remain inwardly ensconced in the castle of God's presence. There is no other haven of safety. No hurt, no disease, not even death can reach you there. That heaven of God's presence is always within you; find it by Kriya Yoga meditation. "Even a tiny bit of this real religion protects one from great fear (the colossal sufferings inherent in the repeated cycles of birth and death)."* In fearlessness affirm: "I am castled in God's presence. No harm can reach me, for in every situation of life—physical, mental, financial, spiritual—I am protected in the fortress of God's presence."

* Bhagavad Gita II:40.

How to Succeed in Finding God

Self-Realization Fellowship International Headquarters,
Los Angeles, April 22, 1937

Close your eyes. Feel that you are Spirit watching your finite body. Feel that the room is filled with joy; it surrounds and permeates you, within and without. Affirm: "Joy and I are one. God and I are one in divine ecstasy. O Infinite Spirit, surcharge my body, my mind, and my soul with Thy heavenly bliss. Give me realization, that I may consciously know Thy presence within me. *Aum,* Peace, Amen."

Repent of your indifference to God. Those who are indifferent to Him suffer. Give unto Him your love. He is your Father; you are His child. It is your duty and privilege to love Him. Offer Him your heart right now. One moment of sincere soul call will arouse God, and His response will surely come if you will continue to call to Him. Friends, name, fame, money—all mortal possessions are ephemeral and will vanish. But with God all joys are real and everlasting. With your heart's sincerity give Him a soul call—a magnet call, a heart-rending call of deepest longing—and you shall receive His mercy.

I shall talk to you tonight as my inspiration comes, on a few points about meditation. If it were possible for me to remind you every day, every minute, about the importance of meditation, I would do so.

Meditation, complete absorption of the attention in God, is the only way to the Infinite. It is so difficult for most people to find God because they don't meditate. They would find Him very easily if only they would learn to meditate in the right way.

The Divine Power of Concentration

Various teachers and paths have differing definitions of meditation. There is a difference between concentration and meditation. Concentration is a necessary preliminary to and component of meditation; it means to withdraw your attention from all objects of distraction and focus it on one thing at a time. Untrained persons do not think deeply; when they are trying to focus on something, their minds run away in a hundred directions. When you are able to absorb the attention completely in one subject at a time, to be lost in one concept of thought, that is called concentration.

The practice of concentration varies according to the object and purpose of concentration. Your mind is usually busy all the time, constantly jumping from one thought to another. It is therefore easier in the beginning to concentrate on one subject with a variety of related thoughts than to try to concentrate on just one thought pertinent to that subject. So the first exercise in practicing concentration should be to absorb the attention in all the thoughts you can about one subject, to the exclusion of unrelated mental wanderings. After you have thoroughly mastered this, then your disciplined mind is prepared to concentrate on one thought alone. Take a single thought from a subject, such as: "I am peaceful" or "I am love eternal" or "I am happiness eternal," and think only that thought without any other relative ideas. If you are able to awaken that thought—to feel it within your heart and mind, so that your whole system realizes the intrinsic truth expressed in that concept, and the attention does not wander—then you have achieved true concentration upon that thought.

Now, what is the use in such practice? The idea is that concentration is power. Everything in the universe required concentrated thought to come into being. When you look at a flower, do you wonder what made it? The thought of God. Everything you see is the product of concentration—either God's or man's. How thoughtless we are! When we admire the wonderful inventions and works of art created by man, we acknowledge the marvelous powers of concentration that were necessary to produce them. But we take for granted the miraculous creation of trees, flowers, human beings—as if they are simply dropped from heaven! But they are the result of God's creative concentration.

When ordinary persons try to put their minds on creating or accomplishing something, they find distractions and give up. But great souls are those who exercise the divine power of concentration that is hidden within them. Concentration is not given to some people and denied to others through heredity; it is an inherent quality of the soul. The power of concentration comes from God and is a native gift in each of us as His children. But persons who live in a state of restless distraction and never exercise their powers of concentration never seem to achieve anything.

Concentration is more than mere visualization. They are two different things. Visualization, employing only the mind's faculty of imaging, produces hallucinations. Concentration brings in the will force of the soul. Focused or guided visualization is one of the parts of concentration, but concentration is the whole. Concentration and will force go together. Will gathers the power of attention; and as it does so, the will force becomes stronger and stronger until it becomes one with Divine Will. This Divine Will Force controls all cosmic energy; it lets loose forces in the ether that change one's environment so that the environment becomes compatible with the strong vibrations of one's wish.

Persons who concentrate a little bit and then give up do not know the power of concentration. They wish to accomplish something before they have sufficiently developed that power, so when obstacles loom they are apt to become discouraged: "Well, I concentrate and still nothing happens." Their attention is distracted by impatient thoughts of the desired result, rather than concentrating on the steps necessary to achieve that result. To concentrate on having a house without making an effort to get that house will not do.

Mind has great power. And concentrated mind is the supreme, all-accomplishing power. I have seen the most marvelous demonstrations of this power of concentration. This power is everything, provided you do not give up.

The Factors Impeding Success

No achievement happens of itself. If some persons have "smooth sailing" it is because they had worked hard before and thereby attracted that seemingly effortless success. But even if you are not one of them, that doesn't mean you cannot succeed now.

First, you need to understand the forces you have to contend with. Every action you perform—physically or mentally—leaves a trace in your mind. Yoga calls them *samskaras*—the habit-tendencies or predisposed moods created by the things you have already done, whether in this life or a previous incarnation. Whenever you try to break out of the mold and accomplish something constructive or new, immediately your past wrong actions try to nullify your present good efforts. But if you keep on trying, and concentrating, that power of concentrated thought will obvert your past actions that are trying to keep you down.

Another thing: company is vitally important—it is stronger than will power. If you mix with saintly people, you think their life is the way to live. And if you mix with worldly or evil people, you think theirs is the only way. Mind is influenced by environment. Do not be a victim of your environment; choose good company that inspires your continuous self-improvement.

Thought is fire; use its concentrated power to consume all obstacles to achievement. Most people are mentally lazy. Physical laziness is sometimes forgivable, because that person may simply need a rest; but there is no justification for being mentally lazy. Most of you never use concentrated mental power to destroy the *samskaras,* the subconscious mental patterns left by your past wrong actions, which are the real obstacles to success.

Concentration and Will Power Can Overcome Subconscious Compulsions

If you let yourself be continuously driven by the effects of your past actions, you will find yourself in a bad way. Suppose you jump into a fast-moving stream or river. Of course you will be carried along with its current, possibly to great harm. But the first act of jumping into the stream was your own fault. You started the cause that brought about the effect. Likewise, you created your stream of wrong thoughts—first allowing them entry into your consciousness and then repeatedly swimming along with them—and now you are allowing yourself to be carried away by their force. You must break away.

How? By use of concentration and will power to bring that stream of conscious and subconscious thoughts under your control. Ordinarily you don't know how restless your mind is until you try to practice concentration and meditation. It is only when you sit quietly and begin to introspect that you see the myriad thoughts coursing through your mind. But if you continue to sit still and practice the yoga techniques of concentration,* refusing to be distracted by the restlessness of your thoughts, you will find suddenly that your mind has become calm. The mind is like a child; you have to patiently humor it without getting upset by it. Gradually it will come under your control. "With the intuitive discrimination saturated in

* The scientific techniques of yoga meditation taught by Paramahansa Yogananda are presented in the *Self-Realization Fellowship Lessons*, available for home study from SRF Headquarters.

patience, with the mind absorbed in the soul, the yogi, freeing his mind from all thoughts, will by slow degrees attain tranquility."*

When as a result of concentration and meditation, your mind comes under your control—when you can step out of the stream of restless habit-compelled thoughts into an inner calmness and quietude—you can attune the mind to constructive positive thoughts of accomplishment. Then it is necessary to use your will to follow through. For instance, when you make up your mind in the morning about what you are going to do that day, you have to use sufficient will power, garnered from concentrated thoughts focused on your intention, to follow through on those plans before the day is over. Thereby, you are actually accomplishing success, not merely wishing for it.

If you are unsuccessful, it is evident that you do not make the effort to go deep enough when you concentrate, and you do not persist long enough to get results. First you have to concentrate deeply and free the mind from the static of restless thoughts. Then you have to wait to feel mental attunement with God's will. If your mind radio has static, you cannot get His message; but when your mind is calm, you can tune your concentrated power of thought to God and receive His broadcast.

Meditation Connects You With God

This brings us to meditation, which is that form of concentration by which you connect yourself with God. Concentration is a broader term than meditation; it can be upon God or upon any other subject. But meditation means concentrating on God alone. Most people apply their mind power to gain specific material things. But if you learn how to meditate and apply your concentration on God first, you become charged with the Divine Will Power. When you have that Divine Will Power you can accomplish anything. Not all the reverses in life can dislodge your goal-directed thought when you are in tune with the Divine. What you will when you are in tune with that Power has to come to pass, because every thought that is given sufficient energy has to express itself. No causation goes without its effect.

Now the question comes, why is meditation the way to the Infinite? Because meditation is the causation by which you tune out thoughts of mortal limitation and attune the consciousness to

* Bhagavad Gita VI:25.

God's presence within you. By meditation you merge in the Fountain of all powers—the Fountain that has given light to the stars and strength and life to the foods we eat; the Fountain that has given beauty to the world and love by which we may love God and one another. This universe is governed by law: thus, every result has a corresponding cause. Deep meditation is that causation whose effect is God-realization. If you set that cause in motion within you, and never give up, the result is scientifically certain. Even if you do not find God right away, it does not matter; if you persevere in meditating and constantly calling to Him, you will unequivocally find His response.

If only you knew how much power you have within yourself! God made you His child and you have chosen to be a beggar. Jesus, by the God-realization of meditation, knew he was a child of God. You can also know that you are His child. You must go to the Source. To have God is to have all power.

This drama of earthly life is to be so played that through it you might learn to know your divine Self. Jesus came, Buddha came, other great souls came, but have they saved you? No. But they have shown you the way by which you can save yourself. Just to believe in Jesus will not save you. You must make the effort to attain what he attained. "The harvest truly is plenteous but the laborers are few." You have to labor for that Infinite Consciousness.

Meditation requires that instead of praying only for the products of God, you turn your attention to the factory, God Himself. Why not go to that Source whence all creation emerges? Meditation is not a vague mental wandering; it is to be so concentrated within that hours slip away without your knowing it. By right meditation, ecstasy comes. Ecstasy is contact with the Source of all power. In ecstasy you touch that state in which anything can be done. If you persevere, a time comes when you find that the assurance and protection of God's power never leaves you. It does not matter if the whole world is against you, if the whole world forsakes you, when you are with God. God will never forsake you. But you need to be sincere in your love for Him. You will not be successful if you seek God with any ulterior motive. It is all right to tell Him of your need, but want God Himself more than all else. Approach Him with complete surrender. Without God's power you cannot think or will or talk or love or do anything. Why should you give more importance to other things than to Him?

How to Convince God to Answer Your Call

God is conscious of your needs. If you appeal to Him with unconditional love and sincerity, He will answer. Do not be discouraged if He does not answer right away. That is His test. If in spite of His silence you still believe He is listening, and still keep on talking to Him, He will respond. He will answer through results. But do not look for the results. Just say, "God, I love You with all my might, with all my sincerity, with all my heart. And Lord, if I am seeking something less than You, forgive me and help me to think of You alone. Without Your wisdom, how could I understand anything? Without Your love, how could I love at all? How could I will to do anything without Your power, which is behind my will and my love and all my feelings? Why are You hiding from me? I must convince You that I love You, that I want You alone. You must reveal Yourself, for I cannot go on in my life alone. Thou art my life, Thou art my Father, Thou art my Mother, Thou art my everything. Reveal Thyself unto me!"

If you go on like this, with sincerity, He will answer. God knows everything that you are doing. You cannot fool Him. The thing He most dislikes is when you try to dissemble with Him or are insincere. Sincerity touches His heart in the greatest way. Where there is sincerity, there is God's response. What have you to be afraid of? Do not think you have to be perfect; that is foolish. Before God, everyone in this delusive finite world can be considered a "sinner." Just pour out your heart to Him, in the humble simplicity of a loving child.

God will not measure your defects or your merits. The preeminent merit is to be sincere with God—sincerity to Him in meditation is most important. At night or anytime you sit to meditate, meditate with all your heart and soul. When you pray with deep sincerity, all restless thoughts fall away, all sensory distractions vanish, and in that stillness you find Him coming to you. Then you will realize how wonderful life is, how great your life is, supported by the omnipresence of God's consciousness that lies just behind your own consciousness.

Everything You Seek Is Found in God

Think how wonderful life will be when you have no compulsion to seek anything at all, because you have found everything you seek in God! Nothing can enslave you then. That is the freedom I am enjoying; and I pray to God that this freedom and grace be always with me. When you *know* that God is a part of your being, you feel no reason to seek from Him any other gain. I sought spiritual power once; but now I don't ask God for anything. I love Him and I know He loves me; I don't want anything else.

Whence did you get your parents and your children; and why is there hunger and nature provides food to satisfy that hunger? These things all come from God. They are part of His purposeful divine plan. His Power is so plainly working all the time in this intelligently ordered creation; and still you refuse to concentrate on that Power. He is giving you all the signs of His presence that you will receive. Why do you waste your time pursuing the gifts instead of the Giver? It is foolish to do so. Meditate! At first you will struggle with your thoughts and then with your body; but if you can go deeper into meditation, your thoughts will settle down and body will become calm and joy will come into the temple of your heart. When joy comes, you know you are contacting God. But you are too much in a hurry about meditation; you do not wait to receive His message. Meditate with calm perseverance; pray and look for His response in your heart center. Pray again and again. When that joy comes, then notwithstanding what you are going through outwardly, you feel that everything is all right. But if you betray that joy of the Divine Presence—ignoring it in favor of material pursuits—then everything will betray you. No matter how convinced you are that this or that will make you happy, you will find that it does not.

You are alone in this world: Nobody is responsible for making you happy except yourself. Let nothing or no one cheat you out of that happiness, that all-satisfying inner joy which you will want to share with all.

You have to work for everything you need or want. Do you receive your wages without working? Do you get anything without working for it? So it is with God. You must prove to Him by your spiritual efforts that you want Him more than anything else. The minute you have proven that, He will come to you. Organizational power and all great achievements of this world are temporary. They will vanish. But the blessing of God is worth having, because that will go with you beyond the portals of the grave. Then why are you sitting idle? You must know that you are a child of God. You don't have to earn that heritage; it is already yours. But you must reclaim it. Make God know that you want Him alone. The time that you spend in idle talk and trivialities should be spent in meditation. Then you will develop.

Everything you have that you were seeking has been given to you by God. So why forget Him? Without Him you would not have love or life or health or anything. He is the cleverest who seeks God, because that devotee is going to receive everything. Having Him, no other gain is greater. As Jesus promised: "Seek ye first the kingdom of God, and all things else shall be added unto you."

Once I had "all things," and I willingly gave them away. I have something far greater—the love of my beloved God. I want nothing—just the joy of existence and the pleasure of talking about Him to others.

The Soul Can Only Be Satisfied by God

As long as the soul is forced to depend on external things it cannot be happy, because these are always changing. The soul can never be permanently satisfied with anything but the love of God. Some people learn this paramount lesson of life through wisdom and discrimination; others must learn through the slow evolutionary process of many incarnations, or by burning their fingers in the fires of sorrow. The moment you realize that in all other pursuits it was God you were seeking, then you are on the path toward your Infinite Home.

It was when I lost my mother that I began to seek God more earnestly.* I sought and sought everywhere, yearning to behold again those beloved black eyes of Mother. I gave poetic voice to my anguish:

She died—
And I cried—
And I sought those lost two eyes everywhere.
I searched in the stars,
Until, bedimmed by my tears,
They twinkled black eyes everywhere.
But they were not those that I lost!†

All love and affection that she gave me seemed to be gone; and I cried, "Doesn't she love me anymore? Where has she gone?" And I cried on. As I went on crying and searching, storming the

* "I loved Mother as my dearest friend on earth. Her solacing black eyes had been my refuge in the trifling tragedies of childhood," Paramahansaji wrote in his *Autobiography of a Yogi*. She died when he was about eleven years old.

† From "Two Black Eyes" in *Songs of the Soul,* by Paramahansa Yogananda (published by Self-Realization Fellowship).

very gates of heaven with my yearning, suddenly the voice of the Divine Mother came, "Many times I have suckled thee through many breasts." In that instant I realized that it was God I was seeking—that behind the love of my earthly mother it was the One Spirit that loved me through her form.

Looking, searching for her everywhere,
I found my Divine Mother;
And in Her love
I found my mother's love;
And in Her omnipresent eyes,
I found those lost two black eyes.

What a wonderful realization I had! All the persons I have loved—all the friends I have had—I see that it is God who is in them, loving me and loved by me. All those who come to me—I see it is God. And where God is, there is my paradise. I seek nothing in preference to Him.

Through incarnations you have sought fulfillment of the soul's longing for love. Sometimes you were an outcast, forsaken by the world; and in some life you have been a martyr who died for a beloved cause; and countless times a lover and a beloved, a parent and a child, and so on. In all these different loves you are like a puppet being danced by hidden strings, until at last you realize that there was only One who loved you behind all other loves—but He never wanted to tell you how much He loved you. He waits for you to discover and love Him freely and spontaneously, without compulsion. I am talking to you of the genuine love of the Spirit.

We Are All God's Children

God reveals Himself to us by His humbleness. We are mere pygmies before Him, but He patiently endures the audacity of us tiny human beings. Despite His sovereign power, He does not compel us in any way. He calls us only by His love. He loves us dearly. Otherwise he would not have sent Jesus and Krishna and other Great Ones to show us the way home. With His infinite love and patience and humbleness, He is waiting for us to love Him.

God is playing hide-and-seek with us, His children. But devotees know the truth of God's promise: "He who watcheth Me always, him do I watch. He never loses sight of Me, nor do I lose sight of him."

One thing you must learn here on earth is that you are a child of God. When you know that, you will know that everyone is a child of God even as you are. What a tremendous realization! that all persons are of God—that everyone and everything that comes to you comes from God! The more you appreciate the divine image in everyone, the more you are alive with God's consciousness. It is not difficult then to love all persons with love that is forgiving and compassionate and good, no matter what they do to you, because you see it is God who comes in the form of every being. In time, as you learn to love God more, you see Him within everyone—friends or enemies. If you can hate anyone, you have not realized God at all. The divine man gives his love equally to all, even as the sun gives impartially of its light.

The most difficult person you have to deal with is yourself. You refuse to work for that which is in your own highest interest. How assiduously people labor in their factories and workplaces, and yet they will not make even the least effort to know God!

Why not surrender yourself to that Power? Take out a couple of hours from your sleep each night and meditate. Make the contact with God. Take my advice. When everybody else is sleeping, fall at the feet of the Spirit. You must throw shells of your yearning at the bulwark of silence. "O God of joy, I know You are here. You are just behind my thoughts—just behind the subconscious land of sleep. Reveal Yourself unto me!"

Every night the Divine Mother comes to wipe away all your mortal sorrows in the subconscious joy and freedom of sleep. But then morning comes and starts to blacken your consciousness again. Meditation brings you conscious contact with that joy. You go beyond the land of sleep and keep that joy with you during the day, so that even when you are crucified by trials you are able to say, "Father, forgive them, for they know not what they do." If you do not lose that joy no matter what comes, then you know you have God with you.

I don't have to try anymore. He is always with me. Once in a while I feel I am in this world, but it is like a forgotten dream—because I live in that eternal wakefulness which is the only Reality. This earth is a school, a motion-picture dream-drama for your education and entertainment. Whether beholding a comedy or a tragedy in the movie theater of this life, remember that it has no ultimate reality. Keep your consciousness attuned to the Lord, and say: "That was a great picture, but I have conquered its illusory power over me. I am not frightened by it, for You are with me always."

That happiness in Spirit is the only thing to live for. Meditate each day; and when you have contacted that happiness, then go about your work. Without that inner awareness of God's joy, you cannot enjoy life—indeed, you are not even truly living.

Someday these things will be taught in schools. The schools do not teach children how to live, how to have that divine happiness. These universal teachings should be given in the schools—not to emphasize any particular religion, but to show that the way to happiness is meditation and contact of God, and that by such contact one may learn from God what one should do.

In order to hold on to your inner happiness, never find fault with others; learn to blame and correct your own flaws. Be sincere with everyone, express kindness and love to each person. Love is the most powerful force that you can have. Love is dynamite. Humbleness is dynamite. Concentration is dynamite. These will destroy all obstacles and barriers to success. Meditation throws your concentration and the shells of your devotion against the walls of your indifference until you break through and contact that blissful Power within.

How to Be Successful With God

My Master shook me with his wisdom; and as I responded that realization came that I was a child of God. Those who love God and seek to commune with Him love to meditate. Here at Mount Washington you must regularly come together to meditate. And use your free time to be alone with God in meditation. There are so many wonderful places here to meditate. What of it if you do not become successful in the way the world thinks of success? To be successful with God is far more important, for that success you can take with you when this life is over. You want that contact of God of which Jesus spoke. If you have that, Jesus' promise that "all things will be added unto you" will be fulfilled anew. Meditate on God. Seek no credit from man. Do not show your devotion to others. In your heart hoard your devotion, concentrate your devotion only on Him; and He shall speak to you. He shall guide you consciously. And in everything that comes, you shall see it is that Power which is loving and sustaining you. There is no greater security than this.

Use your God-given intelligence to find Him. Why have you to be reminded that you are here alone and that a hundred years hence you will not be known? Because you are here today and busy with life, you do not think that anything will happen to you. But "tomorrow" we will be gone. I come not to socialize or talk of useless things, but to awaken your consciousness. Now. Not tomorrow, but tonight. Take some time away from sleep and meditate. And don't give up. Don't succumb to sleep until you have made that contact with God. From tonight begin, and you will succeed. In every little gap of time that you have, talk to Him. And have faith that He is listening to you. He is right behind the darkness of your closed eyes; and as you talk and He listens, you will find that life becomes transformed. You will realize why your parents and family and friends love you—because of God—and you will be day and night drinking of that love direct from His presence.

No matter what weaknesses or faults you have, meditate. Talk to God again and again. And once you can get Him to talk, He will never leave you. Though contact of God may seem to be the most difficult thing, it is the easiest if you will sincerely try. The one who has made up his mind to know God will find Him. God you have already with you. You just have to know Him and receive Him in your consciousness.

It is such a joy to drink His name with all of you. That is why I say to Him, "Lord, I want only those to come who are in earnest in their desire for You and who will faithfully seek You." I glorify not myself but Him who sent me. That is also what Jesus said. It is a beautiful saying; it is alive with truth. Every word in the New Testament is living. Yet people read these words and still want more to stimulate them! That is because they don't meditate on those truths to convert them into their own personal realization.

I thank you for the joy of your attention. Join me in offering our united devotion to the Father. Pray for me, and I shall pray for you, that we all manifest in pure sincerity the consciousness of God. In that selfless consciousness learn to physically help people by service, to mentally help people by kindness and encouragement, and to spiritually help people by radiating the joy of God that you feel. To transmit God's consciousness you do not have to talk much; just feel it, and automatically those around you will be uplifted. Do not seek the acclaim and testimony of man, but the testimony of God. One moon gives more light than all the stars in the heavens. Similarly, one devotee of realization that this organization will produce is greater than thousands of persons who just read Scripture and go to church once a week. So, be loyal in your activities and continuous in your habit of meditation. I do not want to hold you except by your own realization. We are not after anything but to give you realization of that Supreme Power. And that Power shall be revealed to you all if you are sincere in your loyalty, devotion, and desire for God.

By heeding the simple truths I give you, you can find God. You don't need a new religion. You know what God wants; what you need is to live by it. What I have told you tonight, please practice that in your life every day.

Training the Conscious and Subconscious Minds for Success

Compilation of talks on this subject given at Self-Realization Fellowship Golden Lotus Temple, Encinitas, California, April 7 and 28, 1940

Success means the fulfillment of a desire that you have set about to accomplish. But there are two kinds of success: ordinary or temporal success, and truly permanent success. So it is important to analyze and classify your desires accordingly.

Desires for material things—for health, or home, or cars, or money—all these lead to temporal success. You have to leave them at the time of death. That is why the masters discarded the thought of putting their energy entirely on acquiring that which has to be given up at a moment's notice. As Jesus said, "Take no thought for your life, what ye shall eat; neither for the body, what ye shall put on."* He didn't mean that one should go without food or clothing; but rather, one should not pay too much attention to temporal things. We spend too much of our precious time on earth chasing happiness that does not last.

The Greatest Success: Achieving an Evenminded State of Inner Joy

Apart from the legitimate fulfillment of your needs, the greatest success lies in achieving that state in which your mind always remains on an even keel—so that no matter how you have to struggle for health or financial security, your inner joy cannot be taken away from you. Even if you are in need of money or healing, what is the point of worrying? By doing so, you only paralyze your will so that you cannot succeed.

If your conscious mind is weak and afraid, your subconscious mind also takes on those attributes. Why thus poison your subconscious mind, which in turn affects your conscious mind? If

* Luke 12:22.

instead you implant happiness in the subconscious mind, a positive outlook will dominate your conscious mind; and you will be in a position to make a greater effort for success in any endeavor you undertake.

There are some people who, no matter what happens, are never really touched by sorrows. But there are many more who are up one minute, happy, and down the next, sorrowful. If you look impartially into the lives of people, you will more or less see that no one is really happy unless he has consciously trained his mind to be happy all the time. One who has that happiness which can stand against the onslaughts of all trials and still the mind remains untouched—such a person is a real king of peace. That is real success. Analyze and see if it isn't so.

Mental evenness will not only put your conscious mind in a better position to make positive effort, but your subconscious mind will be better connected with the divine consciousness, superconsciousness. And by tapping that consciousness, you will be able to accomplish your goals in life with the power of God.

You have no idea how powerful the subconscious mind is! The conscious and superconscious minds are also powerful; but their potential is suppressed by the subconscious mind if you do not know how to use it properly. Because of this, the average person is only using a very little of the conscious mind, and almost nil of the power of the superconscious mind.

Your Subconscious Mind: Helper or Tyrant?

Everything you do and experience all day—good and bad—is lodged in the subconscious mind. In most of you, that mind operates more or less mechanically, as an automatic device to record your actions and repeat them as habits. But you are meant to control your subconscious mind, to train it with the conscious mind. Instead, you allow that memory- and habit-mind to function passively, absorbing influences from your environment and forming habits indiscriminately, which then enslave your conscious mind.

It is important to remember that the brain is never "unconscious," whether your conscious mind is working or sleeping. Scientists have been able to show this with the electroencephalograph machine, because every brain cell emanates an electrical current. The frequency of the brainwaves during sleep is much less than during the waking state, but every now and then during sleep the rate increases. These surges are called spindle waves.* During dreams, also, the brain activity increases, owing to the influx of more life force into the brain to "project" these mental movies. These varying waves show that the subconscious mind is always awake and engaged in different activities. Like a night watchman at a factory, it remains ever on duty even when the "workers" of conscious thoughts have left for the day. If there is a loud sound or a powerful odor, for instance, very often the subconscious mind awakens the individual, in case it is caused by a fire or some other danger.

In fact, one simple way to learn control over the subconscious mind is to impress upon it a certain time you want to be awakened every morning. Give it a strong command before falling asleep that you must wake up at 5:00 a.m. Experiment by changing that time on different days—for instance, to 5:15 or 4:30 a.m. By practice, the subconscious mind can be trained gradually to do your will.

Before you go to sleep at night, suggest good thoughts to the subconscious mind. And never scold your children or speak harshly to them before they go to bed. Gently speak encouraging words, because your last words to your children before they sleep are impressed on their subconscious minds.

The subconscious mind is very receptive. If you go to a place and sleep where people have murderous instincts and bad vibrations, even if you don't mix with them you will be affected by those feelings. Likewise, when you go to a very spiritual place you receive uplifting vibrations, and they will change you for the better. That is the value of pilgrimages to places where great saints have lived. The subconscious mind picks up those vibrations, even if one does not feel them consciously.

Environment and company have a strong effect on the subconscious mind. Suppose you have been born in a family of mediocre achievements, and they say, "Well, we have always been clerks,"

* Spindle waves were a recently discovered phenomenon at the time this talk was given; their function is still being investigated today. An article in *Psychology Today,* April 21, 2011, reported: "Recent research by Matthew Walker and his research team at the University of California, Berkeley, shows that sleep spindles are associated with refreshment of our ability to learn." A study reported in *The Journal of Neuroscience,* December 7, 2011, stated: "Sleep spindles are an electroencephalographic (EEG) hallmark of non-rapid eye movement (NREM) sleep and are believed to mediate many sleep-related functions, from memory consolidation to cortical development. Spindles differ in location, frequency, and association with slow waves, but whether this heterogeneity may reflect different physiological processes and potentially serve different functional roles remains unclear." *(Publisher's Note)*

or "We have always done menial work." You are likely to absorb the conviction that such a life is all you are suited for. Now, everyone knows their enemies try to lead them astray, and therefore they protect themselves against them. But there are also friendly enemies—those who live near you, perhaps in your own family. They seemingly want to help you, but infecting you with their own subconscious habits of limitations is the wrong kind of help!*

Make it a practice to associate with persons of creative talent, and to read books that will inspire and encourage you. Don't let your life pass away in the wrong environment. Create the best environment you can—by the outward company you keep and by the inward companionship of noble souls whose consciousness lives in great books. A positive environment inspires your initiative-starved thoughts and will to new activity for all-round progress.

No matter how your child is limited in intelligence, never tell him so. If you reinforce that negative thought in his subconscious mind, you end his possibilities for improvement. The subconscious mind will take anything that has been repeatedly given to it through the conscious mind. But a properly trained subconscious mind can bring success in spite of defects of the conscious mind.

The subconscious mind is very helpful when it is nurtured with good thoughts. If you didn't have the memory and habit functions of the subconscious mind, you would have to learn anew how to walk and speak every day. But if you allow the subconscious mind to create bad habits of failure and sickness and limitations, it is your worst enemy; and you must resist this enemy at night as well as during the wakeful hours.

Realize how limited you are by the erroneous habits of thinking that become embedded in the powerfully influential subconscious mind! You think you are a man or a woman; but in reality you are pure Spirit. Why should you impose on yourself the consciousness of limitations of the body? That is why you are what you are. You

* In these words Paramahansaji was not disparaging menial work. He himself set the example of performing any and all duties that presented themselves. His intent, rather, was to caution against mental inertia. "If your work in life is humble, do not apologize for it," he said on other occasions. "So long as you work to please God, all cosmic forces will harmoniously assist you....Work of any kind, if done in the right spirit, gives you victory over yourself. You may clean bathrooms, but if you do it with the thought of serving and helping people, you are showing the right spirit of a man of God. The attitude with which you work is what counts."

are limiting yourself. You don't let your soul express through your conscious and subconscious minds.

If your financial state is chronically bad, it means your conscious mind—instead of exercising free will—is being guided by self-limiting patterns of the subconscious mind. God has given you unconstrained freedom, yet you chain yourself with the consciousness of financial insufficiencies and worry. You walk all the time in those same mental grooves. But you don't have to be like that. You are free. You must train your subconscious mind to be the helper of the conscious mind instead of its tyrant.

Using the Conscious Mind to Break Out of Subconscious Limitations

Never make excuses for yourself if you are always in trouble or unhappy. To do so is to deny the divine capabilities of your conscious mind. Few persons analyze what the conscious mind is truly capable of. Unless you use its potentials, you are more or less an automaton. Most people are like that. They imitate others. They behave in a mechanical way, in their work and in their personal life. They make no free-will effort to change themselves. That is why they don't achieve much success in life. Those who exercise their conscious mind—its powers of will and creative thinking—are the ones who achieve in life.

To think deeply is to delve in the realm of untapped possibility and discriminative guidance. On the other hand, I have seen marvelous thinkers who are not very successful because they do not harness their will and action to their creative thinking. In other words, some people are too lazy to think, and go on acting without thinking deeply about the results of their actions; and others are thinking all the time, but are too lazy physically to bring that thinking to fruition. Success is found neither by the mentally lazy nor the physically lazy.

When you learn to think and will creatively, you find thousands of avenues for success opening to you. Just say to yourself: "What is the matter with me? The world is filled with wealth. All I have to do is connect myself with that wealth." There are always some avenues by which you can create that wealth which nobody else has ever thought of. The ordinary person does not do that kind of deep thinking. But the inventor does. By thought he develops that intuitive searchlight which throws light into many avenues of action and thus finds a way forward. Utilize your moments alone for deep thinking. In such seclusion you can create avenues of action for yourself that you never dreamed possible.

I have had to struggle to support the work of Self-Realization Fellowship. I remember a period during the worst part of the Depression when the work desperately needed money to meet its debts. I thought, "What shall I do?" A business executive suggested to me a commercialization of the work: "Sell more books! Charge more for your courses!" But religion should be a matter of the heart. The teacher should inspire in the students a desire to help God's work, but not be a salesman; though it is all right to sell spiritual things with an attitude of service in order to support God's work. As I wrestled with the problem in the seclusion of my interiorized concentration, an idea came to me: "Well, during this Depression people can do without fancy clothes and fancy cars, but they can't do without food. They always have to eat." So I said, "Let me invent some nutritious food that will benefit people." Because of the Depression many couldn't afford meat, so I gathered together various foods and supplements and invented several kinds of meat substitutes. We sold these and other healthful food products during the Depression, and it helped to support the work of Self-Realization Fellowship.

You too can apply that power of creative achievement. Start by analyzing if the things you want to achieve are for your highest good and for the good of others. To selfishly think only of one's own interest while creating wealth at the expense of others is a misuse of one's powers and will never give you happiness. To make money while serving the welfare of others is the right kind of material goal to pursue. When after honest introspection you determine that fulfillment of an ambition is going to do good to yourself and give happiness to others too, then you can know it is a legitimate desire and can exercise your mind power unreservedly to achieve it.

Discriminate Between Good and Evil Actions

We all want to achieve in this life. From birth we are endowed with certain desires, and we go through life trying to fulfill those desires in various ways. Unfortunately, few are given the training to discriminate between good accomplishments and bad accomplishments.

When you forbid a child to do something, often he looks for the first opportunity to do it! Parents will have better success if they give their children the reasons why they should not perform that particular action. Explain to them that virtue consists of those actions that will positively give one happiness. Evil promises a little pleasure or temporary happiness, but ultimately delivers unhappiness and suffering. Good actions may not immediately appear to be happiness-producing, but always bring beneficial results to the performer of those actions in the end.

Many so-called mature adults are yet immature in judgment. Like ignorant children they go on doing as they please, taking no heed of the result. It seems we never learn until we have suffered. But if we are told that there are certain actions that are going to hurt us and other actions that are going to make us feel better and happier, we are more inclined to listen. Religious teachings must be made more personal. The scriptures were not given to torture people with the burden of an evil conscience, but rather to develop in them that good judgment by which one can tell the difference between evil and good actions. It is in our own highest interest that we expunge from our conscious and subconscious minds the wrong desires and habits absorbed from worldly environments.

When free of negative subconscious influences, the conscious mind finds it easy to perform good actions. But if you train your subconscious mind to do evil, then you will find yourself engaging in wrong actions even if you don't want to do so. All forms of activity—good as well as evil—can be stimulated by the subconscious mind. Through its inspiration and imaginative power, people have written many wonderful things and created beautiful works of art and music. Yet others have committed murders under the influence of an ungoverned, emotionally volatile subconscious mind. Never allow your subconscious mind to rule your conscious mind.

Therefore, not only should you develop your conscious mind and will, but you must train your subconscious mind as well. When you do that, you will have two powers—the conscious and subconscious minds—by which you can tackle every difficulty and find happiness that is lasting.

Training Your Subconscious Mind

In order to instill strength and right thinking in the subconscious mind, suggest positive thoughts and improvements to your mind by the practice of affirmation. It is best to be in a state of half-sleep. Much can be absorbed in the period just before and just after sleep; that is why some people advocate "sleep learning" or subconscious training during sleep.

There was a lady who wanted to cure her husband of the smoking habit. Every night she would stand by his bed and intone: "Day by day, in every way, you are losing the smoke habit." But her husband had not yet gone to sleep. He endured his wife's efforts to cure him as long as he could stand it, and then cried out, "Confound it, I don't want to be cured!" So when you are suggesting a good habit to anyone, be sure he is either willing or is well asleep!

The thing is this: You must not let your subconscious mind hold on to contradictory thoughts as you are affirming. Whatever you are affirming, you must keep on with your mental repetition until all negative thoughts are swept aside. Take your chosen affirmation and repeat it again and again until your consciousness is soaked in that one thought.

For instance, suppose you are sick and in need of healing. You may affirm, "Perfect health permeates all my body cells." Simultaneously there is an undercurrent in your subconscious mind that says, "You are done for. You can't be healthy!" If you go on affirming good health even though your subconscious mind tries to discourage you, you will eventually drive away that subconscious habit of negative thought and start a new mental pattern of good health. Then you can be healed, for the powerful subconscious mind controls all the internal life processes that maintain and repair the body.

Every night before going to bed, affirm very deeply the attainment of anything you want to have. If you want God, affirm just that, every night: "I and my Father are one." If you pray for God, you have prayed for everything else. God knows what you need. If you pull the ear, the head comes with it. In finding God, you find complete fulfillment of all legitimate desires.

Your subconsciously doubting mind may say, "Oh, what is the use of meditating? I have meditated, but God has not come to me!" That was the worst thought-obstacle I had to fight. But as I persevered in meditation, and with conscious acts of will and affirmation again and again resisted my subconscious mind until that thought of defeat was gone, then God revealed Himself to me in the glory of *samadhi*-bliss.

Conscious and Subconscious Tools for Success

So, I have told you how to use your conscious mind in collaboration with your subconscious mind for success. Learn to think before you act. Never use your will until you are sure what you are thinking is right. Reason first, and then feel; for calm feeling is an expression of intuitive guidance. Find out what you want to do; see what you are best suited for; and then use calm feeling to find your way forward. Sometimes it is difficult to choose the right course to pursue. But go on putting the searchlight of your concentration and calmness on many alternatives, and find out where your mind "clicks." When you feel that intuitive assurance from within, then apply your will unflinchingly to reach that goal. Consciously destroy from the mind all subconscious suggestions of limitation, wrong desire, and failure. The greater the will you use, the greater shall be your success. When you have a mountain in your path and you dynamite that mountain with your will to succeed, then you have a tunnel through which you can pass to reach your goal. All through my lecture tours I used these principles of success.

I remember a long time ago, when I first came to Boston, someone was playing a recording of Madame Galli-Curci.* I knew immediately that I was to meet her. I asked who she was; and later, when I went to New York, someone told me that she was singing there and asked me to meet her, but there was no opportunity. Later, in Chicago, a countess told me she knew her and again said, "You must meet her." Then, in Detroit, she was performing while I was in the city to lecture. I decided I wanted to go to her concert, but it was sold out. But my mind was set; I told my secretary to try again to procure tickets. "I am going to that concert," I assured him. "I see myself and you there!" But after several attempts, still he did not succeed. Finally I called the manager myself and told him, with conviction, that I *had* to have tickets. He said, "All right! You can have the two I had reserved for myself. I want you to be happy, so that you don't exert your will power on me anymore!" Galli-Curci and I met after her concert; and ever since we have been great friends. In the early years, I used to spend the Christmas holidays at her home with her and her husband, Homer Samuels—both wonderful souls.

In using the will consciously there is direct causation. Will starts a cause. Your strong will vibration strikes the brains of others and can change them. Will is not the mechanical result of an outside force. It works from the inside, from the inner or causal plane of your being. It is the result of your thought—the power to execute your thought, to convert your thought from a cause into an

* Amelita Galli-Curci (1882–1963), one of the most renowned operatic sopranos of the early twentieth century. She volunteered to be one of the national sponsors of Paramahansa Yogananda's work during the 1920s and '30s and was a devotee of his teachings until the end of her life. *(Publisher's Note)*

effect. I have used this will, surcharged by the superconscious mind, throughout my life; and have never known it to fail. Everything I wanted to achieve in this world, I have achieved. But remember: If you use your will power for wrong purposes, ultimately you rouse contrary forces that defeat you. Always harmonize your will with goodness and righteousness, which are manifestations of God's will in creation.

Limitations of the Conscious and Subconscious Minds

An infinite reservoir of God's power and intelligence lies within the brain. You must learn to draw upon that reservoir. The use of the conscious mind for success means that you use your intelligence to think creatively, independently, constructively. You compare your plans and goals with the experiences of others in order to choose the right avenues and learn from their mistakes. And then you seek those opportunities by which you can manifest your constructive ideas through will power. But even by carefully planned efforts to apply all of these, still you may arrive at the wrong result or fail to achieve your desired goal. That is why it is essential to harness your conscious and subconscious minds to superconsciousness.

The conscious mind expresses its faculties through the physical body. Whenever you are walking or thinking or performing some work in the world, you are using the conscious mind. But that mind is subject to the limitations of the physical body and its material environment, whose conditions it has drawn to itself through the law of karma.

Through your subconscious mind, your conscious mind is reinforced at night by some degree of contact with the superconsciousness of the soul; man could not survive without that. But the subconscious mind is also limited. Though it can support a cause initiated by your will or your environment, it cannot create a new cause of success.

All human beings are harnessed to the law of cause and effect. The health or prosperity or success you have is more or less limited because of your karma (the effects produced by the causes created by your own past actions) and because you have allowed yourself to be ruled by the causation coming from your environment. If you want to change the causation governing your life, you must either change your environment and karma or lift your consciousness above them. In other words, you must learn to utilize your superconscious mind, which cannot be affected by any limitations suggested by the body or its mortal environments.

Using the Superconscious Mind for Success

Now, how does one utilize the powers of the superconscious mind for success? There are several steps. First in importance is to find regular times for seclusion, to still your muscles and senses and thoughts by concentration and go deep into meditation. When your mind is completely still, that is the time you are aware of the superconsciousness of the soul.

Superconsciousness is an intuitive power. It doesn't require investigative thought or deduction or inference or a constant mental process of trial and error. Superconsciousness is direct perception. It is an all-seeing power. One night long ago in India, when this cosmic consciousness came over me, I blindfolded myself and set out for a temple to worship. Seven miles I walked through the busy streets and winding ways, led by that Light which I could see within, until I reached the temple.

That power of intuition always more or less tells me what is going to happen. Life is no longer a surprise to me. When I look at people's faces, I see their whole life written there. In the beginning I began to be a cynic because I looked at people and beheld their evil thoughts, and became somewhat disillusioned. But my master Sri Yukteswarji said, "What is the matter with you? You are always taking pictures of ugly things. Why don't you use the camera of your superconsciousness to take beautiful pictures?"

I learned much from his teaching and realized that I was not to use my intuition to look at the dark side of people's lives, because evil does not belong to man's soul. Now I see every soul as a garden of God's presence. Every soul has some unique quality that no one else has. Every soul is hallowed because in each one there is an individual expression of the Infinite found in no one else. Nobody has a face like yours. No one else has a smile like yours. You are needed in this world just as much as anyone else. If this were not so, you wouldn't be here.

You are eternally made in the image of God. You are higher than the animal or the plant. Trees are bound to the soil, and animals are bound by the cords of instinct, but man has the free will of the soul. Man can soar transcendent in the airship of his inspiration; he can uncover the secrets of the minutest atoms and the farthest stars; he can penetrate into the deepest reaches of eternity. He is free! God has given man divine intuitive power, but whenever man looks on himself as a physical body and identifies with his past habits and limitations, he is a mortal being.

The highest way to achieve success is to go deeper and deeper into the silence within, until you rise above the mortal realm of this earth-plane. You are too busy with this world. You must look behind the surface appearances of this universe, and ask deeper questions: "How are these flowers coming into existence out of a tiny seed? How are planets and stellar systems born and maintained in their orderly dance through the cosmos? How do they give rise to the teeming lives and consciousness and feelings of animals and plants and human beings?" Realize how all material things are enlivened by that Great Light which supplies them with life, that Light and Intelligence of God which is just behind your flesh, just behind all your sensations, just behind your human consciousness, just behind your subconscious habit-mind. Your home is not on these mortal shores. By deep meditation, every day I bid adieu to my body and my senses and everything and go into the land beyond, where the all-creative factory of the universe lies.

That factory, that Intelligence, is within you. You don't have to beg and whine and be filled with self-pity. If you think you are inferior, it is you who have limited yourself. And if you think you are superior, you have also limited yourself, by being satisfied with only a little bit of truth. That is not good enough for you. You are a child of God. Do not have a superiority complex born of self-pride, because it is His power that makes you what you are; but neither should you have an inferiority complex, because God Himself is within you. In the bower of your inmost consciousness, He is hiding just behind your thoughts. How do you know? These things I have told you, you must practice. They are object lessons that will lead you to that realization.

Self-Control Is the Greatest of All Accomplishments

In this world nearly everyone seeks health, happiness, and success as the highest goals to be achieved. But from the beginning of one's search, the true goal should be having control over one's life. In that lies the supreme accomplishment.

You will say that is something difficult to achieve, but it is not—provided one learns to use the combined power of the conscious, subconscious, and superconscious minds. First we must put into effect the right actions that will bring the result of soul-happiness into our lives. By awakening our will power and freeing it from wrong subconscious influences of habit and environment, we learn to conquer evil by good, hatred by love, sorrow by giving happiness. And as we learn to choose rightly between the dualities of good and evil, eventually we rise above both, and attain that state which Jesus and Krishna and the Masters attained—the state of evenmindedness, living always in the bliss-consciousness of God in which no dualities can distress or upset us.

Having health, happiness, and success is not the way to freedom, and you must not be slaves to them. For when you are slaves to them, you will be very happy when you have them and very unhappy when they are taken away from you. The mind must be so anchored in God that when health, happiness, success are taken away, you will still know that you are not harmed, that you are Spirit itself. You will say, "Many times I dreamed that I was healthy; many times I dreamed that I was sick. But now, Lord, I have risen above all the alternating conditions of earth-life." When you can realize that, you are free, as the great masters are free.

Happiness and sorrow are waves that ruffle the waters of consciousness: Today you are happy; tomorrow you are unhappy. Today you are well; tomorrow you are sick. If you are all the time fearful and nervous that when happiness slips away you will be again dumped in the pit of misery, you are not a truly successful individual. You should develop that consciousness within yourself wherein a little happiness or a little sorrow cannot disturb the calm lake of your mind, for a ruffled mind cannot mirror the reflection of God in the soul. Swami Shankara said, "If you want to know the Lord you must make your mind even, for on the altar of evenness the Lord of Creation comes."

Often God shows me that there is no body, there is no pain, there is no suffering, but what one creates through the delusive mind. Suppose I fall asleep and dream that I fell and hurt my foot. When I wake up there is no pain. My mind is disconnected from the experience of that dream. It is not true in my waking consciousness. So when you wake up in God, there is absolute release from pain and suffering. That is true release. That is true freedom, when you see that God has detached you from identification with your body.

How to Achieve the Transcendence of Nonattachment

How are you going to accomplish this? The first thing to learn is detachment from possessions. You always say: "This is my body.

This is my house. This is my money in the bank." Why be limited by identifying yourself with your possessions? Instead, learn to say, "These things are given to me to use." Enjoy them, but do not become attached to them.

This temple that I have given to America is the fulfillment of a desire I had in many lives. It is a place where people may realize that there is a sermon in nature, in the vastness of sea and sky.* The satisfaction that I have is that thousands of people will come here to enjoy the quiet and peace and beauty of this sanctuary. It has been created for all of you; there is no possession consciousness in my heart or mind. As soon as one is attached to anything, it is the cause of misery. Everything I acquired I have given up. At death you must part with all your material possessions; and if you leave any attachment behind, you will be compelled by that desire to reincarnate on this troublesome material plane. Before I went to India in 1935 I gave away everything to the work. And now nothing belongs to me. No bank book do I hold. I am free within. To enjoy everything without being attached is true kingship.

God has given you a sharp sword of discrimination by which you can cut away all limitations and free yourself within. In my mind I am free from everything. I am not bothered by anything. That is true happiness. By that kind of mental strength, one can always feel that he is above everything that happens.

When troubles come, or when people say, "You are no good," just affirm, "I am all right." You don't have to say it aloud, but you do have to be able to affirm inwardly—from a calm, unruffled consciousness that God's image is within you—that everything *is* all right with you. By doing that regardless of what circumstances try to vex you, you ascend from the limitations of attachment to the things and conditions of this earth.

There is a second way of detachment you must practice: from the character flaws and habits grafted onto your soul through the influence of your environment and ungoverned subconscious mind. Introspect daily; sit down and analyze yourself deeply. Find out whether you are a slave to the senses, always controlled by a craving for some pleasure. Each one of you has some particular inclination to conquer. Perhaps you are too greedy or too sexually conscious, or you love flattery or are prone to anger. If you sit quietly and ask

* The SRF Golden Lotus Temple in Encinitas, California, overlooking the Pacific Ocean.

yourself, "What is wrong with me? What am I like, and why am I this way?" you will begin to understand yourself clearly. And once you begin to identify your weaknesses, do not be overcome by discouragement; instead, use your sword of wisdom and discrimination and your will power to get rid of those bad habits.

The man who smokes for the first time never dreams he will get caught by that habit. Yet twenty-five years later he is still controlled by it. But what is that habit? Just a thought in the mind, a thought of twenty-five years standing. If you are bound by a bad habit of greed or sex or anger or anything else, get rid of it now! Affirm that you are free! It is no longer with you! Just one little thought is holding you to that weakness—one thought reinforced by a thousand actions. But when you sit still in concentration and say, "I can do without anything in this world," and then put that affirmation into action by will power, you will see that you have changed that thought and you are free. I do that every morning. I am completely detached from everything. As soon as I turn my back on this world, I see that Eternity is with me.

Third Stage of Detachment: The Transcendent Calmness of Superconsciousness

Now, the third stage is the most difficult. It is the ability to detach yourself at will from restless thoughts and the distractions of outer sensations, so you can enter the superconscious state consciously. One day in my school in India, God gave me a lesson about this. Whenever I sat to meditate, I used to hear the chatter of the boys at their sports and activities. Instead of meditating on God, I was meditating on all those sounds! But on this particular day I was very sleepy; and as I drowsed I found that the noise around me was not reaching me at all. Then I thought, "What is this? Here they are making so much noise and still I didn't hear it? That is the state I must have in meditation!" So I stopped thinking about the noise, and by withdrawing the life force from the senses consciously (not passively as in sleep) I sent my mind deep within to feel the joy of meditation. This is the way to conquer the bondage of the senses and environment.

When in very deep sleep you feel great joy, you have touched superconsciousness; but you are enjoying that state only semiconsciously. When you can bring that state at will, then you are in the real state of superconsciousness. I can enter that supernal transcendence instantly, at any time. It is not imagination. Superconscious bliss is the nature of God; and it is also your true nature as children of God.

Since ancient times, India has taught special methods of *pranayama* (life-force control) by which one can consciously attain superconsciousness. When I enter that state, joy bubbles over my consciousness. And beyond that are further states. When you feel that joy expanding from your little body through millions of miles, when you feel God's creative vibrations and light spread over the whole universe, then you are in an even higher state of consciousness. And why not? The radio can send sounds and pick up sounds from thousands of miles away, and so can your mind when you use its latent power. When you are aware of vast space, and transcendent peace spread over all that space—when you feel your consciousness encompassing all creation—that is called the Christ (or Krishna) Consciousness. But you won't understand what I am saying until you meditate more.

The Meditation Practice That Brings Contact With God and Fulfillment of All Desires

So don't let yourself remain restless. As soon as you sit to meditate, talk to yourself—command the body and mind to become calm. If I try to call New York without a telephone or radio broadcasting apparatus, I won't get in touch with the person I am trying to reach in New York. One has to have a transmitter, and one has to be sure that there is a receiver at the other end. God is an almighty radio, and man can get in tune with that radio of God's consciousness by removing the static of restlessness from his own mind.

Start by concentrating the mind deeply on the thought of love or joy or peace. Go on concentrating until your thought becomes absorbed in that feeling. When your thought process ceases and there is only the great feeling of peace or love or joy, and when you can absorb yourself in that feeling at will, then you have control of yourself.

When that feeling of peace or joy comes over you, mentally chant: "I and my Father are one." Repeat that again and again, broadcasting to Him with ever deeper concentration and devotion, until you feel that joy ever increasing. Then you know that you have tuned in your mental radio with the cosmic radio of God, and that God has responded to your prayer-broadcast.

If you have a desire, that is the time to ask for it. Feeling that consciousness of His presence in meditation, pray to Him: "Lord, grant me good health," or "Let me find peace," or "Fill me with Thy joy." And know that He will bring it to you. There is nothing that can prevent it from coming true. That is why Jesus said: "Have faith in God. For verily I say unto you, that whosoever shall say unto this mountain, 'Be thou removed, and be thou cast into the sea'; and shall not doubt in his heart, but shall believe that those things which he saith shall come to pass; he shall have whatsoever he saith."* This is a true statement.

Being made in God's image, we have all the power that God has; but that power man has not used. That power can only come when your mind is perfectly free from bodily attachments. But you don't make enough effort; you don't exercise patience and perseverance in meditation. Your mind can be compared to a glass of muddy water. If you let the glass stand for a long time, the mud will settle at the bottom of the glass and the water will become fairly clear. So when you sit down for a while to concentrate, your mind is muddy with restless thoughts. But if you sit long enough, repeatedly bringing the wandering mind back to the practice of meditation, you will see that all thoughts settle down; and in that stillness you will feel superconsciousness.

As soon as I sit still, I am calm; then I am just filled with that superconscious bliss. Every cell and every thought is dancing with that divine joy. When you feel that state, then you are in touch with God and you can create at will whatsoever you need.

All my desires have been fulfilled in that consciousness. The Lord gives to every persevering devotee complete satisfaction so that he is ready for the kingdom of God. That is what is meant by, "Seek ye first the kingdom of God; then all things else will be added unto you." You are not ready for the kingdom of God until you feel within the fulfillment of all desires and yearnings of the heart. Jesus had that complete satisfaction; that is why he was not susceptible to any worldly temptation, and told Satan, "Get thee behind me!"

Surrender to the Divine: The Highest Consciousness

If you want to see the power of God, you must practice silence and deep meditation at night. Never go to bed until you have attuned yourself to His consciousness. Now I don't have to meditate anymore; I am in that state all the time. If food comes, all right; if food doesn't come, all right. If people come to the classes, all right;

* Mark 11:22–24.

if no one comes, all right. Whether there is sickness or health, the inner state of mind remains the same.

In the beginning I used to pray for different things, but I pray no more, because I know that to pray is to doubt. Whatever He wants me to experience, it is my pleasure. Be it success, be it poverty, be it power, be it ill health, these are naught but the dream-delusions of life. God is with me through all of these dualities, and He is my haven. That state is the highest accomplishment. "Their thoughts fully on Me, their beings surrendered to Me, enlightening one another, proclaiming Me always, My devotees are contented and joyful."*

When you have found in your consciousness the joy of all joys, the satisfaction of divine happiness, all conditions of this world mean less than what you have within. You love the flowers, but you love the Power behind the flowers more. You love the joy of meeting people, but you love the joy of Spirit behind all people more. You realize that God is working through you—the Joy of joys, Beauty of beauties, Happiness of all happiness. When that consciousness shall possess your heart, you will find Him within and without, everywhere! That is the way to accomplishment through the superconsciousness.

Seek God Through Self-Realization

These teachings of Self-Realization provide you with definite techniques for improvement of body, mind, and soul. Why don't you try them? See if I am not telling you the truth. No material possession or accomplishment can give you that joy that I have found by following these teachings, and I want you also to have that joy divine. For I love you all, and I am here only to tell you of Him. All my sermons have one end—to give you the means to commune with God.

If I tell you about sugar but you don't taste it yourself, you won't rightly know what sugar is like. So it is with God. If you don't taste Him for yourself, you will never know what He is like. I am just here to tell you about Him that you may know He is real, and so that you make the effort to taste Him in deep meditation. You cannot know the sweetness of sugar by attending a thousand lectures on sugar; you must experience it. You cannot realize truth by hearing a thousand sermons, for truth must be cognized within yourself.

* Bhagavad Gita X:9.

My duty is to urge you to seek Him for yourself, so that you all become like Christ; for that is the true nature of your soul. "As many as received him, to them gave he power to become the sons of God." Receive that Infinite Consciousness! If you utilize your vast mind-power at night in meditation, the light of God will shine through you.

These great teachings are enumerated in weekly *Lessons* and are sent out all over the world. Our primary purpose is to give divine communion to everyone, and to remind them that God is the source of all power. You don't need to seek anything else; because when you find Him, you find everything else. We teach the techniques by which you can seek the Giver of all gifts. It is so simple. It is something that can be done by all. It is within the reach of all who will make the effort. Those who want to become a member and enjoy the ambrosia of these teachings, apply for the *Lessons*. When I see people who are taking a real interest in finding God, that is the greatest joy. And as long as I shall speak, I shall say, "Seek God within yourself." That is what India taught me, and that is why the Masters and Christ sent me here—that you may establish in your own consciousness a temple of Christ Consciousness, Krishna Consciousness, the unchangeable *Kutastha* Consciousness. Heaven and earth shall pass away, but nothing shall destroy those imperishable temples, in this life or in the beyond.

I used to give healings, but I found that after receiving healing of the body, people went away and forgot God. But as soon as you heal your soul you will have everything. So start now. Follow the teachings. Become a member. Help this cause of Self-Realization, and help yourself above all. If you study the teachings even theoretically you will know all there is to know about religion; and if you practice them, you will come to know God even as Christ knew Him.

May the Lord bless you, and I pray that you have the one desire to find Him. Worship the living God of Bliss, not the God of punishment and revenge. Worship the God who is templed in the flowers, heaving in the ocean, and who blesses and caresses you in the wind and in the sunshine. God will never forsake you. It is you who are running away from Him. Find Him within. You will behold this world as a dream. Many times I see it that way. Rouse yourself. Forget this dream delusion, for the world offers nothing but sickness and suffering, false security and happiness that is short-lasting. Break your limitations. Be ever awake in Him!

Awakening Will Power for Success and Divine Accomplishment

*January 25, 1935**

The purpose of human life consists in finding out what we really are. We can inquire what human life is because we are endowed with the faculty of reason. The distinctive difference between man and animal is that man has the ability to reason and inquire into the source and meaning of his existence, and of the existence of other forms of life. Yet many human beings behave more blindly than animals, going sheeplike to the slaughterhouse of death without ever having sought the answer to the mystery of life.

Whence did reason come? What is its source? It is intuition, the omniscient faculty of the soul, that fathers the faculties of reason and discrimination. We must daily recharge our reason and good judgment by contact with the soul through deep meditation if we are to achieve true success and fulfill the purpose of our earthly sojourn.

Difference Between "Wish" and "Will"

To wish and to will are different things. In this life we see that people are following many different paths to one common goal: all are seeking happiness. Some want money, some want health, others want fame, hoping that through these they will find happiness. Varied are the desires, but few persons have the will power to accomplish them.

And how desires come and go in the mind! Do you realize how many of them have found a place in your heart? Within every human being lies a great graveyard of unfulfilled desires. Desires that you feel cannot be fulfilled corrode the heart, and are really just "wishes." Sometimes you hear someone say, "I wish I were a

* Much of this talk was integrated into the *Self-Realization Fellowship Lessons* in the 1930s. In preparing it for publication in this volume of Paramahansaji's *Collected Talks and Essays,* unused material from the original talk, never before published, has been added.

king," or something equally unlikely. These are wishes that you know cannot be fulfilled. And not all people have the same desires. In the zoological garden of life roam all kinds of animals of desires; what interests one person doesn't necessarily have any attraction for someone else.

But remember this: To have a desire fulfilled, you must first have the power to fulfill it. A wish is a desire that you think cannot come true. Stronger than "wish" is "intention"—intention to do a thing or to satisfy some wish or desire. But "will" consists of desire plus energy—a motivating desire plus application of energy to bring that desire to fruition. Will means continuous, concentrated action until that desire is fulfilled.

How few persons actually will! Of course one should not use will power to perform wrong actions: that is a violation of the purpose of will within us, and brings us harm. Will should be guided by wisdom. Right desires, and will guided by wisdom, lead to ultimate fulfillment in God.

There is a difference between ineffectual desires and the kind of persistent longing that eventually materializes its object in reality. Desire involves a strong psychological wish; but longing connotes an unbearable, haunting desire that unfailingly gathers to itself the necessary force and knowledge with which to materialize itself. Therefore, dear friends, remember that you will not achieve merely by a series of wishes or desires. You will succeed by nurturing your worthy, wholesome desire into a heartfelt, undying longing; and then manifesting that longing in continuous, introspective, intelligent activity.

Why Do People Fail in Life?

Do you know why people fail? It is because they give up. I often say that if I had no job, I would shake up the whole world so that it would be glad to give me a job to keep me quiet. *You must exercise your will power*. If you make up your mind and go forth like a flame, every obstacle in your path will be consumed. The man of realization walks safely even where bullets fly, for the divine will is behind him.

Let me tell you a story: A and B were fighting. After a long time A—exhausted—said to himself: "I cannot continue any longer." But B thought: "Just one more punch, though I can hardly move." He gave it, and down went A.

If you think that you cannot go on any longer and then you make an extra effort, you will see that divine will begins to reinforce your will. When human will refuses to acknowledge its limitations, then it becomes divine will. Whenever you meet resistance, do not give up. If you go on exercising your will power, you will suddenly find that your will has become linked with divine will.

Rouse this will power from the sleep of ignorance. How can you develop it? Choose some objective that you think you cannot accomplish, and then try with all your might to do that one thing. When you have achieved success, go on to something bigger and keep on exercising your will power in this way. If your difficulty is great, deeply pray: "Lord, give me the power to conquer all my difficulties." You must *use* your will power, no matter what you are, or who you are. *You must make up your mind.* Use this will power both in business and in meditation. There is no greater enemy of your own happiness than yourself when you slouch through life with a paralytic will and an indifferent attitude.

Remember, the power of God's will is in all of you. But some persons are like diamonds and others are like coal. Persons of active will, like the sparkling diamond, make themselves receptive to the sunlight of God's omnipresent power of accomplishment and allow it to flow through them. Ordinary individuals of passive mentality make themselves like the dull piece of coal; the sunlight of God's all-accomplishing will, though shining on them, does not illumine their lives with brilliant achievements. Never let laziness or passivity obstruct your noble material and spiritual goals.

By Will Power, Charge Your Success Thoughts With Dynamic Force

Such will power lies within you that if you really put it to use there is nothing you could not accomplish. Will power has created everything—even your body. It is the will that leads you from one desire to another until with all your might you try to succeed in accomplishing your greatest desires. Rarely do people develop the true potentiality of will power! The will develops in man by normal evolutionary progress, but its evolution may be hastened by right thinking and acting.

Carrying a thought with dynamic will power means holding to it until that thought pattern develops dynamic force. When a thought is made dynamic by will force, it can create or rearrange the atoms into the desired pattern according to the mental blueprint you have created. When you continuously develop your will until its dynamic force manifests, you can heal others by your will power; you can say, as Jesus said to the leper, "I will; be thou clean."* You can control your destiny by will power; you can command a mountain, "Be thou removed, and be thou cast into the sea; it shall be done."†

How to Develop Your Will and Guide It by Wisdom

Many people think they should not use their own will power to accomplish what they desire, lest they interfere in some way with God's plan or the scheme of life. They passively accept that "this is how life is meant to be." It is a great mistake to believe you should not use your will; and in any case, that is impossible. In order not to use will power you would have to lie down and not move at all. If you move even a finger, you are using your will power. You must use will power even to eat. The only time your will power is inactive is when you are under chloroform or are otherwise rendered unconscious. When the power to will leaves the body entirely, one dies.

It is true that human will guided by ignorance is bad; it leads to error and unhappiness. But when human will is guided by wisdom to right actions, and thus tuned in with divine will, it then operates for our highest welfare and happiness. That is what Jesus meant when he said: "Thy will be done." God wishes us to tune in with divine will, that we may be guided by His wisdom to find the real fulfillment of all our desires, in Him.

Some people think that just by virtue of prayer God will listen to them and fulfill their desires. But this is laziness. It is necessary to exercise will power, to strive to tune it with the divine will. When your will revolves continually around one definite purpose, it becomes *dynamic* will. This is the quality of will power possessed by Jesus and by all other great sons of God.

The power behind your will is the will of God. This is the way to develop your will:

1. Before you will to do a thing, reason as to what you should do.
2. Make sure that you are directing your will toward accomplishing something good and helpful to yourself.
3. Pray to God to reinforce your will with His divine will.

* Matthew 8:3.

† *Ibid.* 21:21.

4. Exert your will through right action until you achieve your goal.

Don't be passive. Your will was given to you so that you may use it and become a conqueror. Remember, in your will is the will of God. It is His power that you use.

Your Development of Will Power Carries Over to Future Incarnations

According to the law of karma that governs all human actions, persons who have developed strong will find themselves the possessor of the same adamant will in their next incarnation. According to the law of cause and effect, the effect is equal to the cause. Thus it is good to develop will even to the last stage of life, for then it becomes a very powerful ally of accomplishment in the next life.

Therefore, my friends, see to it that each day you select one wholesome desire and use your will and reason throughout that day until you accomplish your goal.

Technique of Increasing Your Will Power Day by Day

In the morning, before you start working, select a particular longing that will improve your or your family's material, moral, or spiritual well-being; and try to accomplish it with bulldog tenacity and clever planning. Write it down and keep it with you throughout the day. If you can't accomplish it, owing to faulty methods or wrong environment, then seek expert advice. Compare your method and plan of action for that specific achievement with that of others who have demonstrated or proved better plans for action. Change your environment if necessary in order to accomplish your purpose. You, being the proud possessor of dynamic will, must never give up until "by hook or crook," as they say, you are able to obtain the desired results. In this way, as you achieve the completion of even a small but definite goal each day, you will gain more and more confidence in the power of your will and thus increase its accomplishing strength.

You will find most people fail to achieve the necessary necessities of material life, mental happiness, or God-realization because they don't employ the above-mentioned technique of developing will by accomplishing something noble and difficult every day. While thousands remain dreaming by the wayside, or become despondent and give up after a few unsuccessful tries at success, the individual of dynamic will continually moves along the path of success until the goal is reached. I have exercised this will and have accomplished much in this life. That will power shall come if you learn and practice the great truths of Yogoda, the Self-Realization Fellowship techniques.*

The Value of "Won't" Power

There is another factor in developing wisdom-guided will power. The saints say: "Do not be a slave to your senses. Let nothing control you. Your senses are given to serve you, not to be your tyrannical ruler." As soon as your discrimination points out that any sense enjoyment has become detrimental to your health or happiness, remember: that is a "sin" you must overcome by virtue. Virtue means that which bestows lasting happiness and well-being of body, mind, and soul.

In your efforts to govern your life by self-control, try to develop your "won't" power if you haven't yet enough will power. For instance, when you are at the dinner table and Mr. Greed lures you to eat more than you should, and tries to chloroform your self-control and cast you into the pit of indigestion, watch yourself. After partaking of the right quality and quantity of food, just say to yourself with firm resolve: "I won't eat any more," and get up from your chair at the table and deliberately walk away. It often seems difficult to exercise will power, but it is easy to develop won't power. Discrimination, not habit, should be the constant guide of our conduct; and the best antidote for bad habits is won't power.

The Highest Use of Will Power Is to Find God

In your heart you must love nothing more than God, who is a "jealous" God. If you want God, you must have the will to cast away from your heart every desire but the desire for Him. And if you really want God, nothing can touch you to deter you from that desire. Have only one desire: "May Thy love shine forever on the sanctuary of my devotion, and may I be able to awaken Thy love in all hearts." That is my only prayer. I don't even pray for my body. I don't want to enjoy God alone; I want to establish the consciousness of God in the hearts of all. So always remember that the greatest and highest use of will is to will for God alone. God is imperishable and with God everything good will come. Develop your will power. Turn your will power away from worldly desires; it is wasted on

* Taught in the *Self-Realization Fellowship Lessons.*

them. Look at this life as nothing but a dream. Make up your mind to will for God.

If you know that you have got to find God in order to satisfy soul-hunger within; and if you use your will power, then you will find Him. But God will not answer unless you know the law. Again and again you must fire the shells of your prayer and will power to break down the ramparts of God's silence. He is castled in silence, but if you send shell after shell of concentration and meditation, the walls will break and God's glory will burst forth.

When Lord Buddha sought illumination, he sat under a banyan tree and said:

Beneath the banyan bough
On sacred seat I take this vow:
"Until life's mystery I solve,
Until I gain the Priceless Lore,
Though bones and fleeting flesh dissolve,
I'll leave this posture nevermore."

Buddha succeeded in his divine quest. Such a will becomes one with the Divine Will.

That is the kind of will and determination that shall give you salvation. Give these teachings your undivided attention, and continuously cooperate with what I am urging you. Sincere souls who are really seeking God shall find Him who alone can satisfy the unslaked thirst and longings of our hearts. Many thousands have listened to my talks, but few have truly put into action what they have heard. Those who do shall find the mighty Truth—the Love and Glory Divine which is everywhere—manifesting through their consciousness evermore.

How to Smile Away Your Troubles

Self-Realization Fellowship Golden Lotus Temple, Encinitas, California, February 1, 1942

To say we can "smile away our troubles" may seem unrealistically simple. However, I do not mean just ignorantly smiling away at everything, blithely pretending no problems exist. Proverbial wisdom is that "ignorance is bliss"; but to be blind to our troubles until they catch us unprepared may be disastrous. The conquering smiles of which I am speaking are born of the realization that we are souls—eternal, immutable—made in God's image of immortal bliss. Our lives should continuously reflect that ever new joy. I never let anyone take away my inner happiness; and you too should learn that art of intrepid soul living which can smile away whatever troubles may come.

The Spiritual Purpose of Trials and Suffering

Through every trial we grow. All the suffering we experience has a meaning. Though it seems very cruel, it is like fire that smelts the iron ore: the steel that emerges from that furnace is beautifully strong, useful for many purposes. The steel of wisdom that we forge out of the searing fire of trials—that is something marvelous. The Lord is refining away the dross in us, so that we can live in this world as pure, steel-like souls, able to bend without breaking under the pressure of our difficult experiences. We should not lose sight of that truth. There is purpose behind everything that happens under the sun.

Every sorrow and hurt has brought me closer to God. When you behold someone whose face is grossly disfigured with anger and cruelty, it makes you eager to refrain from such ugliness in yourself. Wickedness and hatred desecrate the soul, like a black soot obscuring the divine image within. Hurtful behavior from others should stir in you an increased desire to improve yourself, to exercise more self-control. I have freely followed this principle in my life with rigid observance.

No one wants to be a psychological skunk, shunned by everyone wherever he goes. Be like the orange, which when squeezed exudes only sweetness. No matter how people attack you with ugly words or hatred, respond with kindness in your heart and speech. Sweetness of speech is a marvelous panacea, a magic power of soul magnetism. The way of a divine life is to be so secure in your determination to be good that no one can shake you from it. If in response to hateful behavior only soothing kindness flows from your soul, you will be continually refilled by an inflow of God's love, able to channel a divine flood of happiness to all. Apply that understanding to all troublesome trials, and each one will resurrect some dormant attribute of God's image within you.

Observe Yourself in the Mirror of Introspection

India's *rishis* from time immemorial have carefully analyzed the whole of human existence and advised people how to realize life's highest potentials. Psychology teaches you what you are; ethics tells you what you should be. The sages emphasized both as part of true religious training for spiritual unfoldment in body, mind, and soul.

Every day you look into a mirror to observe your face and body, because you want to look your best before others. Is it not even more important to look daily into the inner mirror of introspection, self-analysis, to insure the proper visage of that which is behind the superficial appearance? All outer attractiveness derives from the divinity of the indwelling soul. And as even a little pimple or scar on the face can spoil its beauty, so are there psychological disfigurements of anger, fear, hatred, jealousy, worry from the uncertainties of mortal existence, which mar the reflection of the soul. If every day you strive to free yourself from these defacements, the beauty of your inner being will shine forth.

By analysis we see that human troubles are threefold: those that afflict the physical body, those that attack the mind, and those that occlude the soul. Disease, old age, and death are the difficulties of the body. Psychological maladies invade through sorrow, fear, anger, unfulfilled desires, discontentment, hate, any fever of nervous excitation or mental cancer of emotional obsession. And the soul sickness of ignorance, which is the most injurious of all, is the underlying condition that makes possible all other troubles.

God Wants Us to Stop Misusing Our Freedom

If we could drive away ignorance from the hearts of nations, there would not be any more wars. Just think, if all the money that is being used to make bombs were allocated for peaceful purposes, so many of the troubles of the world could be washed away.* The enormous expense of war would be sufficient to clear out the slums, build new homes, feed and clothe the poor. Half of the diseases of the world could be eradicated. That is a fact. The Lord has provided enough food and materials to look after all of the peoples of the world peaceably. It is only man's selfish ignorance that causes war and its consequent sufferings, drawing even nonaggressive nations into the conflict.

We do not realize how concerned God is to see how man is misusing the freedom He has given to him. He wants individuals and nations to learn how to behave, to respect the territory-happiness of others, to observe the laws of brotherhood. I know no matter what happens, I could not take up a gun and shoot someone, for I behold God in all souls. If people only knew that glory of the Spirit which dwells in themselves and in all, how much better the world would be. But, instead, man has become more and more greedy for material power and possessions, putting into effect those wrong actions that generate aggression in his field of influence, and at the same time also gradually destroy his peace of mind and the harmony of his inner being.

It is not a simple matter just to smile away your troubles. Catastrophe can overtake you at any time so long as you remain in ignorance of your divine nature. The only true freedom lies in the consciousness of the soul. Analyze yourself and determine to what extent your soul-consciousness has been bound by the roots of ignorance. Real freedom is possible only when those roots are severed.

Persons suffering from obvious physical afflictions are quick to seek a cure; but ignorance and the psychological malignancies of bad mental habits—hatred, anger, jealousy, fear—insinuate themselves subtly into one's second nature, so most people don't even try to eradicate them. Even when treatment is applied, they are found to be very nasty and difficult to get rid of. A diseased psychological disposition erodes the health of not only the mind and emotions but the body as well. Likewise, one's mental make-up is affected by

* This talk was given during World War II. *(Publisher's Note)*

physical ailments, but these are easier to get at. However, even a healthy body and mind does not ensure happiness so long as there is ignorance of the soul's nature.

If You Are Unhappy, Try to Find Out Why

Day in and day out, year in and year out, most people are plagued with unhappiness. They don't know why they are unhappy, but they are. One's first priority therefore should be to learn to analyze oneself—to find out why he is all the time unhappy even though outwardly he seems all right and has a sufficiency to satisfy his needs. Happiness will elude him until that question has been answered.

Your natural state as a soul made in God's image is joy. If you are not really happy within, remember: there is something wrong with your spiritual health. As nonobservance of physical health laws invites into the body harmful agents of disease, so transgression of mental, moral, or spiritual laws infects you with psychological and spiritual troubles. These invisible enemies of your happiness are very pernicious. Do not ignore them; overcome them. Be the doctor of your soul. Dissect yourself psychologically and spiritually to determine where your trouble lies, and then remove and completely destroy the malignancies of bad habits and ignorance. As physical ailments can be cured by medical doctors who understand physiology and anatomy, so, like a spiritual doctor, you need to understand the workings of your inner being in order to know what you must do for yourself in consciously diagnosing and treating your psychological and spiritual ills.

The physical body is only an outer shell for your marvelous inner body of life and consciousness. Just as the physical body has a spine and nervous system, a brain, heart, hands, and feet, so also does your inner body. Reason or intelligence is your inner head; life force for sensory cognition and motor response is your inner nervous system; will is your inner hands and feet; and feeling is your inner heart. If your feeling is not working rightly—for example, if your emotions chronically get the best of you—you have spiritual heart trouble. If you sleepwalk through life like a mechanical man, lacking initiative to achieve, then you have paralysis of the will. If you are restless, irritable, never satisfied, then the life energy in your sensory nerves is overheated. And if your reason is sluggish—if you do things first and only afterward think about the consequences—then your inner brain is malfunctioning.

Applying Your Reason Rightly

Faulty reasoning is the cause of such troubles as the tendency to leap before you look. Many people jump into a marriage because two beautiful faces are attracted to each other; she wears a lot of make-up and he has a nice car, and so they marry. But after a time, they see the marriage was only between the rouge and the car; there was no union of hearts, minds, and souls. People are fooled into following paths of unhappiness because of faulty reasoning.

Reason is also often befogged by prejudices. If your reason is clear, you will not mistake your preconceived likes and dislikes for discernments of truth. Be calm all the time and avoid excitable emotionalism, which brings on faulty reasoning. When reason goes awry, you are liable to do nothing or anything—and painfully regret it later.

In order to be happy, reason must be used rightly. For instance, if in a household the wife every day has to be nagged by the husband to do this or do that in order to keep the house clean, and she says, "Oh, you just want to pick on me," that is false reasoning. Likewise, if the husband neglects his share of the up-keep duties, and every day the wife brings to his attention that he should wash the windows, fix the screens, mow the lawn, and he too says, "Oh, you just want to pick on me," that is false reasoning. You must find out what your faults are. See if you deserve the reminders, the so-called naggings, of your husband or your wife. If either of you feel that you have too many duties to do—that you neglect some of them because you are being run ragged—the best thing is to sit down and analyze your life and begin to cut out those things that can reasonably be eliminated. In other words, live more simply so that you can balance your life and have more time for other worthwhile pursuits that bring satisfaction and happiness. Most people take on too much work, thereby leaving no time to enjoy anything. Having too much to do, they can't do anything willingly and they can't do anything well.

When you learn to think deeply about whatever confronts you, you can find the solution to any problem. Why? Because your mind is a receptacle of the Infinite Mind. It doesn't cost you anything to learn to think deeply, but it costs much if you don't. Day and night people in all branches of life are acting from ignorance—children as well as grown-ups. Sooner or later those wrongdoings bring inharmonies, nervousness, all manner of unhappiness. You see nice rich food and you say, "Well, I know I shouldn't eat it, but I can't control myself." And hours later you are sick; and oft repeated, chronic illness sets in. Wouldn't you have been happier had you thought ahead and exercised a little self-control? Or someone is mean to you, and so to pay them back you treat them with even greater meanness. Is that not faulty reasoning? Just because someone else is angry, or spiteful, why should you inflict that psychological disease on yourself? It makes no sense. No matter what ugliness we see in others, there is no reason to act in like manner.

How necessary it is to analyze why you behave the way you do. Some people are filled with fear; they have made it a chronic habit. They nurture fear every day; and therefore their days are miserable with worry and anxiety. What is the logic of it? We are all going to die one day. It only happens once, and when it happens it is all over with. Then why be afraid of it? Why die every day through fear? When you learn to reason clearly, you discover that so many of your everyday attitudes and actions are foolish; the unhappiness they create is totally unnecessary.

I remember when I was a little child I loved to make images out of mud. Mother used to scold me for getting dirty. But how I loved to do it! When I was older, that childhood enjoyment seemed foolish. That is the way with lots of people who are mentally and spiritually immature: They love to muddy their minds with misunderstanding, and do not want that mud removed. Often they become furious if anyone tries to help them see how unseemly it is. It is impossible for them to understand because they never look in their psychological mirror to see their faults reflected there. Far better it is to clean away your mental and spiritual dirt, so that when others look at you they see the marvelous soul that you are.

Introspection Changes Us Immediately

It is heartbreaking to see people remain the same year after year. Why is it that they do not improve themselves? Because they do not take time to think. As soon as you learn to think introspectively you change right then and there. You have dissociated yourself from your faults and recognized them instead of pretending they do not exist. In that instant a change takes place. Even the desire to be good—to correct yourself—means you have changed.

Spiritual growth is invisible. That is why you may think you have not progressed, unless you have kept a record in your mental diary. Each solar year brings you a certain evolution; if your development were put in figures, you would see how much you are changing. But it requires millions of refinements in your inner being before your soul can be fully liberated in God.

Once I asked a great saint if it were possible to get to God. He replied, "Even the thought of wanting God changes you." If you nurture that singlehearted desire, nothing can stop you from attaining. Even those who have done no more than listen willingly to my words have begun to progress. Some people deliberately go to sleep on the way; that is different. But as long as you have that fervor of willingness, all the shackles of habits and evil will not be able to hold you. So learn to analyze yourself strictly. Don't spare yourself. Cure your mentally paralyzed will.

Think and plan your life, and see how you will change. Try constantly to improve yourself. Seek out good company, company that reminds you of God and of the noble things in life. Be conscious every day of how you are going to change your bad habits; how you are going to schedule your day; how you are going to hold your calmness. And every so often inwardly ask, "Lord, am I wasting my time? How can I get a little free time every day just to be with You?" All the time I say that. And He responds, "You are with Me, for you are thinking of Me."

Start the morning in meditation and praying deeply to God; and after you have meditated, ask God to guide your life and all your noble efforts: "Lord, I will reason, I will will, I will act; but guide Thou my reason, will, and activity to the right thing I should do in everything." Determine to be better in every way that day. If you start in the morning and keep on working at trying to hold on to your calmness, or trying to put into effect some good habit that you want to acquire, thinking of God all the time, then when night comes you can go to sleep knowing that you have put the day to good use. You will know you are making progress.

So think and make plans for success before you do anything. Of course, some people think too much and don't act in the end. Do not be like that. Act sincerely with a determined will according to your thinking. The pledges that I make for myself I carry out before I urge you to follow them. I never have missed morning and evening Energization Exercises, not even one day, since long ago promising myself to be regular in my practice. That kind of resolve is what gives you the conquering power to smile under all circumstances—not the smile of the hypocrite, but the real, sincere smile that comes from your soul. When that smile fills your heart, you will always see how foolish it is to act unwisely.

Happiness Requires a Clear Conscience

Smiling away your troubles requires a clear conscience that harbors no insincerity. It touched me deeply when my dear friend Luther Burbank told his acquaintances: "Swami Yogananda could never deceive anybody." So must you also be like that: By your continuous right behavior, your eyes become so spiritually clarified that everybody can see in them the sincerity of your soul.

Insincerity is never necessary. However, you cannot speak everything to everyone. When you offer guidance to some people they seem invariably to misunderstand your words. To that kind it is best to say nothing; just remain quiet. It is not always safe or wise to tell people when they are wrong; you will only invite trouble. But never be insincere with anyone. If a person is bad, you don't have to tell him he is bad; you don't have to say he is good, either. Unless it is your beholden duty, it is better to say nothing.

Never try to deceive others. If you do not want to tell something, remain silent. But do not dissemble. And hold steadfast to your word. If you say you are going to do something, you should stand behind your promise. Your word should be your bond—redeemable like gold.

Your life is a battleground between the beautiful qualities of your soul and their tenacious enemies of ugly behavior. The battles are fought every day in your interactions with others. The most immediate take place in your own home—you must win the friendship and the love of your family through the sincerity of your soul. I remember in my family, except for my parents, I was like an outcast because I didn't see as they did. But I held no resentment, silently pursuing my supreme love for God. Eventually they one by one became my disciples.

From today on, cultivate sincere goodwill in your heart. Harm no one. Never engage in trickery. Think no mean or jealous thoughts toward anyone. Tell yourself that you need nothing outward in order to be happy; and no matter what happens, say that you can get along just the same. That is a great art and a wonderful way to live. When you are with others, let them see on your face a real smile that is noble and calm and gentle. Guard in your heart that treasure of your smile. Do not make a showy display before others of how much happiness you have inside. When you meet someone who wants to know you, then put on a warm smile of sincerity; otherwise, be reserved. But with those who are in tune with you, share that happiness from your heart.

Learn to Smile From the Depths of Your Being

It is when you know yourself as the soul that you can smile away your troubles. The best way is to think deeply, analyze yourself and your true goals, and act accordingly with joyous anticipation regardless of setbacks. Schedule your life; instead of giving importance to unimportant things, give greatest importance to cultivating through daily soul-awakening meditation your relationship with God and your inner happiness. When you are in the perfect calm of soul awareness, you see God moving in all creation. You do not see the world anymore as a nightmare of troubles, but as an entertaining spectacle to be enjoyed. Then you shall smile from the depths of your being, a smile that can never be destroyed.

Play your role in the drama of this world, but do not be worried or fearful. The show will go on; your part is to make the best of each day. You are in school, and the Lord is the teacher. You have many lessons to learn, and He does not want you to fail in any of them. So no matter how many times you have faltered, if you keep on trying you are bound to succeed. If you have given up trying to change, then you yourself have decreed your own failure. Never cease striving to pass all tests, knowing that with each one you are earning the diploma of God's eternal pleasure.

If you study these teachings you will know everything about practical religion—the science of dispelling every form of sorrow. And if you put the teachings into practice, you will be on the way to becoming master of yourself. You will be able to smile from your heart with the joy of your soul that will vanquish your troubles.

How to Get Out of Mental Ruts

Self-Realization Fellowship Golden Lotus Temple, Encinitas, California, July 14, 1940

Our paramount duty while on earth is to change our status from that of a mortal being to that of a divine being. But this world is replete with alluring playthings—shiny material toys that attract our attention—and myriad are the ways in which our thoughts and behavior are routed into constricting channels of desires. Unless guided by wisdom, we get caught in these delimited tracks and cannot move ahead in soul progress. It is only when we regard the pursuit of the Divine as foremost among all our desires that we find the route that leads to lasting happiness.

Analyze Your Progress in Life: Are You in a Rut?

If you are traveling along a dirt road and your automobile gets stuck in the mud, it takes skillful driving—and perhaps a tow truck!—to free your car from that rut. Likewise, mankind gets stuck in mental ruts; and how to get out of them is a subject that needs our attention.

All of you should periodically analyze your progress in life to see if you are in a rut. First, ask yourself what kind of road you are driving on. Are you traveling a smooth, bright highway that will take you surely to your life's destination? Or are you traveling the hazardous, muddy back roads of evil or wrong behavior? If you are moving along a good path of right actions, maybe the car of your life will not get caught in ruts. Yet even then there is a chance that you are not steering properly. If you are too sure of yourself and carelessly take your eyes off the road, you can veer off course and into a rut by the wayside.

On any pathway in mortal life one can get mired in ruts; they are present everywhere to catch man's consciousness. Some channel your feelings into compulsive anger; some keep you stuck in a mindset of pessimism or despondency; other ruts may hold you in fixed habits of avarice or jealousy or being overly critical, and so forth. And the tragedy is that throughout one's life, a person may think he is progressing when in fact he is firmly stuck in a rut. Just as when a car gets bogged down in mud or sand, and the driver steps on the accelerator, making the wheels spin rapidly, but the car remains in the same place—that is the condition of many persons. Even though their engine of life is running, their wheels are spinning uselessly. The progress and growth of such persons is negligible. They think they have grown up because their body has matured, but their brain, their mind, their attitudes remain stationary—psychologically and spiritually immature.

There are so many detrimental habits that hold you back. Anytime you are compelled against your will to do something evil or harmful, remember, you are in one of the mental ruts of mortal delusion. How to get out of them? Analyze yourself. Introspect to see if you have progressed in any undertaking that you have set your mind upon. Ask yourself in what ways you are in ruts. Practice this review at least once a week, keeping a mental diary. The best way to see yourself is to look through the eyes of conscience: "Have I become more peaceful? Have I become more understanding? Have I become more tolerant? Have I become more loving toward others?" Your friends and relatives may pigeonhole you, saying that you are such-and-so kind of person and always will be. But do not believe them. You can be anything you want to be. You will be surprised to see how life can be changed for the better if you develop the will-to-accomplish attitude.

Mental ruts are fearsome enemies of progress. Man becomes "hard-boiled," absolutely fixed, in his accustomed ruts. He becomes so bound by them that he cannot move onward. That is one reason the Lord has set a limit on the term of mortal life. When one's car of life has become completely bogged down with disease or the disillusionments of old age, so that no further progress can be made, that is when God says it is time to walk away from that no-longer-useful bodily vehicle; so death comes as a blessing. No matter how ossified the mind has become in limiting mental ruts, at the end of life God says to everyone, "Come on, I will give you a fresh start in a new body."

The Purpose of Death in the Soul's Journey

Every hundred years all humanity is taken from the earth. But the inevitability of death should not make us feel hopeless—a mental rut into which most people fall. To them, life often seems so meaningless. They do not see the silver lining behind the cloud.

They do not see the purpose of the darkness of night as helping us to appreciate more the light of the sun. In the same manner, death comes as a reminder to appreciate and make the most of each moment of the life we have been given.

Death seems very cruel when one by one our dear ones and loving friends are snatched away from us. But even when thus confronted with the brevity of life, most persons are apt to remain complacent in the consciousness that their own life will go on forever! This mental rut of false mortal security makes us ignore the fact that all too soon our life will be gone; and so we had better make progress now, gathering a goodly store of self-improvement we can take with us beyond the portals of death.

Death is not the end of life; the soul's journey continues through reincarnation. The effects of your good as well as your bad actions travel with you as subtle tendencies. But if you remembered your past existences, you would not try to improve. The knowledge of all your errors and sufferings of former lifetimes would be so discouraging that you would give up immediately. From that perspective, forgetfulness of previous lives is a blessing. Forgetfulness comes as a sort of panacea and soothing elixir that frees the consciousness from the lacerations and sufferings of past experiences. The Lord is so forgiving and so wonderful that He gives everyone a chance to have a new beginning. That is why I love little children. When I see them running about with new hopes, new excitement, I see that God has given them a fresh start. They have gotten out of their ruts of past incarnations and have come back again with new courage to make another effort.

Children start out on life's path without any obvious prejudices or well-worn channels of habit. But as they grow older, you see the influences of their innate tendencies and of their family and environment forming their thoughts and personalities into mental ruts. Just observe how every person's face is different, reflecting their own unique pattern of mental ruts. If you analyze them, you can easily recognize those ruts. But most important is to analyze yourself.

Are You a Psychological Antique?

You can find out if you are in mental ruts by comparing your life now with what it was ten years ago. I have seen some people, and I am sure you have too, who are today exactly what they were decades ago—no change, no development of their potential. I call such persons "psychological antiques." Year after year they remain the same, bound by certain traits.

You can see this even in some persons who have good training and worthwhile habits and characteristics. They get up at a certain time each morning, work in a certain way, go to bed at a certain time; their lives are organized. But they can also become antiques if they are not moving with the progressive opportunities of the times. Those who have wonderful traits must keep the car of life moving, avoiding mental ruts that preclude advancement, such as saying, "Well, this is what I am, and this is what I shall remain." Or, "What was good enough for my parents is good enough for me." Still, it is beneficial to take good ideas and values from our parents and from the older generations. Look for the best traits in people and apply them in your own life, in a continuous effort to improve yourself.

When you settle into doing the same ordinary things every day, life becomes more or less mechanical. You get used to it, no matter how nice everything is. But eventually you will feel an inner prompting from the soul to get free from that stagnant routine of thought and activity. That is why vacations are good; they are necessary. Vacations on which you can be alone are wonderful. If you want to have a really beneficial vacation, arrange at least some time when you can be by yourself. Do not be with even your nearest and dearest during all of your vacation, because constant association with those who have their own mental ruts makes it more difficult to break out of your mechanical way of life.

Practical Advice for Getting Out of Mental Ruts

There is an art to getting out of mental ruts. Sit in a quiet place away from everybody and talk quietly with yourself. Think about the ways in which you can make your life more worthwhile and interesting, ways to improve yourself. The very best way is to develop a deeper relationship with God by practicing His presence more in your life. It is not necessary to talk to others about what you are doing. Just inwardly be with God. He is the Source of all peace, all happiness. He is ever new joy. By getting to know Him, your life will no longer be dull and boring. There will always be new thoughts of inspiration flowing into your consciousness.

When you see people who are "psychological furniture," never showing any positive change in their nature, you think: "I don't want to be like them!" I used to know someone in Boston like that. She was a wonderful soul, very refined and intelligent. But she had certain negative characteristics. She would dwell on the same fears, react with the same negative ideas and peculiarities, that she held fifteen years before. Don't be like that. Do not become desiccated with negation. You want to be vibrantly alive, not a dead stump! If you take an old rose bush, for instance, and prune off all of the dead wood, water it, and care for it, gradually life force begins to flow up through the bush, and little leaves start to come out. And then as the sunlight pours over the bush, magnificent blossoms appear. With proper tending, it continues to grow and flourish, entertaining us with its beauty and fragrance. You can be like that. Rid yourself of all of the old habits that have paralyzed your progress and made you feel useless. Continuously grow leaves and blossoms of new experiences, new qualities, new improvements in body, mind, and soul.

When the winter of trials comes, some leaves of life fall away. This is normal. It doesn't matter. Take it in your stride. Say, "Never mind, summer is coming, and I shall blossom forth again." God has given inner strength for the tree to survive the harshest winters. You are no less endowed. The wintertimes of life come not to destroy you, but to stimulate you to fresh enthusiasm and constructive effort, which will blossom forth in the spring of new opportunities that come to everyone. You must say to yourself, "This wintertime of my life shall not last. I will get out of the grip of these trials, and I shall throw out new leaves and blossoms of improvements. And once more the bird of paradise shall sit on the branches of my life."

If you find, for example, that you are afflicted with nervousness or digestive trouble or some other stress, do something constructive about it. Even if you suffer for a little while, it will be all right if you don't get into a rut of helplessness. Chronic disease is a form of mental rut that you think you can never get out of. Your mind must not accept any suggestion of sickness or limitation. Naturally, it is unrealistic to think that the body will remain the same always; it can be kept well for a long time, but eventually it will age and weaken. This does not mean your mind must succumb. The mind must be kept free.

When you look at your body it may appear to be old. But close your eyes and look within to your real Self, and you will see that you are Spirit. There is no death, no old age, no material circumscriptions when you close your eyes to the outer shell of life and open your inner eye of the soul. You are pure Spirit. Every night in the freedom of deep sleep you actually behold yourself as such, for you have no form, no weight of the body, no consciousness of being a man or woman or any fixed type of personality. Wakefulness is the overarching mental rut. Controlling that state extricates one from the bondage of material life. Sleep is an unconscious respite; and its effects are temporary. The transcendent silence of deep meditation is the only way to release your consciousness permanently. Through meditation, you learn to retain conscious inner freedom all the time.

When the day is done, sit quietly in meditation and briefly analyze the day's activities. Then mentally make the affirmation, "I am free from all ruts, from all thoughts and experiences that have limited me. My mind is resting in the blissful, boundless peace of God." What happiness comes over one during such periods. No words can describe that joy. But most people do not make the effort. Their priorities are pursuit of material things. And they think they are living because their heart is beating and breath is flowing. But that is not living; that is merely existing. Their wheels of accomplishment have been caught in sandy ruts on the road of life. If you are in that state, put forth a sudden burst of extra power from within, so that the car of your life can jump out of the rut onto the free-flowing highway of steady progress. Then you can rumble along smoothly, avoiding further ditches of distractions, until you come to the vast, beautiful scenery of perceptions of God—of happiness, peace, tranquility—and you can rest there. That vista is real. It is not imagination. But to get there you must enter the deep silence produced by meditation. In that inner stillness, free of mortal thoughts, you will see that your soul is out of all mental ruts.

Do not be in a hurry when you meditate. Relax. Do not be tense with pressure to finish your meditation quickly and get back to your material duties. Set aside, for instance, one hour for silence. And during that period, forget time and go deep. You will have divine peace, divine joy. But if you are focused on the thought, "I have only one hour to spend," then your mind restlessly anticipates the passage of time instead of experiencing the blessings of inner calmness. During that one hour just relax mentally and surrender yourself to the infinite silence, forgetting time and all extraneous thoughts, and you will begin to experience the wonders of divine consciousness.

I remember the discipline my Master [Swami Sri Yukteswar] gave me when I used to visit his ashram in Serampore during my college years. When the time drew near for me to depart in order to catch the train back to Calcutta, my mind became nervously focused on the clock. My Guru knew my mental state; but as though oblivious of it, he refrained from giving me leave to go. One day he said to me: "Either you come here and don't worry about your train time, or don't come at all!" What wonderful training! He had made me miss many trains until I learned the lesson that my restlessness was not necessarily helping me catch trains, but rather taking from me a part of the blessing of being in Master's presence. When I controlled my concentration, matters greatly improved.

The Ultimate Purpose of Existence Is Attainment of God

Why are you always in a hurry? Why are you always in a mental state of worry or fear or anger? Get out of these ruts. Lead a different life, a more peaceful life, a spiritual life.

If you are making progress in anything, material or spiritual, that exercises your will power and initiative; you are getting out of some mental ruts. But if you think that life's purpose is anything other than the attainment of God, you are deeply entrenched in the consciousness of mortal existence. The wise individual does not put anything before God. He realizes that God is the ultimate goal. He may live in the world and carry on many duties, but does not delude himself into thinking they are more important than his duty to God.

Suppose I thought that the organization was so wonderful that I spent all my attention and time serving it, yet forgetting God. This would be gross neglect of my supreme duty to Him; and without Him I would have nothing of lasting value to give to you. The other day I was starkly reminded that nothing of this world is ours forever. I visited a certain ashram whose spiritual teacher had passed on, leaving behind his ashram and all of the things that he had used. And I knew the same thing would one day happen to me. I suddenly felt very much saddened, not for myself or those whose lives are anchored in God, but for the masses of the world who hanker and hope in the mental rut of false security. For at the time of death they suffer terribly, when all the earthly belongings and achievements they consider "security" are wrested away in an instant. But, forgetful of the past, they will have a fresh chance to fulfill their deep-rooted desires. They reincarnate with those desires embedded within them. Even as little children, these hidden desires begin to develop as interests and ambitions: "When I grow up I am going to be this or I am going to be that." God gives everyone repeated opportunities to fulfill their desires by working them out—if not in one life, then in lives to come—until all have been satisfied. But the unfortunate reality is that no fulfillment of any material desire will give complete satisfaction. Thus millions waste their time in this respect. And at the end of life, each one is rudely confronted with this realization.

On the other hand, it is better to be actively ambitious in any direction than to be idle, for the lazy individual is misusing his God-given talents. If you are in the rut of idleness, you have lost yourself. To be idle, to be mentally lazy, is to be dead before one dies. Those who are creatively active avoid mental ossification. But in all your activity, do not get caught in the mental ruts of attachment, material desires that lead to disillusionment. All ambition should revolve around the ultimate purpose of existence: to find God.

See how God is manifest in everything! Look at the beautiful earth, and how nature keeps it in balance—how there is a plan, an Intelligence behind everything in creation. After the patterns of nature had been created, God created man to appreciate this earth. But see how poorly we have taken care of it. We have failed miserably. God made all men as brothers, but they have become blinded by narrow social and national self-interest. Loyalty to one's heritage and country is noble, but the wrong kind of fealty and patriotism creates prejudicial mental ruts that lead to brother fighting brother. War comes; thousands are killed; and then peace is established and men become brothers again for a little while. Then humanity again falls into the rut of greed, of selfishness, of intolerance; and more war is the result.

There are many good families in which children grow up never quarreling among themselves. And there also are many, many families wherein everyone fights one another; and those who are quarrelsome can never be convinced of the beautiful way of peace. But those who are always calm and understanding do not fall into the rut of fighting. Life has become good for them. If only this could be learned by our world family!

A Comparison of East and West

When I look at my many years in America, I feel such joy. At times it seemed extremely difficult, almost impossible to go on. But one thing I am most happy about, that no one could take away my peace, my happiness, my friendship. The unkind things done by others aroused in me greater desire to give love to those who were hateful. When I have witnessed unfriendliness, it has strengthened my desire to be friendly to all. When I have seen anger and greed and misunderstanding, it has given me a firmer desire to forgive and to be calm and peaceful. I have always looked at myself through the eyes of conscience, for eyes of conscience are the eyes of God in man. And I have been happy beyond the wealth of kings. Why? Because I refused to get into adverse mental ruts.

When I returned to India in 1935 some critics initially thought I had become Westernized. But I said, "Why not? I have taken what is good of the ideals of America." But I was not attached to it. I again put on my simple cotton robes such as are worn by monks in India, and often went without shoes and so on, just as I had done during my early years in India before I came to America. Then one night, when I was scheduled to give a public lecture, I found that all my cotton robes were soiled, and I had only the silk robes I used when traveling and lecturing in the West. I had not worn them in India, lest it appear extravagant. Sure enough, the next morning two newspapers came out criticizing my silk robe, stating that Swami is setting a bad example in India.

My friends came forward and said, "You must explain things to these newspapermen and set the record straight!" I said, "No, they are right." So for the next day's lecture I put on my old stained cotton robe. I didn't do it for effect, but because it was right. And then I told the audience this story: In New York in 1923, when I appeared before an audience of thousands wearing the cotton gown I wore in India, they derided me and said I was wearing a nightshirt. But when I began to wear robes of silk (as my Guru had foreseen years before),* their attitude changed—they respected this apparel as appropriate for a spiritual teacher. See how life is? See how rooted in ruts customs are?

Here in America you want to trade in your automobile for a new model every few years. If a businessman drives an outdated car, people think he must be a failure and they don't give him their business. Change has become a necessary condition of life here. These changes in cars are not considered a luxury for you, but an economic practicality; however, in India it would be considered

* "It was a sunny Thursday, I remember, in July 1915, a few weeks after my graduation from college. On the inner balcony of his Serampore hermitage, Master dipped a new piece of white silk into a dye of ocher, the traditional color of the Swami Order. After the cloth had dried, my guru draped it around me as a renunciant's robe.

"'Someday you will go to the West, where silk is preferred,' he said. 'As a symbol, I have chosen for you this silk material instead of the customary cotton.'

"In India, where monks embrace the ideal of poverty, a silkclad swami is an unusual sight. Many yogis, however, wear garments of silk, which retains certain subtle bodily currents better than cotton."—*Autobiography of a Yogi,* chapter 24 unnecessary. To live there in a perceived luxurious way is generally frowned upon. So every country has its national mental ruts. The different nations of the earth need to learn from each other to get out of their particular negative ruts that prevent all-round progress.

People of the East traditionally have not placed undue importance on material progress. The spiritual expressions of their culture, wherein they are not too much troubled by outward things, are good. But their lack of balance is a mental rut that has caused them much suffering.

Here in the West I see a horror of pesky insects and of enduring weather extremes of heat or cold without some artificial intervention. It is wonderful to see how clean your homes are here in America. In fact, I think the Americans may be the cleanest people in the world! I admire that spirit that wants to make life better and progressive; but on the other hand, to be so affected by external circumstances that one loses one's peace of mind is a sure indication of being stuck in a mental rut. When all your time is spent in looking after your material comfort and possessions, you forget to cultivate happiness in your heart.

Manifest Your Divinity by Leaving All Mental Ruts Behind

To remain in any rut—material or spiritual—is to make life static and miserable. How dare you, as a child of God made in His image, go on in the same stilted, mechanical way! There are redwood trees that were present in the time of Christ and are still alive today. But merely to live long, even in good health, is not the measure of a successful life. We are not mindless trees. Man is God's greatest creation, unique beings, capable of continuously growing divine qualities until he expresses all the perfect qualities of his godly image. Man has the power to expand his consciousness to the farthest reaches of eternity and spread the spiritual glow of his life over the entire cosmos. Then he has attained the Self-realization that God intended for him.

Striving to manifest that divine image is the real way to live—not to be bound by nationality, race or sex, disease or weakness, or any other limitation of mortal consciousness. Every day in deep meditation, close your eyes and affirm: "I am out of all ruts. I am not a man nor a woman. I am pure Spirit. I am a child of God, and like an ever-growing perfect plant of divinity, I will continue growing and flowering until I permeate the whole universe with the fragrance of soul qualities."

I have had everything that I ever wanted, but I find that all material things are cumbersome. Whatever has come to me, all the places that I have built, the ashrams here and in India, I have no attachment to them. The only joy that I find is when I close my eyes and go into that state of ecstasy of the Infinite. That is the real happiness. I had a desire long ago for a little hermitage by the sea, but I gave that desire to God. And when I was in India, He arranged for this beautiful place here in Encinitas to be given to us. I had nothing to do with it. It was given as a surprise. How great and good God is!

So remember, all the things that I tell you here on Sundays are the result of my own direct experience with God. I do not come here to lecture to you. In fact, I seldom prepare for these Sunday services. When I entered the hall this morning, I didn't know one word of what I was going to say to you. But when I commune with Him, He tells me everything to say. All these teachings of Self-Realization have been recorded as they have been given to me by God. Real Christianity teaches one to be like Christ. To show you how to attain that universal consciousness is why this great work of Self-Realization has come here. It teaches how, through your own self-effort, you can know God. You cannot get to God just by listening to sermons. You have to know how to commune with Him, and that is a consummate art—how to connect your body and your mind with God in meditation. All these things are taught in the weekly studies from Self-Realization Fellowship.

The more you learn to live in the thought of God, the more you will free yourself from all ruts of fear and anger and unhappiness and disease and death. Speed ahead on the smooth highway of right behavior, right thinking, and meditation that leads to God. Keep on, until you come to the land of the rising sun of joy—of peace, of happiness, of inner strength that can never be taken away.

God-Communion: Man's Greatest Necessity

A talk at the second anniversary celebration of Self-Realization Fellowship Golden Lotus Temple, Encinitas, California, January 7, 1940

War results from selfish patriotism, which does not recognize the kinship of all humanity under the Fatherhood of God. Hence, the preaching of universal religious principles of our oneness in God and the fostering of the ideal of a United States of the World are extremely necessary. It is because of man's ignorance of his divine nature and his lack of spiritual balance that nations are using engines of war to destroy one another. This is why the world's greatest necessity is God-communion, which brings understanding that we are all His children.

In Communion With God, We Realize We Are All One

As I have told you before, the metaphysical cause of this war [World War II] is to bring about the freedom of India, China, Africa, and all the downtrodden nations. After this war you will see greater unity of spirit among followers of the different religions, greater intellectual and spiritual exchange between the races. You will see the dawn of a new expression of the universality of Spirit.

Wars are not engendered by God, misunderstandings are not the fault of God; they are caused by the Evil Force, which foments evil actions in unthinking men. Therefore we must consciously and continuously cooperate with the divine principles of goodness, by which every nation can be brought together under the name of God.

The world will never be united in the material sense of the sameness of all nations, as some may think. There is a reason why God has made the potential of differences among His children of various races and nations: to prod mankind toward greater understanding of the soul unity beneath the outward diversity. That is what will bring a true United States of the World. It is unity in spirit, and acting in harmony with God's universal principles, that is necessary. In actual communion with our common Father, we realize we are all one. When we have fellowship with God, we feel fellowship with all people.

This last Christmas at Mt. Washington, I was so deeply touched to see how everybody—each one coming from a different background—was like one family. That is the spirit I hope you will always keep in our Self-Realization ashram centers, as an example to the world—appreciating the basic unity of religions, the unity of races, the unity of minds in wisdom. We must look beneath the waves of our thoughts and differences into the ocean of Spirit and Truth that underlies our individuality.

Truth is One. All religions should band together against our common enemy, ignorance—and the worst form of ignorance is hatred. I love Self-Realization Fellowship, and am loyal to it as my own; yet I have called this Golden Lotus Temple a "temple of all religions." In Self-Realization Fellowship we revere the great saints of all paths, while following faithfully our own path. Each of you can be a messenger of unity among religions and harmony among nations—wherever you go speak of the fatherhood of God and the brotherhood of man and the coming United States of the World. This concept of a united world was written by me years ago in my *Whispers from Eternity.* Now this idea is being seriously talked about.

This World Will Always Have Imperfections

This world will always have some defects. No matter what wonderful methods are discovered to benefit the human race, this material world will never be completely safe for mankind. Though Jesus could perform miracles of feeding five thousand with a few fish and loaves of bread, and even raising the dead, still he had to suffer for doing good. He showed by his powers that everything is of God, and when we cultivate that transcendent consciousness of Spirit we gradually go beyond all superficialities and realize the One Reality underlying all outer manifestations. That is the only way we can be happy, the only time we can really consider ourselves safe and secure—in sorrow or pleasure, in health or illness, in life or death, in all dualities of existence. We should not expect perfection from ever-changing material conditions, but realize that it is the Father alone who can give lasting happiness.

Suppose you are dreaming that you have a terrible disease and you see someone else in your dream who is strong and healthy. Then you see that you are poor and hungry while someone else has plenty. While you are dreaming, your pain and hunger are real; but when you wake up you smile with relief. So it is with this dream world we live in. I am seeing this all the time. Outwardly I have to contend with the limitations of the body and material existence in order to work for the Father in this dream world of *maya;* but in the inner wakefulness of God-awareness I am ceaselessly enjoying the bliss and unconditioned freedom of Spirit.

All the dualities of this world are the tests of God. He wants us to wake up from the illusion of mortal life, to rise to consciousness of our immortality. Even saints are tested; they have to undergo many trials. Read the life of Saint Francis—how he suffered even while he was healing others, but he never prayed to God for his own healing. Every night he saw Jesus Christ. He was born with sensual habits, but still he rose to sublime heights by his complete surrender to God.

God Is Moved Not by Our Praise, but by Our Love

It is not the ability to perform miracles that makes a saint. Such feats do not impress God; He is performing miracles all the time in everything in this intricate and marvelous creation. He is interested only in the love of those who love Him. To make your heart pure with love for God is the greatest miracle; and nothing else will fully satisfy your soul.

Nor can God be moved by praise, for in Him there is no vanity. When you do not crave attention from anyone but are only interested in true souls who love you, when you understand the meaning of true friendship, when you cannot be moved by words of flattery but only by the love of true hearts—then you know the love that God seeks from you and gives to you.

That is why temples such as this one are important—that we may all change the superficialities of religion into the direct experience of God. The great Jesus Christ and Babaji and Lahiri Mahasaya and my Master conferred together to save the church from churchianity and bring back true Christianity. That is why I am here to serve you. This teaching will be the salvation of each individual. Not all the inventions of convenience in the world will bring you happiness. Coming here from the Orient, I was at first enamored about America's ingenious machines and material progress; but I see that these things have not brought you peace and contentment. Real peace and contentment lie in the bliss of God. No death, no disease, no trouble can ever enter there in the land beyond the dreams of delusion, in the eternal safety of your own consciousness of Spirit.

Be anchored in that Refuge. Establish yourself in that consciousness by deep, regular meditation, and you will find Him there.

Communion with God is the best way to seek happiness and health and prosperity. It is certain that without God you can never find lasting happiness. Then why persist in pursuing something else? That is why Jesus said, "Seek ye the kingdom of God first and all things shall be added unto you." You seek the gifts of God, but you forget Him who is the Giver. Seek Him first. That is my foremost New Year's prayer for you—that all those whom I love and who come to me may find highest favor with God. That is the only thing I am living for. I know within myself that I have done everything only for God and not for my own ambition. His work is my only ambition; and for His work I am ready and willing to suffer, if necessary, to please Him in activity and to please Him in the silence of my soul.

The joy and love of His favor are incomparable. If it were not tangible I would not urge you so. Day and night, mixing with people or alone, you can be drunk with the love of God. Do not love Him at a distance; every night before sleep, talk to Him as your Nearest and Dearest. "My Lord, I am here. Thou art my Beloved. Thou art my Father. Thou art my Mother." Go deep and see what happens to you. You will see how He responds. It is most strange how He fulfills even your slightest innocent desires. From my early years I had admired those little French mechanical singing birds; and this Christmas Dr. and Mrs. B___ gave one to me. I was deeply touched because only God could have known that long-forgotten wish; it was He who gave it to me through them.

We Are on Earth to Find God

We are here for only a little while, and we must make the best of every moment in our life. To talk of communion, and to actually commune with that great Spirit and be a living example of that communion, are very different. No one could satisfy me with mere words. But when I see Saint Lynn completely in ecstasy with God, when I see Dr. Lewis diving in that realm and Dr. Kennell enjoying Spirit, when I see the sincerity of God in the face of each of the true ones He has sent to me, then I am overwhelmed.* When you are

* James J. Lynn, whom Paramahansaji often called "Saint Lynn" because of his marked spiritual advancement through practice of Kriya Yoga. (He was later known by his monastic title and name, Rajarsi Janakananda, and was the first spiritual successor to Paramahansaji.) He spoke after Paramahansaji on this occasion. Dr. M. W. Lewis was one of Paramahansaji's first disciples in America and later served as vice

spiritually thirsty, even reading Scripture cannot give you a satisfying drink. It is only God who can quench the thirst of desires, when we have actual contact and communion with Him.

Life is very tricky. Constantly we see others dropping all around us, and someday our turn will come. This is to make us think about the meaning of this show. We are not here just to do our little dance on the stage of life and then be forgotten. We are here to remember Him, to find Him. But nothing can attract God except our love. He brings vast worlds into being and shatters them into dust again in the endless cycles of creation. And His only wish in putting us in this stupendous show is that perchance we will seek Him. He has given us the power to cast Him away or to accept Him. What else could the meaning of creation be? He is entertaining us through friends and flowers and the joys of life; but we do not like the show when the rod of suffering is beating us down. Eventually we realize that it is our mistakes that create our suffering, and that the only way out of this play of incarnations is to find Him, love Him, worship Him in everything we do. Even when you are sweeping the floor of your home or writing or working in the office—every minute, before action and after action and when you are not active, let your mind be with God. Be conscious always that you are not working for yourself, but for God. The stage of time and the grand drama of human civilizations are His creation, not yours.

As we compare our life with the lives of thousands, it is so tempting to wish for some of the advantages we see in others' lives. But we must be proud of the part we are to play, and play it well—without sorrowing or flinching but with pleasure in our hearts only to please the Father.

The Most Precious Possession Is Love for God

The most precious of all possessions is love for God, that love which the great saints have expressed. That is the consummate achievement of life. For it is not easy to please God, and one cannot do so by absentminded prayers to Him. "He who watches Me always, him do I watch always." Such is the unconditional surrender of the Lord to the devotee who loves Him supremely and remains ever immersed in Him.

God is willing to give you anything you want to see if you will be satisfied with less than His Presence; but when you ask the Father

---

president of SRF. Dr. Lloyd Kennell, another close disciple, was an alternate speaker at the SRF temple in San Diego.

to surrender Himself, He will put you to the test. So strange are His tests! Even the utmost human wisdom or imagination cannot fathom the depths of the Father's mind. In the lives of saints God has manifested all kinds of trials; but His saints say, "Lord, these are but dreams. Thou alone art real."

I often think how fortunate I am. What He has given to me is beyond the wealth of kings. I have prayed to Him, "Father, test me with any conceivable trial, but never test me with obliviousness of Thy love." That is the profoundest curse of all. When we forget His love we suffer greatly. "Devotee knows how sweet You are; he knows, whom You let know."* Once you taste God's love nothing can ever equal it. It is eternal, ever new. Now I don't have to remind myself to think of God—it is just one unbroken consciousness, one intoxication, day and night. That is how you become when you love God. No earthly pleasure can compare. Nothing is more tempting than God; find Him by the practice of His Presence.

That consciousness can never come so long as you are seeking other things. Some want to play the radio or go to the movies or waste time in other diversions. Rather, whenever you have a little spare time, go into the inner silence and talk to God. "Father, beloved God, I am privileged to live here for a little while, to please You by doing Your will. At any time I may be called to another place. But Lord, wherever You may put me, let me remember You always. Be Thou ever enshrined in the temple of my memory and love." When you pray this way, the Father hears. The Father wants you to come home, but you cannot get there as long as you desire something else. God must be your supreme desire. It does not make life stale or uninteresting; it is the unending joy of divine romance.

Some people enter this path talking all the time about the powers that can be attained and the miracles they want to see; but once you have the Lord, as is seen in the life of Jesus and Babaji, Lahiri Mahasaya, and my Master, you are resurrected. Awake in the Transcendent Reality, you find that all desires born of the dualities of this dream world are finished forever.

Dear ones, remember what I tell you. I am talking only from experience. He is more real than anything you see around you. He is the Light behind the candlelight, the Power behind the electricity in the bulb. He is the Wisdom behind your thoughts; the

* From the chant "Thou Art My Life," in *Cosmic Chants* (published by Self-Realization Fellowship).

Discrimination behind your reason; the Vitality behind your hands, muscles, and cells; the Life throbbing in your heart. He is everything. Do not forget Him. God alone can make you happy. God alone is sufficient. God is the joy of meditation, He is the love flowing through all hearts, He is the life throbbing in every living thing. He is the Intelligence that created this universe and runs it in a scientific, mathematical fashion.

If you want to find God, join Self-Realization Fellowship and see for yourself whether or not we are telling you the truth. Meditate every night. You will understand the paradoxes of life. When you see some poor and some rich, some with health and others with disease and pain, remember that He did not create His children to suffer these inequities. He wants you to be free.

True Freedom Lies in Finding God

Even a great country like America cannot give you freedom. But freedom you can give to yourself by finding God. "The harvest is plenteous but the laborers are few." Why waste time? Spend one hour every night in real communion. Never go to bed until you feel He is with you. Then next morning pray even more deeply: "My Beloved, I know that I love You and that You love me. Reveal Thyself!" Go on like this, until day and night you behold the Beloved everywhere. Think what your life will become—fulfilling beyond all the dreams of your expectation.

Never consider yourself unfortunate because of difficult circumstances. You may be on the brink of freedom, even though you are suffering. So keep on. Someday, when you find God, He will explain to you the book of life. Do not lose faith in Him. All this world is a stage, and the one purpose behind everything that happens to you in the drama of life is to teach you to find Him who is the Lover of all hearts. Let us seek the Father who is yearning for the return of all His prodigal children who are roaming through incarnations in this realm of matter. He is waiting to receive us. When we turn homeward, He will prepare a feast with the "fatted calf" of wisdom to celebrate our return. Forget not Him who is ever seeking you even though you are not seeking Him. He is calling you, "Come home, child. Cease your oblivious roaming in the terrible delusions of this world. Come back! I have the eternal manna of joy waiting for you. Come home!"

Man's Highest Achievement

On Sunday, June 10, 1934, Paramahansa Yogananda announced the inauguration of the weekly Self-Realization Fellowship Lessons. *His words on that occasion were taken down stenographically by Sri Daya Mata, as always.*

This afternoon I hope you will give me your undivided and absolute attention, that you may understand the spiritual value of this occasion and respond spiritually, from your souls. I want to bring to you a living message of truth, so that you realize the necessity of knowing God *now*. Let this be your day of awakening! If you concentrate deeply on my words, you shall feel the joy of God.

As human beings you are different from the animals. Make use of your higher endowments of intelligence and reason; don't remain in ignorance and go on suffering. The spiritually blind cannot see the glory of God. When they open their eyes, then they see Him. Tear aside the veil of delusion and know things as they really are.

A Plan for Your Spiritual Awakening

If you listen to my words and the plan that I have for your self-development, you shall say it is true that from this day a new era of understanding and happiness has come into your life. I have a right to say this to you, because today I am going to tell you the practical means we have devised to serve you, to show you how you can achieve—in the highest way—the deepest yearnings you have cherished in your heart.

Day and night for 14 years* I have been thinking how to give to the students a continuous flood of that spiritual awakening which will assure they can never fall asleep again. Students in all parts of the country have asked, "Why don't you give more classes?" So I have planned to send weekly lessons to them. We have been working day and night to get them started. They will start next week and come every week thereafter. You will never find anything anywhere

* Paramahansaji founded his work in the United States in 1920. This talk was given in 1934. *(Publisher's Note)*

to compare to these lessons. Each will have a wealth of immortal information for study. They will also specially feature many instructive stories, each with a wonderful moral. You will find the stories very helpful to yourself as well as to your family members, with whom you can share them. Most important are the advanced spiritual techniques and principles, which will change your life in a way that you will never forget. I have at last found the plan that I know is going to free thousands of souls.

What Is Man's Highest Achievement?

What is your real goal in life? Analyze yourself: Something within you is always prodding you to seek that "something else" which seems to be missing in your life. In the inner self of all human beings is a deep-seated need for achievement. Why? Because we have fallen from the Father's bosom. We have wandered away from our eternal home in God, and we long to regain that lost perfection.

That inner yearning of your soul has become so bedimmed by your ceaseless outer activities and habits of restlessness that you are rarely even conscious of what you truly want. But there is one desire that is common to every human being: happiness. To find lasting joy, that unalloyed Bliss which is God, is man's highest achievement; and he will never be satisfied until he attains it.

Have You Found Happiness?

All of you are trying to be happy, but have you been able to? Your environment influences you to form desires and habits that keep you seeking in all the wrong places. Some of you think that getting rich will give happiness, while others gamble for joy by playing the marriage "stock market," and still others think that fame will give them the fulfillment they crave. The ways and means go on and on. The person who is a money-fiend; the one who is a matter-fiend, enslaved to sex, wine, or sensual indulgence; the seeker of thrills and pleasure—all want happiness. But if they do manage to get a little satisfaction, does it last? No, never.

Why do you go on looking for lasting satisfaction from this mortal world? What is the matter with you, that you cannot learn from experience? I looked at the lives of others and saw that those who blindly set forth on the path to material happiness too often ended up in the swamps of suffering. I made up my mind: "I am not going to follow the world into that pit of misery!" So I searched and struggled, and I found the laws of Self-realization, and I made the effort to know God. And today my heart is filled with the infinite, all-satisfying joy spoken of by the great masters. I have found happiness, complete and unending. My mind is not on how many people come to hear me; it is always absorbed in that bliss divine that lives within me. Life goes on, but no matter what difficulties it brings in my path, still that consciousness of inward joy endures.

To live without God is animality. You have got to find Him some time, for you will have a thousand miseries until you do. If you think that you can live happily in forgetfulness of God, you are mistaken, for you will cry out in loneliness again and again until you realize that God is all in all: the only Reality in the universe. You are made in His image. You can never find lasting happiness in any *thing,* because nothing is complete except God.

The highest achievement in this life doesn't lie merely in financial gain. It is not what you permanently possess, but the ability to create or attract at will what you need that defines true success. But don't be lured by unnecessary "necessities." Analyze the happiness of persons who have luxuries and wealth. What is the use of all that, if it cannot rid us of misery? What does having a million dollars mean if you have not learned to live with your wife and children without having fights every day, or if your nerves and peace of mind are daily slaughtered on the battlefield of unscrupulous business competition, or if your self-respect has deserted you because you have failed to befriend your conscience?

SRF Teachings Show You How to Be Master of Yourself

Highest achievement means to be master of yourself. It means you have learned to govern your impulses by discrimination, to be influenced only by your own good habits and reason. Nobody should be able to tempt you to do anything that you know you should not do. Don't be a slave to anything. Have you that power of self-control? If not, then join Self-Realization Fellowship and you will be taught the art of doing the things you ought to do when you ought to do them. You will learn to awaken dynamic will power. To remain enslaved by habits and impulses that compel you to harmful actions against your will is to guarantee that you will often find yourself in the pit of disillusionment and trouble. Self-Realization will teach you how to be free—to be your own king.

You may accept intellectually that you should know God, but most of you lack the conviction and determination to make the necessary effort. Why? Because you are a slave to your bad habits.

I never go to bed at night until I have conscious contact with God. One day, I remember, the body was much in need of rest and I started to lie down to sleep instead of having my meditation. But even as my body touched the bed, the force of habit took over—my eyes automatically focused at the point between the eyebrows and the first thing I knew I was in *samadhi.* Though I had been sleepy, I was unable to sleep until I had contacted God. The protection of God-habit is marvelous.

Two days ago, after a little meditation, I had just laid my head on the pillow, when a sheet of golden light descended on me and whom do I see? Jesus Christ. At first his expression was very sad; but after a short time I saw him as he was after the Resurrection. His face was divine. When I behold his presence and when I see what it does to my life—that I cannot express to you. The proofs of the presence of God and Christ that come through meditation, I can never forget. That proof comes not through theology or logic but through my own Self-realization. If I hadn't formed the habit of deep meditation, he would never have come—and I would never have had definite proof that he and all the Great Ones are omnipresent in the ether.

Solving the Mystery of Life and Death

Self-Realization Fellowship says, "Why do you wait for death to find God? He will not be any closer to you beyond the portals of the grave than He is now. Why shouldn't you find Him now?" Why don't you try to know the Master of this life and of the afterlife? You are carried away by bad habits and you don't make the effort to know Him.

Highest achievement means to know the mystery of life and death. To realize this, you must make your first duty your duty to God. Remember, you cannot think or live at all without God's life and intelligence present in your body and brain. Therefore, the highest achievement is to know Him. By Self-realization, you will widen the channel of your life to receive the full inflow of His consciousness—His light and power and joy—in your own consciousness.

Wisdom, Understanding, and Help With All Needs

The highest achievement means having wisdom and understanding, when you know everything that you want to know. I can truthfully say that everything that I have wanted to know, God has told me and shown me. After my earthly mother died, God answered my fervent prayers and showed me where she was.* Truth is illuminating. You must be able to *know* that God is with you. Did Jesus have to consult anybody? He knew everything. So must you know. Anything I want to know is given to me. Why couldn't you live like that?

All hearts crave a love that is perfect and everlasting. But that longing can be satisfied only by experiencing the love of God. Without God's love, no human being can really love you. Do you know that? Only God loves you, through your loved ones; for without love borrowed from God, no one could give love or receive love.

When Mother was taken away from me, I felt so lonely and sad that my heart almost died within me; again and again I cried, "God, You must come to me!" When your soul is really ripe with longing, and when you really want God, He will come to you. No one can give you Him except yourself, through your own efforts. If from today you vouchsafe your life for God and work assiduously toward that end, you will never know death. He is waiting for you. He is telling you, "This world is only My movie house. I didn't mean for you to mistake this picture show for Reality. Don't get attached to anything in it; for it is all a play of My light and shadows."

Even if you become the President of the United States and everybody says "hurrah," you may have achieved little in the eyes of God. You may still be torn by worries, sickness, wars, and death. But if God is in your heart, even if you have nothing of the material world, you cannot be hurt or defeated. When you are one with Him, you shall have all the forces of creation at your feet.

I have no fear at all. I never want for anything. Why? Because I have the greatest thing in the universe. God has surrounded me with responsibilities; yet I know He is with me, and that is all that matters. He knows what I want and what I need. I often think He is more with me when I am in trouble than at any other time, because the child in trouble needs the mother more. When you are in trouble, instead of saying, "God isn't interested in helping me," you must believe—you must *know*—that He is with you. That is how I found my realization and salvation. It isn't that the Lord is specially fond only of this institution, so that He takes care of it. He is specially fond of all of you and will show you the same attention, if you cease running away from Him.

* Paramahansaji's beloved mother died of cholera when he was only eleven.

Study the Lessons Each Day

My only purpose is to awaken God within you. As far as you want to go along the spiritual path, I can show you; and if you practice the techniques in the *Lessons** you will never feel stagnation in your progress.

So this is the plan. Fill out the application, and these instructions will go out to you starting next week. Of course, there is a little financial help required to keep this work going. There is no other obligation other than five dollars' initial fee and two dollars per month thereafter. Just the bare expenses of printing, mailing, etc., are being looked after by this donation you give. We are practically swamped from all sides with work. But there is another plan also. To those who find they cannot give two dollars monthly, we are removing the barrier and for a love offering of 50 cents they will receive one lesson a month and our magazine.†

Now I have done my part; it is up to you to do yours. If you will study these *Lessons* for at least half an hour every day, you will soon realize a new goal of happiness, inner awakening, and Self-realization that will forever shed light upon you so that you may live according to the highest standards of existence. You will feel God; you will see Him smiling in the stars and the blossoms; you will see Him templed within every human being and in every good thought and every love that you have.

When you have understood by your own Self-realization the spiritual message given here, you will also realize that within these pages is the best that India has to offer. Theoretical theological teachings will seem as kindergarten studies to you, because in these *Lessons* you are receiving the highest truths of India's scriptures and the Bible, which have been hidden from the masses for centuries. Self-Realization Fellowship brings you the universal technique of salvation, the royal highway to the Infinite.

The Help and Blessings of the Masters

Those of you who shall come into this spiritual fold, I as your humble servant shall give my best possible cooperation to help you.

* The *Self-Realization Fellowship Lessons* are mailed to students worldwide from SRF Headquarters in Los Angeles. More information is available at www.srflessons.org

† Though the cost of the *Lessons* has naturally increased with inflation during the 90 years since this talk was given, they are still made available to all at a minimal charge that covers only the bare costs of production and distribution.

Self-Realization Fellowship has thousands of followers, and the movement is growing fast. It is through these weekly *Lessons* you shall realize you are a perfect being as a child of God. These truths are going to be one of the greatest spiritual awakenings in your life, for they have been written down with my heart's experiences within them. March on with this truth and you shall feel new wisdom and new vitality and strength within you.

This movement has the greatest masters of Self-Realization behind it.* And you can demonstrate in your own life what they experienced. I am bringing the message of the masters and Christ to you. Self-Realization Fellowship is giving you what Christ taught to his disciples—the esoteric truths that he taught. In these weekly *Lessons,* immortal truths will be found. It is very sacred to me, but I am telling you this, that if you follow these techniques and if you meditate unfailingly every day, and once a week have a longer meditation for several hours, you shall find God. That will be your highest achievement.

So let this occasion be the awakening of a new life. Sleep no more! Awaken yourself and realize the powers of the Spirit. If you pore through these pages that come every week, you shall realize they are potent with the light of Self-realization. But after receiving them, you must do your part too, and never go to bed until you have meditated and prayed so deeply that you feel God has heard you.

By your own Self-realization you will be able to see the light of God in all true spiritual teachings; and, most important, you shall behold that light in the greatest way: in yourself. These weekly lessons shall give you the light of Self-realization in which you can know Truth, not just read about it; and wherever you go, that inner light of your own awakening shall silently radiate to establish the temple of God in the hearts of others. Whoever will come in contact with you will feel changed. You won't have to talk, for they shall feel your love and purity.

Using these studies, and meditating regularly, you shall find such happiness, such answers to your problems! Don't be satisfied with words. Have actual experience of truth. Have Self-realization! Keep this living message in your breast. Do not listen half-heartedly and then forget. God cannot redeem you unless you make the effort

* Mahavatar Babaji, Lahiri Mahasaya, Swami Sri Yukteswar. Their lives, and the spiritual teachings and worldwide mission they entrusted to Paramahansa Yogananda, are described in *Autobiography of a Yogi.*

to redeem yourself first. You must bring His consciousness into your own consciousness.

Prayer for God's Blessing

Close your eyes now and say: "O Infinite God, saturate me with Thy light. Baptize me in Thy consciousness, that after listening to Your words, poured through Yogananda, I shall never sleep again."

"Heavenly Father, Jesus Christ, saints of all religions, Babaji, Lahiri Mahasaya, Swami Sri Yukteswarji, Guru-Preceptor, bless me that I sleep no more." As you are saying this, concentrate on the palms of your hands and your fingers. You will feel that energy just like electricity flowing through the antennae of your hands into your nerves and whole being.

"Heavenly Father, bless us, that we sleep no more; that we follow the Self-Realization Fellowship way and weekly instructions that come from the greatest masters of India, which show the universal highway wherein all bypaths of religions meet. Father, bless me that my willingness be kept alive, that I may make up my mind to dispel from my body, mind, and soul all darkness and sickness and poverty-consciousness and ignorance through the light of Self-Realization.

"Father, naughty or good, I am Thy child. Forsake me not, though I forsake Thee. Forget me not, though I forget Thee. Remember me, though I remember Thee not. Father, bless me that I may never sleep again, but make the adamant, determined effort to meditate and follow the light of Self-Realization in these *Lessons,* that I may know I am free. Father, I am Thyself. I am free. Thou and I are one!

"God, Guru, Father, bless us. Baptize us in Thy consciousness, that we may follow Thee evermore. Father, Father, Father, may Thy love shine forever on the sanctuary of my devotion, and may I be able to awaken Thy love in all hearts."

Be Castled in Self-realization, and Be Free

Dear ones, the light of God is moving through me this day. May you remember this occasion always. I am in His sea of Light, in that eternal land. Wherever I am, in this life or beyond, I am always roaming in that eternity. I want you to come there also, for you are my brothers and sisters and I cannot bear to see you left in delusion. Make your irrevocable determination today. Your Father is calling—His golden bell voice is calling you: "Come home, child of immortality! Wander no more in the marshes of disillusionment, led by the will-o'-the-wisp of worldly attractions. Come to Me. You shall never be afraid. I shall free thee; I shall free thee through thine own Self-realization. Make up thy mind. Come home!"

So, dear ones, sleep no more. The dread and fear that comes in my heart when I think what would have happened had I not come to this path—that same fear I feel for you. Don't forget; don't forget! My heart aches with you, bleeds with you; and I plead, sleep no more! Failure, disillusionment, and death are stalking you. Friends, come! Be castled in Self-realization; wear the armor of Self-realization; and laugh at death and be free.

Let us chant *Aum* and be baptized in the great light of Spirit, which I am sending through each of you on this occasion.

Aum! Aum! Aum!

Peace.

Amen.

When Will God Come to You?

Self-Realization Fellowship International Headquarters, Los Angeles, September 19, 1940

God is with you now; you have only to make the effort to realize His presence. Many seekers, when they try to find God and do not succeed, feel a sense of helplessness: "God is away in His heaven, and we are left alone down here." But God is not far away. He is here.

So you ask: "Why doesn't He answer when I pray?" The reason is that your call is not strong enough. A little bit of prayer, a little bit of reading about God, is insufficient to penetrate the mystery screen of creation's laws behind which He has hidden Himself. It is not easy to know God. If it were, then many people would have God-realization.

The World Both Suggests and Veils the Presence of God

Most persons only imagine they have found God. They have found a solace in those saints who have the consciousness of God, and feel that is all there is to religion. But as I have told you again and again, there is a vast difference between imagination and realization of God.

Of course, there are both positive and negative sides to having imagination. Envisioning that sometime we will know God brings us closer to Him. But if you are overly imaginative about what you have not actually attained, you are fooling yourself, for God's laws are not affected by mere belief. Imagining that you are fed does not miraculously supply nutrition to your body. And God certainly does not manifest to you just because you imagine He is there.

A time comes in everyone's life when trials and troubles are so great that one feels like a helpless puppet, pulled this way and that by an uncaring fate. When all your outer resources have been exhausted, you turn within and say, "God, help me!" But does God help? Whether He helps or not, you don't know. Was the favorable outcome from God or from a natural course of events? Suppose it is five seconds before noon, and I say: "When I slap my hand on the table, the clock will chime twelve times." Those events take place as predicted, but there is no causal connection between my hitting the table and the clock striking. My point is that you should not take for granted that a few prayers are the cause if things take a turn for the better. I am not trying to make you disbelieve in the help and blessings of God; I am trying to make you become sure of God. Unless you are sure of Him, you should not fool yourself.

When you behold nature's wonders, belief in an organizing Divine Intelligence comes easily. But when you reflect on the chaos that seems just as prevalent in the world, you are filled with doubt and faith equally. Seeing the inharmonies of disease and destruction in nature, and man's brutal evil against his fellow beings, you think, "Can there really be a God? Is this earth not a torture chamber?" Yet when you calmly muse on the beauty of the rose and the lotus, when vitalizing air fills your lungs and you feel happy and full of life, you say: "Surely there is some Higher Intelligence behind the seeming contradictions of this world." Then when that temporary optimism is shattered by some new trial, again you become downcast in uncertainty about God. Your mind passes through a million difficulties of doubts before you arrive at the settled conclusion that God is.

The testimony of the Great Ones such as Jesus and Krishna must never be discarded. They lived on earth immaculately, willing to endure any cross, accepting without hesitation to go through any difficulty in order to bear witness to Truth—they testify that God is. He created this earth filled with righteousness, but we have covered His goodness with a terrible veil of ugly delusion—misery-making ignorance.

Don't Allow the World and Its Temptations to Distract You From God

If there were no God, why would even a thought of Him persist in man's mind at all? In the universal human desire for happiness, in man's unceasing quest for knowledge and understanding, lies a clue that there must be some Higher Power from which our consciousness and intelligence came, and which prods us incessantly to overcome our limitations. But I am not talking tonight about various proofs of the existence of God; I am talking about how He can be found.

To the individual in ordinary worldly consciousness, God is both unknown and unknowable. Some talk of Him eloquently; some listen about Him intently; but few know who God is, or what God is, or how to find Him. Most persons live on earth in a state of stupor—so busy with worldly "necessities" that they have no time for God. This world with its tempting objects of desire; its diseases and suffering; the proliferating distractions accompanying the growth and progress of this age, which lure man to dissipate his energy in useless pursuits; the degrading influence of unwholesome company; and above all, one's own bad habits—these are the enemies that prevent one's realization of God.

How repetitious is the story of mankind! Father and mother fall in love; children are born; they feel this life is going to last forever. Then one by one the children get married and have their own children, and the parents grow old and pass away. Over and over again the drama is repeated. Some reason, "Well, that is life—birth, marriage, children, and then death." But I say that life should be more than that. Those who are wise seek the purpose of their recurring roles on the earth-stage: to find the Maker of this play, and to please Him by enacting only the noble parts that lead to eternal freedom.

The temptations and distractions that keep man from God are very great. There is no denying this. This world may be a play to God, but it is not a play to those in delusion. It is very real. And because He remains hidden behind the scenes, it seems all the more doubtful that there is a God. That is why people do not seek Him. Instead, when they are in trouble they say, "If only I can get more money, my problems will be solved."

Life is so tricky. Some persons appear to be very happy because they have lots of money and good health, and you think your life should be the same. So you work hard to acquire these things. You may devote all your energies to getting rich, then suddenly find you are stricken with a violent disease and cannot enjoy your gains; or perhaps the stock market crashes and you lose all of your wealth. Or you might have a healthy body, but no money to feed it; so again you suffer. And you ask, "What is this? I did nothing wrong. I am as deserving as the next person." But that is the way life is. On the surface, there seems to be no justice, no equality. As soon as you compare your life with someone else's, and find that your life is less than his, you want something more. But that is very foolish reasoning. You have to take life as it is. If you don't, you are going to be moaning and grieving all the time instead of making the most of what opportunities you do have. Remember, just because one does not have money and health does not mean that that person's life is not worthwhile—perhaps it is even more so than that of the person who is well-endowed. The individual of scanty means who is sick and blind, who may be at death's door, but still he fixes his mind on God alone, is a much better person, much nearer freedom, than the one who lives to an old age in opulence and health, but in utter oblivion of God.

In this country, most teachings of self-improvement keep you subject to life's dualities rather than giving you the means to retain inner happiness no matter what your circumstances. The modern psychologist says, "Demonstrate health, demonstrate success; that is the way to happiness." It is all right to use your God-given powers to achieve these things; but no matter how much health and wealth you acquire, someday you will have to dump this body. The lover of his body is in delusion. That is why Christ said, "Take no heed for the body...." The Lord shows you every night in sleep that your real Self cannot be bound by consciousness of this mortal form. By meditation, establish that freedom and body-aboveness in waking consciousness, too; because body-identification is the source of all suffering.

The Realm of the Soul, and of God, Is Not in This World

Behind the gross atoms of the body is the realm of the soul, the kingdom of eternal happiness. Why don't you make the effort to enter the portals of meditation to that happiness which lies within? All the doors of the senses lead to the valley of misery. This does not mean you should blind yourself to the world and withdraw from everything, but that you should lead a controlled existence. This requires discrimination, realizing that no lasting security or happiness is to be found in a transient existence on this ever-changing earth. We are travelers, here for but a little while, but our ultimate destination is God.

In India we find the divine romance with God. That land is blessed even amidst its poverty and suffering. I have met many of the great ones there, renunciants of worldly goods, yet they are the real kings, the real souls. When I was younger I used to wonder if they took any notice of the poverty and suffering around them. Then I saw that life is very two-faced and treacherous—it is always up to something to test us. I realized that such God-knowing souls are the only ones who really know how to train the heart and soul to be strong against the pulverizing trials of life so that they are not touched by anything. They teach us that no earthly castle is safe. There is nothing you can depend upon with certainty except God, because if you rely on anything else, you will be disillusioned. Those who are young take for granted their vitality, with no thought of getting old; and those who are old with shattered dreams can no longer imagine what it was like to be young. Life is a ridiculous medley of contrasts. Yet when you close your eyes and go very deep in meditation, you do not mind what is happening to the body.

So never be afraid. Those who are wise do not grieve at what has gone by or fear what is yet to come. With evenness of mind they move through the world and perform their duties. When any disturbance comes, I see myself apart. My joy no one can take away, for I realize that this is only a show.

Everyone's life is different. But no matter how nature treats you, either through karma or through the tests of God, if you say, "Well, I am all right, Lord," and your heart remains calm through all trials, then you have won. You will find Him now and then, in almost everything you see. An advance notice will be given to you about everything that will happen in your life. God will not remain obscure. If He is obscure now, it is because you have not made the effort or given time to Him. That is why He does not come.

God can be found in one life if the will is there. If you can meditate deeply three days and nights, and pray unceasingly, completely oblivious of the world, you will feel His presence. But will you do it? You will have a thousand excuses. The body will rebel, and you will reason how everything else is important and that you do not have the time to make that effort.

I say to you, the most important thing is to find God first, for then you will understand His play. Make Him your priority. Do not continue to procrastinate, because, in truth, you have relatively very little time. There is no certainty to human life. There is more predictability about the life of a tree—for instance, the redwood tree lives for hundreds of years. But your life is like a dewdrop precariously perched on the lotus leaf of time. When it will slide off into the shining vastness beyond, you don't know. Anyone who thinks that anything is more important than God is in delusion. In your heart you must understand that the only real necessity is that Divine Consciousness; there is no engagement more urgent than your engagement with God, because no engagement is possible without the power borrowed from Him.

Dear ones, God is not a myth to me. He is not merely an object written about in the scriptures; nor am I seeking Him anymore, for He is with me. Every moment of my existence—in life and death, health and sickness, no matter what comes—He is with me. And from His joy I speak. You too should seek until you find Him. Don't wait. You have wasted too much time already. You have not been serious about God, and that is why you have not found Him.

As you go along in life, always try to be honest with yourself. Have you sought God as strongly, as determinedly, as continuously as you have followed temptation or the fulfillment of your material desires? Not many of you can stand up and say that you have done so. Your desire for God and pursuit of Him has been intermittent, occasional. It has not been a steady, continuous seeking.

If you plan to drive to New York and you wander all over the countryside in a roundabout way, it is easy to lose sight of your intended destination. That is the approach some persons take on the spiritual path. They say, "Well, it is Sunday. Let us go to church." But by the time they get home, the inspiration and wisdom for which they went in the first place is forgotten, and their mind is on the nice Sunday dinner waiting for them. I call that kind of superficial worship "graveyard dispassion." I was told that when people attend a funeral service, confronting the reality of death makes them very philosophical. But their sober detachment from the world lasts only as long as they are present. When they leave the service, they want to head straight for the cocktail bar!

Use Discrimination in the Face of Desires

Discrimination must be constant. By always discriminating about your desires, guide your reason to the realization that God is your true goal. Unless you apply that discrimination, you have no will power to persevere in spite of life's distractions.

Inwardly renounce desires, except the desire for God. Even then He will test your nonattachment. Be pleased in whatever position He places you. Don't complain; that increases desires and is the sure way away from God. If you want to be away from Him, create desires. Like a chain reaction, they are never-ending; they can never be completely satisfied through material means. Everlasting fulfillment lies within, in the soul's realization of God. Every outward desire, whether it is a good or bad one, takes you away from that inner happiness. And when you wander away from the soul's happiness, you cannot find peace of mind or contentment.

Desirelessness does not mean that you should not have ambition. You must not be lazy. You should be ambitious to accomplish good in this world, but with the desire to please God, not yourself. In doing good works, be able to sacrifice anything for God. Take the life of the Lord Buddha. He was a prince who had great wealth, a kingdom, and a beautiful wife and a son. And he renounced everything for God. The renunciation of many monks and nuns cannot be eulogized as is the renunciation of Buddha, because they did not have anything to renounce. Everything renounced them, and so they decided to become monastics!

It is not one's outer pretense of renunciation, but what is hidden in the heart that God looks to. In a secluded forest monastery, one may be a man of the world; and in the business world one may be a monk at heart. It is harder to be in the world but not of the world, but it can be done. Many are only rationalizing, however, when they say, "I live in the world, but I am not attached to the world." As soon as something is taken away from them, they realize how attached they are. There are so many ways the devil fools us. Test yourself. Do you think you could go into the forest and renounce all material comforts and possessions? Right away you would miss having your warm bed, and your bath and toothbrush in the morning. The dog has no toothbrush, no toothpaste, but that does not make him a renunciant! My point is that you should not fuss so much about outer conditions.

Yoga teaches that whether you live in an ashram or in the world, meditate deeply. And in your heart renounce everything, so that wherever you go will be your monastery. That is the inner renunciation extolled in the Bhagavad Gita. Day and night you carry on your outer duties, whatever they may be; but inwardly you know only One—the Lord, and the joy of His presence.

In ashrams in India the young boys are taught to sleep on the floor and still be comfortable, even without a pillow and sometimes without a blanket. It is a wonderful training. The mind gains an inner adaptability under all conditions. To have that freedom from desires is greatness. As soon as you surround your life with complexities, you feel you are so important that the world cannot go on without you. What a delusion! That delusion keeps you away from God. If you want to find Him, you must put Him first in preference to everything else. It is not difficult if you train your will and discrimination to remember that you are here for just a little while. You are in the world only as a player in this drama created by God. That is the only logical conclusion a thinking person can reach. Every saint who has found God has understood that this earth is only a show, and so he is ready to leave it anytime God calls. Why should you be attached to this treacherous life? Suddenly you become sick, and it is all over. Without any notice you are pulled away, without any time to make plans. Why should we leave this world that way? Such is the fate of the man in delusion.

Steps in Conquering Delusion

How to conquer delusion? I have told you the necessary steps: First of all, there must be yearning for God. Your heart must have that desire to renounce for God instantly. The minute you understand that something is a temptation, walk away. That is real renunciation. But are you prepared to do it? When you are ready to do it, that is the beginning. Then you have truly started on the path.

Next, after making up your mind that God is the supreme goal of your life, you must have determination to seek Him with unbroken effort. That kind of determination the Buddha had, when day after day he sat in meditation. Many temptations were sent to him. One day after great struggles he saw before him dancing maidens sent by Satan to break his determination, and still his mind soared beyond all temptations. Then he said, "I have conquered *maya.*" On that day he received illumination. He became the Buddha, or enlightened one. So you too must have that dogged determination. Then if disease comes you will not say, "I am too sick, and I give up." Or if poverty comes, you will not say, "I cannot do it, God."

Then the third point is that you must have knowledge of the right method of meditation. Follow the right guide, or guru, who himself has found entry into the kingdom of God. He can help you reach that consciousness quicker than if you try to go it alone. He will hasten your evolution and assist you in avoiding those difficulties that may well confront those who think themselves spiritually self-sufficient.

When God Will Come to You

So when will God come to you? When your desire for Him is as urgent as the drowning man's desire for breath, as strong as the miser's yearning to get back all the money he lost, and as deep as the love of the lover who is ready to die for the sake of the beloved—when you have that degree of desire in your heart for God alone, you will find Him without fail. It is the urgency of the heart, the depth of the love for God in the heart, and the continuity of your search for Him that will bring Him.

No one can give you God; He can only be had by individual seeking. It is possible for you to have Him now. But will you make the effort? Shankara says, "The child is busy with play. The youth is busy with sex. And the aged is busy with worries. How few think of the Lord." Do not forsake Him; rather forsake your desires, for they are blind alleys. Look upon this life as the cosmic movie of God; and do not identity yourself with the part you play. Otherwise, when tragedies are being enacted and when diseases and troubles try to break you, you will lose your balance of calmness. You must so strengthen your mind and soul that in the face of all crucifixions you will be able to say, "Father, forgive them for they know not what they do." Be so deeply immersed in the thought of God that troubles of life will not upset you. Instead, you will laugh at them and say, "Lord, it is all right. Thou art with me: Thou art my own. Thou art my mother and my father. Thou art my friend. Thou art my beloved. Thou art my ambition. Thou art my health and wealth. Thou art my home, my garden, my flowers. Thou art my life—my breath and joy and peace and will. Thou art everything that I have sought." Then He will come.

[At this point in his talk, Paramahansaji's mind became so withdrawn that he spoke directly to God:]

"Beloved Lord, God of our hearts, Glory be Thy name. May the dance of *maya* forever be banished from our consciousness. Be Thou the only King sitting on the throne of all our desires. Be Thou the Ocean into which all the rivers of our desires flow. Be Thou the only Love in our hearts, the supreme Desire of all desires. Mighty King of the universe, our own Father, we seek Thee not because Thou art great and powerful, but because Thou art our own. Being made in Thine image, only by finding Thee can we live our true nature and be happy in Thee. I mind not where Thou hast placed me. I am happy in whatever Thou hast made of me. May my will and actions and thoughts, everything, be only what pleases Thee. Beloved One of my heart, Beloved One of the ages, Neglected One of incarnations, finding Thee as the Self of my little self, Life of my life, Joy of my joy, Love of my love, Reason of my reason, Desire of my desires, I seek Thee alone, naught else. Reign in my heart forever. O Lord, delude us not with Thy delusion; Thou art more tempting than all other temptations. Be supreme in our hearts. And whoever is here, open his or her heart with one love for Thee. May they find Thee—Thou who art the end of all trails of incarnations. Do not delay our evolution. Do not delay our meeting Thee. Every day that passes away is lost without having Thee. Bless us all, that we be with Thee evermore. *Aum. Peace. Amen.*"

Dear ones, the saw that is used in the workshop to cut wood to build furniture can also be converted into an instrument to produce beautiful musical sounds. So it is with us. We can convert ourselves, our matter-of-fact workaday life, to vibrate with the song of the Infinite. Spiritualize yourself, so the divine melody will flow through your life no matter what your outer activities.

You should be able to utter the name of God just once with such devotion that it will bring a great joy in you—God will become manifest in you. That consciousness is indescribable. But keep your love for God sacred within you. Let no one know that love of God which you keep hidden in your heart. When you pass a certain stage in your spiritual growth and God wants you to speak to inspire others, that is all right. But God will not come to you as long as in your mind you are trying to impress others. His love is very sacred, very private, and it is in secret that you will find Him. Secrecy is the price of God's consciousness. Where there is no one watching to praise you, there you will find God.

All these things I tell you, you can only know by testing them. You cannot know by theory. Study the *Self-Realization Fellowship Lessons.* There you will find many answers you are seeking. You will not find God by emotionalism, intellectualism, or by following the popular beliefs of the crowds. In India the teacher sits in his hermitage, and the students come to him. There is no talking. They meditate, and the teacher inwardly directs each soul. In the same way I direct those who are very devoted and earnest in seeking God and who are in tune with me. It does not matter where they are. Here in these teachings is the key. Follow them, and you will find that what I say is true.

Live the Life Shown by the Great Ones

Self-Realization Fellowship Golden Lotus Temple, Encinitas, California, July 23, 1939

If you can realize God in this life, then your work is finished. When God comes, you see your body, mind, and soul transformed into the consistency of God's nature. Being made in the image of God, you can and should reflect that image in the incarnate instrumentality of your threefold being.

Let us meditate. Feel that you are charged with the creative, life-sustaining energy of God. Feel that the everlasting consciousness of God is manifesting in your body, erasing the mortal consciousness of past failures, fear, disease, old age. Repeat this thought with deep attention: "Father, Thou art present in my body, in my mind, in my soul. I am made in Thine image. Bless my body, mind, and soul, that they shine with Thine everlasting youth, power, immortality, and joy. *Aum.* Peace. Amen."

God is our Father and Mother, our Friend and Beloved. Many religionists teach you to fear God, but that is wrong. No matter what our mistakes, He knows them and forgives us. He is waiting right around the corner of life to greet us, if we would only acknowledge our mistakes and seek Him through love. "Father, Thou art ours. We seek Thee not through fear but through love. It is our privilege to love Thee. We are made in Thine image, and we love Thee from our hearts—first, last, and always."

Don't Be Busy With the Faults of Others

From childhood, there should be emphasis on the importance of educating our young people in developing their moral and spiritual consciousness. That training is essential, because the universal principles of virtue are the foundation of a happy and successful life. And among the first lessons is to learn how to introspect to keep a watchful eye on the correctness of one's own thoughts and behavior, and to avoid the divisive habit of criticizing and judging others. One should criticize and change oneself first.

A woman is standing at a window looking at the passersby. A kindly man comes along and thinks, "She is waiting for her son." A sensual man goes by and thinks, "She is waiting for her lover." A sociable person passes and thinks, "She is waiting for a friend." So it is in this world, that the state of consciousness you have created within will impose itself on all your perceptions.

What you spitefully criticize in others is often a reflection of some flaw within yourself. Therefore, do not busy yourself with others' faults; be busy changing your own. If you follow this effort to perfect yourself, you will find God. Those who have found God, who have been asked by Him to be gurus, are the ones whose job it is to be busy with correcting the lives of others. A guru has ironed out the troublesome mental kinks of his own ego, and can therefore see others with eyes of soul-wisdom and divine love. Without that self-mastery, if you try to be a "guru" of others you will lose yourself. That is why in Self-Realization Fellowship we emphasize individualized study.*

As Jesus taught, "Judge not others....Why beholdest thou the mote that is in thy brother's eye, but considerest not the beam that is in thine own eye?"† If I were to dare any one of you to stand up in public and speak of all the wrongs you have done, you could not bear to subject yourself to such humiliation. Those who have erred do not need your kicks of denunciation; they need your loving hand in assistance. "He who is without sin, let him cast the first stone." So before you cast aspersions on anyone else, always ask yourself, "Am I without error?" Then, mindful of your own need for love and forgiveness, give that love to all.

Seek the Certificate of God's Approval

Only love can redeem the world. That is the rallying cry of Christ. It is not necessarily those who call themselves Christians, but rather those who live Christlike lives, who are recognized by Christ. Recognition from man means nothing. Jesus didn't care what people called him. Despite all the people he divinely helped and healed, many nonunderstanding persons said he did those works in league with the devil. Yet today millions follow him, because he

* I.e., Paramahansa Yogananda's *Self-Realization Fellowship Lessons.*

† Matthew 7:1–3.

lived by his ideals, unafraid of popular opinion. He was conscious only of having the certificate of God's approval.

This is God's world. Dedicate yourself to Him. I no longer do anything of my own will. I have dedicated my body, mind, and soul to Him; and as He leads me, I follow. I stand against the world if the Lord so commands me. Life is simple when God's will, not our own desires, becomes the criterion by which we choose our actions.

As human beings endowed with free will we have some independence; but it is when we use our free will to attune ourselves with His will that we feel our divine nature as His children. Then we become like Him. Otherwise we are just puppets of *maya*-delusion and past karma. Worldly persons forget that. Instead, they are like little Napoleons! They behave as though their ego were the supreme authority in life. They assert their little power for their own wishes, not God's, and sooner or later the karmic hammer falls on their head to wake them from that delusion.

Even a Moment of Yearning for God Will Ultimately Save You

Do not be afraid of God because of what you have done in the past. The past is gone; it is beyond your control. What is done, is done; you cannot go back and change it, so why continue to berate yourself? You can atone only by becoming better now. Live the life shown by the Great Ones. And remember: All those who are wandering in the valley of dark delusion, whoever among them has given even a little thought to God—even a momentary yearning for Him—that desire shall ultimately save them.

There are millions today who do not want God. They could not use their brains for one instant without the power of God that invisibly sustains them; yet they shudder at His name. God does not punish them, but they punish themselves; for, being made in the image of God, if we do not live a pure life we will suffer. Our souls are divine; and unless we reflect that godly image in our thoughts and actions, we can never be lastingly happy. Marriage, wealth, health—nothing will satisfy. If you are not trying to achieve the purpose of life—realization of your innate divinity—happiness will elude you. There will always be some canker, some void of unfulfillment.

Suffering, created by your wrong living, is the call of God. When you suffer, it is a reminder not to stray from the heavenly consciousness of your true divine nature. But you should not need painful reminders. God prefers that you instead heed the call of wisdom. Realize that even though today you are so filled with life, enjoying the world around you, sooner or later you will suddenly be snatched away by death. Nothing in the world will be able to bring you back. Why wait until it is too late to reflect on the purpose for which you are here? You are not an animal; you have the power to think and reason and plan; and that power you must use to find God.

Finding God in Your Busy Life

India shows the way. Of all the nations in the world, India has for millenniums been the most sincere in seeking God. Some of her saints have sat fifty years in secluded caves, seeking Him day and night in meditation. They found the answer—the practices that scientifically bring communion with Him—and that answer tells us how to find God in this busy life.

Those who will meditate and love God shall see Him. You make excuses, saying: "O God, if I had a little more money, or if I had a little better health, or if this or that were different in my life, then I would seek You." In this way you are always missing the goal—never finding happiness, never understanding the purpose of life. But why beg to have small favors or material conveniences? Have Him who is the source of all things. Have Him!

The Lord says: "To men who meditate on Me as their Very Own, ever united to Me by incessant worship, I supply their deficiencies and make permanent their gains."* This has been demonstrated in my life. Five or six times I have parted with everything I had; but I received everything again direct from His hands. When God gives, He gives from His heart. He gives in abundance.

Heed the Wisdom-Call of Divine Awakening

In India we seek spiritual guidance from those souls who know God. We don't follow just anybody. "The blind cannot lead the blind." Would you make an important purchase from a salesman who misrepresents a product because he does not understand what he sells? A teacher without some God-realization is merely a spiritual victrola that may grind out a sermon, but doesn't know what it is all about. It is the greatest farce to pose as a spiritual representative unless you are making a sincere effort to commune with God and realize the truths you preach. I received that exhortation from my Master, and I live in that communion with God and truth day and

* Bhagavad Gita IX:22.

night. That is all I live for. Now I know it was God who loved me through my parents and relatives and friends. Having His love, I have everything.

So, find Him. You will never be happy until you do. That is the keynote of life. He is calling you. Each one of you who is sympathetic with that thought has responded to the wisdom-call of God within you; and that is why you are here in this temple today.

Some persons sleep very deeply, and others are easily awakened. Some awaken for a little while and then go back to sleep. And there are those who awaken in the morning and get up, but as soon as they are left alone they go back to bed. Finally, there are those who wake up at dawn and jump out of the bed, ready to take on the day, with no inclination to go back to sleep again. In the same way, there are those who are totally asleep in delusion and never respond to Truth; and those whose interest is aroused for a little while when coaxed (by a spiritual teacher or by suffering); and those who take up the path for a longer time, but lack the will to persevere and eventually drift away. But blessed are those who respond at once to the call of God, and taking up the search for Him in earnest, never waste time anymore.

God Will Guide You in Everything

I am speaking the philosophy that will save you. And I want to give you the techniques that will teach you scientifically how to commune with God now. If you follow this path and meditate in the right way, you can know Him. The scientist does not get his inventions or discoveries merely by praying for them. He has to apply the laws pertinent to his area of research. So must you apply the spiritual laws that will enable you to progress scientifically and surely toward God. Sermons alone will not suffice. They are given only to whet your appetite for God. Practice of the scientific techniques of meditation, and love for God, will take you to Him. Again and again meditate and pray at night with all your heart, forgetting everything but Him. That is how you will find Him.

When by consistent practice your meditation begins to deepen, you may see a little light or hear the astral sounds or see a vision of some saint. At first you tend to discount it as only hallucination; but as you go on with yearning and devotion, applying the law, you see that wonderful things begin to happen in your life in mysterious ways. Five years before this place [the Encinitas Ashram Center] was given to us, I saw in vision the large central hall of the Hermitage, and I told someone it would one day be ours. In the same way, God is responsive to you; He will sustain and guide you in everything—in the selection of your friends or business partners or in everyday decisions—when you will be in tune with Him.

Why should you look for Him in some distant heaven beyond the skies? Our hearts would not beat without the indwelling life of God. We could not speak without borrowing His power and intelligence. The yogi realizes: "O Father, Thou art just behind my vision with which I see Thy beauty without."

When you really feel divine love, you are nearer to God than at any other time. He is so near, and yet so far away—farthest of the far to those that are constantly rambling and wandering in the wilderness of delusion, and nearest of the near in the heart of the yogi who loves Him and who sees Him within.

So follow this path of Self-Realization, whose techniques give you that personal realization of His presence. Let us give thanks to the Heavenly Father with all our hearts for giving us Christ and the Great Ones as our examples to follow. May all God's children follow their example, that a United States of the World may be established with His guidance leading us to His kingdom. His divine emissaries have told us to live as brothers. Christ wanted us to feel "the peace of God, which passeth all understanding."* May that peace reign among men, and the havoc created by wars of nonunderstanding and selfishness be smoothed out by divine love.

Meditate. Feel the great love of God in your heart, and extend that love to all nations of the earth, that it contribute toward removing the cause of wars.

Now affirm with me: "Father, Mother, Friend, Beloved God, I feel Thy divine love within me. I extend that love to all the nations of the earth, that they may stop fighting and be merged and soothed and saved in the infinite peace and divine love of Thine Omnipresent Consciousness. May Thy peace and love reign on earth forever and forever."

* Philippians 4:7.

Living the Divine Existence God Planned for You

Self-Realization Fellowship Encinitas Ashram Center, July 26, 1939

The history of man and the history of man's relationship with God—these are things we should study not only from the scientific but from the metaphysical point of view. We find that man has grown independent of his Creator. He has forgotten that he owes everything to God, and consequently he leads a life that is far different from the divine existence God had planned for him. Although God sent us into this world and although He is putting us through the fire of trials, He did not forget to endow us with His saving grace by putting in man the stamp of His image. Thus man has within him the key to his liberation. Self-realized saints declare: "You do not have to acquire anything for salvation; you merely have to *know* what you are." You do not have to struggle to reach God; but you do have to struggle to tear away the self-created veil that hides Him from you.

The solution to man's problems lies in understanding what the real troubles are, and the ways and means to overcome them. Most people think that by increasing worldly wealth man would find the solution to his problems. But his predicament cannot be solved so simply. Everyone thinks they have to acquire material things in order to be successful. That is recognized as the law of the material world. And those who make the effort through a combination of determination and will power do meet with some success. But if you scrutinize the material world, you will see that very few people are consistently happy, very few are consistently healthy, very few are consistently successful. There is always some trouble. That is why Jesus said, "Seek ye the kingdom of God first, and all things will be added unto you." In the kingdom of divine consciousness you do not have to acquire anything. When you change your status from a mortal being to an immortal being, you will know you have everything in this universe. Man must divert his attention from his environment, and the limitations of his environment, to the image of God within. Until he finds that image, he will not find freedom.

"Thou art That." This is what the Sanskrit scriptures say. Jesus in the Christian Bible says, "I and my Father are One." He was persecuted for that; but it is not wrong to say "I and my Father are One" if you have attained that oneness. A certain saint in India was worshiping the Divine; and suddenly illumination came, and he began to put the flower offerings on his own head, saying, "I bow to Myself within my Self." When the consciousness of God comes, you realize He is within your Self, not merely somewhere away in heaven or in nature or in temples. You find Him within your heart and within your soul.

However, there is a great deal of difference between the state of ignorance and the state of godliness. First, by meditation, gradually try to identify yourself with God; and when you have found that image within yourself, only then can you in truth know, "God has become myself."

Your restless mind is a veil of ignorance between you and God. When you are calm, your consciousness becomes transparent, revealing God. When you are calm, you feel His image within. That is why the Lord gives us sleep at night, to help us remember we are made in His image. Every night in sleep you realize in the deep dreamless state that you are not a mortal being; you feel that vast kingdom of God. But when you wake up you forget that kingdom. Try to retain that soul-peace you had in deep sleep; otherwise this waking world is a nightmare to you.

It is very hard to forget the suggestions of the daytime. From morning till night, you have so many experiences; your mind becomes restless due to the sorrowful or happy experiences you have had. This restlessness is destructive to your consciousness of your divine image within.

Yoga: Scientific Way to Realize God

So how can you know you are Spirit; how can you find that image within? By meditation. There are many ways to get to New York from Los Angeles. If you take a stage coach, it will take many months; and if you go by airplane, it will take just a few hours. So is the Self-Realization way the fast way to God.

Prayer alone will not do. People wonder why they pray so hard and still do not get a personal response from God. They do not know how to meditate. That is why yoga is necessary. If you practice the

Self-Realization yoga techniques, you will get there. Yoga does not tell you merely to believe and you will be saved; it teaches you the scientific laws and techniques by which you can feel God in your own consciousness. It is only when you actually commune with God that He will respond openly. Not before. He can't. When your consciousness is closed behind the door of your ignorance, God cannot enter in. When you will open that door, God will reveal Himself; and in that realization all things become possible. However, you have to make the effort. You won't find God if you sit for meditation and your mind roams about on different subjects. But if you practice the techniques regularly, you will find Him.

Devotion is also necessary. Follow the scientific technique of meditation which we have taught, with devotion. That will take you much farther than you can imagine, for God will answer only through law plus devotion.

Let no one tell you that yoga meditation can be harmful, that it can cause you to become mentally unbalanced. The masters have given these scientific techniques to free mankind. Negative criticism takes root because Satan does not want souls to go back to God. Some persons are fully ready to have a mental breakdown through either abuse of sex energy or some emotional complex, and they seek religion—not only yoga—to find relief. It is not the religion or spiritual practices that brings on their trouble, but their own karmic predisposition. Religious congregations provide a sort of mutual psychological support for those who seek God because of troubles—mental, emotional, physical, or material. In fact, most people do not wake up to the need for God until some form of sorrow comes. But there are also true devotees who have a great devotion for God and seek Him unconditionally because of love for Him.

Four Stages of Spiritual Seeking

Spiritually, there are four types of people. Many are completely asleep spiritually. When you talk of God, they ignore or laugh at you. Some are a little awake; you talk to them and they understand, but that is all—they do not want to make any effort to know God. Then the third type read lots of religious ideas in books and think they will know God; or they read a little and pray and go to church or perform their *pujas.* They do not want to go further; they are satisfied. But it is not the satisfaction of blind belief that can get you there. God reveals Himself only to those who make the effort to *know.* If the scientist does not make a systematic effort, applying nature's laws, he does not reach his goals. Similarly, the superficial seeker cannot have God just by external worship and blind prayer. There must be understanding of the laws by which his mortal ignorance is dispelled.

In India we have made the spiritual search a definite science. There is no speculation about it. But here in America so many are just seeking some solace, and so they take to anything. Some teachers use religion to exploit others to make money. I never expose them, for they will fall of themselves. But you must be aware, for "the blind cannot lead the blind." In India, we go to places where great saints live and are in contact with God. It is only by following the example and guidance of those who have found God that you can find God.

In India I met a great many men and women of illumination. But when I have gone into the churches in the West, I have seen good souls who have a little inspiration, but they have not divine realization. To find truth in the forest of theology, we must have a proper guide. As you must study with a creditable teacher in order to know about medicine or science, so you can never realize truth or understand the mysteries of God without a qualified mentor who himself has attained that realization.

When the initial desire for truth comes, someone gives you a book or you seek out a teacher to awaken you further. But when the desire is very strong, God sends you a guru, one who is much more than an ordinary teacher. The guru must have some credential from his own God-knowing guru, and from God. Through that messenger, God will bring you back to Himself. No one can go back to God without this aid of a God-ordained guru.

God is more tangible, and more desirable, than all things in this world. The Masters have shown me that. And how to know for yourself? When you become a member, spiritually, of the fourth class of people, a devotee who can say, "I have been praying and have tasted a little divine joy within me, but I know that is not enough. Lord, I have to find You." Then your heart day and night pursues Him, and you do not feel joy in anything unless God is there with you.

Do not be satisfied with a little devotion; every day and night practice the scientific method of meditation, and then concentrated prayer and communion become easy. What is the use of listening to sermons and then going home and falling asleep spiritually—not applying what you hear? If you want to find God in this lifetime, and if you want to know you are made in His image, you must make a sincere effort. You must seek wholeheartedly by throwing yourself at the feet of God. That deep effort can best be done at night when all are asleep and you are free of daytime duties.

Do not think you can get ascension in a moment. It takes years! Salvation can come only by the strength of your determination. It cannot be known by the weak-minded. But it is much easier and faster if you know the science of meditation. If you are a member of that fourth class of people who cannot be satisfied with reading a book about God, or listening to a sermon, or feeling a little devotion, you will find Him.

Persevere to Advance Through the Progressive States of Calmness

Not only should you meditate, but you should strive to destroy the veil of mortal delusion and restlessness by practicing during activity the calmness felt in meditation. When you first begin to meditate, you find it hard to concentrate. Ordinary man is always restless. Even in sleep, he is not at rest. But by a little meditation, the mind will remain calm for a little while and then go straying again. That is the second state. That is where millions stay. If you make greater effort, you will reach the third state: The mind is half the time restless, half the time calm. And then after more effort, in the fourth state, the mind remains mostly calm; only a little restlessness comes back from time to time. I never blamed anybody else when in the beginning I didn't get results. I knew it was my own fault, and that I must persevere. In time, the effects of my meditation habits automatically began to be poured on me. As you go on meditating, in the fifth state the mind and consciousness are raised up in unruffled calmness.

God made us in His image. The way to remember the image of God within us is to retain the state of perfect inner calmness. He who is calm is fit for the kingdom of God. His mind is always still; never restless. I never could dream that I would attain that state. The struggle in the beginning seemed so difficult. I knew others who would not get that state because they did not give the time to the struggle, nor have sufficient desire for God. Again and again those others compare my life with theirs and say, "I am sorry I didn't follow the example of your life."

I sat hours and hours in meditation seeking God—and then at last I found Him. Sometimes, even when I sought with the most urgent effort and expectation, still I didn't find Him. But when the heart was filled with great devotion and was drunk with His love, then He was there. Yet when I would try tangibly to hold on to Him, He would slip away. He wants to make sure whether we want Him or His gifts. That is the drama of life—to choose God or the offerings of the world. Every day I tell Him, "Lord, Thou art mine. And because Thou art mine, I want naught else but Thee." You must convince God that you love Him alone. Show Him silently in the fullness of your heart, "Lord, I love Thee more than everything else." He will test you; and if you pass His test and still say you love Him supremely, then the Lord will come to you.

Day by day is passing and you must feel the urgency to find Him now. But you must be patient. Without perseverance you will never find God. With continuous patience and continuous prayer, and ever deeper and longer meditation, you will realize the glories of the Spirit. "Ask, and ye shall receive." By continuous asking, the presence of the Spirit is revealed within us.

First, you feel always restless; then sometimes calm; then by practice you feel half the time restless, half the time calm; and then as you develop you feel more calm and seldom restless; and last, when you are all the time with God, there is no more restlessness. That is the state I am enjoying. When you realize Spirit as your own Self, you no longer have to seek the Infinite within Its myriad manifestations. When you become one with God, you do not have to meditate on Him anymore. You are that Infinite Self. Nothing else is more important. Nothing else is necessary. If I don't wish to eat, I don't eat. If I don't wish to sleep, I don't sleep. I remain in that continuous devotion—the boundless joy of God's love. When we turn on the light of devotion, it may be put out by doubts; but when God puts the light of His love in our hearts, it can never be extinguished.

Each one of you, no matter how restless you are, if you follow the laws of spiritual realization and meditate in the way I tell you, you will get realization much quicker than you can ever imagine. "Then life is sweet, and death a dream; then health is sweet, and sickness a dream; when Thy song flows through me." That is the state you want to enjoy. Then you know you are not destroyed with the death of the body. Suppose you are dreaming that you are as strong as a Sandow, lifting a motorcar; and suddenly your heart collapses, and you die.* When you awaken from that nightmare, you

* Eugene Sandow (1867–1925), famous for his physique and physical prowess, died at fifty-eight when a blood vessel in his brain burst as a result of his having raised a car singlehanded.

realize it was but a dream and that you are not dead. You *know* you are alive. That is what will happen to you when you are awake in God. You will realize that all of life's experiences are but a dream, and you are free of that dream. That is what God reveals to you.

God showed me this truth during the Civil War in Spain, when bombs were falling on innocent people and helpless children. I prayed, "Lord, why does this happen?" He replied, "Son, I cannot prevent the misuse of man's free will, which causes disasters." But then He showed me what freedom these innocent ones received through death—freedom from starvation and fear. In this vision God said, "See how they are all jumping out of their bullet- and bomb-shattered bodies and entering My everlasting bosom. There is no suffering for them anymore." Then I said, "Lord, glory be Thy name that I can understand this truth."

I realized that the Lord is infinitely Good. He even gave man unconsciousness to alleviate suffering. That is, man does not experience torture beyond a certain limit. The mind detaches itself from the body and is no longer conscious of it at all. God gave sensitivity to man's flesh merely to protect the body lest in breaking a limb or cutting the flesh man would not take care of it. Human nature has magnified that sensitivity into pain by fear. Man has made himself much more sensitive to pain than is the animal.

God's Plan for Harmony Among the Nations

There will come a time in the distant future when there will be no physical disease or material suffering; but the world must become much more spiritually evolved than it is now. There was such a time in ancient India when harmony, peace, and prosperity existed. The masses were following spiritual laws. But gradually they fell away from that consciousness; and inharmony, disease, and poverty resulted. The conditions that caused the Great Depression and the ongoing inharmonies in the modern world are, likewise, the results of man's wrongdoing, metaphysically and psychologically. There is enough food and other materials to supply the needs of the entire world. Why is there suffering? Because of selfishness. Jesus taught caring and sharing. But everybody wants for himself. Selfishness and greed bring fear and discord.

We must seek to understand the divine plan of God. First were the cavemen; through the impulse of sex, man and woman were drawn together and formed a family unit. These units protected themselves against the aggression of other family units. Then, to protect themselves against more widespread aggressions, family units came together to form clans. And then clans joined together to form a nation with common interests. But why stop there? It is by understanding others' needs and uniting a nation's interests with others' needs that man furthers the divine plan of God. But it seems man does not understand this drama of life. He constantly foments conflicts.

War consists of unheard-of cruelties; and when you are directly involved, it makes your heart tremble! In the days of the kings, war for the good of the kingdom was thought to be chivalrous; but after World War I, war was condemned—nations began to realize that brother was killing brother. Nations must cease actions based on hatred and adopt measures that are only constructive. Hatred is the instrument of Satan. The best way to conquer is by the power of love. Jesus showed the example. He said, "Father, forgive them, for they know not what they do." People do wrong under satanic impulses. Any act that desecrates the image of God within you is wrong.

As soon as nations, tempted by the evil force, become greedy and selfishly aggressive, they lose the image of God. But the image of God is trying to establish Itself in the world. The world is marching on—it is not going backward as many think.

The nations of the world will find that there is some purpose to this trouble that is going on now.* In spite of everything, out of this chaos you will see that all those weak nations that have lost their independence will regain it. All these wars will never stop until enslaved nations, such as Egypt, China, and India are free, completely. God always takes the side of the oppressed. Even the most powerful nations will fall where there is rule by tyranny—any nation will fall if it uses tyranny. When you have the pulse of the world, you will see that the power of God is working there. The power of evil travels with the wind and the power of good travels against the wind.

Power should be tempered with wisdom; power governed by spirituality. True and lasting peace will not be arrived at by force; it must be accomplished by spiritualizing mankind. If everyone in this world were spiritual, not by religiosity but expression of soul qualities, the result would be perfect harmony. I love America and I pray that—along with India—she be a spiritual example. Goodwill

* The beginning of World War II.

to all—that kind of patriotism is real Americanism. Follow God and Christlike principles. Spiritualize the nation, and that will save many, many troubles for your country. And you will set an example that many other nations will want to follow. The image of God is slowly coming in the heart of nations. That is what will gradually take place. But God has all eternity; He is not in a hurry to give salvation to the world.

Give Your Time and Concentration to What Is Truly Important

You must convince God that you absolutely refuse to be treated like a human animal, bound to the slow progress of natural evolution. Show that you are willing to make the effort now to remember your divine heritage as made in God's image. You do not want destiny to gamble with your life. You must be able to take command of your life, even of death, as Jesus commanded the storm to cease. The Masters teach you how: Become a master of your Self. If you practice these teachings of Self-Realization Fellowship you will know that all I have said is true. Be like Jesus' disciples by practicing kindness and love and renunciation of too many desires so that you can find God. That is what you want.

See the difference between the great man and the ordinary man. The ordinary man is lost in a myriad of little things, but the great man concentrates on what is important. That is how you must be if you want God. Those who do not meditate, or who do not read or think deeply—their consciousness is always external. They are constantly running here and there, wanting diversion. They go to the movies for a little entertainment, but it is always the same thing—a hero and a heroine and a villain. The villain gets killed and the couple supposedly live happily ever after. There may be a different background—Indian, African, American—but the same old story is there. And it doesn't tell of all the battles and troubles that the couple have during the "ever after"!

Just look about you at the brevity of human love! You see two young people very much in love. Then picture them an old couple sitting together, bored with each other, no communication. A little emotion there may be; but where went that exhilarating love? The one thing that never goes away is the love of God.

God is playing hide-and-seek through human hearts, so that ultimately you will understand that it is His love you are seeking in your human loves. If you omit God from your human loves, love fades away. But by bringing God into your daily life, ordinary human love changes into divine love, manifested from the image of God within you. Transform your love into divine love. Then human relationships become sanctified.

In divine love, you see God not only in your friends, but in your enemies as well. You treat everyone as a child of God. I am filled with such love, especially when I see people who are imbued with harmony and devotion. I worship Him in all of you. All the great ones that I have seen are humble, because they see God in all, having found the image of God in themselves. That is realization.

Why Choose to Remain in Spiritual Darkness?

Remember, that divine state is already yours, right within you. The need is not to acquire, but to know. As soon as you know, you will be freed. The sun shines, but if I close my eyes I see only darkness. When I open my eyes, the sunlight is there. It was always there; the darkness existed merely because I had my eyes closed. That is the way it is with the light of God's presence. Your eyes are closed; but if you open your spiritual eye by meditation, you will behold Him shining within you and everywhere.

For those who choose to remain in darkness, life is fraught with troubles and sorrows, interspersed with a little happiness. And then death comes and wipes away that particular dream. If there were no death, there would never be any respite from sorrow and suffering. Death is not as terrible as you think. It comes to you as a healer. Sleep is nothing but a counterfeit death. What happens in death we can picture in sleep. All our sufferings vanish in sleep. When death comes, all our mortal tortures cease; they cannot go beyond the portals of death.

After some time in the greater freedom of the astral world, if your desire for the sensory experiences of a physical body becomes very strong, you are drawn back to rebirth on earth. But if you finish all your desires, you do not have to reincarnate, forced here by your unfinished desires. Who wants to come back that way, starting out as a helpless baby to grow up and go through all life's troubles again? Why not finish your desires now? Show God that you are fit to enter His kingdom. Wash yourself completely clean from all the soil of your mortal desires so you can return to your Father and say, "Lord, I was Your prodigal son. Receive me now. I want to enjoy throughout eternity the festivity of Thy kingdom."

God is not partial. His spirit is as fully within you as it was in Jesus and the great Masters. Find it by making your mind more transparent, more receptive. The more you meditate and remember that image of God, the more you will feel God's harmony uniting all things. Meditation and holding on to God's presence in that inner calmness all day long is what is necessary.

If You Follow These Teachings, You Can Know Him

I am extremely enjoying my time in Encinitas. The more I have God, the more I am able to give Him to you. In the indescribable beauty of Encinitas, with the fragrant flowers, the blue sky, the temple domes, and the breath of the sea—everything speaks of His presence. Time and time again people have told me how they have felt the presence of God on these grounds. Nature's scenery is the perfect representative of God. This beautiful Self-Realization Encinitas Center is an ideal environment to help you find God. Divine communion is difficult in busy places. You should now and then get away for silent retreats. Jesus went to the mountains for his solitude. So make regular visits to Encinitas. One moon gives more light than all the stars. If you make the real effort to find God, you will accomplish more good than all superficial seekers.

Here in Self-Realization you are connected with a great movement that has come through the lineage of our Great Gurus and is blessed by them. It was Jesus and Mahavatar Babaji who sent this work to America that devotees worldwide might find fulfillment of the Christ-promise of receiving the Holy Ghost. If you follow these teachings and meditate deeply, and then compare these teachings with any other, you will see that they are several hundred years ahead of their time. They herald the coming of a higher age of enlightenment. You are learning truths that can be applied and realized now in your daily life. Every moment that I am with you I shall urge you to seek God; and if you listen, you will find Him. This work will take you as far as you want to go. You must have the desire and the zeal. It is the voice of God that is speaking to you, reminding you that you must redeem yourself. Self-Realization Fellowship will show you how—by personal fellowship with God you can know Him. Do not delay, for you have to go a long way; and who knows when you may be snatched away by death? Find redemption now.

Come along! I found Him, my Beloved, my Lord, my Intoxication night and day; and I can show you how to become intoxicated with Him. It is through His grace that I am speaking to you; otherwise I would remain silent, because I have no desire for students and a following. I am concerned only with your soul, and I want only those souls who want God; and it is for their own highest good that I am here, and for naught else.

So, dear friends, study the *Lessons* and magazine and stay here in Encinitas whenever you can. We do not want any persons who are inharmonious; we only want those who are in harmony with us—who meditate regularly, eat simple healthful foods, and practice calmness.

Mount Washington is the mother who gave birth to Encinitas. Enjoy the environment of these spiritual places. I don't need these centers for myself; they are my contribution to God's work in America. When I will be received in the bosom of God, you will realize somebody came here from India, not to take anything away, but to give to peoples of America and the world the realization of God.

Your cooperation with this work is just as important as anyone else's. It is all for you. I have given every penny to this work. I do not keep any bank account of my own. I live the spiritual law of renunciation just as I lived in India; everything has been given to the work. I am free, as free as when I came to America. My life is God, my home is God, my prosperity is God.

Self-realization: Knowing Your Infinite Nature

Compilation of two talks given at Self-Realization Fellowship International Headquarters, Los Angeles, August 1933 and March 1934

Peace fall upon you, peace abide with you, joy permeate your being within and without!

An ocean of eternal power is around you and within you. Just as a corked bottle floats in the ocean, so you are surrounded by God and peace. Wherever you float in the ocean of life, you will always be immersed in that Great Power and Life. Realize that!

As you become more and more aware of God and the eternal power within you, the focus of life becomes reversed. Instead of constantly feeling the processes of the body, you feel the Eternal Silence behind the flesh. The man of realization knows himself as the Formless and yet as the form of everything.

You are concentrated on the isolated wave of your body and its finite life; thus you forget that infinite omnipresence of God. But when you realize that the life in all bodies, and in all manifestations in nature, is nothing but outbursts of God's consciousness, then you are in His eternal presence. God is ever in the stars, and in the clods of the earth, and in our thoughts, feelings, and will; and when you perceive this, then you realize your connection with Infinity. That is Self-realization: You feel yourself no longer as a little wavelet of life, but as the Ocean itself.

Throughout the day, you are constantly working through the body, and so you become identified with it. But every night God removes from you that imprisoning delusion. Last night in deep dreamless sleep, were you a woman or a man or an American or Hindu or rich or poor? No. You were pure Spirit. In the daytime you are conscious of being so many pounds of flesh and bones, a bundle of nerves and muscles; but in the semi-superconscious freedom of deep sleep God takes away all your mortal titles and makes you feel that you are apart from the body and all its limitations—pure consciousness, resting in space. That vastness is your real Self. Meditation is the process by which you become fully conscious of the freedom of that forgotten Self.

Why do I ask you to be silent, to meditate? To compare that vastness and freedom with the confining consciousness of being tied to the body. With eyes shut in meditation, you do not see your body; you are gazing into the sphere of darkness behind closed eyes. As you become calm and your meditation deepens, the sensations and awareness of the little body recede. You feel an expansion of your being beyond the boundaries of the mortal form. The vast inner space becomes bigger and bigger; you begin to feel that you *are* this space, boundless consciousness pervaded with ever-increasing happiness and peace. It is then that you realize you are something much greater than the body.

If you can retain this consciousness of joyous vastness instead of losing it again in the delusion of the body, you will realize your true Self. Isn't it strange that you do not know who you are? that you do not know your own Self? You define yourself by so many different titles applicable to your body and mortal roles. But are you the body? No, because you can exist without the body. Every night you do it. Though you are not aware of the body in deep sleep, still you know you exist. Anything that you can subtract from your consciousness without losing your sense of "I-ness," you are not that. You must peel off these titles from the soul. "I think, but I am not the thought. I feel, but I am not the feeling. I will, but I am not the will." What is left? The you that *knows* you exist; the you that *feels* you exist—through the proof given by intuition, the soul's unconditioned knowing of its own existence.

That is what I learned in India: to be centralized in the Self and constantly remain in that unbounded attitude. Always the great masters that I knew there never identified themselves with the body. In the divine man the body is just a manifested finite part of his infinite being. He doesn't feel for the body as ordinary persons do. When you are walking you do not feel identified with any particular part—your hair, your fingers. You have a general feeling that you are carrying a body. So it is with me. I am aware that I have a body, but I know I am the soul.

Such is the change the great masters wrought in me. Now there is one consciousness alone: I am conscious of my real Self. The vastness of my soul has spread wings into everything and I am conscious of all things.

I will tell you how I live and work in the world. My body and the world are my office; and my inner Self is my home. My mind always dwells within. I live from day to day. There is no consciousness of past or future; I am living in the eternally happy present. It is not a mundane happiness, which becomes boring after a while so that you welcome a little difficulty just for a change. The joy that has come upon me is a thousand million times more intoxicating—ever-changing, ever-new. In that consciousness you feel all the happiness in the world passing through you. Your love is all-encompassing. That is the experience of God's love. I see people suffering from sickness and poverty and all kinds of misery, and I yearn to bring them all where I am: Whether I laugh or cry at the scenes of this earthly drama, a current of bliss is ever moving underneath my outer consciousness. At first it was different. I would try to be happy, but then some sadness would come inside. But I continued in meditation to make the effort to know God, and now it is happiness all the time. My body and mind respond to what my heart feels. It is filled with divine love no matter whether I talk to people of peace or business—always God's joy bubbling within me. And the wisdom! As soon as I pick up a book I perceive whatever truth it contains, or whether it is only a product of misguided imagination. I do not accept anything just because somebody else has said so. If it is truth, I feel it; and if it is not, I disregard it. The whole library of the cosmos can be found within the soul. I rarely read a book, and yet the things that are given to me overpower me. As I am speaking to you, I am drawing on that inner source of cosmic wisdom. I don't have to try. All I do is put mental obstructions out of the way.

Refining Your Consciousness for Cosmic Perception

All truth is in God—in His cosmic consciousness. Truth means the nature and history of everything on earth, everything in the universe and beyond. Man's faculties are capable of being greatly expanded. However, to encompass the totality of knowledge would require a correspondingly vast mental development. By natural evolution of the body and its instruments of knowing and perceiving, it would take a million years of living in perfect health—free from physical disease and mental inharmony—to refine the chemical and cellular composition of the brain sufficiently. By the mortal way of development, with its inevitable setbacks of negative conditions, this takes untold rounds of earthly reincarnations. But by the divine way it is possible in one life for the body and mind to become fit receptacles of Cosmic Consciousness. That is the purpose of the Kriya Yoga higher art of realization that I teach.

Nature's snail-paced process of evolution develops the physical body and thereby the brain; but India's masters anciently found that any development that is approached *from* the brain *to* the body gives vastly quicker results. By mastery of the intelligent life currents in the brain and spine, with their divine astral centers of life and consciousness and their physical counterparts in the central nervous system, the body and brain can be purified and refined in three to six, twelve to twenty-four, twenty-four to forty-eight years. When by Kriya Yoga meditation you understand the mysteries of the cerebrospinal centers, where the powers that control the universe are enshrined to control the microcosm of the body, then any effect you initiate there will quickly change the body and its consciousness. Thus with the help of this technique of Kriya Yoga the adept can in a few years attain Cosmic Consciousness.

If only you could see what I see, and feel the joy I feel! You can, if you meditate. I have practiced this spiritual science; and I know whereof I speak.

The Scientific Highway That Leads to God

The teachings of all great religions lead toward God; but their varied outer observances are bypaths that must eventually bring the seeker to the one inner highway of meditation. Withdrawing the consciousness from the body and finite world and merging it in the Divine is the only way to liberation in God. Jesus meditated. To the crowds he taught moral and spiritual truths—the necessary first steps toward God; but to his close disciples he taught the higher science of meditation for actual union with God.

It is not the technique of meditation alone that will bring you freedom; your character must be strong and pure. Your whole life and behavior must be in harmony with the laws of truth. The first rules of the yoga path of meditation are *yama* and *niyama*—certain things you should not do, corresponding to the Ten Commandments ("thou shalt not kill," "thou shalt not bear false witness," "thou shalt not commit adultery" and so on); and also the positive prescriptions you should follow: purity, evenminded contentment, introspection (self-study), devotion to God, and self-discipline. To progress in meditation, you must be working to free yourself from pride, wrath, greed, jealousy. You must not be insincere with people; say nothing you do not honestly feel. Do not selfishly seek anything from others; if you have no expectations, then what can people take from you? No one can hurt me because I have no ambition except for God. I wish anger on no man, and no one can provoke me by a display of anger. So strive to be peaceful, self-controlled, and sincere. Otherwise, the wrong behavior will negate the propitious effects of meditation.

Every spiritual thought you think will be your eternal friend. And every evil inclination you acquire will be your enemy for a long, long time; it will pursue you until you slay it. Remember that. I am pointing out to you the step-by-step methods to God. First, free yourself from wrong thoughts and habits. Second, establish good habits and perform good deeds.

The third step is *asana* or posture: The body must be under your control in order to meditate deeply. Then comes *pranayama* (control of *prana* or life force), techniques for calming the body and mind, breath and heartbeat. *Pranayama* is the primary art of realization. You cannot find God unless you can master the mortal breath. Breath ties the mind to the sense plane. As your breath becomes calm, your mind goes within. Breathlessness is the way to God. Practice *pranayama* and you will know how to meditate—how to perceive God and be one with Him.*

The interiorization of the mind that comes through *pranayama* is called *pratyahara.* That is the next step: The consciousness is turned within, away from the senses. Then true meditation begins. When your attention is freed from distractions of breath and body and outer sensations, it is able to focus single-pointedly on God. That is called *dharana,* concentration, the sixth step on the eightfold yoga path. In the inner stillness, one hears the mighty voice of Spirit as *Aum,* the Word or Amen. As you listen to and merge in that great, comforting Cosmic Vibration, the consciousness expands with it into all space. That is *dhyana,* meditation on the conception of the magnitude of God. And as the concentration and perception of meditation becomes deeper, one reaches the ultimate state, *samadhi,* in which the meditator, the process of meditation, and the object of meditation (God) merge in oneness. In *samadhi,* you know by direct experience that God and you are One.

* The highest *pranayama* techniques are part of the science of Kriya Yoga, taught to students of the *Self-Realization Fellowship Lessons.*

The Inner Heaven of Oneness With God

Most people think of heaven as a glorious land of angels, with streets paved with gold; or as a place of exceeding pleasure with laughing-eyed girls serving banquets on golden platters. Man idealizes according to the nature of his desires—his overall level of consciousness. I think that if a fish could speak to us, his conception of heaven would be a place where there is lots of water and food-filled coral reefs! But the real heaven is more transcendently beautiful than any conception of your imagination. It is oneness with the Infinite Consciousness; indescribable, eternal Bliss. In that heaven of Cosmic Consciousness God is calling us. And man is resisting His call by preoccupation with wrong thoughts and earthly desires. It is for us to attune our thoughts to His resonant voice within.

"The ignorant, oblivious of My transcendental nature as the Maker of all creatures, discount also My presence within the human form."* By your delusive attachments, you absolutely shut out that Infinite King who is within you. A caged bird regards its confinement as its home, with its accustomed comforts and sense of security. It shows no interest in the broad horizon beyond its cage. Our love for our body-cage is nothing short of that, even when disease and ignorance impinge on our peace and happiness. Why not inquire what is behind the darkness of closed eyes? That is the escape route to explore. "The light shineth in darkness; and the darkness comprehended it not."† Vast light and cosmic forces of the Almighty are moving there in that darkness, awaiting the command of your emerging true Self. Make the effort to see what it is all about. Meditate! Free the soul-bird of life from the little cage of the body, that it spread its wings and soar in the eternal skies of Self-realization.

In Seattle I was sitting by a waterfall, enjoying the sunlight shining on my face; inwardly I prayed, "Lord, what is this light? Is it comparable to the effulgence of Your presence?" As I thought this, a glorious ray of light divine came over me, cool and soothing in its effect—a marvelous thrill of happiness. All the visions I saw in that light came true afterwards. If you persist long enough in meditation, you will find to be true what I am telling you of this wondrous science of God-communion.

* Bhagavad Gita IX:11.

† John 1:5.

In nature, the aurora borealis has the closest resemblance to the light of God. If you remain quiet in meditation for a short time and see a little light, you think, "That is all there is to it." No, it is not. As you spend more time at night and really make up your mind that you must know what lies behind the obscuring wall of material darkness, eventually you will behold vast worlds, infinite life, emerging from the factory of silence. That hidden factory is the source of creation; stars, planets, blades of grass, all beings, all things come from the vastness behind that wall of darkness. Do not be satisfied with a little light and temporary peace in meditation; and don't be constantly identified with the body if you want to know the greatness of your soul. To be with God is to be richer than Croesus. To be with God is to own the whole universe and be its master. To be with God is to free yourself from misery and fears for all eternity. To be with God is to know all that is to be known. These attainments cannot be had by a mere few minutes of silence. You have to put your whole attention to work.

Meditation is the only way. Jesus taught, "Pray unceasingly." What does that mean? Not just to sit for five minutes of scattered prayer and then rush off; but to meditate until you have received an answer to the cry of your soul to know God. As the infinite Transcendental Absolute, He is impersonal. Yet as the Father-Mother-Friend of all, that Supreme One is intimately personal; and as such, He will answer you. He is silent in the beginning; but if you are persistent in your demands, He will reply. I can feel that some of you are nearing the place where He is about to whisper to you.

Do not give up until God responds: "You must speak to me, Mother Divine. I die a thousand deaths if You do not talk to me." When you convince Her that you are absolutely sincere, you will find the fulfillment of what I am telling you.

Make your meditation so intense that its effect lasts throughout all the day's activities. Do not be too busy to seek the One who created you. If you become king of the world, what then? If you conquer all nations, what then? One day you will find you are dying and helpless. Why should you crave to own worldly things? They can be taken away from you anytime—as they surely will when you pass through the portals of death. Rather, make the effort to know that Something which can never be wrested from you. God is the most uncertain to those who do not meditate, yet the yogi knows Him as the most dependable Certainty. And "great will be their reward" who find Him.

Real happiness I have seen in the great yogis of India. Their earthly abode may be only a humble cave; but they are kings smiling with the joy of God, the King of kings, secure in their power over all creation. Realize that to attain this consciousness of God is your ultimate and most worthwhile goal; I am telling you all the steps so that you know how to get there. It is not just sitting quietly and saying a little prayer that will give you God-realization; it is churning the silence with your prayer and desire for God. The result will be something wonderful. You must make the effort: I am not here to feed you with words, but to nourish your soul with the love of God.

From my researches in the laboratory of life, I have found eternal pleasure. Modern life is becoming very unsatisfactory. It does not give you happiness. There are too many things, too many desires. More nice cars and dresses and entertainments—and more worries! Free yourself from these so-called "necessities" and spend more time with God. Make your life simple. Be happy in and by your Self. And when you want to be with others, join them with the distinct consciousness of helping them, or of sharing friendship in God, but don't waste your time. Instead of spending hours in idle socializing, read good books and thereby keep company with the great souls whose consciousness lives on in the wisdom they have written. And meditate! The song of truth that can be heard within you is much more charming than any book can tell. If you want to hear the magnificent songs of the greatest souls—those who are one with God—you must go into the temple of meditation. The saints and masters are all there. They will come to you.

God is the Supreme Spirit of the spirits within all created things that makes them attractive. Why wish for anything else than God? Tune your mind to the presence of God. Go deep into meditation, so that you merge into the Infinite. When I meditate, one by one I close the doors of the senses, lest the aroma of the rose or the song of the nightingale distract my attention from God. That ability and freedom from body-consciousness came by hard labor; it did not come just by wishing for it.

When others are wasting time, the yogi meditates. Every day you feel you have some duty that is the most important thing you should do. And after you finish that duty, you find another and another equally pressing engagement. So the whole day passes; and by the time you have finished, sleep is upon you. You must save yourself for God, for communion with Him in the secrecy of inner silence. Let no one tamper with your time for God. Then you will know what this life is all about.

Be with God instead of with your worries. If you can apply the same zest for God that the miser feels toward his money, that the lover feels for his beloved, with which the drowning man gasps for air—when you concentrate those strong cravings upon God, then you will know Him. Be intense! Wholly immerse yourself in meditation. Start by spending half an hour in meditation, then increase it to one hour. The more you become accustomed to meditating longer, the more you will like it.

Why do you permit yourself to remain entrapped in the cycles of births and deaths and their untold miseries? How many lifetimes will you helplessly go through all this? Don't waste your time. I condemn anything that keeps you away from God. To seek Him is the eternal way of happiness. This, every man and woman should realize.

Anyone who is successful in making money does so by spending much time learning the means to his goal, then adopts the right method, and then persists with determination until he achieves. That same systematic effort must be applied to finding God. Self-Realization Fellowship gives you the method. If you take my advice and follow the *Lessons* sent from our headquarters, and meditate night and morning, you shall see what wonderful changes happen to you. I will show you the way again and again until you get it. We are here for Self-realization, to know the truth now. Some are already achieving that through these *Lessons* and their meditations; I know who they are. Why shouldn't you, too, have that fulfillment?

No matter how you feel, whether you are happy or unhappy, remember, try to meditate. You will find the joy that is within you. Throughout the day, carry with you the peaceful aftereffects of meditation. Do not think of yourself as the body, but as the joyous consciousness and immortal life behind it. And at night intensely meditate. Once a month—or every week, if you can—have a day of silence, when you get away from everybody and give yourself uninterruptedly to your relationship with God.

To retain your spiritual consciousness, keep your awareness always at the point between the eyebrows; feel the superconscious state of the soul. The sleeping person has his mind in the subconscious state, and the eyes are cast down. The meditating yogi's eyes are uplifted and his breath more or less still. And even when active in the outer world, his mind dwells in superconsciousness, focused always at the Christ-*Kutastha* center between the eyebrows.

In that consciousness, I am always happy. Even death is no threat to that inner joy. I never miss any dear one taken away by death, because I feel my existence spread through the very depths of the Divine Sea, while on the surface our individualized wave-forms are all dancing. Do you see what I mean? If I am the ocean, then I feel all its waves. Whether soul-waves disappear in the Sea in death or reemerge in another wave of life, I shall feel them. When I meet these souls again, I feel the same unbroken joy. They are ever with me in that great Divine Spirit. When we are tossed together as companion waves on the bosom of the Ocean of God, we are happy together. And when we are flung apart into distant reaches of that Sea, still in God we are always together.

I am not here with any desire to be a lecturer or a minister. I am just one of you, and I humbly bow to the God templed within you. As I speak, I see a vision of God's light pervading each one of you. You are little bubbles of light in His effulgence of Eternal Power. Everything is melting in that great Light. All is God, God, God. In that Infinite Consciousness, body, breath, everything becomes still—just as though I were dead, and yet I am living.

I have come not to sermonize, but to give you realization—to strike fire in your hearts, to blaze the flame of devotion! I speak what I feel of the Infinite God. The joy of all souls I feel dancing within me. Omnipresent joy! That is what I want you to feel. Someday I shall wash my hands of everything connected with this mortal body, that I may be free and say, "No more am I teaching; I am everything."

Dear friends, I have told you something very sacred today; and if even one of you out of this congregation is inspired to start in earnest on this path, my sermon this morning is a blessing both to you and to me.

Remember, we are immortals, divine children of the King of Infinity, sent here to play and to dream and to be entertained; but not to become enmeshed in the tangle of life. If you forget God, it will not be God who will punish you; you will create your own misery. If you know God, He will reveal to you that this life is only a drama and that you are immortal, that you were never sick, that you were never dead, and you were never unhappy. It was all a dream. There is no other way to find God except through meditation practiced in the way the masters teach it. Follow that method. Veils will fall from your mind and every thought and every thing will be a window through which you will behold the face of the King.

The Divine Art of Erasing Age and Creating Vitality

Compilation of two talks given at Self-Realization Fellowship Temples, July 23, 1939 and November 14, 1943

To remain in abundant good health is an art that is not known by most people. There are two aspects to this art: the physical methods and the divine methods. The physical ways of looking after the body-machine are numerous; countless books have been written on the subject. Still, that knowledge alone is of limited effectiveness in keeping this machine in perfect condition. We must also know how to apply the divine ways in order to keep ourselves well.

The joy and vitality of youth are not related to one's physical age. God is ever youthful, and He is eternal. But in the general sense we can say youth is with us until about the age of thirty. After forty, the body-machine begins to change; its natural endowment of vitality and ability to restore itself starts to wane. You can choose to be either the body's doctor or its enemy. To the degree that you can avoid inflicting damage on your body-machine, you can hope to preserve it much longer in a healthy condition. By the right physical, mental, and spiritual methods, much of the unwelcome effect of the body's aging can be erased.

Cleansing the Body From Within

Health is easier to maintain if you know and practice the laws of keeping the body well, rather than starting the effort to heal yourself only after you have become sick. The Chinese tradition was to pay their doctors to keep them well; and if someone fell ill, the doctors had to pay the bill. You, too, should apply the wisdom in the adage: "An ounce of prevention is worth a pound of cure."

When you buy an old car, you want it to run like new. The best thing to do then is to get it thoroughly overhauled so that it is in good running order. You have to spend a little bit more money initially, but you can then expect it to run reliably for a long time. So it is with your body. Those whose physical vehicle has been weakened by age—perhaps their liver is out of order, or their kidneys or digestive organs—should know the way to overhaul that human machine thoroughly. The first step is to get rid of the poisons that have accumulated in the system. Fasting is an ideal method of accomplishing this—for example, three days on orange juice and ground almonds, with a natural laxative. Repeat this after one month. If you spend the time and effort necessary to cleanse the body from within, you will quickly find the truth of what I am telling you about preserving youth.*

Most of you are dying of disease because of overeating day after day, and eating the wrong foods. The less meat you eat the better—especially after you turn forty, because it takes much energy to clean your own blood as well as what you ingest from the animal's, which may carry many toxins or harmful chemicals. Meat has some good qualities, but it is better to eat meat substitutes. Meat takes too long to digest and pass through the body; and that undigested protein creates an acid condition in the body that is destructive to the kidneys. Many persons have kidney trouble and do not know it; yet the impaired functioning of these purifying filters inevitably hastens old age.† Fruits and vegetables, including raw salads of lettuce and other greens, help to counteract harmful acid-forming foods—as well as aiding elimination.

Make it a habit to eat more fruit. It is made for you by God. It is packed with energy and healing power. You will not have constipation, which is one of the worst enemies of health; and your body will not look haggard. Fruits have a definite effect upon the mind. Vibrationally, fresh fruits in the diet help to produce spirituality, even more than vegetables. An abundance of fruit will make your mind much more clear and calm. Watermelon, for example, is helpful for those who are cranky. More fruits and vegetables will get rid of whatever headaches and pains and cranky disposition come because of eating too much meat. Of course, these conditions may also be caused by other factors; but the point is, to retain youthfulness and

* Various highly beneficial cleansing regimens can be found in the *Self-Realization Fellowship Lessons* or from a health professional experienced in these matters. Lengthy fasts or cleansing diets should only be undertaken with expert advice and supervision. *(Publisher's Note)*

† According to the Centers for Disease Control and Prevention (a U.S. government agency) in 2024, more than 1 in 7 U.S. adults are estimated to have chronic kidney disease (CKD); as many as 9 in 10 adults with CKD do not know they have it; and 1 in 3 adults with severe CKD do not know they have it. *(Publisher's Note)*

calmness in body and mind, you should eat those foods that lessen and remove the accumulation of toxins in the body.

Another point is to change the type of meal you take at night. It is best to take the heavier meal at noon, not late in the day. In particular, drop the habit of eating much protein at night. Instead, have more fruits or light vegetable dishes for the evening meal.

Healthy Blood Is Necessary for Optimum Vitality

In Venice I saw the canals that provide transportation and prosperity to the city's residents—and how all the refuse from the homes along their banks is dumped into them. So also the "canals" in our bodies carry blood plasma that brings nutrition to all the cells, as well as take away the waste products that are dumped by the cells into the bloodstream. Healthy red blood is of utmost importance in order to keep well—and plenty of exercise and fresh air.

Many persons do not exercise at all. Working is not real exercise. Of course, any physical activity does some good and is better than a sedentary life; but if it doesn't use all the muscles, you are not truly exercising. Scientific exercise means working the entire muscular system. That charges fresh blood into the blood vessels in all parts of the body, and as a result it washes away poisons and gives life-force-laden oxygen and food to cells throughout the system.

You do not know how wonderful are the Energization Exercises* that some of you have learned here. By tensing and relaxing all of the body parts as taught in this system, you shut off and then open little valves in the blood vessels and thereby direct a tremendous supply of oxygen through the blood to all of the major muscles and organs of the body in turn.

The red blood corpuscles not only carry oxygen, but also life force, *prana,* to the cells. The Energization Exercises teach you to reinforce the flow of that life force by the conscious direction of the will. Every corpuscle is a tiny battery of life energy. That is what most people don't know. This is why when you lose blood, energy goes. Unless your body is strong, you should never give your blood; it is a mistake to do so. If you are weak, the loss of even one pint of blood may injure you in unsuspected ways by lowering your body's overall life energy. If your body is strong, then it is all right to give blood.

* A unique system developed by Paramahansa Yogananda and taught to students of the *Self-Realization Fellowship Lessons.*

The blood is an amazing thing. It knows how to throw off anything it does not like—anything foreign to the health of the body. Being a vehicle of life force or *prana,* it carries the subtle intelligence innate in that creative energy. Some of the chemicals in medicines are not good for you, with the result that potent tonics are sometimes filtered out rather than absorbed by the blood. The blood takes in oxygen more readily than anything else. That is why proper breathing is so important to keep your blood charged with vitality. You receive more tonic from oxygen than from anything else—especially if you have good habits of proper breathing.*

Learn and practice this method: First, throw out the breath with a strong double exhalation (one short and one long breath). Then, inhale in a double inhalation (one short and one long breath), filling the lungs as full as is comfortable. Hold the air in the lungs for a few seconds, allowing the oxygen to be fully absorbed and converted into *prana*. Then repeat the double exhalation, followed by the double inhalation. Practice this method in the fresh air 30 times in the morning and 30 times at night. It is very simple. You will be healthier than ever if you follow this. This exercise brings in a great deal of extra life force; and also decarbonizes your blood, promoting calmness. Remember that. I want all of you to be healthy and well. Those who will use the practical knowledge you are getting here will find they have truly benefited. There are many of our Self-Realization Fellowship students who are aged fifty or more but look half their age, because they follow these principles.

The ultraviolet rays of the sun are also easily absorbed by your blood, and recharge it with extra power and vitality.† Try to take ten-minute sunbaths at least twice a week. If you can do it every day, fine; but if not, take five minutes on the front and five minutes on the back twice a week. That is all you need. In my busy life, sometimes all I get is ten minutes of sunlight. Practiced with yogic concentration as taught in the *Lessons,* the energy absorbed lasts for at least one week.

* See SRF Lesson 14, "Preventive and Curative Techniques for Good Health."

† Dr. Richard Hobday describes many benefits of ultraviolet light in his book *The Healing Sun: Sunlight and Health in the 21st Century.* Sunlight penetrates far enough into our skin, he writes, to irradiate the blood passing through the capillaries that lie near the surface, increasing its capacity to deliver oxygen to the tissues and speeding the elimination of toxic chemicals from the body. *(Publisher's Note)*

Eating bananas will help to increase the health of your red blood.* They are one of the most beneficial of God's foods. Taking half an avocado daily with your meal will also greatly help in giving you the right nutrition. Your body will feel just as strong as if you had meat—and without creating meat's harmful acid condition.

The foundation of divine healing is to live naturally. This is not just a physical method of healing; it is a divine method, because God wants you to depend on His creation more. To maintain health you must use nature's laws. Sun, fresh air, pure water, fruits, and vegetables—all these were given to you by God to keep well. Base your diet on natural foods that are easily assimilated by the life current in the blood. And remember to exercise and go on cleansing fasts periodically. I keep myself well because I try never to overload my body by overeating or wrong eating; and most of all because of contact, through meditation and Kriya Yoga, with the Divine Life.

When I think of all the diseases that beset us in this world, there is so much to tell you that there is hardly enough time to give you other sermons! Every day remind yourself how to keep well. Practice what I have taught you, and the body will remain healthy even when everybody else is getting sick.

There is a harmony between the physical and divine methods of healing. My Master [Swami Sri Yukteswar] was so balanced; and so was his guru, Lahiri Mahasaya—they never condemned anyone for seeking the help of physicians instead of relying solely on spiritual methods.† Lahiri Mahasaya loved the doctors he knew, as did Master; and so have I attracted many doctors who follow these teachings. The doctor is trying by physical and psychological laws to help mankind, while the spiritual teacher is working by the laws of Spirit. Both can be combined, by knowledge of the underlying Divine Principle that works through material as well as spiritual forces in creation.

* Bananas are a good source of dietary iron and folic acid, lack of which reduces the red blood cells produced by the bone marrow. Bananas and avocados are high in Vitamin B6, which (in addition to combating infection) is essential for the body's synthesis of heme, the iron-containing part of hemoglobin (the molecule that carries oxygen in the red blood to all the body cells and removes the carbon dioxide they produce as a waste product). (*Publisher's Note*)

† See, for example, the story of Lahiri Mahasaya's divine healing of one of Sri Yukteswarji's friends, recounted in *Autobiography of a Yogi*, chapter 32, "Rama Is Raised From the Dead."

Divine Principle Behind the Human Heart

With all the healthful foods you eat, you are still ultimately dependent upon the ticking of the heart. This little machine is much more wonderful than any made by man. It goes on and on working. A mechanical clock is wound each day; but the heart is wound once by God and it goes on ticking throughout life. Every time it contracts, it produces enough pressure to push out one ounce of blood. In one day that little heart pumps seven to eight tons of blood; and you can well imagine how much it pumps over a lifetime of many years. Often when I put my hand over the heart, I think how peculiar it is that everything in the body depends on that little ticking. When it stops, you have to go. We think we are keeping ourselves alive and well by food and oxygen, but no—it is the heart that keeps the body living. If your heart stops, no amount of chemicals can maintain conscious life in the body.

What is that power which beats in the heart? The Divine Principle. The Infinite Life and Mind. That is the secret. Mind is the secret power that produces any chemical that the body needs. Without that intelligence inherent in bodily *prana,* how could the cow—by eating only hay—obtain all the elements it needs to maintain its massive frame and great strength? While the doctors tell us various things to do to keep the body well, still, they don't know the mystery behind the physiology of the heart that keeps it ticking and circulating the blood through the system, with its nutrients and life force.

The heart is not only a pump. The heart is a seat of divine life. It is the seat of the Universal Mother Principle. That Principle manifests in the heart as love and compassion. When we love somebody, though the current comes from the brain, it centralizes in the heart. Every organ in the body is a counterpart or a vehicle of the Infinite Life and Mind. The Infinite Presence of God as manifested in man's body is secreted in the subtle divine center of God-consciousness in the brain. From there It radiates Its various qualities throughout the whole being through specialized functions in six subtle centers, subdynamos, in the cerebrospinal axis. Every organ in the body, relative to the specialized functions in these divine centers, is thus an instrument, or conduit, of the Infinite Life and Mind of God. Behind the heart is the Love Principle of God. And behind the brain is the Wisdom Principle of God. Cultivating pure love and true wisdom greatly enlivens the heart and brain—physically as well as spiritually. And the harmonization of the Love Principle in the heart and the Wisdom Principle in the brain creates a magnetic force that draws healing energy into the whole body.*

If your heart is good and your brain is clear, you will attract unto yourself all the right ideas by which you can keep well. But most people are either too intellectual or too emotional. Either kind of imbalance is destructive—destroying the natural harmonious expression of the Divine Principle in man's being. If you cultivate heart as well as reason, you will always be well. The Divine Principle will be working throughout your bodily system. When love and reason are balanced, then the life in the body is balanced. The intellectual principle, when used to imbibe divine thoughts of Truth and immortality, brings as much energy as the heart principle does; so if you are all heart and no reason you are starving yourself. Likewise if you have too much intellect and no heart. You have to balance reason and feeling; then you draw from the Divine Source the proper amount of current necessary to keep all the cells in the body vibrant with life and health.

With the calmness that comes from perfect balance between feeling and reason, you will enjoy tremendous vitality in your body. That vitality is the manifestation of the Divine Principle—the real source of health. When anyone comes to me with pains and aches, as soon as I touch them through that Divine Principle the pains will leave. Many have thereby been convinced of the power of divine healing. Pains can be taken away almost instantly. In one incident in Mysore, someone was complaining that he had a splitting headache. I felt the divine permission to free him from it. So when he came to me I said to him, "Where is the headache? It is gone." And his suffering ceased in that moment.

So remember, the balanced mind—the mind that is calm—is the heart of the Divine Principle. Meditation is the supreme way to create that inner calmness and balance. When you can hold on to that calmness even after meditation, you will be able to feel the power of that Divine Principle always with you. And you will be able to direct it to persons who are sick and they will be healed. I

* "Healing" and "wholeness" are etymologically and spiritually related. Paramahansa Yogananda explained that the unification of the masculine and feminine (reason and feeling) components of human nature restores the soul's original divine nature, "made in the image of God"—the natural human condition before the fall of "Adam and Eve." See *Autobiography of a Yogi,* chapter 16, and *The Second Coming of Christ: The Resurrection of the Christ Within You,* Discourse 62. *(Publisher's Note)*

rely on no other principle but that Divine Principle; and its healing light flows steadily through my calmness.

Most persons are opaque with restlessness; that is why they are always a sort of annoyance to other people. You should be a transparent jewel through which God can shine to others. Try it out. It is most wonderful to be balanced; and the only way to have this balance between feeling and reason is to have inner contact with the Divine Principle through meditation, and to control your emotions and not permit moods. Free yourself from them! My Master gave me such excellent training in ironing out moods. So many people do not analyze themselves and take the steps to overcome their destructive emotions and moods.

If you have devotion, every time you come to these services you will receive twice as much. It isn't what I say, it is what is behind me that will change you. You are not joining an ordinary church; you are joining with the great Masters. As you follow them, and practice their teachings, you will receive the power to keep your body and mind well; and in time you will be able to heal others of their worries. Isn't that much more important? Because worry and mental trouble create much disease—they help disease to stay in the body more than you can imagine. The holy man is the happy man and the healthy man.

The Cells of Your Body Adopt the Mood of Your Mind

When you are happy, all the cells of your body are relaxed and recharged with life. The cells put on the mood of your mind. Each cell has a mind; you are not alone in your body. If you are sad, all your cells are devitalized. Persistence in a negative mood devitalizes the whole body.

By making yourself unhappy and succumbing to worries all the time, you can turn your hair gray and your eyes will be dimmed. Look at your life and health and see if this is not so. If every day you say to yourself, "The world is treating me badly," your face and whole body will begin to sag and droop. Instead, say: "Well, Lord, You know what it is all about. I am going to make the best of life. It may be a cloudy day but I am going to enjoy it just as much as the sunshine." No matter what happens, say: "It is all right. I am happy within." God has given you the power to be a king of kings, to be happier than any rich man who ever lived. You can walk through life like a king, or like a mental skunk who throws off the odor of unhappiness and gloom on everyone.

Health and youthfulness depend on being happy within. As your body ages, so your mind, through bad habits, puts on the condition of the body and also begins to grow old. Why allow this? Your mind can remain young in spite of the body. And if you can make the mind youthful, the body will put on the same mood. Thoughts are marvelous. If you affirm a thought strongly enough, it will become real to you. Always think: "In my mind I am ever young. I am lasting youth, untouched by time. There is no reason for me to be otherwise, for I am Spirit. I am mind; I am consciousness. Consciousness is ever young. I can be old right now if I choose to be so; and I can be young in mind and heart, no matter what my body goes through, if I choose to be so. Lord, make me as happy as Thou art. Make me realize I am made in Thine image." Try affirming these thoughts for six months and see what happens. Everyone you come in contact with will be drawn to your magnetic aura of youthful vitality and happiness.

Happiness is like the iceberg—three-fourths of it lies within, while one-fourth is revealed on the surface. Be happy within. Fill yourself with the abundance of joy that is deep within your heart. Meditate! The illumining presence of God has been obscured by the dark veils of ignorance and worry that you have thrown over yourself. Tear those veils away forever. Let the spirit of God shine through you—through the transparency of healthful living, through the transparency of your smiles, through the transparency of your meditation-born peace. Let that Divine Light shine through you, driving away all dark shadows; and let that Light shine through you to others, keeping them well and happy. Divine healing is not far away from you. God's healing light is always knocking at the gates of your mind. Do not clog the flow of life in your body with poisons from wrong foods, and don't create mental obstructions of worries. Keep yourself pure in mind, body, and soul; and the rays of His all-healing light shall be always there to keep you well, and will also touch whoever comes into your presence. Be an aurora of healing light!

The Cardinal Virtues: Faith, Hope, and Charity

This article is based on a discussion between Paramahansa Yogananda and one of his advanced disciples, who had asked, "Which is the most important: faith, hope, or charity?"

Hope Is an Eternal Light on the Pathway of Incarnations

Hope really belongs first on the list, for hope is the preliminary to real faith, which in most persons is undeveloped and has yet to be cultivated.

Hope can arise in the mind when there is reasonable expectation of some happiness or success; but in essence hope is much more than a result of human reason. It is a manifestation of soul consciousness. People hope blindly, or without a conscious reason, because the latent inner divine voice of the soul intuitively reminds them: "All is not lost forever." Failure, disappointment, and death are not final experiences. Behind the dark clouds of temporary disillusionment awaits the silver lining of eternal fulfillment. We must keep hoping to know God, even to the last breath, for we have all eternity in which to hope for the best and the highest. The greatest insult to the soul is to attribute to it the consciousness of final despondency.

Hope is the eternal light held aloft by the soul as man travels the pathway of incarnations to reach God. Never extinguish hope, for you would then have to wait miserably in darkness, unable to resume your journey toward the Divine until you chose to raise once again your searchlight of hope.

Most people hope and try for a while, but if they fail more than a few times they cease to hope and become despondent. Earnest students of Self-realization never stop hoping, for they know that they have all eternity in which to materialize their dreams. They know that death is not an abyss of eternal oblivious sleep, but a caravanserai where souls rest for a while so that they may, with fresh hope and energy, journey on until they reach the mansion of eternal fulfillment in God.

To kill hope and be despondent is to put on an animal mask of limitation that hides your divine identity. Instead, hope for the highest and the best; for as a child of God nothing is too good for you. Keep on hoping! Move in that light as you travel on pathways of incarnations to your luminous home in God. Hope is born of the intuitive consciousness in the soul that sometime or other we shall remember the forgotten image of God within us. This intuitive consciousness is faith.

Faith Is the Proof of Things Unseen

Faith, or the intuitive experience of all truth, is a native quality of the soul. It gives birth to human hope and the desire to achieve, but it may also hide behind the wall of spiritual ignorance. Ordinary human beings know practically nothing of this intuitive faith latent in the soul, which is the secret wellspring of all our wildest hopes.

No hope is too grand or impossible for this all-seeing intuitive faith to bring into manifestation. The eye of faith, or intuition, bestows the ultimate perception through which we know all things as they are. In ordinary mortals we see only the manifestation of hope. When hope is used properly, to work for the acquisition of what the soul's hidden intuition knows, then faith, or intuitive Self-realization, progressively develops.

Faith Versus Belief

The word *faith* is often erroneously used for *belief,* as: I have faith in him. A belief is problematic and may be followed by disillusionment. Belief is the initial experimental feeling about the truth of anything. Untested belief often crystallizes into dogmatic sentiment or, if discouraged, it may change into skepticism or unbelief. When belief turns into dogmatic sentiment or skepticism it is destructive.

Constructive belief is the attitude of mind necessary for initially testing the truth about a thing. The person who refuses to believe in anything refuses to test and experiment, but these are the only means by which to know truth. Constructive belief is good when one continuously believes and experiments to prove a particular truth until its real nature is revealed. *Destructive disbelief* is limiting, because one disbelieves for the sport of doing so. Constructive disbelief, or doubt, is all right if one assumes an attitude that says; "Well, I cannot believe your statement, but I am willing to accept it if you can prove that it is true."

All phenomena of visible matter can be recorded by the senses, but not invisible substances such as subtle cosmic vibratory forces and astral lights, which are unseen, unknown, and unregistered by the limited power of the senses. According to Saint Paul, "Faith is the substance of things hoped for, the evidence of things not seen."* Faith is inner light, in which the presence of all the finer forces, invisible to the eye and the senses, is revealed as true. That is, the proof of the existence of all the subtle forces, and of God as the final Substance, lies in faith. This instantaneous, all-knowing, all-seeing, intuitive power of faith is developed through deep meditation and conscious realization of one's soul and, through that Self-realization, communion with God.

"For verily I say unto you, If ye have faith as a grain of mustard seed, ye shall say unto this mountain, Remove hence to yonder place; and it shall remove; and nothing shall be impossible unto you....Whosoever shall not doubt in his heart, but shall believe that those things which he saith shall come to pass; he shall have whatsoever he saith."†

If a fanatic or madman or religious zealot without God-realization strongly believes that he can move a mountain into the sea, and for years tries to do so, he can never accomplish the feat. Also, if a man says, in a meek, squeaky voice: "Mr. Mountain, please go into the depth of the sea, for Jesus said it was possible to make you move, although I myself don't believe it," the mountain will not listen to that either. If, however, one has faith in, i.e., intuitive knowledge of, Cosmic Consciousness as the prime mover of all atomic creation, then, through that all-pervading consciousness one can act on or control any portion of matter on the earth or on a distant star.

Just as your consciousness is omnipresent in a microcosmic way in every part of your body; and as you can swing an arm or move your muscles, thus causing consciousness to act in any part of the body; so when your faith attunes you to the omnipresent Cosmic Consciousness, you can cause any portion of matter to respond to your command. You can "move mountains," heal disease, or banish delusion and realize God.

"The Greatest of These Is Love"

After regaining the latent cosmic intuitive faith through continuous hope and efforts in meditation, one may become selfish and

* Hebrews 11:1.

† Matthew 17:20 and Mark 11:22–23.

want to enjoy the acquired kingdom of God alone. That is why one must also cultivate a consciousness-expanding love.*

Love is born of sympathy; and sympathy is born of the consciousness of omnipresence, in which advanced souls can transfer their consciousness to souls in other bodies and experience their limitations and sufferings. When one does this, then the loving desire to offer help springs forth.

Selfishness cramps and confines the omnipresent soul in a prison of limitation. Selfishness defeats its own purpose: instead of producing happiness it brings on misery. Often it shuts out—with a fog of desire for imperfect, limited worldly happiness—the desire for the perfect unlimited joy to be found in God's omnipresence.

I used to want salvation only for myself, until my guru, Sri Yukteswar, said to me: "Do you want the whole divine *channa* for yourself alone?"† He made me understand that the ultimate joy in my own salvation would come when I shared it with others.

From that time on I wanted salvation so that I might give it to everyone. I wanted to drink God's omnipresent nectar not only through my own soul-mouth, but through the countless mouths of all other souls. I wanted to share Him with all. That is love. But spiritual aspirants should remember this: You must first have God yourself before you can give Him to others.

* "Now abideth faith, hope, charity, these three; but the greatest of these is charity [love]" (I Corinthians 13:13).

† *Channa* is a cheese made from curdled fresh milk, often served in Indian cuisine.

Christ Consciousness Versus Human Consciousness

Self-Realization Fellowship Temple,
San Diego, California, December 10, 1944

Whenever you sing to God with utmost sincerity—forgetting your body, mind, and all other thoughts—He will respond. But most of you are not sincere enough. You have no idea what security, what joy, comes from God. There is no security anywhere in this world; at any time your consciousness may be forced to give up the body by disease or misfortune. But once you are established in God, then in life or death you know that you are safe and secure in Him. "O Arjuna! this is the 'established in Brahman' state. Anyone entering this state is never (again) deluded."* You know and can say: "I cannot die, for I am upheld on the ocean of Eternal Existence. I am ever with Thee, my Lord, my God, my Beloved."

So, anchor your love not in this world, for it is all illusion and delusions. Rather, build your mansion of lasting happiness on the rock of the Infinite, a mansion of silence and God-communion, and you shall never regret it. "Seek ye first the kingdom of God, and all things that your heart craves will be added unto you. Nor be ye of doubtful mind."† This is the message of the Lord—the clarion call for all of you, for He loves you as much as He loves Jesus Christ. And even though He loved Christ, He did not come to rescue him in his hour of crucifixion until Christ had overcome; then He received him. Jesus had the power to perform all miracles, but still he had to be put through the "third degree" to see if he would use that power to destroy his enemies. That was his greatest temptation; but he overcame it. So must you overcome. Love your enemies; love all unceasingly. Believe in God's goodness. And whatever trials or

* Bhagavad Gita II:72.

† Paraphrase of Jesus' words in Matthew 6:33 and Luke 12:29–31.

tests He puts you through, remember: It is not that He wishes you harm, but so that you seek and receive all things from His hands.*

So go to Him within. Every night offer the choicest flowers of devotion to Him on the altar of silence. Don't waste your life. In these days of struggle, it is very hard to attain God, for your days are spent in restless activities and business pursuits—which mean nothing in the end but loss of time, and unhappiness. Spend your time with God, in utmost joy. Use your nights to be with Him. Don't sleep away your life. To sleep too much is an insult to your soul. Why should you feel your soul only unconsciously in sleep, when by learning to go deep in meditation you can feel it consciously? Awake, sleep no more!

Our spiritual Christmas is coming on the 23rd. I want you to come to meditate with deepest devotion. Celebrate Christ first in spirit, by giving one whole day to meditation and communion.† Then have the social celebration of his birthday by exchange of gifts on the 25th. This year we have chosen the 23rd for the meditation. Each one of you who will meditate deeply will feel the presence of Christ, and many may see him on that day. Each Christmas, Christ has visited me several times. Those who will meditate with that same depth and devotion will receive his spirit.

Realize the Consciousness of Universal Brotherhood

"O our One Father, teach me to feel that all men are my brothers. Teach me to love all brother-nations as much as the nation in which I am temporarily placed by Thy grace. Teach me, above all, to love those who love me not. Teach me to see Thy presence in my erring brothers. Teach me to heal ignorance-stricken brothers as eagerly as I yearn to be healed myself."

Think of the meaning of this prayer. We call one another Hindus and Americans and so on, but we are only in these bodies for

* Referring to the poem, "The Hound of Heaven," by Francis Thompson:
"All which I took from thee I did but take,
Not for thy harms,
But just that thou might'st seek it in My arms."

† The All-day Christmas Meditation is a spiritual custom begun by Paramahansaji in 1931 and observed annually in Self-Realization Fellowship ashrams, temples, and centers throughout the world. It is held on December 23 at the Mother Center and other ashrams, whereas SRF temples and centers generally arrange to hold it on the Saturday prior. More information is available on the SRF calendar of events, found on our website www.yogananda.org.

a short time. We don't belong to any nation. Our souls belong to God. When you shed your body, you are buried and forgotten by your nation. But God honors you by taking you to His bosom. So you must learn to love all, regardless of their temporary nationality. America became great because it is a melting pot of all nations, as India is a melting pot of all religions.

To love those that love you is easy. To love those that love you not is not so simple. If you want to change anyone, set a better example. Show more kindness, more understanding, more love. That has a sure effect. To those who are not kind, show kindness. To those who are mean, show bigness of heart. Though it is sometimes unavoidably necessary for society to imprison wrongdoers to protect itself from their evil actions, still the right attitude is to pray: "Teach me to feel that even he who does me mortal injury is my brother, made in Thine image; he is only temporarily in ignorance. Destroy in me the vengeful 'tit-for-tat' spirit."

Didn't Jesus Christ manifest that when he said, "Father, forgive them, for they know not what they do"? That was the mightiest of all his miracles. He worked many wonders, and modern science can also perform things that would have seemed miraculous in Jesus' time. But to give love and forgiveness to those who would destroy you is a greater demonstration of God than any other display of power.

Jesus could have slain his enemies by a mere glance of his eyes. Just as you can put out all the lights of a city if you know where the main switch is, so Christ, understanding the flow of astral energy that sustains living beings, had the power to switch off the life in his oppressors if he wanted to. But he would not do that. When captured and taken away to be crucified, he told his disciples, "If I would, I could borrow twelve legions of angels from my Father, but I will not."* Instead he gave love. That was a demonstration of Christ Consciousness.† Humanity would not have been inspired by or loved a Christ who was a tyrant; but all can love and emulate a son of God who could say, "Father, forgive them."

* See Matthew 26:53.

† The infinite, unchanging consciousness and love of God that pervades all creation and was incarnate in Jesus, Krishna, and other avatars. In Christian scripture, it is called the "only begotten son," i.e., the only pure reflection in creation of God the Father; in Hindu scripture, it is called *Kutastha Chaitanya* or *Tat,* the eternal consciousness, or cosmic intelligence, of Spirit everywhere present throughout the universe. Great saints and yogis commune with that consciousness in deep meditation.

Sometimes people try our patience and forbearance very hard. I have never intentionally hurt anyone in my life, though many have tried to harm me and thwart my efforts to do good. But I have never sought to harm any of them, even in my thoughts. I could have borrowed the power to do so from my Father, because He is all-powerful; but if you love God you cannot hate anyone, for you behold God even in your enemies. And when you receive power from God and react revengefully, you lose the consciousness of God, you lose the love of the Father.

Make Sure of the Love of God

So never let go of the love of your Father. You must have that first, last, and all the time. When I went to a great saint in India, he asked me first, "Are you married?" I said, "No." He replied, "Then you are on the safe side." He happened to be married, and he went on: "Marriage is not incompatible with the path to God; but if one is not married, it is better first to establish the habit of seeking God before becoming entangled in the world, lest He be forgotten."

Seek God first. Then if He directs you into the path of the householder, that is all right. Follow His will. But it must be His wish, not the voice of your desires. Whether or not you are married, get to know Him. Because if you prefer anything to Him, He will not come to you; and without the consciousness of His presence there is no end to the miseries and heartaches that you face. Of first importance is to make sure of that love which will never disappoint you, which will never deceive you; and that is the love of God. When I saw others being deceived that way, I made sure I would not be deceived. I made sure of the love of God. The consciousness of Him who has given me boundless love and security, as nothing else in this world could have given—that is called Christ Consciousness.

Make the effort to acquire that consciousness. We are thrown into this world, and its changeful show is so engaging—sunshine, clouds, rain; breakfast, lunch, and dinner; activity, sleep, a little happiness; on and on, day after day. The world keeps us drugged with delusion, thinking our lives are going to last forever. A sage once said: "The strangest thing of all is that everyone knows death is inevitable, but no one thinks it is going to happen to him!"

Death seems very dramatic if you are thus entangled in the world, but to me death means nothing more than the changing of an overcoat—or moving from one house to another, to a bigger mansion than this one. Every night you have a mini-death. Every night you drop the consciousness of physical existence; three hundred and sixty-five days a year it happens, and three hundred and sixty-five days you are reborn. To wish for death is weakness; death is a pension that you earn only after completing the hard work of life. But when it comes of itself, it is a blessing. You do not realize how terribly limiting the body is until you die; for when you move in space, free from the body, then you say, "How wonderful! No more do I have to drag around that old carcass, constantly subject to disease and suffering and pain." I behold this all the time in Spirit. Every night in sleep a little glimpse of this freedom is given to you. That is why saints don't like to be identified with their bodies in the daytime.

I have told you of a saint in India who had diabetes, with sores all over his body and seemingly just a few months to live. He couldn't sit still for five minutes, but he made up his mind he was going to meditate until he had a response from God. Gradually he became able to rise above his bodily difficulties and meditate unmoving for eighteen hours in the lotus posture. When he ceased his meditations, he again felt the pangs of his disease; but he kept on, day after day. He prayed, "O Lord, wilt Thou come, just once, into this broken body temple?" And he told me: "At the end of three years, I found the Infinite Light blazing within me." With his finger he wrote on the ground, "Here I met Him," meaning God. He found that his disease was gone; and he said in gratitude, "Lord, I didn't pray that you heal this body. All I asked was that You come into my broken temple. And now that temple is made whole by Your mercy!" Is that not a beautiful example of love for God?

Illness and trials may come to you because of your karma, effects of past actions—but it isn't your karma that God cares about; it is your love for Him. Many persons have wonderful, healthy bodies as strong as an ox. They never suffer. But they don't find God, because they have no desire for God. And many people think that spiritual persons attract suffering. That isn't so. Spiritual people are usually those who have suffered much, so they have turned to God. And sometimes as you advance, God tests you very much. But why shouldn't you be able to meet His tests, since you are made in His image? If you say inwardly, "I love God forever and forever, and nothing shall take this love away," what can destroy that love? Nothing!

That love is your redemption. Why did God create man and woman and all the things of this world? He had one purpose. God is seeking something from you. He owns everything in the universe;

worlds upon worlds He controls. Why did He give us independence? To see if we would freely choose to love Him and seek Him above all else. Love is the only way to win Him.

I sometimes wish He had not given us such independence, because we abuse that free will and suffer for it. We throw Him away and get hurt and bloodied by our disregard of His laws, and then we want to run back to Him to fix things. But even then, most people don't learn. Jesus spoke of the foolishness of seeking anything but God first. He said, "If thy hand offend thee, cut it off"—cut out of your life anything that prevents you from meditating and finding God.* But that lesson does not sink into the soul when one is drugged with delusion. Such persons go on making the same mistakes every day.

Some say, "I am too old to change." But what is old age? It is an attitude that has crept into your will. You are "old" only if your will has become mildewed and rusty. Persons in that state are as good as dead. So never let your will die. Will to seek Him! Will to find Him! Never let sleep claim you at night until you have meditated. You won't die; but even if you did, what of it? Many times you have thrown this body garment away. Why are you afraid of it anymore? Seek Him with all your might. "Wilt Thou come into this temple? Night and day, night and day, I look for Thee night and day." As often as I say this, just like an aurora borealis His light pours over my being, and I laugh at this body.

This world is like a motion picture of light and shadow, of which your body is a part. One philosophy is that the body has no reality; but philosophy alone does not show you how to realize this. Self-Realization gives you the actual techniques of communing with God, so you can know that all matter is unreal—a movie show made from His Light and Consciousness. Such was the consciousness demonstrated by Jesus and all Christlike masters.

Human Consciousness Is Bound by Attachment to Possessions and Family

What was the consciousness of Jesus Christ? He was born in a human form; he ate, he slept—and yet he was able to walk on water and change water into wine, and showed all the signs of omnipresence. Though he was a man with a body like ours, he obviously had some other kind of consciousness than the consciousness you

* Mark 9:43.

possess. Let us compare the consciousness of the ordinary human being and that of Christ. That will give you a definite picture of how to develop that consciousness which was in Christ.

Human consciousness, ego consciousness, dwells on property—"my this" and "my that." That consciousness seeks to possess things, and expects those possessions to last forever. "This is my land, this is my child, this is my home, this is my money." But property consciousness or possession consciousness is very foolish, for we own nothing—not even our bodies; we are merely given the temporary use of things.

Emerson spoke of the powerful illusion of possessiveness: There was a farm by a river, owned by a man named John. He said, "This is my farm." But John died, and Periwinkle moved onto that land; and Periwinkle said: "The birds sing my praises, and the very winds say this is my farm." But when his life was over, Thompson came and possessed the farm. And he said, "Look at the hills: My name is written on them! How sweetly the leaves of the trees are singing to me. This is my place." But he too was only a temporary resident. And Emerson points out: "Here is the land, here are the trees and hills, here is the river. But where is John, where is Periwinkle, where is Thompson? They are gone like foam on the river."*

Human consciousness limits the expression of Christ consciousness in the soul, the image of God in man, by attachment to material possessions. Divine consciousness is free of such delusive identifications. I have no consciousness of property or ownership. All I know is that in my temporary role in this outer show, God has given me nice places to live and to carry on His work. When I look within, there is no attachment to these places. I am only building them for Self-Realization Fellowship to fulfill the mission given to me by God. And after this life, it will be wonderful to return and sit in the back row and see how you are all carrying on.

Along with property consciousness, the ordinary human being is limited by consciousness of family and relatives. He thinks in terms of "us four and no more." But that, too, is a foolish consciousness. Two people marry. They have a son and a daughter, and they say, "These are our own." But who implanted that love for one another in the parents and the children? God did so. You couldn't love anyone

* Paraphrasing the thoughts and imagery in Ralph Waldo Emerson's 1846 poem, "Hamatreya," which was based on a passage from the Hindu scripture *Vishnu Purana*. *(Publisher's Note)*

without the love of God. And why does God make love between parent and child instinctive, automatic? So that you might have a first inkling of what love is—and then expand it into love for all persons as your own.

The ordinary person evolves a little from being property-conscious (selfishly preoccupied with his own possessions) to being family-conscious (concerned for the wellbeing of at least a few others). His consciousness is identified with his home and family, then his neighbors, then his race and religion, and finally his nation. And there he stops, his little ego circumscribed in these ways. And he behaves accordingly. That is human consciousness. Again, let us compare that with the consciousness of Christ.

Jesus said, "Is it not written in your law, I said, ye are gods?" He saw God in all. He didn't see human beings as different races, different creeds, different colors. As his disciple St. John said, "All those that received him (the Christ Consciousness), to them gave he power to be the sons of God." But ordinary consciousness says: "Here is a Jew, here is a Hindu, here is a Christian, and so on."

Look at the horrors perpetrated by so-called Christians during the Spanish Inquisition. Would Jesus or any of the Great Ones emphasize Judaism or Hinduism or Christianity? Rather, their universal teaching is: "All humanity is made of one blood."* As long as the consciousness of sectarianism, racism, and nationalism will remain, war and the greatest miseries will visit the earth. That is why we must cultivate the vast consciousness of Christ that embraces all. Do you think war is caused by bombs or machine guns? No. It is the divisiveness of human consciousness that causes wars.

The Most Practical Teaching for World Peace

Human consciousness—ego consciousness—is a most dangerous state for people to live in. Christ consciousness means to treat all humanity equally. All peoples of the earth must have food, provisions, and sanitation. It is man's selfish consciousness that has caused this World War, more than anything else.† Family consciousness, race consciousness, country consciousness are bad when they

* "God hath made of one blood all nations of men" (Acts 17:26). More anciently, the scriptures of India also spoke of the world as one family: "Only the narrow-minded discriminate, saying: One is a relative; the other is a stranger. For those who live magnanimously, the entire world constitutes but a family" (*Maha Upanishad* 6:71–72). *(Publisher's Note)*

† This talk was given during World War II.

exclude the rest of humanity. That is why Jesus said, "Love God with all your heart, with all your soul, with all your mind, and with all your strength; and love your neighbor as yourself."

Neighbor means whoever comes into the environment of your life. He may be any race, of any religion, but love him as yourself. That is practicing Christ consciousness. It is the most practical teaching in the world for bringing real peace and happiness. Jesus lived it; all great masters have lived it; and I have lived it. I have no race consciousness. I don't think in terms of Americans or Hindus, though my body was born in India. I practice the consciousness that everyone is my relative, for we are all the children of God.

That is what Christ taught, and that is how Mahatma Gandhi feels. He has said: "Whoever loves India and India's ideals, I consider a Hindu. And anyone who does not live that ideal, even though born in India, is not a Hindu." Gandhi does not restrict his consciousness to any race. He said, "If India gets her freedom by shedding the blood of English brothers, let her be drowned in the Indian Ocean." Such is his love for all mankind. That is the ideal of Christ Consciousness. That ideal is livable. It must start by our destroying race and hereditary caste consciousness.*

In India we give Brahmins such respect, yet still they cook in their own places, and won't lower themselves to sit and eat with others. Just as in America, you white people let Negroes cook food for you, but you don't like them to sit and eat with you. The foolishness of humanity would be the funniest thing, if it were not so terrible in its consequences! Christlike souls like Lincoln work to abolish such injustice. To hate any class of human being is to hate God. Who is in the body of the Negro—in the bodies of all human beings—but God? You must not outlaw God. He has taken the forms of different races, castes, and classes to see how you treat Him—or whether you mistreat Him—in his various disguises.

God could send "hellfire and brimstone" to destroy us when we misbehave, but He doesn't. He gives human beings a chance to evolve by learning from their mistakes. We are the architects of our

* In his writings, Paramahansaji explained in detail the spiritual principles pertaining to nonviolence and the question of whether war is ever justified. See his commentary on Bhagavad Gita II:32 in *God Talks With Arjuna: The Bhagavad Gita* (published by Self-Realization Fellowship).

He also explains the real meaning of "caste" according to the spiritual ideals practiced in ancient India; see his commentary on Bhagavad Gita II:31 and IV:13. *(Publisher's Note)* own fate. When you understand this, then you will see the great justice of God. We punish ourselves and create these fearful wars. Why? Because of our human consciousness: "This is my property, this is my neighborhood, this is my country, mine, mine, mine." That consciousness was behind America's abuse of the Indians and Negroes; and in India they behaved similarly to the aboriginal peoples there. And see how we are paying for it! Metaphysically speaking, that is why you were drawn into this present war. The war would never have been part of your karma if you had not done such injustice to the American Indians and had such hatred for the Negro. I have traced these things and noted the actions of the different nations and what their karmic effects will be; I could write a book on the imbalances in the various nations, which cause wars, calamities, and mass suffering.

It is wrong to think, "My race, my people, and no more." Christ came on earth to develop in humanity the consciousness that he has. In the words of a poet: "Love and I drew a circle and took in the whole world."* That is what we must think and say and live; that is Christ consciousness. And what is human consciousness? "Love and I drew a circle around 'us four and no more,' and threw the rest of the world out!" Do you see the contrast?

At Mt. Washington this last Thanksgiving, so many souls were sitting with me; and I felt that all of them were my large family. I thought of the little family in which I was born in India; I remembered how one was fighting for more than the other. And I saw the contrast with this family I have created here in the ashram through God's help. Here we have people gathered together from all different religions, different nationalities; but mixing in complete brotherhood. There is no consciousness of race, no consciousness of division. That is the spirit of Christ Consciousness. If Jesus, Buddha, Krishna, and all the Great Ones were together, they would feel and express toward each other only divine love and brotherhood. Here we are practicing that love in our lives. We are not just talking about it, but trying to live it.

* "He drew a circle that shut me out—
Heretic, rebel, a thing to flout.
But Love and I had the wit to win:
We drew a circle and took him in!"

(From the poem "Outwitted," by Edwin Markham [1852–1940], Poet Laureate of Oregon and a beloved student of Paramahansa Yogananda's during the Guru's early years in America.)

Jesus said, "Who is my brother, who is my sister, but those who love God?"* The sunlight shines on both the charcoal and the diamond, but the diamond reflects the sunlight more. So in those souls who are devoted to God, you find greater brotherhood; you feel a closer kinship. It is easier to cultivate spiritual consciousness in fellowship with those who are thus akin—much better than to go among devilish human beings. It is good to see God in those individuals, too—but from a distance! If you have the spiritual strength and courage to change them by going among them, then do so. But don't be like the doctor who was trying to cure a patient and contracted the contagious disease himself! You have to be spiritually strong yourself before trying to help everyone else. Until then, you can still pray for them and send thoughts of healing and harmony to their souls.

Characteristics of Christlike Behavior

All the time we must contrast the behavior of ordinary human consciousness with that which is characteristic of Christ consciousness. Christ taught us to "turn the other cheek" when we are slapped. He taught forgiveness for all. The ordinary person, when he is slapped, wants to give two slaps in return. And still he thinks of himself as a Christian. He may be on Sundays, but if you give him a slap, watch out! It is not weakness to practice these teachings of Christ. It takes greater strength not to hit back when somebody hurts you. What is the use of mere talk about the transcendental Christ Consciousness? Why shouldn't we practice it every day? If you do that, you will find yourself closer to God than ever.†

Always remember the qualities of Christ. Never get angry. Love all people with the consciousness of Christ, with the consciousness of brotherhood and forgiveness. Go on doing good no matter how much you get slapped by others. There are thousands who will appreciate your efforts, and a few who won't. When they crucify you with unkindness, that is the time to say, "Father, forgive them, for they know not what they do." Continue to do good to please God, including efforts at resolving the misunderstanding.

* A paraphrase of Matthew 12:50.

† In his writings on the Gospel passages where Jesus counsels his followers to "turn the other cheek" and "love your enemies," Paramahansaji explains the practice of these teachings in more detail. See Discourse 27 of *The Second Coming of Christ: The Resurrection of the Christ Within You* (published by Self-Realization Fellowship).

Don't be a doormat or cooperate with evil, but in your heart separate them—their souls—from their misguided actions, and give them love sincerely. Thereby you will attain self-mastery—a peace within yourself that cannot be destroyed by the actions of others, and a love for all that is lasting. If you express that Christ-peace and Christ-love—doing good to all, feeding the poor and thinking of others' welfare, thinking of them as your own, taking an interest in them—then you will be manifesting Christ Consciousness.

Meditate to Realize the Infinite Consciousness

Last of all, dear ones, remember: Meditation is the scientific way to expand your consciousness beyond egoistic identifications that limit your soul, going step by step to superconsciousness, Christ consciousness, and cosmic consciousness. When you meditate, go so deep within that you get away from the consciousness of the body and its material surroundings, so that your mind doesn't waver any more or flit restlessly about from one object of distraction to another. One-pointed fixity in interiorized, concentrated meditation is the first step to divine consciousness. When I turn my attention within and put my mind at the Christ center,* it remains there. At once I am in the kingdom of God within, and I remain locked in that great joy of Christ.

When you can rest in the consciousness that you are all joy, all peace—and when your mind doesn't waver at all and you are absorbed in the divine love of God and Christ that fills your soul—that is superconsciousness. Then, when you remain in that state for a long time, with your mind perfectly still and calm, you will see the Infinite Christ come into your life. You will behold the splendor of God that pervades all creation. And your body will be just like a speck in that vastness. When you have that perception, the whole universe appears as a light-image—and you behold yourself and all things as one with the Cosmic Light pouring out of the Divine Source.

The trouble with most of you is that you don't meditate deeply enough to get beyond the restlessness of your mind. If you meditate long enough, with sufficient concentration, you will see a little

* The *Kutastha* or *ajna chakra* at the point between the eyebrows, center of will and concentration, and of Christ Consciousness, in the body; seat of the spiritual eye—the singular eye of spiritual perception, of which Jesus spoke when he said: "If therefore thine eye be single, thy whole body shall be full of light" (Matthew 6:22).

light at the spiritual eye. But as you persist and go deeper, in time the whole universe becomes filled with light like a radiance of moonbeams. When your awareness spreads unbounded over this whole electric universe—when you know by realization that everything is formed of luminous astral "electricity" and that nothing is solid—then you have real Christ Consciousness. Then you can perform the miracles of Christ.* And you can know and feel what is happening everywhere. Lots of times these experiences have come to me. In the omnipresence of Christ Consciousness you know what is going on in India, on Mars, everywhere. If you are one with that Light, you can create a body just like this one that you have now, if you wish; and return to earth again after death, as Jesus did. There is absolute freedom. All eternity becomes yours.

In superconsciousness and Christ Consciousness, you can see the astral world—the subtle realm of light and color and energy that is behind the material universe. But when you go higher still, all images—all separate manifestations of *maya*-delusion—vanish. You come to a realm beyond, where there is naught but pure eternal Joy. In the highest state, *samadhi,* you behold God as pure formless Bliss, pure transcendental Consciousness beyond all finite creation—and experience yourself as one with that Infinite Being. That is Cosmic Consciousness. No one can describe that state. But in scripture it is called "God the Father," and "God the Son" is His intelligence—the Christ Intelligence—within creation. And the Holy Ghost is the vibratory substance of creation—the "Word" of God by which all things are made and sustained.†

When you meditate, first you feel within your body the peace and joy of the Holy Ghost, the great Comforter; and you hear its great vibration of *Aum*. Expanding with that all-pervading sound, your whole consciousness is translated from the body all over the universe, and you intuit the presence of the Infinite Christ, the intelligence and love of God in creation. Then all creation melts away, and you are in the uncreated, transcendental vastness of Spirit. Eternity and you become one. In that state you can say, as did Jesus: "Before Abraham was, I am" and "I and my Father are one." You

* See *Autobiography of a Yogi,* chapter 30: "The Law of Miracles."

† "In the beginning was the Word, and the Word was with God, and the Word was God....All things were made by him; and without him was not any thing made that was made" (John 1:1–3). See explanation of these verses in Discourse 1 of Paramahansa Yogananda's *The Second Coming of Christ: The Resurrection of the Christ Within You* (published by Self-Realization Fellowship).

realize that you exist eternally, that you are eternally conscious of that existence, and that your very essence is infinite, unqualified Bliss (*Sat-Chit-Ananda*).

As the Lord says in the Bhagavad Gita: "Whoever realizes Me to be the Unborn and Beginningless as well as the Sovereign Lord of Creation—that man has conquered delusion and attained the sinless state even while wearing a mortal body."* But you must begin from the beginning. First, remember that you are made in the image of God. You are not made in the image of a Hindu, or an American, or any other nationality; you are not a brown- or white- or dark-skinned human being. You are made in the image of God.

When you close your eyes and shut out this world, you are just at the threshold of the Infinite. It is right before you. You must go ever deeper into that region. In that expanding consciousness, you go from planet to planet, through solar and stellar systems and galaxies and all space, like an eternal fire rolling over the universe in joy—knowing that nothing can break you, nothing can cut you, nothing can harm you; no gas, no smoke, no heat or cold can reach you there.

Let us meditate. First, look at your body. Now close your eyes, and fix your attention at the Christ center between the eyebrows. Repeat with me, and visualize and feel: "I am infinite. Above, below, left and right, within, without, I behold eternity, boundless eternity. I am that. I am not a little body in this finite world of dreams and illusions. I am spread over eternal space. I am a great light shimmering over the universe. I am immortal, eternal Bliss."

That is what you are. Why should you do things and behave in such a way that diverts your attention from what you really are? You are not here to be circumscribed by property and possessions and family. Without God, these things will bring only trouble. First have God. Seek God, find God, be one with God!

* Bhagavad Gita X:3.

(Left) The SRF Lake Shrine in Pacific Palisades, California, founded by Paramahansa Yogananda in 1950. Each year thousands of people from all over the world enjoy the tranquil beauty of this scenic location. On the grounds, set amid verdant hillsides and flower gardens, are a hand-carved stone sarcophagus that enshrines a portion of Mahatma Gandhi's ashes, and a hilltop temple where Self-Realization Fellowship services, meditations, and classes are held weekly. An SRF Retreat overlooking the Pacific Ocean provides SRF members and friends with a year-round retreat program, allowing them to share in the spiritual atmosphere of this sanctuary. *(Right)* The SRF San Diego Temple, established by Paramahansa Yogananda in 1943, where he gave many lectures and led meditation services during the 1940s. Today the temple continues to serve many SRF members and friends in the San Diego area, offering weekly services, meditations, and other programs.

(Left) Paramahansa Yogananda, 1929. *(Right)* Paramahansa Yogananda with James J. Lynn at the Self-Realization Fellowship Golden Lotus Temple, Encinitas, California, 1938. Mr. Lynn received the *sannyas* vow from Paramahansa Yogananda in 1951, and was given the Sanskrit name Rajarsi Janakananda. A highly advanced disciple, he contributed much to the Guru's growing work both spiritually and materially; after Paramahansaji's passing, he became the second president of Self-Realization Fellowship/Yogoda Satsanga Society of India.

The Mystic Tree of Life

Self-Realization Fellowship Temple,
Hollywood, California, December 17, 1944

"The Mystic Tree of Life" is a very deep subject and a most interesting subject, as I shall explain to you. This symbol has come down to us from antiquity. In the Occident, one example of this symbol is the Christmas tree, but most people have not understood the spiritual meaning of that symbol or how it originated. In the Orient, we see the Tree of Life represented in carpets, in architecture, everywhere, because there its significance is understood.

Understanding the True Meaning of the Scriptures

What is the spiritual import of the Christmas tree of the West and the Tree of Life in the East? In the Book of Genesis in the Bible, it is written that the Tree of Life stood in the midst of the Garden of Eden, and that God commanded Adam, saying: "Of every tree of the garden thou mayest eat freely, but of the tree of the knowledge of good and evil thou shalt not eat of it, for in the day that thou eatest thereof thou shalt surely die." Eve, the Bible says, was tempted by a serpent who lived in the garden, so that she partook of the forbidden fruit and shared it with Adam; and for doing so Adam and Eve as criminals were driven from Paradise. And not only were the guilty pair punished; all of us, too, who had no share in the eating of that "apple," were driven out of the heavenly Eden. Now, taken literally, isn't that a most unsatisfying explanation of the sorrows and woes to which everyone on earth is subject?

When I first heard the Adam and Eve story presented in the Christian teachings, I refused to read the Bible; but when I heard the right interpretation from my Master, Swami Sri Yukteswar, I knew the Biblical account to be a true revelation. I came to understand the real meaning behind the confusing symbolism and terminology in Christian teachings: the promise of Jesus to send the Holy Ghost, and of the second coming of Christ; the meaning of the Genesis story of creation; the deep yogic experiences metaphorically described in the Book of Revelation. That knowledge is spreading faster than you know, through the Self-Realization Fellowship teachings that my guru and *paramgurus* sent to the West through me. We are building a temple of souls—those who have realization of the true Christ-teachings and speak with the authority of their own direct experience.

I once asked an orthodox missionary to tell me how Eve could be tempted by the serpent to eat the apple. Do you know what he told me? "Well, in those days serpents could talk." I took my hat off to him and said, "I bow to your colossal ignorance." Darwin and other scientists of evolution never discovered talking snakes. We are living in a modern world and we must understand the real meaning of the metaphysical truths written in the scriptures. First I will give you a little background on the genesis of creation, so you will understand.

How the Physical Cosmos Materializes From Intelligent Life and Energy

The whole universe—the cosmos and all the planets—is created in spherical form. Why? Because force, when it emanates from a central point, takes an even radius and creates a sphere. The creative vibration sent out from Spirit formed a great spherical mass of light, vibrating cosmic energy, made up of individualized sparks of the intelligent light of life force. These were condensed or "frozen" into atomic particles, the building blocks of matter. Thus, out of that creative light and cosmic energy emanating from God was produced the solid mass of matter, of all the planets and the earth.

The tendency of energy is to radiate; it wants to express itself. So the intelligent life force that was materialized into the earth began to evolve plant and animal life and human beings—all created from those sparks of cosmic life and energy frozen into atoms and aggregated into increasingly complex cells and tissues. Life is ever seeking greater expression, greater freedom, instead of remaining locked in matter.

From the seemingly inert minerals that compose the earth came the plants and vegetation that covered the globe in a mantle of living, growing matter, which was yet more or less rooted to the earth for its life and sustenance. In the animal kingdom we see that radiating light and energy taking on more freedom of expression and movement, no longer tied in stationary forms to the life-giving earth. The human form was a special creation by God, built after the pattern of the earlier creations but not a direct product from them. Darwin's evolutionary theory is wrong in that respect. God created the bodies of "Adam and Eve" by direct materialization, uniquely endowed with astral-causal instruments of consciousness and will that enabled man to reproduce his own kind by that same immaculate method, and to express unlimited spiritual freedom and consciousness of immortality even while incarnate on earth.

The Tree of Life in the Human Body

In the scriptures of India, the human body is compared to an upturned tree, "with roots above and branches beneath."* The hair and cranial nerves are the roots, the cerebrospinal column is the trunk of the tree, and all the different nerve systems are the branches. Trees in the plant kingdom evolved as a result of the rays of life energy emanating out of the earth, and are fed through roots that draw sustenance from the earth. But when God created man, the "upturned tree," the creative rays came from above—from the higher astral and causal planes of spiritual existence. The hair of the head is nothing but condensations or materializations of fine rays of astral energy. In the brain and medulla oblongata are the "roots" of this upturned tree, through which man draws into his body the cosmic energy by which he is principally sustained. Thus, the cerebrospinal axis is called the "tree of life" because life energy is distributed from the brain-roots to all the organs and parts of the body through the "trunk" of the spinal column and its outward-branching nervous system.

The Biblical account in Genesis tells us: "And the Lord God planted a garden eastward in Eden; and there He put the man whom He had formed." The human body that God created was intended to be a paradise, "Eden." Metaphysically, "east" refers to the front of the body and specifically to the spiritual eye at the point between the eyebrows.† The consciousness of the original man always faced "east." That is, it was always centered in the spiritual eye of divine perception, which is the door to heaven.

* "They (the wise) speak of an eternal *ashvattha* tree, with roots above and boughs beneath, whose leaves are Vedic hymns. He who understands this tree of life is a Veda-knower" (Bhagavad Gita XV:1).

† The single eye of intuition and omnipresent perception at the Christ or *Kutastha* center (*ajna chakra*) between the eyebrows. The deeply meditating devotee beholds the spiritual eye as a ring of golden light encircling a sphere of opalescent blue, and at the center, a pentagonal white star. The spiritual eye is the entryway into the ultimate states of divine consciousness.

The Fall of Man and How We May Return to Divine Consciousness

The Bible says that in this "Garden of Eden"—which is the body—God gave Adam and Eve permission to "eat of the fruit of the trees," except that of "the tree which is in the midst of the garden." There are several "trees" inside the body, each one a system of nerves branching out from its roots in the spine or brain (the main "Tree of Life" in the garden of the body). There is the motor nervous system, with its myriad branches controlling activity in the muscles and organs, and there is the sensory system with its optic, olfactory, gustatory, tactual, and auditory nerves. Adam and Eve were to enjoy all the "fruits" of these trees of the bodily garden—including the sensations of sight, smell, taste, touch, and hearing—while keeping their consciousness in the paradise of the spiritual eye.

There is a reason why the "tree which is in the midst of the garden" is so important. The meaning is that they could partake of all the senses; but were cautioned to be careful of sex—to beware of indulging in the sensations of the sex nerves situated in the center of the body (midway between the feet and the head). "But of the fruit of the tree which is in the midst of the garden, God hath said, Ye shall not eat of it, neither shall ye touch it, lest ye die." "Die" means changed from immortal status to the state of body identification that results when the consciousness is dragged downward from the centers of divine perception in the brain. In other words, their consciousness of immortality would be lost, and they would place themselves under the law governing physical beings: bodily birth must be followed by bodily death.

According to Genesis, in the garden was a serpent, "more subtil than any beast of the field which the Lord hath made." Of all the senses in the bodily "field," touch—and especially sex sensation—is the most difficult to control. Sex temptation is stimulated by the "serpent" or coiled life energy at the base of the spine, known in yoga treatises as the *kundalini* force. Yoga describes how cosmic energy flows from the brain down into the different plexuses in the spine, empowering man's bodily instruments of knowledge and action, and comes to rest in a coiled passageway at the base of the spine. When that energy flows outward into the sex region, the desire for sexual union ensues. This coiled energy is thus symbolized in the Bible as the serpent that tempted Eve (the feminine or feeling aspect of human consciousness). But when that current is lifted up into the brain, through practice of yoga techniques of meditation and *pranayama* (life-force control), it bestows mastery over self. Jesus said, "As Moses lifted up the serpent in the wilderness, even so must the Son of man be lifted up, that whosoever believeth in him [the Christ Consciousness] shall not perish but have eternal life."* All human beings have the power to do the same thing and regain their divine consciousness as immortal children of God.

Concentrate on the Spiritual Eye

The serpent intimated to Eve that by eating of the forbidden fruit—"the fruit of the tree of knowledge of good and evil"—their eyes would be opened. "She took of the fruit thereof, and did eat, and gave also unto her husband with her; and he did eat. And the eyes of them both were opened, and they knew that they were naked." That is, they lost the ability to use the one spiritual eye of divine perception and "opened," or developed a dependence on, the two physical eyes, through which man cognizes only the material world of painful limitations and duality ("good and evil") that mortal beings endure under the spell of cosmic delusion.

If you concentrate on the spiritual eye at the Christ center you will find heaven. If you concentrate on sex you will lose control and be overpowered by it, and you will find it the cause of great misery of body and mind. Adam and Eve not only fell long ago; modern Adams and Eves are falling every day—throwing themselves out of paradise by yielding to the temptation of sex impulse. To have absolute mastery over that force is the greatest thing in life, and that means to control the thoughts as well as actions.†

If you could see with the spiritual eye, you would see the whole universe as divine light. "The Light shineth in the darkness but the

* John 3:14–15.

† Paramahansa Yogananda did not teach that celibacy in marriage is necessary for spiritual progress. In his book *The Second Coming of Christ: The Resurrection of the Christ Within You* (Discourse 62) he wrote: "Neither Jesus nor any other great master would expect celibacy from persons unprepared spiritually and emotionally for such lofty discipline. Wise counsel is rather that of gradual overall sublimation of physical consciousness, including sex, into spiritual consciousness through daily practice of scientific methods of meditation along with cultivation of pure soul qualities." He taught that promiscuity or overindulgence is debilitating physically, mentally, and spiritually; and that abuse of sex for sensual gratification is to be avoided. "In marriage," he wrote, "spiritual aspirants should observe moderation in physical relations, and above all the culture of a spirit of love, service, loyalty, and divine friendship between husband and wife." This subject is taken up in more detail in the above mentioned book and in the *Self-Realization Fellowship Lessons. (Publisher's Note)*

darkness comprehendeth it not." I always grieve for people who when they close their eyes see nothing but darkness. If you would only make the effort to open your spiritual eye! When man lost the use of the spiritual eye by concentrating on sex and the physical method of reproduction, he was forced to rely on the two physical eyes. Thus he lost his spiritual freedom. In meditation, you concentrate on the spiritual eye to reawaken it.

Jesus said: "When thine eye is single, thy whole body also is full of light....Take heed therefore that the light which is in thee be not darkness."* With the vision of the "single" or spiritual eye, a light comes all over inside the body; and you can see the light of astral life energy radiating through all the branching nerves and illuminating the seven astral centers of higher consciousness in the cerebrospinal axis. That is what is meant by the "seven stars" and "seven churches" referred to in the Book of Revelation, which also says: "To him that overcometh will I give to eat of the tree of life, which is in the midst of the paradise of God."† By self-discipline and practice of yoga meditation techniques, you can restore your lost consciousness of the immortal tree of divine life just behind the façade of the fleshly body.

At the top of your Christmas tree, you place a shiny star. The spiritual significance of that is to symbolize the spiritual eye at the top of the Tree of Life. This is the "star of the East" followed by the Three Wise Men to find the Christ. As you prepare your Christmas tree in order to celebrate the birth of Christ, never forget this explanation of the Tree of Life which God is giving you today.

Remember always that you are made of immortal sparks of divine light; every atom and cell of your body is glowing with that light. Light also forms the nerve fibers, which are condensed rays of cosmic energy emanating from the astral Tree of Life. You are not a frail fleshly body; you are the divine electricity within the physical form. If only you could realize that! If you could open your eyes and see that Light Divine filling all space—all things as waves of light dancing around you—you would know that God is in His creation and all is well. Otherwise we can find no justification for what is going on in the world—disaster and suffering and the mass murder of war, thousands upon thousands killed and the victors rejoicing over it! War or no war, how can we rejoice at killing thousands of

* Luke 11:34–35.

† Revelation 2:7.

people, no matter which side they are on? Isn't it better to follow the way of Christ-love and truth than to be killers? Sometimes it is necessary to fight to defend one's country against an evil aggressor; but the world's greatest need is for the Christlike virtues of love and peace, which come from God-communion. If all Europe were really Christian, if all nations of the world practiced those universal virtues, this war would not have come about.* And already there are hints of a third war to come. Are we going to follow the politicians or gather the spiritual blessings of the Tree of Life?

This Tree of Life infuses your body with power, which can be destructive if you are controlled by the senses. Concentrating too much on sex and material things is the way to destruction for individuals and society; it produces the fruits of body-bound selfishness and mortal consciousness. That does not mean that you should maim your senses, that you should not taste or touch; but that you should have control over this Tree of Life and the kind of physical and mental fruits you eat from it.

Cultivating Right Thoughts and Feelings on the Tree of Consciousness

In the human body, the physical tree of nerves is a gross manifestation of the astral tree of life energy within. These two trees are condensed out of the even subtler tree of human consciousness.† This tree of consciousness in the bodily "Garden of Eden" has its roots in the divine intelligence of the soul, and has three main branches: thought or reason, feeling, and will. Those are all sending forth branchlets of power that yield fruits of joy or disappointment according to the use you make of them. Every thought and feeling and action produces a fruit on these branches of the tree of consciousness.

From the heart, the tree of consciousness sends forth branches of love. If that tree bears only the fruit of transitory human love, it gives disappointment—through the inevitable separation brought by death, boredom, or disloyalty. Cultivate instead the truly satisfying fruit of divine love and selflessness in the garden of your life, that you may eat always of its blessedness.

* This talk was given during World War II. *(Publisher's Note)*

† Yoga teaches that underlying and sustaining the physical body is the astral body of life energy, which in turn derives from the causal or ideational body—the thought-matrix of elemental ideas that covers the indwelling soul. These three body-vehicles work together to enable the incarnate soul to cognize and express in the material world.

The love of relatives is only your first experiment in the laboratory of divine love. For family members you usually feel love automatically, instinctually; those loved ones are given so that through them you may without effort glimpse what love is, and then learn by further experiment and training in the laboratory of everyday life to expand that family love into divine love and understanding for all.

Divine love and friendship must be unconditional. Be very careful to whom you give your affection and loyalty; but when you give it, let it be unconditional. Never in my life have I betrayed friendship. On two or three occasions, I have lost the friendship of those who proved unable to respond to that ideal. I was their friend, but they were not mine. Except for those few, I have never lost a friend.

Eat of the fruits of love, but don't mistake attachment for real love. If you are attached to a person you want to possess them, to stifle them. If in your love for a rose you squeeze it and destroy it, you did not love the rose—you loved yourself.

Let not your tree of feelings produce poisonous fruits of selfishness or attachment. Eat the fruit of divine love and you will enjoy it; but do not cultivate possessive love, for it will give you unending misery. And never confuse sex attraction with love. From the tree of the nervous system enjoy the wholesome fruits of the senses, but do not poison your self-control by indiscriminate indulgence or unbridled attachment to sex. Nature made the sex instinct very powerful to insure the propagation of the species; therefore, sex has its place in a marriage informed by spiritual values, wherein there is cultivation of divine love and harmonious exchange of soul qualities between man and woman.* But without that spiritualizing and transmuting influence, sex keeps the consciousness too much on the plane of physicality and gradually erodes mutual respect, friendship, understanding, and true love. So, from the tree of the heart choose the divine fruit, not the poisonous fruit that grows on the same tree.

Reap the Good Fruits From Your Tree of Life

On the same tree grows the fruit of selfish attachment and unselfish love, of sense enjoyment and self-control, of laziness and healthful exercise. The slothful individual prevents the growth of the good fruits of this tree, but the one who is progressively active in a balanced way enjoys the fruits of health and all-round well-being.

* Paramahansa Yogananda explains this in more detail in Discourse 62 of *The Second Coming of Christ: The Resurrection of the Christ Within You.*

If your body has a "bay window," so that you have never seen your feet in ten years, you have misused the tree of flesh. Restore your connection to the Tree of Life within. If ill health comes, born of past bad karma, bear it bravely; but do not create more fruits of disease by continuing to sow seeds of wrong actions.

Jesus said, "Let the dead bury the dead." The ones who were burying their deceased companion were also dead, spiritually speaking. So many are dead long before they die and they don't know it. If you are always morose—with no energy, lifeless—you are absolutely misusing the tree of astral energy. Live with enthusiasm; let your eyes sparkle with joy, so that those who come near you feel your magnetic personality.

With the Tree of Life, God gave you the powers of action and knowledge to cultivate and enjoy the fruits of sight, hearing, smell, taste, and touch; and to create a vibrant personality. Do not burn up that Tree of Life by indiscretion and wrong behavior until there is nothing left but a dead tree that everybody shuns—a person who repels everyone and makes everyone nervous. If you are always nervous and making everybody around you nervous, you are not properly tending the astral tree of life force behind your nervous system. Such persons bring discord and inharmony into their environments. If you throw one pebble into a lake of perfect calmness, the whole lake is disturbed into ripples. Do not be the kind of person who affects his home and surroundings like that; rather, bless those around you by the vibrations of peace that are the fruits of tending your Tree of Life with discrimination and wisdom.

So from the Tree of Life in the body that God has given you, try to reap all the good fruits and avoid the evil fruits. Control the senses so that they won't control you. When you tell your mind and body to shun temptation, your command must be final. Do not crave the fruits of material sensations with possessiveness or attachment. It is all right to look at a rose and enjoy it; but if you say you can't live without that rose, you are misusing the fruit-bearing power of your Tree of Life, which is meant to feed you with higher perceptions, joy, and freedom.

You can live in the Garden of Eden now, if you take care of this tree of flesh and do not produce evil fruits—indulging in things that destroy the tree of the nervous system—and if with the astral tree you do not produce moroseness, peevishness, and the other fruits of wrong living. When you meet a person vibrant with life and look into their inner garden and see there a tree of love, a tree of peace, a tree of joy, a tree of forgiveness, a tree of kindness, then you know they are in Eden. By yoga and meditation you can forsake the bad fruits of the tree of the flesh, and go beyond it to the astral tree with its centers of divine life and consciousness in the spine. Then beyond that you see the tree of consciousness; and beyond that you enter the garden of heaven.

Do you see now what is meant by "The Mystic Tree of Life"? In the garden of your life, all these mystic trees must bear fruit: the body must produce the fruit of vitality; the life-current in the nerves must be used to bring the fruit of calmness; and the tree of consciousness must be laden with the immortal, ambrosial fruits of joy and peace and divine love. If you cultivate in your garden all these fruits, you shall live with God in a heavenly Eden while on earth; and if not, your earthly sojourn will be a hell. The best fruits of the tree of consciousness are Self-realization and intuition. When you taste of them, you find God. Meditation is the way.

The Self-Realization Way to God

So when you enjoy the Christmas tree, remember the mystic Tree of Life. When you place your gifts under the tree, do so with the consciousness that you are worshipping the Tree of Life, that you are placing at the foot of that tree all the packages of your material desires, so that Christ will take them and deliver you from the evil fruits of your unspiritualized tree. Concentrate on the star at the top of the bodily tree, the spiritual eye; and upon the Christ-spirit of universal brotherhood, which is the way of peace. Will you remember that when you place your gifts under the tree? that you are surrendering your material desires, and turning to the star of the spiritual eye for freedom? To give you that experience is why I have instituted an all-day meditation at Christmastime, that you may experience the joy of Christ-communion in a greater way.

What you have heard today is given to you by God; these truths are not of me. Give yourself a present of the *Self-Realization Fellowship Lessons*. Study the *Lessons,* and practice them, and see what your life becomes. The truths taught therein are the living Bible for this age. Jesus and the great masters were sent to bring Christ Consciousness into your consciousness. How can you get the whole lake into a cup? The cup must be made as big as the lake. So if you want Christ to come to you, you must expand your consciousness to be able to receive that infinite consciousness. That is the real "second coming" of Christ. By the practice of Kriya and the other meditation techniques I have taught, you will gradually achieve.

Christ promised especially to send the Comforter, the Holy Ghost, after he had ascended to the Father. The Holy Ghost is the Holy Vibration of *Aum,* the manifested presence of God in creation, which you can consciously contact through the techniques taught by Self-Realization Fellowship. Always think of the presence of the infinite Christ Consciousness in this universal vibration of the manifested universe.

These teachings will go all over the world, and they will spread like wildfire after a while. They were given to me by God; and if you follow them, you will receive more than from all teachings of ordinary "churchianity" put together. Start the Christmas season and New Year with a new light of understanding. Meditate daily, and one day a week dedicate several hours to deep communion and talking with God; and you will have a life that you never before thought could be yours.

The practice of Kriya Yoga meditation brings results. If I were to read to you some of the testimonials of spiritual awakening I have received, you would weep. People all over the world write me how they are benefitted and uplifted; how they had searched everywhere in vain, but now are realizing God. One woman wrote me, "I was sweeping my floor when all at once the great joy and light of God came over me, and everything was drowned in that light. It was not a dream or hallucination; it was real."

By cultivating a love for the Infinite you will see a different world. The Lord wants us to realize that all this war and suffering we see is just a make-believe show, a cosmic movie—nothing but that. Through the experience of communion with Him all these things come to light. That is what I am experiencing now all the time. Sometimes when riding in the car I am translated into another world. And at night I altogether forget the outgoing power of delusion, by which this world is made manifest to us and which is almost as strong as the attractive power of God's love. In that consciousness the material world and all its paradoxes and disappointments vanish; and naught but God is real to me—His love, His glory, His bliss.

The cosmic movie of delusion came from Him, but He didn't intend that we take it as real. You must develop such remembrance of God that delusion does not possess you anymore. The true devotee does not want to remember anything but God. He sees, touches, hears, tastes, and feels only God; and works on earth, as did Christ and the great masters, to share God with others—to bring the complete brotherhood of man under the Fatherhood of God.

The Spiritual Celebration of Christmas

The following remarks were given on December 17, 1944, prior to Paramahansaji's talk on "The Mystic Tree of Life," to focus the attention of the congregation on the spiritual significance of the upcoming Christmas observances.

Each year at Christmastime there are strong vibrations of Christ Consciousness in the air. Those who are attuned by their devotion and by deep, scientific meditation will receive in their own consciousness these vibrations of the universal consciousness that was in Christ Jesus. It is of utmost importance to every man, whatever his religion, that he experience within himself this "birth" of the Universal Christ.

The universe is the body of Christ: everywhere present within it, without limitation, is the Christ Consciousness. When you can close your eyes and by meditation expand your awareness until you feel the whole universe as your own body, Christ will have been born within you. Clouds of ignorance will be dispelled as you behold, behind the darkness of closed eyes, the divine cosmic light—the aura of the Infinite Christ.

"As many as received him, to them gave he power to become the sons of God."* If you expand your mind to receive Him, you will be blessed with the universal consciousness. You will know that your body is the whole universe, and that your mind is a little wave of that ocean of Cosmic Consciousness in which Christ dwells.

Just saying, "Jesus! Lord! Lord!" is not enough. You must invite him within your consciousness by your concentration and devotion. Then he will accept you and he will come; you will feel the birth of his consciousness within you.

Jesus was born in an Oriental body; but it was the Occident who adopted him as their guru and preceptor. The Orientals, in turn, have accepted the leadership of Western nations in science, except

* John 1:12.

where there is a wrong employment of science for the purpose of killing and destruction. East and West have concentrated on spiritual or material development, respectively, so that each lacks what the other has to offer. The uniting of East and West was part of the divine purpose of Christ being born in the East and his teachings taking root in the West.

"Behold, I bring you good tidings of great joy, which shall be to all people. For unto you is born this day in the city of David a Saviour, which is Christ the Lord."* This little child was not a helpless babe; the angels stood watch over his body in which the whole universal consciousness was manifest.

That spirit of Christ must be born in the cradle of your own consciousness. Visualize the whole universe as far as you can mentally picture it—above, beneath, to the right, to the left, and all around you. Just as your consciousness pervades your whole body, the consciousness of Christ is equally present throughout the cosmos—in every tree and plant, in every bird and animal, in all human beings. "Are not two sparrows sold for a farthing? and one of them shall not fall on the ground without [the sight of] your Father."† Saturate yourself with that consciousness. Meditate on the presence of Christ in the vibration of the manifested universe: the great *Aum* or Amen, the Cosmic Vibration or Word.‡

Repeat with me: "The vast consciousness of Christ is born this day within the cradle of my universal body, the cosmos. Unto me a child is given, unto me a child is born. I celebrate the birth of Christ in spirit and in body. The consciousness of Christ is all-pervading. Within the cradle of the universe, Christ and I are one." *Aum. Peace. Aum.*

Last night I saw Christ. I beheld his face; and just as he passed out of my vision I perceived also the delusive evil force manifest as Satan. It was a strangely awesome experience—those two universal forces passed through my body: one of them as the infinite joy and peace of God, the other as the great outgoing power of Cosmic Delusion. That satanic force could not harm me, only try to frighten me. In exalted states of consciousness experienced as one goes toward

* Luke 2:10–11.

† Matthew 10:29.

‡ "In the beginning was the Word, and the Word was with God, and the Word was God....All things were made by him; and without him was not any thing made that was made" (John 1:1–3).

Spirit, those two forces are beheld distinctly as the essential duality of manifested creation; but in the highest *samadhi* I see there is naught but Spirit, the Unmanifested Absolute. On the relative plane, however, one sees at work in the cosmos the power of evil and the power of Christ Consciousness, the power of Satan and the power of God.

Jesus conquered Satan's delusion in the highest way; and in doing so an unseen monument of love for Christ has been established in all hearts. Napoleon, Genghis Khan, Hitler, we know as villains who ruled by ruthlessly destroying their human brothers; but Christ reigns immortally in our hearts because he conquered through love. Even when his enemies sentenced him to a cruel death, he would not use his divine power to harm them.*

Do not think that Jesus only was crucified; everyone in some way has his cross to bear daily. Those who try to do good in this world know what it is to be crucified by enemies. When one gives love and gets treachery and hate in return, those wounds of the heart are sometimes harder to endure than wounds that injure only the body. When misunderstood or mistreated, that is the time to live by the divine example set by Jesus on the cross: "Father, forgive them"—love even thine enemies as thyself. Sick in mind or asleep in delusion, they are still thy brothers.

Greater than adoration of Christ is to love Christ—to feel the love of Christ Consciousness that is born in your heart when you dwell in the Infinite Consciousness that was in Jesus. The sun sheds its light equally on the diamond and the charcoal, but only the diamond reflects the light. Though God's light is present in all, it is unseen and unrecognized in a charcoal mentality. But when the consciousness has the transparency of the diamond, then it receives and radiates the light of God, the light of the Infinite Christ.

Concentrate on Jesus throughout the Christmas season. If you want to experience the joy of the presence of Christ, follow the star of Bethlehem, the star of the East. Join with Self-Realizationists for deep meditation on December 23rd; or plan to meditate privately in your own home. May you experience a Christmas joy that you have never felt before! Many who have attended the annual Christmas meditations held in Self-Realization Fellowship temples have seen

* "Thinkest thou that I cannot now pray to my Father, and he shall presently give me more than twelve legions of angels? But how then shall the scriptures be fulfilled, that thus it must be?" (Matthew 26:53–54).

the Christ. He has graciously given me a special visitation each year on the day of our Christmas meditations.

Spread this idea wherever you go: that Christ must be worshiped in truth—first in spirit, by meditation; and second in form, by perceiving his presence even in the material world. You must meditate on the real meaning of the coming of Christ, and feel his consciousness drawn within you by the magnet of your devotion. That is the real purpose of Christmas.

I saw an advertisement telling people to celebrate Christmas with a special brand of wine, to make that the gift placed under the Christmas tree. What a desecration of the observance of Jesus' birth! Another time a student in my classes bought an air gun as a Christmas present for her son. She changed it when I reminded her that killing birds is not in the spirit of Christ's message of love. To give useful material gifts is all right; but it is of more benefit to give spiritual gifts also, such as inspirational books. Spiritual gifts will last; material gifts will not. And remember, the spirit of Christmas giving is not to expect a bigger gift in return!

Exchanging gifts and writing letters of greeting are only part of the celebration of the birth of Christ; the real meaning of Christmas has been largely forgotten. We must celebrate a spiritual Christmas first; a social Christmas can be celebrated afterward, on the 25th, with gaiety and the exchange of presents. Self-Realization Fellowship teachings are inculcating in the hearts and minds of SRF students the deeper meaning of Christmas. We have started the idea of devoting one day at Christmastime entirely to meditative worship of Christ, and that idea shall never die. The spiritual custom of Christmas meditation will be adopted everywhere—I predict it.

Know the Real Meaning and Joy of Christmas

*Introductory remarks given by Paramahansaji before his Sunday talk at the Self-Realization Fellowship Golden Lotus Temple, Encinitas, California, December 22, 1940**

As Christmas is approaching, I extend to you my deepest blessings for a very spiritual Christmas and a wonderful New Year. May they create in your heart a strong impetus to begin anew.

The idea behind great occasions is to give us such incentive and strength that life receives a fresh start. Make a strong resolution that your life will be different from this Christmas on. Resolve that you are going to make the supreme effort of your will to do away with those wrong attitudes that have disheartened you—those psychological bad habits that have been clinging to you like cancers. Cut them out. Lead a healthy life—physically, mentally, and spiritually—during this Christmastime and the New Year. You can and you must. If you allow your life to go on in a desultory or misdirected way, there will be repercussions. Every year your life will be more burdensome. The energy of the body will grow weaker and your mind more defeated. Now is the time for strong resolutions to make of your life what it should be.

The birthdays of great souls are not to be passed off as merely times for socials and ceremonies. They are auspicious occasions, which are observed also in heaven, to honor great souls who came on earth for the upliftment of mankind. God and the masters manifest in form and rejoice together, celebrating with astral lights and fragrances. This truth is unknown to the unawakened man, but known to those who are in communion with God. Whoever will take spiritual advantage of these sacred events will find his resolutions helped by the vibrations of those great souls whose anniversaries are being observed. Their vibrations are stronger and easier to tune in with during the holy seasons dedicated to them.

* The main talk, "Making Religion Scientific," is published in *Man's Eternal Quest*, Volume I of Paramahansa Yogananda's *Collected Talks and Essays.*

So remember that Christmas is a wonderful divine event. Receive the blessings of Christ to spiritualize your life. You can be old, mentally stagnant, and refuse to progress, if you choose to be that way. Or you can be young and accomplish whatever you put your mind to, if you so determine. It has nothing to do with the body. Your spirit must be absolutely independent of the conditions of the body. When we realize this, we are free.

Jesus' body was slain, and still he knew he was immortal, that his spirit goes on. He said, "Destroy this temple, and in three days I will raise it up." The life of Jesus demonstrated immortality—that although the body dies, we never die. When the garment is cast aside, the wearer does not cease to exist. Jesus knew he was not the body, which is only a shadow. The lesson is that we are not the body, but unconquerable Spirit.

In this world there are lots of truths that are stranger than fiction. Human life is the receptacle of all the wonders of heaven and earth. Those who take the life of Jesus seriously, and demonstrate within themselves the experiences of Christ, know how to solve the mystery of existence and realize the glories of heaven. Such are the experiences I am having now, by the grace of God. I was sitting last evening in my room at Mt. Washington, and suddenly heaven opened up and I saw many saints. Do not despair if these wonders are not yet revealed to you. When you unceasingly reach out to God, He will one day reach down and lift you up. Never give up!

Constantly keep the mind aloof from material consciousness. Be in the world, but not of it. You give too much time to useless things. Don't make unimportant things important. Cut out the nonessentials in order to make time for God and those spiritual habits that will give you true peace. I cut the world from my life because it made unimportant things seem important. Life is too short to waste time. You can't afford to do so. You cannot fly away from your duties, but you can avoid personal ambition. Do everything to please God. To be motivated by egoistic desires, attachments, and ambitions is dangerous to your true happiness. But when you try to pattern your life after the example of Jesus and the great ones, who lived only to do the will of God, then you see that life is divine and full of joy.

In this coming year, you should completely change your life. If you make up your mind to do it, that determination will be helped by the vibrations of Christ at this holy time, when he reaches out forcefully to wake up mankind from the sleep of delusion.

Prepare your mind to commune with Christ. At the Self-Realization headquarters we meditate all day on the 24th of December.* If you cannot attend one of the group meditations in our centers, meditate at home. Many people who hadn't been able to feel God's presence before have found communion with Him on that day. We don't think of time. The hours seem only a few minutes. If you have the will power and strength to meditate deeply on that day, you will feel the presence of God and Christ.

In time, this custom of observing the spiritual Christmas will spread like wildfire. People will realize that it is a desecration of Christ's birthday to celebrate only with material pleasures, going even so far as to include wine and drunkenness. To give nice gifts to cheer others and to express your love for them is all right. But the real celebration of Christmas is to experience something of Christ's presence—to know that he is born in the cradle of your awakened meditation.

The idea of an all-day Christmas meditation was really given to me by Christ, that he might do something for you. He wants to bless you, but his hands are tied if you are not receptive. He wants to come to you, but he can't if the portals of devotion, through which alone he can enter your life, are closed. Wherever he finds sincere souls, he tries to come to them; but how can he get in when the doors of calmness are shut, and the latch of restlessness has locked up the soul? Yet if you meditate long and deeply, and call to Christ with all the love of your soul, removing all barriers of restlessness and doubt, you will find him willingly entering in. You will know the real meaning and joy of Christmas.

* In subsequent years, Paramahansaji began holding the long meditation on the 23rd of December. *(Publisher's Note)*

How to Perceive the Infinite Christ

Words of inspiration addressed to Self-Realization Fellowship students and ashram residents during an annual Christmas meditation at SRF Headquarters, Los Angeles, December 24, 1934

As you meditate, watch the growth of happiness, the feeling of lightness, the sense of expansion in all space. As your silence intensifies and your joy grows in meditation, so will your recognition of Spirit grow within you. As your intuition increases in meditation, so will your joy in Christ increase. The deeper your meditation, the deeper your contact with Christ Consciousness. As you feel happiness growing within, know that Christ is approaching nearer and nearer to you.

Coax Christ today with your songs and the devotion of your heart, and then coax him with your deepening Self-realization. With all the intensity of your zeal and inner perception, merge your consciousness in the happiness within. Forget time. When you feel joy spreading within you, realize that Christ is hearing your song. You are not identified with Christ if your concentration is merely on the words. But if your joy is singing within, Christ is listening to you.

Keep your flesh harnessed to the guiding power of Spirit. Let not the Spirit be carried away by the flesh. A steady, ever-increasing flame of devotion and Self-realization will bring you to the perception of the Infinite. The Lord is burning like a great fire, destroying all darkness from our minds. With united hearts let us offer the homage of our prayer unto Christ, unto God:

"Father, Mother, Friend, Beloved Lord, come to us in response to our soul cries, to our importuning devotion. Test us as Thou wilt, but do not punish us with oblivion of Thy presence.

"O Divine Mother! come out of the cave of my silence. My darkness melts in the fathomless wisdom of Thy dark eyes. My cry is Thy cry; my joy Thy joy. My soul is lost in Thy Spirit. My heart has lost its throb in Thy throb. My hands are but Thy hands, my brain Thy brain, my thoughts Thy thoughts, my feelings Thy feelings, my soul Thy soul, my love Thy love. Divine Mother, my errors, my virtues are Thine; but my love for Thee is mine. My heart feels only Thy love, my love dreams of Thy love, my love drinks of Thy love with the lips of silence. Mother Divine, Mother Divine, it is Thou who hast become Christ, Krishna, and the saints of all religions. Divine Mother! Divine Christ!"

With Each Breath We Imbibe the Spirit

Every time you take a breath you are inhaling the presence of God, of Christ, into every part of your body. Inhale, exhale; concentrate at the point between the eyebrows. Feel, feel! Within, all is immersed in the peace of Christ; without, all is filled with the peace of Christ. The peace of Christ within is joined with the peace of Christ without. The ocean of Divine Mother's love is flooding the little cup of life within and without. "Beloved Mother, Father, God, in the silence of my soul I cry, with all my gathered tears I silently cry, Mother Divine, take possession of our souls, manifest Thyself as Christ Consciousness to all. Divine Christ, forget us not though we forget Thee, remember us though we remember Thee not, be not indifferent to us though we are indifferent to Thee. May Thy love shine forever on the sanctuary of my devotion, and may I be able to awaken Thy love in all hearts."

Indifference Hides the Jewel-Presence of God

Just as gems are hidden in a mine, so the jewel-presence of God is hidden under the soil of our hard indifference. We have to dig through that soil again and again with the pickax of meditation.

Behind the vibratory veil of thoughts, feelings, sensory perceptions, and outer noises lies the wisdom of God. The less your consciousness moves in these vibrations of restlessness, the more you live in God. As you live more deeply in awareness of Him, even the greatest pleasures of the senses gradually lose their attraction. Once, after deep bliss in God, I started to eat a sweet orange; it seemed as if a thousand scorpions had stung me, so gross was its sweetness.

Just behind your thoughts and feelings is God. The Spirit that is talked about and wondered about is right here. It is through His voice that I am speaking to you of the happiness that I have in Him, joy indescribable, happiness immortal. Divine perception has everything within it. All the joy of the world is contained in Spirit. The delight you feel in sensory pleasures is only an imitation of divine joy. How fortunate we are! Many have talked about God, but we are feeling today that Ineffable Being throbbing in our bosoms.

Though this earth is an illusion, created out of the consciousness of God, it was not intended to delude us. God meant it to be an entertainment for us, His immortal children. Beware, as you play your part in His dream creation, that you do not develop ensnaring desires for sense happiness, for they will cause you to fall into the pit of disappointment and misery. The only happiness that is lasting and worthwhile is the joy found in meditation. When you meditate long, old worldly habits drop away, and the glory of the Divine shines forth. You realize then that all along there was something tremendous within you, and you had not known it.

Keep a room apart for God, and whenever you deeply meditate in it you will see that what I am telling is true. It is such happiness to know the Lord! The whole ocean of divine joy rolls beneath the little wave of your consciousness. Who shall believe except those who are devotees?

Remember the experience of Christ that you have had today, and make every day like it. All the time I am filled with this joy. But I had to work for it. As a little boy I cried night after night for God; He seemed not to respond. Then, little by little, He began to play hide-and-seek with me; now and then I saw images of saints. I wondered if they were hallucinations, but when those visions came true in life and I met my divine Guru and other masters in the flesh, I didn't doubt anymore.

Divine Love Is Matchless

What the company of the great masters of India taught me! When I saw the Divine in their faces right in front of me, and when I saw them actually talking with God, what could I say? Doubt fled, doubting itself, before the living presence of the Lord. But this realization comes only by continuous meditation. Just as young people are concentrated on human love, and the miser is always seeking money, so should your love for God be your supreme preoccupation. Meditation gives birth to the love of God, because by meditation you are able to feel His presence. How can you feel the love of God without the presence of God? That divine love no human being knows. When my mother died, I cried inconsolably. But no pain of human separation can match the longing I feel now when I cry for my Divine Mother.

Beholding in Vision a Blue-Eyed Christ

God granted my prayer that Christ come today. I saw his face. But I was much astonished, for he had blue eyes! the most beautiful

I have ever seen. I used to scoff at the idea that Jesus, an Oriental, would have blue eyes and golden hair, as he is often depicted in Western art. But Christ spoke to me today and said, "You didn't know that I can have blue eyes, too!" Then, as I gazed in wonder, his eyes became dark and he spoke again: "Why do you want to see me in form? See me as Infinite."

Think what a Christmas we are enjoying today! We have something more beautiful than material gifts to attract us. No man-made temple can produce the Spirit we are enjoying today. Wonderful music couldn't produce this joy. God is the music of all music, the nectar of all nectars, the happiness of all happiness. If only people could picture His joy! If the Lord should come even once to you, nothing else would matter to you anymore. Don't let the world fool you. Fool the world. The drunken man is always drunk wherever you put him. So is the divine man. Whether talking to people or meditating, he is intoxicated with the love of God.

God—Source of All Happiness

Instead of the supernal security of Spirit, Satan gives man delusive desire for money. In place of the joy of meditation, Satan substitutes worldly attractions, to keep our consciousness turned away from divine bliss. But once the love of God comes to you, Satan will no more have a hold on you. So no matter how much pleasure you find in sense perceptions, remember that in God-perception there is more happiness. Live in the world, but be not of the world. In the world you must play the game; but you can beat Satan at his own game. It is a question of what you want.

Whoever tells you that to have a family is supremely wonderful, or to have money is supremely wonderful, or to be a great businessman is supremely wonderful, is lacking in true wisdom. For every worldly dream will terminate after a time. Suppose you become a great singer; then you grow old and people lose interest in your voice. Or perhaps you amass money; you will have to leave it when death comes. But God is wealth you cannot lose. If you think human love is wonderful, it will someday bring you unhappiness, when the beloved dies. Divine Joy outlasts everything. It is enduring. When all else melts away, that Joy remains.

Everything has its place; but when you waste time at the cost of your true happiness, it is not good. I dropped every unnecessary activity so that I could meditate and try to know God, so that I could day and night be in His divine consciousness. If you want to be different, you must really work to be different. When the masters warned me, I arranged that not one evening slipped away without meditation.

Meditation Strengthens Desire for God

The minds of most worldly people are "shot" by the age of 30–35. If you don't meditate when you are younger, you will find that from the age of 35–40 onward it will be more difficult to know God. But even if you have passed that age, if you keep trying to meditate no matter how discouraged you may be, after a few years your desire for the Lord will become very strong. Angels will be with you. Though the whole world be plunged into suffering, you will know what is going to happen, and God will be with you.

Seeking God Should Be a Relentless Pursuit

At first the soul is very desirous of exercising its power to know the future. But after a while this knowledge palls. Knowing what is going to take place is no fun at all. I have given all my powers back to God. I am living like a child, just to please Him. I have no ambition of my own. Why should I torture myself with desires? I have given them to Him; whatever He wants me to do, that is my happiness. But it is nevertheless very difficult to carry out His wishes when He tells you to do things you don't like to do! You must have undiscourageable faith in Him. You must know that you are His.

Let no one tell you that anything else is better than God's joy. All men seek happiness, but do they find it? Meditation, long and deep, is the way to attain true joy. Nothing else can compare to meditation. Don't be satisfied with a little silence. Go on endlessly. It must be a relentless pursuit, day and night meditating. When you are in His joy, sleep doesn't matter.

Stay more by yourself. Remember, the only real happiness is in meditation. And the proof is obtainable by you. If you meditate the Self-Realization way for two or three hours at night, and then sing and talk to the Lord, undismayed if there is no answer, suddenly a divine light will come. Mysteriously, a fragrance will come. This is the way God lets you know that He is near. But you must be persistent, until He Himself comes. Then you will never fear anything anymore.

"In the Cradle of Our Consciousness, the Eternal Christ Is Born Today"

Guided Meditation, Chanting, and Ecstasy at Christmastime

An especially blessed annual occasion at Self-Realization Fellowship International Headquarters is the all-day Christmas meditation. Paramahansa Yogananda inaugurated these services in 1931, and personally conducted them each year. During these meditations, his words flowed extemporaneously: sometimes an expression of his own divine ardor intimately addressed directly to God; sometimes an appeal to the Lord on behalf of, or as one of, the assembled devotees; sometimes spiritual guidance for those present—the spontaneous inspirations of a soul in deep communion with God.

"After Gurudeva's return from his 1935–36 trip to India, his consciousness was fresh with many visions and superconscious experiences," recalls Sri Daya Mata, who recorded his talks stenographically. Following are the Guru's words at the all-day Christmas meditation held December 24, 1936—just a few weeks after he had arrived back at Mt. Washington from that momentous journey—as he guided those present deeper and deeper into a blissful communion with the Divine.

"The meditation was conducted by Swami Yogananda, who was in ecstasy for seven hours without intermission," reported Richard Wright in SRF's magazine. "Those who joined this meditation felt the seven hours pass like seven minutes of unending joy."

[Paramahansaji begins the meditation by invoking the presence of the Self-Realization Fellowship line of Gurus, followed by an opening prayer:]

"*Aum,* Babaji; receive the homage of our souls. *Aum,* Lahiri Mahasaya; receive the homage of our souls. Beloved Guru Swami Sri Yukteswarji, receive the homage of our souls. Guru-Preceptor, receive the perpetual loyalty of our souls. O Christ, O Krishna, and saints of all religions, receive the devotion of our souls. We offer with this incense our deepest devotion unto you all. *Aum, Aum, Aum.*

"Heavenly Father, awaken within us the birth of Jesus, the birth of Krishna, as the *Kutastha Chaitanya,* the universal Christ or Krishna Consciousness.* Bless us that we may arouse within our souls the great light expressed in all Thy true sons—in Jesus, in Krishna, in Babaji, Lahiri Mahasaya, Swami Sri Yukteswarji—and may our consciousness be united with their consciousness. May we all be one in Thy Spirit evermore. Be Thou with us evermore, O Spirit Divine. We are blessed that Thou hast brought to us Thy glory. Father, Thou art our very own Beloved Spirit. What more shall I pray, but to feel Thy love in my heart?

"We all offer our love unto Thee, O Father. Delude us no more with this world. If it is Thy pleasure to leave us in this world, all right. Our bodies may be here, but our souls are in Thy kingdom. And may we remember that our bodies, our minds, and our souls are but the reflection of Thy Spirit. May we behold Thy divine light; may we behold Thy Spirit behind our lives.

"Father, Mother, Friend, Beloved God, oh, what joy, what joy, what joy! Rivers and oceans of joy! Joy eternal, joy eternal, joy eternal possesses us. Joy eternal flows through us. O River of Ever New Joy, flow through us. Flood us with Thy consciousness. Melt us in Thy joy. Destroy the habits of incarnations that encrust our souls. Naught else do we want but Thy strength, Thy consciousness, Thy wisdom, Thine ambition, Thine ever new joy, evermore. Our bodies, our minds, our souls are translated into Thy bliss, O Spirit. We sing to Thee our song of love with devotion. With our reason, with our love, we sing our soul song unto Thee.

"Father, Thou art with us. Every thought is directed toward Thy presence. Every feeling is drunk with Thy consciousness. Every wisp of consciousness is filled with the fragrance of Thy joy, O Spirit. On the united altar of our hearts, reign Thou forever. Lift us into Thy grace, O Father, into Thy consciousness, that we may realize we are of Thy Kingdom. O Father, we bow to Thee again and again. *Aum,* Peace, Amen."

* The projected consciousness of God immanent in all creation. In Christian scripture it is called the "only begotten son," the only pure reflection in creation of God the Father; in Hindu scripture it is called *Kutastha Chaitanya* or *Tat,* the cosmic intelligence of Spirit everywhere present in creation. It is the universal consciousness, oneness with God, manifested by Jesus, Krishna, and other avatars. Great saints and yogis know it as the state of *samadhi* meditation wherein their consciousness has become identified with God's Intelligence in every particle of creation; they feel the entire universe as their own body.

Dear ones, go deeper and deeper in meditation. Do not lag behind and fall into the ditch of delusion. Go on marching to the eternal kingdom of joy, and you will forever be free of the jungle of sorrow, the swamps of ignorance.

Those who go deep today will be blessed by God and find it difficult to be restless. As you offer to God your devotion, offer it with sincerity. Pray to Him, "O Lord, You know that I am sincere; You must listen to my prayer." Sometimes the Lord plays tricks on us. He is right behind our thoughts, talking to us; but we do not hear His message. But when a devotee is sunk in humility, then when he least expects, God will come. He manifests to the devotee as Light or as ever new Joy, or as a poetic inspiration, or as Wisdom. Above all, He comes as Love.

"O Lord, I want to tell all of Thy blessings. I want not to enjoy them alone, selfishly, but to share with others. Bless all with Thy consciousness. O Jesus Christ, O Jesus Christ! O Joy, Joy, Joy! Beloved God, Beloved Mother-Father, open up the heaven that lies within us."

Concentrate at the *Kutastha* Christ Consciousness center between the eyebrows. Now practice Kriya Yoga, very slowly.* Feel the life currents and consciousness ascending and descending in the spine, whose centers of light are the altar of God. While the opportunity is at hand, make the effort.

[As the assembled devotees follow these instructions, Paramahansaji beholds a vision of the infant Jesus:]

The baby Christ is born right now in that divine Light at the *Kutastha* center. He is bathed in that eternal Light.

Concentrate at the point between the eyebrows, and go up the spine mentally chanting *"Aum"* at each of the centers: coccyx, sacral, lumbar, dorsal, cervical, medulla, Christ center. Now mentally go down the spine chanting *"Aum"* at each of these centers. Go deeper and deeper in concentration, up and down the spine, mentally feeling the centers and mentally chanting *"Aum."* As you do this, you see that your consciousness is no longer locked in the external awareness of the body, but becomes centered in higher spiritual perceptions in the spine. Relax in God. Don't be tied to the consciousness of the body. Let your mind go deeper and deeper in the thought of God.

* Kriya Yoga consists of certain specific techniques for realizing the immanent presence of God, taught to students of the *Self-Realization Fellowship Lessons.*

[A period of meditation follows, and then the chant, "Engrossed is the bee of my mind on the blue lotus feet of my Divine Mother."*]

This song I sang all the way coming to Los Angeles from New York, and Divine Mother was all the time with me as I chanted. You see, every song to God should be sung until it is spiritualized; and all songs that you will sing with that devotional yearning, the Spirit will respond to. That hunger for God is eternal in the soul, and the joy that comes from God is eternal. That is His response. Some devotees of great devotion, who love worshiping God, hold on to that hunger for God all the time; others in divine union enjoy the joy of God. Never think there is an end to that Joy, for it is eternal. Man's real nature is to be day and night happy in that joyous love of God. Because you are away from your true nature, you suffer in this world. The nature of Spirit is joy; and the nature of your soul is joy. He who is afraid of sickness is in delusion. Both health and disease are delusion; all that has to do with the body is delusion. It is better to cast aside the dreams both of health and ill health and be above them, in the consciousness of the soul, your true Self.

All the joy of my beloved God is coming over me. "O Lord, Thou alone art real. Thou art the only reality of life. Take away this veil of delusion, O Lord. No more do I want to care for the body. Take away this delusion. Let me enjoy Thy joy. Let me share this joy with devotees day and night. Day and night, day and night, I look for Thee day and night."

In sleep I feel Thee, night and day, night and day.
In joy I feel Thee, night and day, night and day.
While awake I feel Thee, night and day, night and day.
I enjoy Thee night and day.

Without breath I feel Thee, night and day, night and day.
Ever flowing I feel Thy love, night and day, night and day.
Night and day I love Thee, night and day.
O Lord, Thou art mine, night and day, night and day.
Thou art mine, night and day;
I am Thine, night and day.

Night and day, Lord, Thy love flows through me, night and day.
Ceaseless joy, Lord, night and day. Ever new joy, night and day.

* "Blue Lotus Feet," in Paramahansaji's *Cosmic Chants*, published by Self-Realization Fellowship.

All desires I give unto Thee, O Lord, night and day, night and day.
For Thee, O Lord, I forsake all else, night and day, night and day.
For Thee I surrender all, O Lord, night and day.

My time is Thy time, my Lord.
Be Thou mine, be Thou mine! O beloved Lord, be Thou mine.
My time is Thine, O Beloved, my time is all Thine.
For senses, no time, no time. For matter, no time, no time,
For my time is always Thine, always Thine.

All is Thine, O Lord, all is Thine.
Night and day, night and day, I feel Thee night and day.
Continuously, night and day, Thy joy, O Lord, Thy joy;
Ever new joy night and day, ever new joy night and day!
*Aum Guru, Aum Guru, Aum Guru, Aum Guru. Aum Kali, Aum Kali.**

"O Spirit, let us have no other preaching than Thy preaching, Thy Word vibrating through us! No longer the mock truth of intellectuality; no other voice but Thy voice, speaking through us! No other love but Thy love, loving through us! No other consciousness but Thy consciousness, flowing through us! No other spirit than Thy Spirit, radiating through our souls!

"Mother Divine, bless all with Thy continuous joy. All things I place at Thy feet. All desires I burn in the flaming love of Thy presence. No other duty more important than to love Thee. No other romance but the romance with Thee. No other work but the work for Thee. No other reality but Thee, O Mother Divine. Thou alone art real; all things else are illusion. Mother, in the reality of Thy presence, all the audacity of unreality shall vanish forever.

* In India, "Kali" is one of the names given to God as the Cosmic Mother Nature. In Hindu art She is represented as four-armed. One of the divine hands symbolizes Her powers of creation; the second hand, the universal principle of preservation; the third hand, the purifying forces of dissolution. Kali's fourth hand is outstretched in a gesture of blessing and salvation. In this fourfold way She leads all creation back to its source in Spirit.

The aspect of the Cosmic Mother as Kali is especially dear to the hearts of Bengalis. During his yearlong visit to India, Paramahansaji was deeply immersed in the joy of experiencing once again the spiritual atmosphere and traditions of the blessed early years of his life in his native land. Thus his frequent references to Divine Mother as Kali during this period of worshipful meditation.

"Oh, such joy, such eternal joy! Blessedness eternal! Mother Divine, my voice shall speak Thy voice. My love shall declare Thy glories. Mother Divine, look into my heart; if there is anything there but Thee, cut it out. Guru divine, I lay my life at thy feet. Nothing I keep for myself—not even the body, not health, not any desire. Take them away.

"I found at the end of each trail of my desires that it was Thee I was trying to find, O Spirit. Such love, such love! I stand between life and death beholding the Kingdom of all joy. O Lord, make us love all things that are good. Divine Spirit, You know we are not of this world; why do You keep us believing that we belong to this world? We don't belong to it, but to Thee. Divine Spirit, O playful Child, don't run away; come unto us. Escape not through the back doors of our minds. How mankind lives without Thee, I know not, O Father, Mother, Friend, Beloved God!

"O Spirit, bless those that are here that they preach naught else but Thy presence alone, for Thou art health and wealth and joy eternal. O Guru, unite our hearts. We open wide our hearts to thee. O Lord, You know whether we are sincere. We surrender our hearts unto Thee. We seek no glory of organization or power. What is Thy wish, we will do. Bless St. Lynn;* bless us all. O Lord, Mother Divine, Father Divine, all I want is to preach the glory of Thy name. Nothing else do I crave. Whatever is for Thy glory, that alone I want. Put us in a palace or under the trees, it does not matter; but promise You will be with us always, for that will be our heaven.

"O Spirit, I pray with my heart, with my soul. The tiny bubble of my breath breaks into the eternal Cosmic Life. The tiny bubble of my thought melts into the vast ocean of Thy thought. The tiny bubble of my love melts in the ocean of Thy love. The words I speak are not mine; I only borrow Thy voice. All credit belongs to Thee.

"O Spirit, I open my heart to all. Let my agony be shown for all those who do not think of Thee. Oh, this is my prayer, Mother Divine: Make them see the folly of clinging to selfishness. Wherein they desire to use selfishness, that breaks my heart. Make them unselfish, and show them how blessed it is to be the lowest of the low, the humblest of the humble.

* James J. Lynn, exalted disciple of Paramahansa Yogananda on whom the Guru later bestowed the monastic name Rajarsi Janakananda, and who succeeded Paramahansaji as the second president and spiritual head of Self-Realization Fellowship/Yogoda Satsanga Society of India.

"O Kali, Kali, Kali, Divine Mother, Divine Kali, blessed Mother Divine, Kali, Mother Divine! O Mother, Mother, I was reluctant to come to America, lest in its materialism I lose sight of You. Mother, no body, no name, no fame do I acknowledge. What You have done through me, I don't know. I am dreaming on this earth, and living in Thee. I am walking in sleep on this earth, awake in Thee, O Divine Mother.

"I offer my life at Thy feet, O Lord. All those whom You have worked through from the beginning, both here and in India, bless them. I offer all my love, O Beloved, at Thy feet.

"Divine Mother, bless each one who is here. What joy we have in poverty and prosperity, when all comes from Thee, O Spirit. If it is Thy desire to leave us in poverty or in prosperity, may we realize both come from Thee, and may we love Thee always. They are but dreams, and Thou art the only Reality, O Spirit.

"O Ocean of Love, Ocean of Joy, what shall I utter but bliss eternal, joy eternal, eternal flame of light! We want no other prayer, no other meditation than to concentrate upon Thy love. *Aum,* Christ, Christ, Christ! *Aum,* Krishna, Krishna, Krishna! *Aum,* Kali! They are all one. All are waves of Thy one Being; all saints come from Thee, O Ocean of Love. A fragrant bouquet of saints have come from the garden of the Infinite; and through our devotion on these sacred occasions such as Christmas, they remain in the vase of our hearts."

Death, fear, disease—these exist only in delusion. Seek reality. Only the reality of God's consciousness will destroy delusion. No matter if there is disease, don't be afraid of it. When you are in the nightmare, cling to the Divine Spirit and that nightmare will go. Throw yourself at the feet of Divine Mother. A saint in India had diabetes, owing to some karma from his previous incarnations; but his will for the Divine Mother was very strong. He couldn't sit for five minutes in meditation, but he made up his mind that he would make every effort. His love for God was greater. Gradually he conquered, until eighteen hours he could sit in lotus posture, meditating deeply. And what happened? It took some time, but his body was made whole. His determination, his spirit of devotion, overcame the body; and he became united with God.

The body that you are all enjoying, suddenly the day will come when you have to dump it in the fire of death. Don't give it too much attention. I never think of the body; I see the Eternal Flame behind it. Meditate, and one day you will see that your mortal existence is but a dream. And if you are jerked out of this dream of flesh, you will be in the eternal flame of God's love. So fear nothing. Know that you are in the presence of God right now. Every wrong thought that you have comes from Satan's influence. Fear nothing, fear nothing; for God is more powerful than Satan. God is trying to win you with His love. When you renounce everything for God, you will see that God's light will work through you.

Listen to the guidance of Guru. If you resent my words, how my heart bleeds; for if I say anything to you, it is for your own highest good.

"Mother, I killed all egotism so that You could come into this temple. Mother, there is no end to this joy, no end—eternal joy! O Mother, what grace, what pure joy! We are all Thy devotees, and You, O Mother, are so great. You are the ocean, and You are the millions of waves of human beings. Mother, we are Thine always. Make us realize we are in Thee always. *Aum* Kali, *Aum* Kali. As long as we surround ourselves with darkness we cannot see Thee. When the darkness is lifted, then we behold Thee."

When the darkness of body consciousness and breath is gone, Divine Mother is revealed—the Beloved Mother who is there always.

"O Divine Mother, with folded hands we worship Thee. We are Thy children; we are Thy babes. Before Thy wisdom my wisdom is little. Before Thy power, my power is little. Before Thy strength, my strength is little. And before Thy love, my love is little; for all love, all knowing, all strength, all power, come from Thee. Nothing is mine. All is Thine. With our souls, with our hearts, we love Thee.

"May this consciousness we feel today be a cradle for the universal consciousness—a cradle for Christ, for Krishna. O Guru, O Christ, let our consciousness be the cradle for the supreme consciousness that was within Jesus the Christ, in Lord Krishna, Babaji, Lahiri Mahasaya, and Sri Yukteswarji. *Aum,* Guru; *Aum,* Guru; *Aum,* Guru. Lahiri Mahasaya, beloved Lahiri Mahasaya! Oh, what joy; endless joy; eternal, everlasting, ever new joy. O Mother Divine, scatter the joy in my heart unto all!

"O Mother, spread the science of meditation over the earth, that true seekers may meditate in centers all over the world. Let there be a new spiritual awakening in mankind. Destroy hatred from the hearts of men. We are a small band of devotees—a small hive, but filled with the honey of devotion for Thee. Let us gather souls to be filled with Thy name, with Thy love—not with intellectuality, but with Thy presence. Mother, I bow to Thee."

[A long period of meditation followed. Then Paramahansaji spoke again:]

As a lamp with a dimming apparatus can be gradually turned lower and lower, and then suddenly turned up high so the light shines forth again, so can you dim the outwardly directed lamp of life in your body and then bring it forth within to reveal the Divine Mother. Our bodies are but the bulb; our life and consciousness are the electricity in that bulb. We want to switch off the dim lights of the senses, and bring forth the blazing light of divine consciousness.

Close your eyes. Tense the whole body slowly. Now relax the life energy from the muscles; let go and let the body feel totally relaxed. Inhale deeply, then throw the breath out; forget it. Switch off the energy from the senses and the heart. Let your consciousness retire into the "tree of life," the spine. Now bring your attention slowly up the spine to the medulla, to the Christ center. And now let your consciousness flow out through the Christ center into the infinite bliss of God.

Now again bring your consciousness back through the Christ center, the medulla, down the spine into the heart, into the lungs and breath, and into the muscles of the body. Once again flex your muscles; feel the energy and consciousness infusing the little body.

[Paramahansaji leads the devotees in the above exercise three times, then says:]

Now concentrate at the point between the eyebrows and then mentally go up and down the spine, chanting "*Aum*" at each of the centers.

[Meditation follows. After a while, the Guru speaks again:]

Visualize a great fire of wisdom (in India this is called *yajna*), around which all the Masters are standing. Now feel that you have cast into that fire of wisdom all your past karma.

[Here Paramahansaji has a vision:]

There is Divine Mother standing right before the flaming light, and all the Masters are standing there. "O Kali, O Kali, oh, such bliss, oh, such joy! Babaji, Lahiri Mahasaya, Swami Sri Yukteswarji, Guru-Preceptor, Mother Kali, Mother Kali, Divine Mother, before us is the fire of wisdom. And in that fire of wisdom we offer all our past karma and the karma of all nations. Let that bad karma be consumed forever. *Aum Swaha. Aum Swaha. Aum Swaha.*"

[A period of meditation, followed by singing of a chant:]

Paramahansa Yogananda, Self-Realization Fellowship International Headquarters, Christmas Day 1933

(Above) Paramahansa Yogananda standing in front of the SRF International Headquarters building, Los Angeles, 1934; *(below)* an aerial view of the building and surroundings taken in 2022. From this 12 ½-acre site, lovingly named by Paramahansaji as the Mother Center, his teachings on Kriya Yoga meditation and the underlying unity of the world's great religions are disseminated worldwide.

My Krishna is blue, the tamal tree is blue,
So I do love thee my tamal tree.
And when I die,
Do put me high
*On a branch of the tamal tree.**

The highest love was expressed by the devotees of Krishna. Even the close disciples of Christ abandoned him. Peter denied his guru three times. Yet he quickly recovered his faith, and so great was his devotion for Christ that when he himself faced crucifixion, he had himself crucified hanging upside down. What great love all these devotees felt for their guru, whose only wish was to show them the way to God, to help them attain their salvation. There is no comparison between divine love and human love; only if you have tasted of divine love can you compare. If you place human love first, you can never know the meaning of divine love. But if you have divine love first, no matter what lesser love comes along you know it cannot compare.

Many people say it is wrong to worship personalities, but that is not necessarily correct. If you worship only the physical form and characteristics of a great soul without attunement with the meaning and inspiration of his life, then that is idol worship. But how can you develop love for God if you are not first introduced to some of His divine qualities in those who knew and manifested God, such as Lord Jesus and Lord Krishna? If you wear a cross in reverence for Christ or have an image of him, it isn't that you are worshiping those relics or those actual images; rather, those symbols are reminders of what his life and message means to you. Likewise in India: To perform ceremonies before an image of Krishna or some other divine one without a deeper actual perception of what that image represents is idol worship. But to be reminded of the divine attributes made manifest in that great one's form is not wrong. Behind the wave is the ocean. Reverencing the waves of godly lives, we come to behold the ocean of Spirit behind them. That is the role of the guru: God sends someone to show you the way. The whole purpose of such a one is to point your attention toward God. The disciple is to follow the guru's guidance with complete devotion; and the guru directs that devotion not toward himself, but to God.

* "My Krishna Is Blue," from *Cosmic Chants.* Scriptural lore of India relates that Bhagavan Krishna left his body while seated in a blue-blossomed *tamal* tree, after being accidentally shot by a hunter's arrow.

If any teacher fails to do that, he himself loses sight of God. Those who are caught up in egotism may tell you to worship them. But Jesus had no such desire. He was never emphasizing himself, but his Christ Consciousness, which was one with God.

Without loyalty to the guru whom God sends to help you on the path, you cannot find God. And without love and devotion, you can never know God. If you cultivate love for God and pure devotion, know absolutely that He cannot stay away. When your love is not wet by material desires, it is like a dry match—when you strike it on the soul, it produces the flame of God-consciousness.

"O Lord, let us burn away the darkness of this world with our love for Thee. Mother Divine, Mother Divine, we are not of this world; we are of Thy kingdom. Father, Mother, Friend, Beloved God! Father, Mother, Friend, Beloved God! Ever new joy, ever new joy, ever new joy! O Kali, Mother Divine, bless all with Thy love, with Thy joy!"

God comes to the devotee as love. Then He comes as wisdom. Then He comes as ecstasy. In divine ecstasy all desires are melted away in the supreme desire for God. If you will have desire for anything but God, He will slip away. But if you have God, if you love God, then you will love everything. The devotee sings, "I love the blue sky, because my Krishna is blue. I love the *tamal* tree because that is where Krishna sat." With divine love you love God in everything.

"O Lord, in deep, ever deeper meditation we are nearing Thine eternal life. So much time has gone by, but we are nearer to Thee. Tossed on waves of life or death, we are yet in Thine ocean of immortality, O Spirit. Bless us and make us pure. We are all baptized by the birth of a baby Christ within our souls. O Divine Christ, how shall I thank Thee? Hours and hours pass in meditation and I know them not."

My dear ones, when you know the Spirit, then even when this body is snatched away there is joy eternal, bliss eternal; endless joy, endless happiness. Why do you stay behind? Come, my children, come on. Make the effort. Receive! Go within and enjoy the festivity of that inner bliss, that inner joy. *Aum,* Guru. *Aum,* Brahma. Such joy in God!

Forgetting God is destruction. Forget everything else, but not God, for those who love Divine Mother do not have to be afraid of anything.

"Divine Mother, Divine Mother, O Guru, Divine Mother! Divine Mother, make us like little children—free us from too much intellectuality, from pride that keeps us away from Thee. Commune with us in the secrecy of silence. We renounce everything for Thee. Divine Mother, the devotees, the organization, all things I love, I love only for Thee. May Thy love shine forever on the sanctuary of my devotion, and may I be able to awaken Thy love in all hearts. Mother Divine, Guru Divine, enthrall us with Thy light. Ignite our ignorance with Thy wisdom. Sanctify us in the purity of Thy divine flame.

"O Divine Mother, I behold the crucifixion of Christ tonight. O Kali, Christ, Krishna, Babaji, Lahiri Mahasaya, Sri Yukteswarji, Guru, saints of all religions, all are One everlastingly—one Love to worship. O Spirit, sometimes I behold Thee as Kali, sometimes as Jesus, sometimes as Krishna, sometimes as Babaji, Lahiri Mahasaya, Sri Yukteswarji, Guru, saints of all religions. In the cradle of our consciousness, the Eternal Christ is born today. And tomorrow as we celebrate the social Christmas, be with us in the firmament and behind the screen of all space. O angels, listen to our prayers for the birth of universal Christ Consciousness in our consciousness. This is my prayer with all my heart. May everyone here behold the Infinite Christ born in the cradle of their hearts.

"Divine Mother, our hearts, our minds, our souls rejoice in Thee, for Thou art here. Bless us in Thy name, sweet Mother, that we never forget Thee. And I pray from my heart that only those come to me who come only for Thee. May they learn to renounce everything mentally, to place Thee first above all else. Mother Divine, all those who have come here, let them be saturated with Thy joy. Let them speak of Thee and of the magnetism of Thy love. Transform them, O Mother Divine. Look after their necessities that they may not be diverted from Thee, O Divine Mother.

"O Mother, O Mother, I want to fly away from everything. I want to shed my tears for Thee in silence, in solitude. Years and years of struggling; but You have given me much more than ever I lost. And everything given to me I have given to You, only for Your work. Naught else do I want but Thee. Divine Mother, O Divine Mother, You have freed me tonight, Mother Divine. O Mother, every time you come to me as Kali, I am filled with such devotion. O Kali, *Aum* Kali, O Kali."

[Another period of meditation follows. Then Paramahansaji addresses the disciples:]

The valley of humbleness is filled with the joyous presence of God. When you enter the valley of meditation, you find it filled with the consciousness of God. When you enter the valley of divine love, you feel it filled with the loving presence of God; you feel a devotion that never ceases, a devotion that is ever satisfying. The ordinary devotee seeks God when prodded by suffering; that is conditional devotion. Unconditional devotion is when the devotee seeks God not for any selfish reason, but because he loves Him. So remember: With the raft of devotion and wisdom you shall cross the sea of difficulties. Much is forgiven that devotee who appeals to God with love.

What is love? It means that you never think of yourself, but only of the joy that comes in serving God selflessly. And it means serving Him also in human beings; help them because they are your brothers and sisters. Those who are sunk in the depths of error need your love and sympathy more. We forgive ourselves our own errors more than we forgive anybody else. Rather, we should heed Jesus' words: "Love the Lord thy God....and thy neighbor as thyself." The raft of our love shall surely take us across the sea of ignorance.

"Father, Mother, Friend, Beloved God! Eternity of prayer, eternity of love, the endless love of our hearts through eternity we give unto Thee. Receive! These are Your gifts. What more shall we give but what we have received from Thee, O Spirit? Punish us not with oblivion of Thy Spirit. In life or death, disease or suffering, health or ill health, let us know that all waves of duality vanish forever in the vast ocean of Thy presence. Father, we think not of ourselves as beggars, but as Thy children. As Thy children, it is our privilege to love Thee, for Thou art our Father and our Mother. We live in Thy joy, in the consciousness of Thy love. May Thy devotion, wisdom, joy, and faith be spread unto all Thy children. Father, Thou dost not reveal Thyself unto the wise, but unto babes. I know You are listening to the voice of my prayer. Why, O Father, do You keep the veil of darkness in so many? Father, You are so humble, that is why You are our Father. How shall we please You? You don't require to be pleased; You want our heart's purest love. O Father, You are like a little child, so easy to please.

"I know Thou dost not want our reverence. Thou art our Eternal Friend. But loving Thee as a little child, Yasoda knew Thee. Krishna's devotees knew Thee as the greatest Friend. Ramakrishna knew Thee as Divine Mother, as Kali. Lahiri Mahasaya knew Thee as the Great Spirit.

"I sought Thee, calling for Thee, everywhere. The cold sky never answered, and the ocean roared at me, and the sun blazed, and the moon stared; but when I meditated and called unto Lahiri Mahasaya, beloved Lahiri Mahasaya, Thou didst come through knowledge of the law and practice of the law.* Such joy, such happiness, such communion, endless joy!

"With my finite prayer I worship my Infinite Mother. Receive this joy, and in this joy we celebrate the festivity of Cosmic Mother Kali and the Omnipresent Consciousness of Jesus Christ, beholding them as one.

"Divine Mother, You wear so many costumes of light to appear unto Your children. I don't know if You are Guru or Kali, for I see that You are one. O Kali, You are our Guru, and Guru is Kali. *Aum,* Kali. *Aum,* Guru. *Aum,* Christ, *Aum,* Krishna. I see that You are all one in Her.

"Mother of Finitude, when will that day come when from infinite perception in ecstasy we shall come down as human beings and, with our finite eyes, weep finite tears for Thy finite expression as Mother Kali in all nature? O Kali, Thou hast danced on the twinkling billows of nature, on the soft cushion of our love. O Kali, ever dance on the sacred sanctum of my devotion.

"Oh, what shining light glimmers in Thy face, Mother Divine! Kali, Kali, Thou art the only reality; all else is unreal. Life is a beautiful dream, O Mother, only when we are awake in Thee. When we are asleep in Thee, we dream the nightmare of mortality. Divine Mother, it is You who are causing this dream world. And Divine Mother, it is You who are behind my prayer for the liberation of all souls. It is You who are behind this endless love in my heart. Mother Kali, if it is Thy pleasure to take me away, take me; for I have no attachment to this world. Kali Divine, all faces are filled with Thee, so I am attached to everyone; and I am attached to no one. Mother, I offer unto Thee this fragrant bouquet of souls. Bless them all."

Dear ones, feel Divine Mother's presence, for Divine Mother is here. She is a silent vibration passing over the shoulders and head. Feel Her as a gentle presence on the top of the head, back of the head, down the spinal tree of life. Her divine life is going back and forth, up and down this tree of life.

* Reference to Mahavatar Babaji's gift to the world through Lahiri Mahasaya of the science of Kriya Yoga, the law that unravels the mystery of the universe by bestowing personal realization of God.

"O Divine Mother, where is my body? Where is my breath? The consciousness of body and breath, the consciousness of this world, they are but Thy dreams. Take this dream body away, take this dream breath away, for Thou and I are one. Divine Mother, it is You who are holding my hands. You are dancing through my thoughts. *Aum,* Kali; *Aum,* Kali." Oh, such joy you cannot know!

[A final period of meditation follows.]

"O Divine Mother, all is finished. Such joy! Such joy! Such pure souls are here tonight. Kali Divine, I pray that all those who are here tonight will never forsake Thee.

"Mother, we thank Thee for this day. This day is a true Convocation of our souls—the cementing of our souls in Thee!

"*Aum, Aum, Aum.* Peace. Amen."

Resurrect Your Spirit

From an Easter Sunrise Service given on March 25, 1951 at the SRF Lake Shrine. An audio recording of the complete talk is published by Self-Realization Fellowship under the name Follow the Path of Christ, Krishna, and the Masters.

On this holy occasion, in this beautiful SRF Lake Shrine, with the sunrise, on the occasion of the resurrection of Christ, I, Paramahansa Yogananda, will say a few words which come from my heart. I bless all our SRF students and friends who are gathered on this occasion to celebrate the resurrection of Jesus Christ.

The Eternal Cycles of Creation and Cosmic Resurrection

Resurrection of Jesus Christ has two significances: The macrocosmic (cosmic) significance consists in the thought that when only Spirit existed as the ever-existing, ever-conscious, ever-new Bliss, there was nothing else in the universe. No planets, no stars, no Milky Way blinked their eyes, and only the Spirit existed everywhere. But when Spirit became God the Father, He spumed out of Him Mother Nature—His consort—ornamented and decorated with stars, with dusts of light, with all kinds of luminaries, planets, and our earth. And in this womb and consort, Cosmic Nature, was reflected the presence of God the Father as the Christ Intelligence—the Cosmic Son.

So, originally God the Father existed beyond creation. God the Father became Cosmic Nature, as His consort, and in Her womb existed Christ Consciousness, the Son. But when the Spirit withdraws Cosmic Nature, when Cosmic Nature is crucified with ignorance, then the Son within it—the Christ Intelligence—is crucified, and he is dissolved in God the Father, and God the Father is dissolved into Spirit.

Many millions of years pass after the cosmic dissolution....But then again Spirit creates God the Father, creates His consort—the Holy Ghost, Cosmic Nature—and again the Christ Intelligence, the Son, is resurrected in the bosom of Mother Nature.*

* The scriptures of India describe these endlessly recurring cycles of universal creation and dissolution: "They are true knowers of 'day' and 'night' who understand the Day

The Resurrection of Jesus Christ

This same analogy can be carried to God the Father, Son, and Holy Ghost. God manifested Himself in the body of Mary who was one with Holy Ghost, as the Christ Son. This Christ Son [Jesus] was reborn from the great Christ Son. When Jesus Christ was born, in him was manifest the Cosmic Intelligence which is present in creation.

When Jesus Christ was crucified by people who didn't understand him, he said the greatest of all miracles that he would perform was: "Destroy this body and I shall build it again."* He knew the body was made of atoms, and that the atoms of his body were controlled by his own soul, which was one with the Spirit of God. And as such, after three days—that is, after three periods of time, when he withdrew his soul from his physical body, from his astral body, and from his causal body—he became again one with the Cosmic Intelligence in all creation. After finding himself as the Cosmic Intelligence in all creation, he took some atomic forces and built them into a physical body, astral body, and causal body, and he again appeared as Jesus Christ on earth.†

The True Celebration of Easter Is to Resurrect Yourself

He is risen on this holy occasion; risen again. As after the death of leaves on a tree, new leaves grow; as from old stars which are dead, new stars are reborn—so Jesus Christ, after the death of his body, rebuilt another body to show that all those who receive God truly can be sons of God like him. And on this holy occasion may you all remember how to resurrect your spirit, resurrect your body in Heaven, even as Jesus Christ did.

---

of Brahma, which endures for a thousand cycles (*yugas*), and the Night of Brahma, which also endures for a thousand cycles. At the dawn of Brahma's Day all creation, reborn, emerges from the state of nonmanifestation; at the dusk of Brahma's Night all creation sinks into the sleep of nonmanifestation" (Bhagavad Gita VIII:17–18). See Paramahansa Yogananda's commentary on these verses in *God Talks With Arjuna: The Bhagavad Gita* for more explanation. *(Publisher's Note)*

* "Then answered the Jews and said unto him, 'What sign shewest thou unto us, seeing that thou doest these things?' Jesus answered and said unto them, 'Destroy this temple, and in three days I will raise it up.' Then said the Jews, 'Forty and six years was this temple in building, and wilt thou rear it up in three days?' But he spake of the temple of his body" (John 2:18–21).

† Paramahansaji gives a wondrously detailed discussion of the metaphysical process by which Jesus achieved the resurrection of his crucified body in Discourse 75 of his book, *The Second Coming of Christ: The Resurrection of the Christ Within You* (published by Self-Realization Fellowship).

Friends, students, on this holy occasion in this most wonderful SRF Lake Shrine, surrounded by ocean, mountain, and lake—Christ is reflected there: in every blossom, in every little fish in the pond, in every little flower, in every true soul who is present there. And may you all make it a mecca, a place of pilgrimage—this great SRF Lake Shrine, which is second to none, wherein pilgrims and devotees from all parts of the world will come and are coming. You must live the life of Christ, so that all those that come to this wonderful shrine may feel His presence. I have left my spirit there in the ether; and all those that will have true devotion will feel my spirit in Christ and the masters and God.

For the wave is the ocean and the ocean is the wave. We are all souls—waves of the ocean of Spirit, waves of the ocean of Christ Consciousness, and we must not forget it. And remember, just as important as Jesus Christ in the body is Jesus Christ without the body. Saint Teresa was persecuted when she said, "I have seen the formless Christ." Then they found out that Thomas Aquinas had also spoken of the formless Christ. So as you worship Christ with form, you must not forget that the real Christ is the formless Christ, behind the form of Jesus which was on earth and which was resurrected again.

On this holy occasion, fill yourself with the Spirit—and the thought that death is but the falling of the wave in the ocean, and that the same force of the storm and the same ocean can revive that wave on its bosom. There is no death for us, for we shall all be resurrected, even as Christ resurrected himself. His was the example for all to follow.

Proof of Resurrection in Modern Times

The great Lahiri Mahasaya, my preceptor's preceptor, resurrected himself on the next day after his passing, in three places. I knew "the saint with two bodies," whom I describe in my *Autobiography of a Yogi*. He saw Lahiri Mahasaya resurrected. He told me, "I got his letter beckoning me to come to Banaras promptly on a certain day. But," he said, "I was one day late. And next morning at ten o'clock, in my room—when I was arranging my baggage to go to Banaras—suddenly the latch of my door flew open, and Lahiri Mahasaya came walking in."

Then, with great excitement, Swami Pranabananda ("the saint with two bodies") said, "Master, Master, how happens it that you are here? Am I seeing a vision?"

Lahiri Mahasaya replied, "No, I am risen. What are you doing?"

He said, "Master, I got your letter, but I am one day late."

Lahiri Mahasaya said, "No use going to Banaras. My body is not there anymore."

And as Swami Pranabananda started crying, Lahiri Mahasaya said, "How foolish of you to cry for me! For see: I am the same." And Pranabananda Swami touched his body. It was flesh and blood, just as before. And after a long conversation, Lahiri Mahasaya blessed Swami Pranabananda; and right in front of his eyes he saw the latch of his door fly open, and Lahiri Mahasaya vanished, and the door closed of itself and the latch fastened the door.

Though the story of resurrection as we hear in the life of Christ is twenty centuries old, Lahiri Mahasaya also resurrected his body, as is known from unassailable authorities.* Read the *Autobiography of a Yogi* and you will see how many great souls have testified to the truth to which Jesus Christ testified in his life. If we cannot testify to the truth in the life of Christ, then it is no use worshiping Christ.

Become Christlike Yourself!

Christ came that we may all remember: "All those that received him, to them he gave the power to be the sons of God."† The charcoal and the diamond both receive the sunlight, but the charcoal does not *really* receive the light of the sun. The diamond receives the light and reflects it and becomes resplendent. The ordinary man shuts his eyes to God, and does not see or receive God's light. He roams in self-created darkness. But when true devotees in the company of masters open their eyes, they see the Sun of Omnipresence, and they become diamond-like souls. Charcoal under high pressure can be made into diamond. So, ordinary souls, under the high "pressure" of deep meditation, can become diamond souls, reflecting the Spirit.

On this holy day, think of Christ, and become Christlike yourself.

Peace! *Aum*, Christ, *Aum*, Christ, *Aum*, Jesus Christ. We bow to you.

* Lahiri Mahasaya's death and resurrection are recounted in *Autobiography of a Yogi*, chapter 36.

† John 1:12.

The Easter Message of Immortality

An Easter Sunday service conducted by Paramahansaji at Self-Realization Fellowship International Headquarters, Los Angeles, April 21, 1935

[Paramahansaji led the congregation in a period of meditation:] With great devotion invoke the spirit of Christ within you. Remember, you too have been crucified, by ignorance and your bad habits. Now you are risen in Christ. You have a new birth in His consciousness. Let every cell in your body be resurrected with Christ Consciousness. Let every thought in your mind be resurrected with Christ Consciousness. Let your soul be lifted and resurrected in Christ. Fill your mind with Christ-power and wisdom. Fill your soul with Christ-bliss. Fill your body with Christ-vitality. Fill your consciousness with omnipresent Christ Intelligence.

Christ must be felt. I want you all, with utmost devotion, to feel His presence. Fill your entire body and brain with Christ Consciousness. Fill your heart with Christ-bliss; envelop your whole being in Christ-bliss. Behold Christ Consciousness enveloping the stars and the hills, and the gardens filled with flowers. Behold Him in the devotion of all churches. Worship Christ with the spirit of Jesus. As Christ Consciousness was manifest in the body of Jesus, may that Christ Consciousness be manifest in us, resurrecting us from disease and ignorance.

Joy within, joy without. O Christ, be awakened within us. We crucified Thee with our ignorance. Be resurrected within us again as everlasting wisdom and perennial bliss—eternal wisdom, eternal bliss!

Aum! Aum! Aum!

Jesus Was an Ideal Example Sent for Us to Follow

[Following the meditation, Paramahansaji spoke:] This is a very happy morning, for Easter celebrates the victory of life over death. To inspire us we have the golden trail of Christ—the trail of immortality. What he could achieve, we too can achieve. Saint

John said: "But as many as received him, to them gave he power to become the sons of God" (and, as sons of God, attain victory over death). When we achieve that Christ Consciousness, by spiritualizing our thoughts and actions, we shall be resurrected in the immortality of Christ, and shall laugh at the dream of death.

The mortal death of Jesus should not be emphasized. Jesus did not perish, even though his body was crucified. He went into the ocean of Spirit and came back again, replete with the power of God, to show that all life is immortal. Very few of us are fortunate enough to have that experience.

Jesus was both human and divine. It is inspiring to know that we, although human, can also be divine like him. In Shakespeare's play, Hamlet describes death as "the undiscover'd country from whose bourn no traveler returns." But Christ proved that this idea is wrong.

Jesus suffered, Jesus struggled, and Jesus won. From the cerements of human frailties he rose up to declare: "I am immortal." Jesus was the ideal sent for us to follow. He did not come on earth to enact the drama of life and death in an ordinary way; his mission was to show us that what he could do, we too can do—provided we meditate as he did, and provided we love God as he did.

Whatever is valuable, precious, and great has to be achieved through self-effort. It takes willingness, and paying the price, to become like Christ. When your consciousness is like his, when you are able to give up your life for all, as he did, the infinite Christ Consciousness will manifest within you. The Unseen will be seen, the Invisible will be visible.

Worship of Jesus Christ without trying to be like him is meaningless. We should adore Jesus because he gave us an example by which we can pattern our own lives. You think that you are just a mortal, someday to be shattered by the hammer of death. Pluck that thought out of your mind and realize your everlastingness! The whole world may not know you, but if Christ knows you, you are eternally a spiritual king.

In one sense, God hides Himself; and yet He advertises Himself in the flowers, in the gentle breeze, in the birds, and in all other lovely things. In every lily and in every gentle fragrance you can perceive His beauty. You do not see His Name written there; but you behold a hint of His presence. He says, "Follow the trail of beauty. I am hidden somewhere in its heart. I am Harmony, I am Love, I am Beauty, I am Fragrance, I am Joy."

The Lord has designed for Himself some striking advertisements: the sun and the moon and the stars. Even through you He is advertising His presence; your very conscience is the voice of God.

Jesus came to show that the universal Christ spirit could be manifested in the human body. Jesus the man and Jesus the Christ were two different entities. Within the body of Jesus existed the universal Christ spirit; the body of Jesus was a vehicle for the infinite Christ Consciousness. But to think that Spirit manifested Itself only in the body of Jesus is to misunderstand God's plan for all mankind.

Resurrection means that the universal Spirit present in all creation as the Christ Consciousness is constantly being resurrected—awakened or manifested—in everything. Whenever you do away with ignorance and think good thoughts, Christ is being resurrected within you; that is, the Christ Consciousness that was fully manifested in Jesus is awakening within you. Resurrection is not the power of Spirit in the body of Jesus only; Spirit is in everyone. Nor does man have to die in order to resurrect Spirit. The physical resurrection of Christ was only part of the lesson of his life. Every time you give up a weakness and feel happy in being good, Christ is resurrected anew. You can bring Christ Consciousness within you right now.

For your own benefit and joy you should emulate the life of Christ; you should try to bring him closer. Do not keep him away by wrong thoughts and actions. If you meditate deeply, you will realize him. You cannot find him without meditation. You must "pray without ceasing," as Saint Paul said.

God Reveals Himself Through Our Devotion and Meditation

There is no offering you can make that will persuade God to reveal Himself except real devotion and meditation. When the ordinary child cries for its mother and she brings it a toy, the child is satisfied and forgets what it was crying about. But the naughty child who cries persistently, refusing to be satisfied with toys, forces the mother to come and give of herself. So if you want the loving presence of God, of Christ Consciousness, you must be like the persistent child: Throw away satisfaction with worldly toys and cry for God only. Destroy the parasites of desires; conflagrate them in the desire for Christ Love. If you can arouse that burning zeal—that ardor by which you are determined to prove to the Lord that you want Him more than playthings—then He will come. I am telling you this out of my own experience. Out of the silence of my own soul-crying, Christ Consciousness was born.

Any time you want to be attuned to Christ, think of him and look in the inner spiritual eye between the eyebrows. That is the center of Christ (or Christna) consciousness.* Your human consciousness has a location in the body, and this Christ consciousness has a location, in the spiritual eye in the center of the forehead. When you are deep in thought, your eyes naturally turn upward and your brow becomes wrinkled, to focus the eyes and attention on this center.

A few months ago I thought: "I have not for a long time seen Christ." Immediately, within the spiritual eye, amidst a mass of light, I beheld his face, looking sad. "Don't let me see you sad," I implored. At once his face became beautiful with smiles.

I have been experiencing wonderful realizations these last few days. They are a great landmark in my consciousness and in my development.

Although I have beheld the land of Christ at a distance, in visions, I want to touch the sod that Christ once walked upon, and to feel his experiences.† In India I sat where Buddha sat, and saw with inner vision what he did and felt. In Banaras I touched the place where Lahiri Mahasaya sat, and saw and felt his experiences.

Meditate deeply if you would know Christ, or Krishna, or any of the great avatars. When your soul becomes attuned with the Spirit, then the Silence begins to speak. You can mentally experience the life of Jesus—all his emotions and trials and spiritual victories—or those of any other great master who has attained liberation. If you can meditate deeply on God, some day you will be able to undergo any experience in the Christ-conscious state; and having resurrected your soul wisdom you will know how to rise above and conquer all mortal experiences. You can even mentally go through the crucifixion and resurrection of Jesus, and you will realize, as Jesus did,

* "The title 'Christ' is more anciently found in India in the word 'Krishna,'" Paramahansa Yogananda often said. "Sometimes I purposely spell 'Krishna' as 'Christna' to show the correlation." He explained that both titles refer to the universal consciousness of Spirit pervading all creation. See *Christ Consciousness* in glossary. *(Publisher's Note)*

† A few months after delivering this talk, on his way to India in 1935, Paramahansa Yogananda visited Jerusalem and many of the other sites associated with Jesus' life. Some of his experiences there are described in *Autobiography of a Yogi,* chapter 39. *(Publisher's Note)*

the lesson for the world conveyed by this supremely selfless act. It can be done. But you must meditate deeply upon it. You can attain understanding and devotion by meditation upon any of his experiences. So bring Christ Consciousness closer. With every kindness and every good action that you perform you are being resurrected; and you are immediately in tune with Christ's divine consciousness. You have then made a new altar for Christ. He will in that instant commune with you through your goodness.

You must, in truth, fully resurrect yourself in meditation. Compare your state of consciousness before and after meditation. You do not know what joy lies beyond the screen of the subconscious mind. Do away with restlessness and bodily sensations, and sit quietly praying: "In the heaven of silence, O Christ, be born within me." Then on that altar of silence He will come. The joy of Christ and God is indescribable. When the lips of every cell are drinking the nectar of Christ Consciousness, when every thought imbibes the joy of Spirit, you have the proof that Christ is ineffable joy—joy that no changing dream of life and death can ever take away. Be resurrected in that Christ Consciousness. This *can* be experienced if you meditate deeply and practice the highest meditation techniques of Kriya Yoga given by the Masters.*

But this I say to you: You cannot know Christ Consciousness without making daily effort. Meditation is the struggle to rise from the tomb of indifference and material desires. You can be like Christ; it is in your command. Practice the teachings I have given you and see if this is not true. I could have been like others; but I followed the way of the Masters and now I am different. Each of you can achieve that victory. By a strong will the flesh can be conquered; you can rise above the consciousness of the imprisoning bodily limitations. The easiest way to attain that resurrection is by regular deep meditation and right action, doing good, every day.

Let your evil habits, indifference, and restlessness die daily. Do not delude yourself by believing that you are your human limitations. Think of the example of Jesus and other Christlike lives. Meditate. Man's cross is his heavy burden of bad habits. If you will try by deep meditation to get through the fog of restlessness, then you will see that you have come to the vast luminous soul kingdom of eternal happiness within. That is the resurrection I want you to experience.

* Taught to students of the *Self-Realization Fellowship Lessons. (Publisher's Note)*

Christ was resurrected not only on Easter morn; he resurrects himself in the dawn of the awakening of the soul within each human being. Every morning I feel the resurrection of the Christ's Infinite Consciousness within me.

"Today You Can Have a New Birth"

Our souls "die" when buried in the tomb of ignorance. Let this be the day of your own Christ-awakening. You can not only experience the life of Christ in visions, but you can practice this resurrection every day in your life. Forget your old weaknesses and troubles. Just think: "Christ was resurrected, and I am resurrected with him. I am no longer my old self."

You may believe that you are wicked, but today you can have a new birth. If you believe this, your belief will transform your consciousness. You can be what you want to be, regardless of your past. Persist in your determination. I pray that you believe what I am telling you today. Cast away all your old habits and weaknesses. Feel that today you are resurrected, that you have become divinely different.

With Christ, be able to say, "I love all." I shall feel happy for having told you this if you are inspired to seek that consciousness. It is not difficult to do so. You will feel great strength of spirit if you can carry out your belief and resolution. In your heart you must be good to yourself. Forget the past. Will to be the very spirit of goodness. Know that you are good.

Why do people do wrong? Because they do not use their will power to carry out their resolutions. Sometimes in the morning I make up my mind to do something and then find I am unable to carry out that plan; but I perform some other good action later in the day, to satisfy myself that in some way I have carried out my intention.

Strengthen your good resolutions today and carry them out. Be faithful to them. You have dropped your old self. You were dead within the sepulcher of hopelessness, but today your divine consciousness has risen at the awakening touch of Christ.

Life is glorious, life is beautiful, if only you can find God hidden behind the gross debris of matter. Concentrate not on the changing picture of life and death, but keep your inner eye on His creative beam of Immortality. It is the most joyous realization that you can experience.

Pray with me: "Heavenly Christ, saturate our consciousness with Thy consciousness. Give us a new birth in Thee.

"*Aum* Christ, *Aum* Christ, *Aum* Christ." Cast your ignorance and consciousness of limitations into this vibration.* Be healed. Be healed of ignorance. Be saturated in Bliss.

Affirm and feel:

"Heavenly Father, awaken me in Christ Consciousness.
Christ and I are one.
Joy and I are one.
Peace and I are one.
Wisdom and I are one.
Love and I are one.
Bliss and I are one.
Christ and I are one. Christ and I are one. Christ and I are one."

* The sacred Sanskrit mantra *Aum* (or *Om*) invokes God as the Cosmic Creative Vibration—the "Word" or Holy Ghost—that underlies and sustains all creation. Immanent in the *Aum* Vibration is the Christ or Krishna Consciousness (*Kutastha Chaitanya*), Spirit's pure reflection in creation.

Follow the Path of the Great Ones!

Excerpts from talks given by Paramahansa Yogananda to Self-Realization Fellowship monastic disciples and members in 1950 and 1951—some of his last public talks before his mahasamadhi. *Deeply moved by the Guru's words on these occasions, after his passing the disciples compiled key points from audio recordings made of these events and shared them with students of the* SRF Lessons *and in* Self-Realization *magazine.* The publication of this volume of Paramahansaji's* Collected Talks and Essays *is an opportunity to make them available for the inspiration of all.*

Though my physical body is not there, my spirit is ever with you, and my voice is with you now, talking to you from my heart, my soul, my spirit.

Remember the illustration I have often given: A man was so thirsty that he wanted to drink a whole lake; but he quickly found that he could not take more than three glasses of water. Similarly, your mind has to be expanded if you want to receive the Ocean of God. Otherwise, even if God came to you, you would not be able to receive Him. The cup of your consciousness must be enlarged like Christ's; then God can be appreciated and fully apprehended.

Understand the Help That Comes From the Gurus

Spirituality cannot be bought in a marketplace. God must be earnestly sought. When you are very desirous of finding Him, the Lord sends you a guru. A true guru is a direct link with God. The guru has only one purpose: to introduce you to the Heavenly Father. When you are in tune with a true guru you are in tune with the Lord. The relationship is eternal. Even after death, a guru continues to help his disciples (i.e., those who recognize him as their guru and who faithfully follow his teachings). That is a spiritual law.

* Two of these digitally restored audio recordings, *Follow the Path of Christ, Krishna, and the Masters* and *Self-Realization: The Inner and Outer Path,* are available from Self-Realization Fellowship and online audiobook services. For the latter talk, he spoke from the seclusion of his third-floor apartment at the Mother Center, and his voice was transmitted to the disciples assembled on the first floor—to which he refers in his opening remarks of this compilation.

Hence every SRF student should understand and respect the significance of the link of SRF Gurus—Mahavatar Babaji, Lahiri Mahasaya, Sri Yukteswar, [and Paramahansa Yogananda,] in communion with Jesus Christ and Bhagavan Krishna—with whom all SRF students are connected by affiliation with Self-Realization Fellowship.

Those who desire the help of these Gurus in finding God should follow the way that the Gurus have shown. Students who do not follow the teachings should not expect spiritual benefits just the same; it won't work! But those who practice the SRF techniques of meditation daily, with sincere devotion to the Lord, will find by their own Self-realization the validity of SRF teachings. SRF asks no one to believe blindly, but to *practice* the methods offered in these sacred teachings. By being loyal to the Gurus in this way, you make it possible for the Gurus to guide you surely to the Divine Goal.

Be the Master of Your Body and Mind

An SRF student should never go to bed without first giving his deepest attention to God. You won't die! But die for God if it is necessary.

Control the body and mind until you are their master. Then when you sit to meditate you will not be restless, you will not nod. Practice these Kriya Yoga teachings and you will make your body a fit temple to receive God. The human body has to be made ready to receive the divine power. The state of consciousness has to be right. Then God will come to you!

But the Lord may not respond right away. Only when He is convinced that you seek Him not for the satisfaction of temporal desires or for spiritual glamour and glory—but simply to be His, unconditionally, forever—will He open the door. The devotees who are faithful to the end are those for whom He will open the door. But only He can tell when that day of final beatitude will come.

God does not always appear before us just because we have meditated deeply for several years, or for whatever we consider a proper length of time. If there is some flaw in their love, even saints who have meditated for incarnations may be chastened by God's failure to appear. But to those who make no demand, who just keep on striving, saying, "Lord, I will wait for You, no matter how long it takes," He will come. The greatest factor for success with God is to have that resolute desire. Lord Krishna said, "Out of one thousand, one seeks Me; and out of a thousand that seek Me, one knows Me."* Those who last to the end of the path will be the first to find Him.

When We Love God, We Become Brothers and Sisters of All

Develop the love of God so that I see in your eyes you are drunk with God and not asking, "When will I have God?" When you ask that, you are not a devotee. The devotee says, "I have Him. He is listening to me. My Beloved is always with me. He is moving my hands. He is digesting my food. He is gazing at me through the stars."

God is caressing you through the breeze, in the sunshine. He is the food that you eat. He is the One that nurtures you as father, mother, and relatives. He is the only Eternal Relative.

No one belongs to another person. We have all come from God. On earth we are seemingly strangers; it is only when we love God that we become truly brothers and sisters of all. Only in God does that relationship hold in the hereafter.

That is why Jesus said, "There is no man that hath left house, or brethren, or sisters, or father, or mother, or wife, or children, or lands, for my sake, and the gospel's, but he shall receive an hundredfold now in this time, houses, and brethren, and sisters, and mothers, and children, and lands, with persecutions [the resistance of delusion to one's progressive spiritual efforts]; and in the world to come eternal life."†

The Futility of Life Without God

Salvation is for those who love God, those who go on seeking Him to the end—not just to "stick it out," but because they love Him.

"Seek ye first the kingdom of God" was Jesus' advice—not only to monks, but to all people. Man was not made merely for producing children and for selfish hunting of money. Millions have thought that, and millions at death have left this world bewildered and dissatisfied, their soul hunger unappeased.

The Lord one day showed me as I was driving along the street: "Look at these little houses; they are like human chicken coops. In their coops the chickens are born, they produce eggs, they peck and eat and love, and finally become fried chicken! Do you want to be like those in the human chicken coops?"

* Bhagavad Gita VII:3.

† Mark 10:29–30.

And I said, "No, Lord! I am with You. I came with You; I remain with You; I go away with You. I am content."

Commune With God in Meditation and Serviceful Activity

The Heavenly Father has fulfilled all my wishes for the organization. Personal wishes I did not have. Our churches are without debt, but it has not been easy to be here with so many responsibilities, sometimes without a penny. I have no bank account of my own. I parted willingly with everything I had. As a monk I came to this country, and the same I am still. I have a little box, that is all. It is never empty, by the grace of God. That demonstration was given in my life because I live for Him. I did not have one eye on Him and one eye on the money. My two eyes were on God alone. God alone supported me. When I needed anything, it was there.

God loves that devotee who not only meditates but works for Him in the world. It is not those who give lip service that move my Father; it is he who works for Him.

Disciples of Self-Realization Fellowship have one thought: to cultivate God-awareness in the heart, in seclusion and meditation and while you are working. If you are working for the beloved God and the Masters and Guru, you never know time. That is how I have rejoiced to work for Him; I could not work for myself. And I work for you all—those who have clung to my God, to my Father, and to my Gurus.

Self-Realization Fellowship teaches the highest principle of spiritual living: meditation combined with right activity. Everywhere people are working, but they have forgotten God. In our ashram centers we work for Him and live in an ideal environment, with the consciousness of God in our bosom.

When you work with the thought of God—thinking of God in activity—that is just as good as meditation. But apart from working for God, you must meditate deeply. Do not sleep too much. Night is the only time you have in this world to make love to God. At night you must use your Kriya Yoga and deepest meditation to be with Him, so that all day when you work you will be drunk with God. That is the way I have led my life. If my body and mind worked hard I never knew it, because I was drunk with God.

When you think of serving Him, all work is a pleasure. I want you all to have that consciousness of the blessed presence of God. But without work, without divine service, you shall never get there. You cannot get there by meditation alone. Meditation means meditation on God in seclusion, and meditation on God in activity—because that is meditation, too.

There are an inner and an outer circle of devotees—those who are steadfast and those who come and go. I prize most the bouquet of souls who have come to serve God and the Masters steadfastly; and that bouquet of souls I offer to the Heavenly Father. I do not care who comes and goes. He who follows me, follows not me but Him that sent me.

The Masters don't want disciples; they don't want anything except to do the will of God. Think of my own Guru. Everyone except myself and three little boys left him, because he didn't flatter them. He didn't suit their fancies. But I didn't leave him, and see what he did for me! By converting me he has converted millions.

The Masters pay no attention to those who come and go. Jesus said, "Who is my mother? and who are my brethren? Whosoever shall do the will of my Father which is in heaven, the same is my brother, and sister, and mother."* I recognize all as brothers and sisters in a metaphysical way; but those that love God, I know as my own dear brothers and sisters.

Realize Your True Self, One With God

I know in time this work will move on and on, as it has already now spread over the different parts of the world. Our "ambassador," *Autobiography of a Yogi,* which Lahiri Mahasaya predicted, has done the duty of spreading the message everywhere. He prohibited his disciples from writing any book about him; and he predicted that later somebody would come to spread his message in the West for the first time—my humble self, as Babaji told Lahiri Mahasaya.

And all credit belongs to the great Jesus Christ and Babaji, who together sent this work to unite original Christianity as taught by Christ and original Yoga as taught by Krishna, the greatest masters of the world.

When you reach the final realization, there is no difference between any master and any other master. In heaven there is no captain or assistant captain and soldiers. In heaven all those who have become one with the Father are equal. They do not suffer from jealousy because they are equally one with the Father. "All those that received Him, to them He gave the power of becoming sons of God."†

* Matthew 12:48.

† John 1:13.

Jesus, Krishna, and the Masters, through their oneness with the Christ Consciousness, are great reflections of God, perfect examples for you to follow in order to know that you are also a potential child of God. All waves of the sea belong to the ocean; there is no difference. Only some waves have drawn themselves into the bosom of the ocean and expanded in oneness with the ocean; and some waves remain on the surface, playing with the storm of delusion and getting farther and farther away from the ocean bosom of Infinity. We are all children of God. We are all sons of the one Father. But you have to *realize* that! May that consciousness be impinged on you now and forever.

Do not call yourself a sinner any more. Sin belongs to the past; it is no longer yours. God is yours! Christ, Krishna, and the great Masters are yours! Hold that truth in your bosom, in every thought you have, and one day you will find that you have only *dreamed* you were a man, and you woke and found you are a god, an eternal reflection of the Infinite Spirit! The greatest sin is ignorance of our oneness with God.

Original Christianity and Original Yoga

How shall you seek Him? Through Self-Realization Fellowship, the great dispensation sent forth into the world by Jesus Christ and Mahavatar Babaji to unite original Christianity and original Yoga, to bring real God-communion in all lands. Christ felt the lack of real God-communion in the churches. They are all doing good, but they must show people how to seek God. That is why Christ and Babaji sent me here, and why Self-Realization Fellowship teachings are the new dispensation that was promised in the scriptures. Christ promised to send the Holy Ghost after he had departed. "Holy Ghost" means the sacred cosmic vibration that is the structure of all creation, the vibration you can hear by practicing the SRF meditation technique. SRF is bringing that which has never before been given in the churches. When you practice that technique and hear and commune with that sacred vibration (the *Aum* or Amen), you will be one with the Lord through the Christ Consciousness immanent in it.

So, my good friends, remember: Self-Realization Fellowship is a combination of the original Christianity of Christ and original Yoga as taught by the great prophet Krishna. And if you sincerely follow this path of Christ, Krishna, and the Masters, you won't want anything else, for Self-Realization Fellowship will take you to your highest goal—our own Beloved—God!

"Whoever Shall Receive This Message Shall Not Go Away Unfulfilled"

Egoity is the greatest sin in this world—for by ego we hold ourselves apart from God. He who shall honor the ego shall lose God.

As the Heavenly Father is in me—for I killed "Yogananda" a long time ago—it is He that speaketh. It is not good to say, "I am God." No wave can say "I am the ocean," because the ocean can remain without the wave—any wave. But you can say, "I am a wave of the Ocean of Spirit; the Ocean has become my wave, my being." That is correct. Don't be afraid to say it. And with that feeling, that realization, I am saying that my hands, my feet, my voice and speech, my mind and thoughts and will, no longer belong to anyone. It is He who has worked as Mukunda. It is He who has worked as Yogananda. And it is He who is working as Paramahansa. It is He who is my being; there is no one else. No other self I acknowledge, for egoity is division and separation from Him.

I want to remain steadily in the spirit of God, that I can give you something, that I can saturate you, bathe you, and change you forever, forever, and forever in this infinite ocean of Light that I behold.

Jesus Christ, Babaji, Lahiri Mahasaya, Sri Yukteswarji, I bow to you all again and again. It is your message from God that has permeated me. Whoever shall receive this message from me with an open heart shall not go away unfulfilled. His or her heart shall become a wonderful cup of realization that will gradually expand to receive the ocean of Infinity, the power of the eternal Spirit.

May His light surcharge you! Everywhere you go, live God. Practice your Kriya, be intoxicated with that communion with the Spirit, and whosoever sees your eyes shall change.

I am only His humble servant; I know only Him. And I am always serving you. May you all be surcharged with the great power that is emanating from me as the power of the Father, none else. My hands, my feet, my mind and thought, my meditation and *samadhi,* all belong to the Father.

Lord, bless all through the Masters, and bring them to Thy consciousness, that we may live in a new world without war. We are come to open heaven in every heart, that war may be gone and His one united world may be established, through the instrumentality of our great America, India, and all nations that are loyal to God.

Pray with me: "Heavenly Father, May Thy love shine forever on the sanctuary of our devotion, and may we be able to awaken Thy love in all hearts."

Aum, Aum, Aum, Amen. God bless you all!

"I Have Wished for You the Highest"

A birthday celebration held at Self-Realization Fellowship International Headquarters in Los Angeles on January 5, 1940, was the second observance in America of Paramahansa Yogananda's birthday. It was celebrated with the SRF ashram monastics and other residents, along with specially invited guests. The first birthday observance was at a small intimate gathering on January 5, 1939, in the Self-Realization Fellowship Hermitage in Encinitas, during the visit from India of the Guru's younger brother, Bishnu Charan Ghosh. It was from Bishnu that the disciples received confirmation of the date of Paramahansaji's birthday, a date that had previously remained undisclosed by the Guru.

*Paramahansaji's remarks during the 1940 celebration recorded here were intimately informal and conversational, expressing an aspect of his personality that was known and revered by the close disciples privileged to be present during such gatherings. The program began with an Indian ceremony: The ceremonial mark of the spiritual eye was placed on Paramahansaji's forehead, and a crown of flowers on his head. A garland was placed around the Guru's neck while the devotees sang "Aum Guru," and then one by one they came forward and took the dust of his feet. After everyone was seated, they were led by the Guru in chanting to God "I Have Made Thee Polestar of My Life."**

Paramahansaji speaks: It overwhelms me to see your enthusiasm, and your kindness. I didn't think much about my birth in this world; but to be able to receive so much kindness is something that makes it worthwhile to be born.

[After a cake is brought for Paramahansaji to blow out the candle and make the traditional birthday wish, refreshments are served and gifts opened.]

My wish on this day is that you all find highest favor with God.

It is awfully sweet, unbelievable, all the ideas you have adopted for celebrating my birthday. I didn't know you had learned about so many Indian customs concerning the guru's birthday.

* From *Cosmic Chants,* by Paramahansa Yogananda (published by Self-Realization Fellowship).

Dr. Lewis speaks: You came here from distant India, and gave up everything that we might find truth. You not only came, but suffered persecution from those who were ignorant; and by your great heart and goodness, took on the karmic burden of many of us so that our path might be easier. That is the greatest thing. We surely appreciate it, and we are glad you were born on January 5, 18-- what was the date?* *[Laughter]*

We thank your mother, that she gave such a good son to the world; and we are thankful to God and the Masters for such a great Master.

Paramahansaji: First of all, I want you to stand and salute her who gave me a spiritual birth into this world, my great mother—and him who gave me spiritual life, my revered guru Swami Sri Yukteswarji. I thank you all for this appreciation.

This has been a very strange experience for me. For these many years I have avoided my birthdays, because I have always recognized that I was in Spirit—never born, although my sojourns on earth in a body have been many. Birth and passing away are just like waves coming out of the sea and receding again. But as the sea remains constant, so God within us is ever constant. With that idea in mind I have not acknowledged birthdays. Another thing—I know so many people that if I started celebrating birthdays I wouldn't have time for anything else.

I am glad you didn't try to pry into my age! You have placed only one candle on this birthday cake, which made me think of the infinite age of the soul and the light of Spirit.

I didn't know what was coming with these birthdays when last year I was surprised with the first little birthday party in Encinitas. I was deeply touched. It is overwhelming to see you celebrating my birthday, which I thought nothing of. But it gives me an opportunity to be with you all.

Many times I have come to you mentally and blessed you and prayed for you that you find the highest realization in God. That is my greatest gift to you—a meager way I can return your kindness—in that I have wished for you the highest favor in God, as He pleases and as He condescends to listen to the prayers of this humble devotee.

* Through the years it became a tradition at Paramahansaji's birthday gatherings that Dr. Lewis would try to cajole the Guru into revealing his age, with the Master smilingly declining to acknowledge anything other than that as an immortal soul, his age was infinite. *(Publisher's Note)*

While I am grateful to my parents for giving me birth, I am even more grateful to my Master Sri Yukteswarji and Lahiri Mahasaya who gave me spiritual birth. Physical birth would not have been enough—though my birth to such good parents inspired me to follow the spiritual path, for they, like my Master, were disciples of Lahiri Mahasaya. My mother was a God-known person, as also my earthly father. It is wonderful to have been blessed with such parents.

My desire for anything of this earth was very little, even from the beginning of my life. But there was an intense desire to be of service to my fellow human beings, and for the privilege of serving them I feel very humble. This occasion makes me realize even more the importance of this great task and the responsibility to all my fellow beings—a world family which I have made my family. I have no other family than all of you and the world.

For your motherly kindness and goodness to me I am more than grateful, but most of all because you follow my ideals—more so, perhaps, than those with whom I was born, with a few exceptions. That is why I feel this birthday so deeply.

So it is a great occasion to be with you all; but really, I felt very guilty to receive gifts from you—that you had to take so much trouble for me. Yet I know to you it was not trouble, for you did it with love. I want only the gift of your kindness; so if ever you celebrate my birthday in future, know that I do not look for any gifts from you except the gift of your goodwill and the joy of being with you all.

Even if my body is not here, still your appreciation of the birth of this body glorifies the Great Ones at whose feet I am but a link.* This wonderful spirit that you all show now is what makes me so happy. In India I have gone to many hermitages, and I have met great souls and lived with them; and as devotees of God you are no less than any of those. It is hard to find even one good soul in the world—but here you are good both inside and outside. It is my good fortune that I was brought to America and found such a wonderful family as is this family of Self-Realization.

It is God who has created the diverse drama of life, and it is He who is bringing this unity amongst us. And remember this: in observing this birthday, keep the same spirit as you felt at Christmas.

* Reference to the Self-Realization Fellowship line of Gurus, which includes (in addition to Paramahansa Yogananda) Mahavatar Babaji, Lahiri Mahasaya, Swami Sri Yukteswar, in communion with Jesus Christ and Bhagavan Krishna. *(Publisher's Note)*

That spirit which we had was so wonderful. We had no limiting thought at all of who were our physical relatives. Always make your Christmases like that—a spirit of divine unity. We are tied together with the one bond of Spirit. Blood ties are only temporary, for one incarnation. But the bond of Spirit cannot be broken. That bond is what we feel here; it is something unforgettable. The spirit of brotherhood that ties us is everlasting. It comes from God. It is God's "blood" that runs through us, His life and love that bind us to one another in an immortal relationship.

So this birthday has been a joyous day, for I have been born in this wonderful family here. My body was born elsewhere; my spirit was born anew in you.

I have appreciated all your loving thoughts and gestures. I didn't think you knew of this custom of touching the feet, which is an Eastern tradition practiced in India. I felt very much ashamed at first, when my thought was of the ego, the little self; but when I looked within and became one with Spirit, I saw you were touching Him in me. It was the same when we tried to touch Master's feet; at first he would pull away, but later on he let us do so.

To see God in each other is a glorious thing. The true guru never thinks of himself as a guru. He sees only God in the various human forms, and he can never think of anyone as less.

There is a scientific reason behind the custom of touching the feet of great souls. There is a contact between the souls, a current that flows between positive and negative poles. The disciple is usually the negative pole, while the master is the positive. When the disciple touches the feet of the master, he receives a vibration of spiritual blessings.* You will remember that Jesus washed the feet of his disciples. This is the same idea, the meeting of positive and negative poles—Jesus the positive, the disciples the negative.

So, it deeply touched me to realize that you adopted and introduced here an ancient spiritual tradition of blessing between guru and disciple.

And as Dr. Lewis gave me a crown of flowers and the spiritual eye mark (*tilak*) of initiation before the pictures of the Great Ones, I felt so unworthy. But as I stood there I thought, "It is God whose glory is extolled—it is He who has given me the power to speak to you of His wisdom and love. 'It is You, Lord.'" Then I saw that

* Not only the feet, but the hands and eyes of a God-knowing saint are spiritual magnets that emanate vibratory currents of blessing. *(Publisher's Note)*

Light within me; and I placed the crown on the picture of my Guru, to whom the honor rightfully belongs.

I thank you for making this such a beautiful occasion. I thank you all individually for everything here tonight. And I thank those disciples who planned this*—they were always secretly whispering; and whenever I approached them, they would become mysteriously quiet. I didn't realize what happiness birthdays could be!

The gift I want from you all is your love, that I may give it to God. I cannot wrest that love from you. It must be given freely of the heart. So that gift of your kindness which actuated you to do so many things for me really touches my heart.

Since I am not able to give you material presents, I shall try to give you a spiritual present from my soul, which shall be greater than any material gift I could give. This lamp that you all have given to me, may it be a spiritual lamp in the astral world, guiding you in the kingdom of heaven toward God. May God grant you a special dispensation by which you may receive His light quicker through Kriya Yoga.

This is indeed a day of great rejoicing that we are all here together. I often try to be with you more; but regardless, I am always active for you and thinking of your future, of your home here, of your spiritual welfare, and of your entire future life. Not a day passes that I don't think of the future welfare of you who are here and all others throughout the world.

By the virtue of God we have forgotten our individual marks of material life and have erased family distinctions and become part of the divine family of Self-Realization Fellowship. The material family has ties that last only if brought into the spiritual family. God gave us family ties that by learning to love family members and to make unselfish sacrifices for them we may learn to practice that same love and unselfishness with the whole world. There could be no other reason for which God would create such tremendous instincts between people. One by one they are taken away that we may not lose the universality of our love in only a few souls. Family love must include the world.

So this celebration is a combination of my birthday in the family in which my body was born, and in my greater spiritual family here. You have made me very happy. I was reluctant to come, because I

* Among whom, the primary instigators were Sri Daya Mata, Sailasuta Mata, Ananda Mata, and Durga Mata. *(Publisher's Note)*

thought of the trouble you were going to on my account. But your efforts very deeply touch me, and what makes me happiest is that you all enjoyed this birthday too.

So, I am glad I am here with you; and your kindness poured on me surely shall be an everlasting memory in my consciousness. Though these flowers will fade, and the candles will blow out, and our bodies may melt away, still the joy that we receive tonight in Spirit shall be an everlasting monument in the kingdom of God.

All good comes from God alone, and all good returns to Him. So all the good and kind thoughts you have showered on me certainly came from the Father, and to the Father I return them. But we are blessed that His kindness comes back to you and to me. As my great Master said, "We are all His instruments. But there are willing instruments and there are unwilling instruments. God works only through willing instruments; and when He does, those willing instruments become Godlike."

As I talk to you, I feel the presence of the Father within and without. He envelops me like a great Joy and Light. "May Thy joy, O Spirit, fall upon all—that they may realize that beneath the outer surface of material waves is the ocean of Thy presence.

"Heavenly Father, we thank Thee for our human relations and for our spiritual relations—we thank Thee for giving us our parents, and, above all, we thank Thee, Father, for giving us Babaji and Lahiri Mahasaya and Sri Yukteswarji through whose grace and instrumentality we are all here to celebrate our mutual joy and companionship in this spiritual family.

"Bless us all that we may realize everlastingly our birth in Thee. We thank Thee, O Father, for the joy of this evening. Bless us. Saturate us with Thy presence."

[After a period of meditation, Paramahansaji said:]

The Eternal Spirit is within us. Him we perceive everlastingly.

"We thank Thee, Father, for Thine infinite presence within us, and for the joy of this occasion and the manifestation of Thy presence." *Aum*. Peace. Amen.

How to Weave God Into Your Daily Life

*Self-Realization Fellowship Second Temple, Los Angeles, September 12, 1937**

God-saturated, God-inspired, let us all rejoice in the presence of the great Father. Let us give our hearts to that Almighty Power who is the fountain of life and consciousness beneath all our mental and physical activities. Please pray with me:

"Divine Father, teach me to enjoy Thee in spirit, that I may enjoy the world and my earthly duties with Thy joy. Help me to train my senses so that they may enjoy all good things. Teach me to enjoy earthly pleasures with Thy joy. Teach me to weave Thee into my daily activities."

I am very happy that you are gradually understanding your own highest interest by studying these teachings. By their study and practice you are connected with some of the greatest masters of the world, who have sent this highest sacred science of God-realization beyond the shores of India to spread all over the earth.

Every nation specializes in something. Germany has specialized in science, and America in business and industrial utility, and England in diplomacy and building of empires. And India has specialized in spirituality; that is undeniable. What Self-Realization Fellowship teaches has been tried and proven through the centuries in India. If you are serious about investigating these teachings, you will attain great spiritual understanding.

Our aim should be to bring God into our national life, our social life, and our personal life to such an extent that we feel the spring of God's presence flowing continually beneath the fountain of our existence. That should be the intention of every seeker of Self-realization. The question then is how you may seek and serve God in your daily life.

* Much of this talk was integrated into the *Self-Realization Fellowship Lessons* in the late 1940s. In preparing it for publication in this volume of Paramahansaji's *Collected Talks and Essays,* unused material from the original talk has been added.

Why Desire to Know God?

First of all it is necessary to understand why you should want to know God. Those who don't understand say, "See how many people there are who don't think of God at all, and they are getting along all right in the world." But are they? There are a great number of suicides among the very wealthy, who are "getting along all right." The trouble is that they use most of their time for the accumulation of money, thinking that it will give them everything they want. When it does not, they become disillusioned. But when God is with you, you do have everything. Many times I have gone someplace without money in my pocket, but the Heavenly Father has always supplied my needs.

Jesus said that if one leaves father, mother, and friends for God, one shall have a hundred times more, and persecution, perchance; but hereafter, everlasting life. I have found that to be true. Everything that I forsook for Him has been given to me again in some form. And I am not waiting for everlasting life, because I feel it in every cell of my body and in every fiber of my thought, *now*. I am speaking of That which dreams the body—the eternal Spirit. That alone is real.

Every one of you, in your heart, has some strong desire. Some want to get married, others want money or jobs. Some want healing. Some want to fulfill artistic ambitions. Meanwhile, every day, life is creeping forward. What are you doing besides wishing? Are you progressing spiritually or are you merely being swept along toward death? Analyze yourself; analyze your life. Like a child, you cry for so many things that you never will find. Why don't you try crying and yearning for God? Of course, a mere show of devotion won't do; He knows what you are thinking. But if you really cry for Him, the Lord will come to you, sometime, without fail.

The satisfaction brought by name, fame, and money does not last. Nothing in this universe can permanently quench the thirst of your heart but the supreme attainment: God.

Again, ask yourself: "Why should finding God be my greatest ambition?" Because without Him you cannot fulfill any other ambition. Think of it! Perhaps you will say: "Paramahansaji is talking of dreams. Today we are busy with new inventions, new pursuits. This is a practical world."

The idea that God is not for this age is not true. I thought the same thing once, but I wish I could show you all the things I have since learned. To him who says that it is not practical to think of God, I would reply: "It is not practical to forget Him." If it were, there would not be so much suffering endured in the world by those who have forgotten Him.

Single-Hearted Effort Is Necessary

Only when you shall purge from your heart every other ambition except the ambition to know God—when you shall say: "On the throne of my ambition lies only the desire for God"—only then shall you know Him. I can show you that Spirit, without fail, if you will follow me and practice what I teach you. I promise you that, because I have found Him. But God does not wish those who know Him to use miracles to draw His other children to Him; you must make your own effort to find Him.

It is possible to know God just as well as you know your dearest friend. That is the truth. Now you are thinking, "Why don't you show Him to me?" Well, if it were God's will that I should do so, I would; but He has decreed that you find Him for yourself. I can only show you the path to follow and the techniques by which you can overcome obstacles.

Don't blindly follow anything or anyone. Investigate and compare their relative value. There are many "Pharisees" in the religious marketplace who practice nothing more than spiritual racketeering. There are some who are trying to sell heaven just as if it were a patent medicine. They have the nerve to tell you that you can find heaven in a few minutes. No one can give you God-consciousness that way. If that had been possible, Jesus Christ would have given it to everybody. Instead, he said, "The harvest is plenteous but the laborers are few." The harvest of spirituality is plenteous but few are the laborers who make the effort to find that realization.

Those who come and tell you that you can know God through some magic formula—and all this in a minute—lie to you. You cannot know about Him without your own effort, without expanding your own meditative consciousness. No one can give you ascension or divine transmission in a minute, unless you yourself have prepared your consciousness for that divine contact. When you have shown God that you want Him above all else, and purified your heart and mind, then through the guru that transmission of God-consciousness will come.

Spiritual truth cannot be found by proxy. You have to use your own brain. On the other hand, many seek but they don't find God because they have no one to point out the way. But through faith in the Heavenly Father they will find the way. You now know the way, and if you will but try you will succeed. The Heavenly Father is your eternal heritage. The kingdom of the Father is your own. By finding God you can find everything. Follow the truths taught by Jesus Christ, Bhagavan Krishna, and the great masters of Self-Realization,* and you will find Him.

Your Only Eternal Relationship Is With God

My one desire has been to give my time to God—my God, your God, our one Father-Mother-Friend and Eternal Companion. Those friends and relatives of whom you say, "They are mine!" shall be taken away from you. Seek Him who gave you the power to think, the power to love. You wouldn't be able to think or love or gather knowledge without the power of God. Cultivate His acquaintance.

Those whom you think are your own are yours because of the Divine Mother. When your mother or sister or wife says, "Come and eat your dinner," it is the Divine Mother who has taken form to serve you. How much more you should love your Divine Mother! So shy! She lets you think that your visible mother loves you, while it is really Her love which is being expressed. Your human mother could never have loved you if she were not an atom of the omnipresent Divine Mother.

So it is with other relationships. It is the Heavenly Father that you see in the mortal father. She whom you call "My wife, my love," is not your wife. It is the Divine Spirit that has taken the form of the beloved to offer love unto you. He whom you call your servant is not your servant. It is the Divine Spirit taking the form of the servant to serve you. He whom you call your friend is not your friend. It is the Divine Spirit expressing through your friend.

Then why do you look up to God in the clouds? He is so near—so real. He receives your kind thoughts and returns kindness and love through your companions. And so I feel His love and service through my disciples and students. Who gives me love, who gives me attention, who gives me service? Only God, through them. What if God switched off the life current from these loved ones? They would be sitting like statuettes, neither heeding nor caring for you or for me.

So why look above for Him? God is right here. Why should you try to find Him? Because He loves you more than anybody. He loves

* In addition to Paramahansa Yogananda, they are Mahavatar Babaji, Lahiri Mahasaya, and Swami Sri Yukteswar—whose lives, and the spiritual teachings and worldwide mission they entrusted to Paramahansaji, are described in *Autobiography of a Yogi*.

you more than your father, mother, or beloved because He gave them to you. He is the beloved; He is the father and the mother.

If you should die and be buried, and then be reborn in the house right next to your old one of the former incarnation, will your former father and mother recognize you? No. But God knows and loves you through thousands of incarnations. To love any being without loving God is meaningless, but to accept the love of family and friends as part of the love of God makes it so real!

In my heart I love everybody. Why? Because I see God in all. God is expressing Himself in the soil, in the metals, and in the flowers. God calls to you and says, "Right behind the petals I am hiding." God is right here. Why do you think of the flower as apart from God? I see it as God—I see every human being as God. If you have this realization, you cannot dislike anyone. If you once saw God in some form, or experienced cosmic consciousness for even a moment, then you would love everybody. It is a strange experience. It makes you love everybody just as your own family.

When I returned to India and saw the people among whom I was born, I could not see that they were any different from anybody else. I thought I would find that my family was my own, but it was not so. I saw that every person was my relative. I felt that the whole world was mine. I did not exclude my family, but I found that inside and outside the family circle the relationship was the same. It is a wonderful life when you have that expanded consciousness. Such joy comes to your heart in seeing people and in serving them. That is why you should love God. It is because most people do not consciously serve Him that the world is full of suffering.

You must realize that you came to this earth alone and you will leave it alone. The only One who accompanies you is God. He is serving you all the time. God made the sky and the sun and the moon; everything that we use in life, He made. That is why you should love God. And when you die—when your family says goodbye and your nation and earth are left behind—then God alone is with you. Why shouldn't you love Him? God will be with you when all things else shall forsake you, if you will only love Him now. Having Him, you shall have eternal protection.

Find the Answer to the Mysteries of Existence

In time you will learn that counting on the changing material world is folly. When, while visiting India, I saw all the things that I used to do, I was absolutely disillusioned. I couldn't find joy in those things anymore. I went to my old school, and in my mind I could see all my old playmates. But the old friends were gone, and the new students did not recognize me. Yet God had not failed me! I saw Him everywhere.

People have married and lost their love. People have attained success, and then lost their money. There is only disappointment in store for those who follow such paths. So I forsook the way of the crowds, and in meditation tried to find the answer to the mysteries of existence. Such joy I found, such happiness, such truth! You can taste it also. But you cannot find it quickly by yourself. You must find the right teacher, and the right teaching. The right teaching is here. Follow it. I am telling you of the way that I found. What assurance, when you see heaven open within yourself!

For there is a heaven, and it is composed of "many mansions" or astral planes. Just as there are myriad sounds going on in the world, some of which we can hear only by means of radio, so behind the ether of the conscious mind God is hiding with all the saints. But you must tune in. Every restless thought is static. If your radio is out of order, you cannot get the program of God. This, I have often told you.

Be Determined When Restless Thoughts Invade the Mind

So, develop your desire for God; and when you are meditating, every time a distracting thought comes, remember that it is only static. Tune it out. If you are praying to the Heavenly Father, and suddenly you think that you should be in the kitchen working, just say mentally to that intruding distraction: "Get out!" Start meditating again, and affirm: "Heavenly Father, Thou art with me."

Then again you may hear the neighbor playing the piano, and you wonder what kind of piano it is, and the memory thought of Grandma's piano arises, and you begin to wonder where Grandma is and how she is. Your mind has wandered again. Mentally say to those thoughts: "Get out!" And bring your mind back to the techniques. Don't give up.

Throw out all invading thoughts: *Oh, what a problem I have with such-and-so! No matter what I do, that person doesn't respond.* "Get out!" *This chair is not just right. Let me find some cushions and fix it.* "Get out!"

In this manner, the mind will go on wandering from one thing to another for hours, if you permit it! Mentally dismiss such thoughts, with all the force of your will, whenever you catch your mind straying from the object of your concentration in meditation.

Pray deeply and intensely until God reveals Himself to you. Do not make a mockery of prayer and meditation. Keep on with ever-increasing concentration: "Father, reveal Thyself!" Just keep hammering at the door of silence and He will answer. Only when you have that contact with Him can you ask for anything and know that your prayer will get a response.

God Intended You to Live in Joy

Therefore, my friends, learn the techniques taught in the *Lessons*. Practice the methods diligently; don't just try them out. Why spend so much time on other things, which are useless? Why not try to know God? That is really worthwhile to you. It is an injustice to God to imagine that He planned life to be full of hunger, sickness, and disappointment. On the contrary: He intended you to live in the consciousness of joy and immortality.

Everyone can find God, and He is Bliss. How can you find Him? Again, first of all you must continually keep in mind the reasons you should seek God. Remember that money gives only temporary release, health gives only temporary joy. But when disease has come, and when doctors are of no further help, what do you feel? You rebel against the world then; and if you have not contacted God, you fear the time when you will drop into the unknown.

Death is the greatest insult to your intelligence, to your real nature as an immortal child of God. Jesus Christ trod on that insult. He said: "Destroy this bodily temple and I will build it again in three days." And he proved it by his resurrection.

You may think, "Well, if Jesus Christ was so great why doesn't he talk to me and advise me? If Krishna was so great why doesn't he appear anymore?" Still, in your heart, you know these avatars didn't tell lies. They did not just speak of immortal life; they exist today. In fact, in every generation there are some devoted disciples who hear and see them. But as yet you don't know how to get in touch with them.

My own master, Swami Sri Yukteswar, also resurrected himself; I beheld him in flesh and blood weeks after his death. When I touched him with my hands, I knew that these things are true. This wasn't centuries ago, but just last year.*

* This divine experience is described in detail in *Autobiography of a Yogi,* chapter 43.

All those who have gone before are just behind the ether, but you don't know yet how to attune your consciousness with them. I have seen Jesus, St. Francis, and other great ones many times. So this is not a myth; but unless your heart is tuned by meditation, you cannot know the presence of God or the masters. You must know the art of tuning in with these great souls. Pursue the path of Self-Realization and you shall be able to contact them.

Two Worthy Ambitions

Two ambitions should reign supreme in your life. The first is to know God, and the second is to play your part on earth as His perfect child. If you know God then you will play your part well, and vice versa. If you do your part well only when it is a pleasant one, you have gained little. If you don't even *try* to play your part properly, then you have accomplished nothing. Yet, many are drunk with oblivion of truth, drunk with *maya* (delusion), drunk with sorrow. The flesh is tender and weak. You ascribe to yourself all these errors and frailties. The only way to get rid of every suffering is to find God. So the first thing is to continually remind yourself of all the reasons you want God-realization. Jesus and other avatars have said so, St. Francis said so, my Master said so, and I am telling you: God is the only Reality.

Why do you so often insult God by your indifference? He who loves you—He who never punishes you for forgetting Him, but gives you life just the same. Instead, while you are playing the part He has assigned you, try to gain His attention and approval.

The certificate of the Father's approval means everything, and in your consciousness you know whether or not you have that. And if you haven't reached Him consciously then you haven't found that, so beware of becoming self-satisfied. Keep seeking and you will find Him and obtain it. It is better to spend the flesh to buy Bliss in eternity than to enjoy the flesh and forget eternity.

Surrender Yourself to God

Self-Realization Fellowship teaches you the highest path. You have received in the *Lessons* concentration and meditation techniques which, when practiced correctly and with ever-deepening devotion, can surely lead you to God-consciousness. Therefore why make life so complicated? Why not make life simple and try out my recipe for living?

Every night, before going to bed, meditate until you feel that your mind has gone beyond the static of your thoughts. Yet even that is not enough. After interiorizing the mind, then pour out your devotion. You must surrender yourself completely to God. Then suddenly you will feel, "I've reached Him!" A great light will appear, or suddenly you may see a figure, or be aware of a delightful fragrance, and then you will know that God has manifested.

And not only that, but you will better understand the meaning of everything that happens in your life. That is the proof of your experience. Or perhaps, while you are meditating, peace will envelop you. Then if you keep on, suddenly all thoughts will be gone and a great joy will come upon you. Some students give up before they reach that state—millions of people don't even know of it. And beyond these states there is even greater joy.

In the Background of Your Mind, Keep the Desire for God Alive

Now I shall tell you another way by which you can find God. If you put aside all other desires you can find Him. Every day when you are walking or working or waking from sleep, have but one desire in your heart, to know Him. This will not interfere with your duties; in fact, you will be able to perform them better. Just say, "I want to be a success at my work," and then work, but constantly retain your desire for Him at the back of your mind, just as the eager lover remembers the beloved. Then, at night, meditate. You shall succeed. Continuous desire for Him will bring an answer. When you have the same desire for God as the drowning man feels for air, you will find Him.

It is also necessary to eradicate certain character faults before you can succeed. You can't love God and be unkind to your associates. You can't love God and be full of wrath. You must keep His commandments.

And remember, above all, there is one commandment you must keep: Love God with all your heart. Most people profess love for God only when they want something from Him. But no matter what you are doing, you must think of Him and love Him with all your heart, and mind, and strength.

To love God with all your mind means to give Him one hundred percent of your attention when you meditate and to think of Him in all that you do. You must own your mind—that is, you must be able to govern your thoughts. You cannot give your mind to God unless it belongs to you. Learn concentration. Bring your mind under your control. Practice that control in meditation, and then keep your meditative consciousness of God's presence during all your activities.

Snatch your mind away from the world, that you may offer it to Him. "One by one I close the doors of the senses, lest the aroma of the rose or the song of the nightingale distract my love from Thee." That is loving God with all your mind. And the greatest way of doing that is to love God with all your strength—that is where the techniques of Self-Realization Fellowship come in. It is done by switching off the life force from the senses. You do that every night unconsciously, but now you must learn to do it consciously. Only then can you know God.

The kingdom of heaven is right *here.* Why shouldn't you take advantage of it by learning to enter at will? Then, when you know God, He will come in any guise you prefer. He will come in any way you want Him to—as Jesus Christ or as the Lord Krishna or Buddha or as any saint you desire to see. Until you have accomplished this, don't stop.

Be serious about finding God. Through these teachings you will be able to find God if you want to pay the price in perseverance and sacrifice. If you study the weekly *Self-Realization Fellowship Lessons,* you will know that for the first time the greatest spiritual teachings of the world have been scientifically systematized. If you want to know God, make the effort, give your time, practice what you learn in the *Lessons*. If you do this, you shall find that I have been truthful with you. For I have made the effort for a long, long time, and I have traveled this path. It is not always easy, but it can be done.

Every little throb of your consciousness is part of Spirit, part of God, for it is Spirit which has become the throb of your consciousness. On the lotus leaf of your life is trembling the dewdrop of God's consciousness. Realize that! Find the connection between the dewdrop and its Infinite Source and you shall find Him. Only by complete surrender can you make God answer. He is very humble. Only in humbleness can you find Him.

I know that my words tonight will awaken many of you. The truths I am telling you are not from any book; they are from my own experience. Those who come to me with love for God shall receive Him. I am blessed by Him to tell you this, because I love Him with all my heart; I have forsaken everything else for Him.

If each one of you had for even five minutes the joy that I feel, you would follow this path and leave forever everything that diverts you. But most people lack determination. What you haven't experienced, you don't miss. That is why you should constantly compare the small material happiness you experience with the unending bliss of higher spiritual experiences.

The Way of Freedom and Bliss

You are here to seek freedom—that consciousness by which you can be liberated forever from the bondage of material delusion and desires. Do not be like the materialistic individual, who is inclined to be shortsighted and to look only for things that are disillusioning, forgetting those things that are imperishable. Because of the limitations of the body, you are in the habit of wishing for things that are limited. Instead, you should strive for things that are lasting: wisdom and happiness through Self-realization.

If you succeed in this primary duty, you will then be ready to perform your secondary obligation in life, which is to do your best to bring other "prodigal sons" of God back to their spiritual home. Awaken souls, relieve them from ignorance; throw the current of love and draw them back to God. There is no other work that pleases God more than to bring your erring brothers and sisters back home through your example. But first you must acquire the pearls of wisdom. Then, as you wear them, their gleaming will give light and joy to others. That is the way of Bliss.

ABOUT THE AUTHOR

Paramahansa Yogananda was born Mukunda Lal Ghosh on January 5, 1893, in the north Indian city of Gorakhpur, near the Himalaya mountains. From his earliest years, it was clear that his life was marked for a divine destiny. According to those closest to him, even as a child the depth of his spiritual awareness and experience was far beyond the ordinary. In his youth he sought out many of India's sages and saints, hoping to find an illumined teacher to guide him in his spiritual quest.

It was in 1910, at the age of seventeen, that he met and became a disciple of the revered Swami Sri Yukteswar. In the hermitage of this great master, he spent the better part of the next ten years, receiving Sri Yukteswar's strict but loving spiritual discipline. After he graduated from Calcutta University in 1915, his Guru bestowed on him the formal vows of a monk of India's venerable monastic Swami Order, at which time he received the name Yogananda (signifying bliss, *ananda,* through divine union, *yoga*).

In 1917, Sri Yogananda began his life's work with the founding of a "how-to-live" school for boys, where modern educational methods were combined with yoga training and instruction in spiritual ideals. Three years later he was invited to serve as India's delegate to an International Congress of Religious Liberals convening in Boston. His address to the Congress, on "The Science of Religion," was enthusiastically received.

For the next several years, he lectured and taught on the East Coast and in 1924 embarked on a cross-continental speaking tour. To the tens of thousands of Westerners who attended his lectures during the decade that followed, his discourses on the unity of "the original teachings of Jesus Christ and the original Yoga taught by Bhagavan Krishna" were a revelation. The *Los Angeles Times* reported on January 28, 1925: "The Philharmonic Auditorium presents the extraordinary spectacle of thousands...being turned away an hour before the advertised opening of a lecture with the 3,000-seat hall filled to its utmost capacity. Swami Yogananda is the attraction. A Hindu invading the United States to bring God in the midst of a Christian community, preaching the essence of Christian doctrine."

Later that year, he established in Los Angeles the international headquarters of Self-Realization Fellowship, the society he had founded in 1920 to disseminate his teachings and perpetuate the work he had begun.

"Paramahansa Yogananda brought to the West not only India's perennial promise of God-realization, but also a practical method by which spiritual aspirants from all walks of life may progress rapidly toward that goal," wrote Quincy Howe, Jr., Ph.D., Professor of Classics at Scripps College. "Originally appreciated in the West only on the most lofty and abstract level, the spiritual legacy of India is now accessible as practice and experience to all who aspire to know God, not in the beyond, but in the here and now.... Yogananda has placed within the reach of all the most exalted methods of contemplation."

The *Cincinnati Enquirer* reported on December 1, 1926: "Yesterday in the Hotel Sinton, Swami Yogananda was greeted by over a thousand men and women, hundreds being turned away. In this enthusiastic throng, there were litterateurs, medical men, leaders of fashion, clergymen, and indeed followers drawn from many walks of life. The Swami was continually interrupted with responsive applause, his words being listened to with profound attention." And according to the *Washington Post,* January 25, 1927: "Approximately 5,000 persons crowded the auditorium to hear his initial lecture... at the Washington Auditorium, where the Swami has broken all records for sustained interest."

After fifteen years of teaching in the West, Sri Yogananda returned to India in 1935. There he had a long-awaited reunion with his guru, Swami Sri Yukteswar, who honored him with India's highest religious title, *Paramahansa,* bestowed on those deemed to have achieved irrevocable union with God. While in his native land, he traveled and lectured and met with many spiritual luminaries, including Mahatma Gandhi, who requested initiation in *Kriya Yoga* from him.

Returning to America at the end of 1936, Paramahansaji began to withdraw somewhat from his nationwide public lecturing to devote himself to building an enduring foundation for his worldwide work and to the writings that would carry his message to future generations. His life story, *Autobiography of a Yogi,* was published in 1946 and substantially expanded by him in 1951. Recognized from the beginning as a landmark work, the book has been in print continuously through Self-Realization Fellowship since its publication more than seventy-five years ago, inspiring new readers decade after decade.

On March 7, 1952, Paramahansa Yogananda entered *mahasamadhi,* a God-illumined master's conscious exit from the body at the time of physical death. His passing occasioned an outpouring of reverent appreciation from spiritual leaders, dignitaries, journalists, friends, and disciples all over the world. The former religion editor of the *Los Angeles Times,* Dan Thrapp, stated in 1992: "All through history you can find people who come along—Jesus, Buddha, and other people—who are inspired, and who have a way of expressing it and have charisma with other people, so that their influence spreads. I think Yogananda was one of those people....He was inspired...one of the greats. He showed the way for people into a purer, unadulterated type of faith, a universal faith."

The Government of India issued a commemorative stamp in honor of the renowned guru in 1977, which was accompanied by these words: "The ideal of love for God and service to humanity found full expression in the life of Paramahansa Yogananda.... Though the major part of his life was spent outside India, still he takes his place among our great saints. His work continues to grow and shine ever more brightly, drawing people everywhere on the path of the pilgrimage of the Spirit."

Scholars and journalists have echoed this appraisal of Sri Yogananda's continuing influence. "Few books have had a greater impact on popular theology than Paramahansa Yogananda's *Autobiography of a Yogi,*" notes Phyllis Tickle, former religion editor of *Publishers Weekly.* His teachings "made an indelible mark on the course of American spirituality," wrote Dr. Robert S. Ellwood, former chairman of the University of Southern California's School of Religion. "Yogananda has become an image—a remarkable, deep, sweet, poetic, ecstatic man enraptured of cosmic life—who has changed the map of American religious life."

Today, the spiritual and humanitarian work begun by Paramahansa Yogananda continues under the direction of Brother Chidananda, president of Self-Realization Fellowship/Yogoda Satsanga Society of India.* In addition to publishing Paramahansa Yogananda's books and his other writings, lectures, and informal talks—including his *Self-Realization Fellowship Lessons,* a comprehensive series for home study; and a magazine, *Self-Realization*—the

* In India, Paramahansa Yogananda's work is known as Yogoda Satsanga Society.

society guides members in their practice of Sri Yogananda's teachings; oversees temples, retreats, and meditation centers around the world, as well as the monastic communities of Self-Realization Fellowship monks and nuns; and coordinates the Worldwide Prayer Circle, which serves as an instrument to help bring healing to those in physical, mental, or spiritual need and greater harmony among the nations.

An award-winning documentary film about Paramahansa Yogananda's life and work, *Awake: The Life of Yogananda,* was released in October 2014.

Paramahansa Yogananda: A Yogi in Life and Death

Paramahansa Yogananda entered *mahasamadhi* (a yogi's final conscious exit from the body) in Los Angeles, California, on March 7, 1952, after concluding his speech at a banquet held in honor of H.E. Binay R. Sen, Ambassador of India.

The great world teacher demonstrated the value of yoga (scientific techniques for God-realization) not only in life but in death. Weeks after his departure his unchanged face shone with the divine luster of incorruptibility.

Mr. Harry T. Rowe, Los Angeles Mortuary Director, Forest Lawn Memorial-Park (in which the body of the great master is temporarily placed), sent Self-Realization Fellowship a notarized letter from which the following extracts are taken:

"The absence of any visual signs of decay in the dead body of Paramahansa Yogananda offers the most extraordinary case in our experience....No physical disintegration was visible in his body even twenty days after death....No indication of mold was visible on his skin, and no visible desiccation (drying up) took place in the bodily tissues. This state of perfect preservation of a body is, so far as we know from mortuary annals, an unparalleled one....At the time of receiving Yogananda's body, the Mortuary personnel expected to observe, through the glass lid of the casket, the usual progressive signs of bodily decay. Our astonishment increased as day followed day without bringing any visible change in the body under observation. Yogananda's body was apparently in a phenomenal state of immutability....

"No odor of decay emanated from his body at any time.... The physical appearance of Yogananda on March 27th, just before the bronze cover of the casket was put into position, was the same as it had been on March 7th. He looked on March 27th as fresh and as unravaged by decay as he had looked on the night of his death. On March 27th there was no reason to say that his body had suffered any visible physical disintegration at all. For these reasons we state again that the case of Paramahansa Yogananda is unique in our experience."

Aims and Ideals
of
Self-Realization Fellowship

As set forth by Paramahansa Yogananda, Founder
Brother Chidananda, President

To disseminate among the nations a knowledge of definite scientific techniques for attaining direct personal experience of God.

To teach that the purpose of life is the evolution, through self-effort, of man's limited mortal consciousness into God Consciousness; and to this end to establish Self-Realization Fellowship temples for God-communion throughout the world, and to encourage the establishment of individual temples of God in the homes and in the hearts of men.

To reveal the complete harmony and basic oneness of original Christianity as taught by Jesus Christ and original Yoga as taught by Bhagavan Krishna; and to show that these principles of truth are the common scientific foundation of all true religions.

To point out the one divine highway to which all paths of true religious beliefs eventually lead: the highway of daily, scientific, devotional meditation on God.

To liberate man from his threefold suffering: physical disease, mental inharmonies, and spiritual ignorance.

To encourage "plain living and high thinking"; and to spread a spirit of brotherhood among all peoples by teaching the eternal basis of their unity: kinship with God.

To demonstrate the superiority of mind over body, of soul over mind.

To overcome evil by good, sorrow by joy, cruelty by kindness, ignorance by wisdom.

To unite science and religion through realization of the unity of their underlying principles.

To advocate cultural and spiritual understanding between East and West, and the exchange of their finest distinctive features.

To serve mankind as one's larger Self.

Additional Resources on the Kriya Yoga Teachings of Paramahansa Yogananda

Self-Realization Fellowship is dedicated to freely assisting seekers worldwide. For information regarding our annual series of public lectures and classes, meditation and inspirational services at our temples and centers around the world, a schedule of retreats, and other activities, we invite you to visit our website or our International Headquarters:

www.yogananda.org

Self-Realization Fellowship
3880 San Rafael Avenue
Los Angeles, CA 90065
(323) 225-2471

Self-Realization Fellowship Lessons

Personal guidance and instruction from Paramahansa Yogananda on the techniques of yoga meditation and principles of spiritual living

If you feel drawn to the spiritual truths described in *Solving the Mystery of Life,* we invite you to enroll in the *Self-Realization Fellowship Lessons.*

Paramahansa Yogananda originated this home-study series to provide sincere seekers the opportunity to learn and practice the ancient yoga meditation techniques that he brought to the West—including the science of *Kriya Yoga.* The *Lessons* also present his practical guidance for attaining balanced physical, mental, and spiritual well-being.

The *Self-Realization Fellowship Lessons* are available at a nominal fee (to cover printing and postage costs). All students are freely given personal guidance in their practice by Self-Realization Fellowship monks and nuns.

For more information...

Please visit www.srflessons.org to request a comprehensive complimentary information packet about the *Lessons,* which includes:

- *"An Overview of the Self-Realization Fellowship Lessons: Information About Paramahansa Yogananda's Home-Study Series"*
- *"Highest Achievements Through Self-Realization," by Paramahansa Yogananda—a thorough introduction to the teachings presented in the SRF Lessons*

Also published by Self-Realization Fellowship...

AUTOBIOGRAPHY OF A YOGI
By Paramahansa Yogananda

This acclaimed autobiography presents a fascinating portrait of one of the great spiritual figures of our time. With engaging candor, eloquence, and wit, Paramahansa Yogananda narrates the inspiring chronicle of his life—the experiences of his remarkable childhood, encounters with many saints and sages during his youthful search throughout India for an illumined teacher, ten years of training in the hermitage of a revered yoga master, and the three decades that he lived and taught in America. Also recorded here are his meetings with Mahatma Gandhi, Rabindranath Tagore, Luther Burbank, the Catholic stigmatist Therese Neumann, and other celebrated spiritual personalities of East and West. *Autobiography of a Yogi* is at once a beautifully written account of an exceptional life and a profound introduction to the ancient science of yoga and its time-honored tradition of meditation. The author clearly explains the subtle but definite laws behind both the ordinary events of everyday life and the extraordinary events commonly termed miracles. His absorbing life story thus becomes the background for a penetrating and unforgettable look at the ultimate mysteries of human existence.

First published in 1946 and enlarged by Paramahansa Yogananda in 1951, the book has been kept in print continuously by Self-Realization Fellowship. It has been translated into more than fifty languages and is widely used as a text and reference work in colleges and universities. A perennial best-seller, *Autobiography of a Yogi* has found its way into the hearts of millions of readers around the world.

Available in hardcover, paperback, ebook, large print paperback, and audiobook.

* * *

"A rare account."—**The New York Times**

"A fascinating and clearly annotated study."—**Newsweek**

"There has been nothing before, written in English or in any other European language, like this presentation of Yoga."

—**Columbia University Press**

"Sheer revelation...should help the human race to understand itself better... autobiography at its very best...told with delightful wit and compelling sincerity...as fascinating as any novel."

—**News-Sentinel,** *Fort Wayne, Indiana*

OTHER BOOKS BY PARAMAHANSA YOGANANDA

Available at bookstores
or online at www.srfbooks.org

Self-Realization Fellowship
3880 San Rafael Avenue • Los Angeles, California 90065
Tel (323) 225-2471 • Fax (323) 225-5088

God Talks With Arjuna: *The Bhagavad Gita—A New Translation and Commentary*

In this monumental two-volume work, Paramahansa Yogananda reveals the innermost essence of India's most renowned scripture. Exploring its psychological, spiritual, and metaphysical depths, he presents a sweeping chronicle of the soul's journey to enlightenment through the royal science of God-realization.

The Second Coming of Christ: *The Resurrection of the Christ Within You—A Revelatory Commentary on the Original Teachings of Jesus*

In this unprecedented masterwork of inspiration, almost 1700 pages in length, Paramahansa Yogananda takes the reader on a profoundly enriching journey through the four Gospels. Verse by verse, he illumines the universal path to oneness with God taught by Jesus to his immediate disciples but obscured through centuries of misinterpretation: "how to become like Christ, how to resurrect the Eternal Christ within one's self."

Man's Eternal Quest

Volume I of Paramahansa Yogananda's *Collected Talks and Essays* includes 57 selections, covering many aspects of his "how-to-live" teachings. Explores little-known and seldom-understood aspects of meditation, life after death, the nature of creation, health and healing, the unlimited powers of the mind, and the eternal quest that finds fulfillment only in God.

The Divine Romance

Volume II of Paramahansa Yogananda's *Collected Talks and Essays.* Among the wide-ranging selections: *How to Cultivate Divine Love; Harmonizing Physical, Mental, and Spiritual Methods of Healing; A World Without Boundaries; Controlling Your Destiny; The Yoga Art of Overcoming Mortal Consciousness and Death; The Cosmic Lover; Finding the Joy in Life.*

Journey to Self-realization

Volume III of the *Collected Talks and Essays* presents Sri Yogananda's unique combination of wisdom, compassion, down-to-earth guidance, and encouragement on dozens of fascinating subjects, including: *Quickening Human Evolution, How to Express Everlasting Youthfulness,* and *Realizing God in Your Daily Life.*

Wine of the Mystic: *The Rubaiyat of Omar Khayyam—A Spiritual Interpretation*

An inspired commentary that brings to light the mystical science of God-communion hidden behind the *Rubaiyat's* enigmatic imagery. Includes 50 original color illustrations. Winner of the 1995 Benjamin Franklin Award for best book in the field of religion.

Where There Is Light: *Insight and Inspiration for Meeting Life's Challenges*

Gems of thought arranged by subject; a unique handbook to which readers can quickly turn for a reassuring sense of direction in times of uncertainty or crisis, or for a renewed awareness of the ever present power of God one can draw upon in daily life.

Whispers from Eternity

A collection of Paramahansa Yogananda's prayers and divine experiences in the elevated states of meditation. Expressed in a majestic rhythm and poetic beauty, his words reveal the inexhaustible variety of God's nature, and the infinite sweetness with which He responds to those who seek Him.

The Science of Religion

Within every human being, Paramahansa Yogananda writes, there is one inescapable desire: to overcome suffering and attain a happiness that does not end. Explaining how it is possible to fulfill these longings, he examines the relative effectiveness of the different approaches to this goal.

The Yoga of the Bhagavad Gita: *An Introduction to India's Universal Science of God-Realization*

A compilation of selections from Paramahansa Yogananda's in-depth, critically acclaimed translation of and commentary on the Bhagavad Gita, *God Talks With Arjuna,* this book presents truth-seekers with an ideal introduction to the Gita's timeless and universal teachings. Contains Yogananda's complete translation of the Bhagavad Gita, presented for the first time in uninterrupted sequential form.

The Yoga of Jesus: *Understanding the Hidden Teachings of the Gospels*

A selection of material from Paramahansa Yogananda's highly praised two-volume work, *The Second Coming of Christ,* this concise book confirms that Jesus, like the ancient sages and masters of the East, not only knew the principles of yoga but taught this universal science of God-realization to his disciples. Sri Yogananda shows that Jesus' message is not about sectarian divisiveness, but a unifying path by which seekers of all faith traditions can enter the kingdom of God.

In the Sanctuary of the Soul: *A Guide to Effective Prayer*

Compiled from the works of Paramahansa Yogananda, this inspiring devotional companion reveals ways of making prayer a daily source of love, strength, and guidance.

Inner Peace: *How to Be Calmly Active and Actively Calm*

A practical and inspiring guide, compiled from the talks and writings of Paramahansa Yogananda, that demonstrates how we can be "actively calm" by creating peace through meditation, and "calmly active"—centered in the stillness and joy of our own essential nature while living a dynamic, fulfilling, and balanced life. Winner of the 2000 Benjamin Franklin Award—best book in the field of Metaphysics/Spirituality.

How You Can Talk With God

Defining God as both the transcendent, universal Spirit and the intimately personal Father, Mother, Friend, and Lover of all, Paramahansa Yogananda shows how close the Lord is to each one of us, and how He can be persuaded to "break His silence" and respond in a tangible way.

Metaphysical Meditations

More than 300 spiritually uplifting meditations, prayers, and affirmations that can be used to develop greater health and vitality, creativity, self-confidence, and calmness; and to live more fully in a conscious awareness of the blissful presence of God.

Scientific Healing Affirmations

Paramahansa Yogananda presents here a profound explanation of the science of affirmation. He makes clear why affirmations work, and how to use the power of word and thought not only to bring about healing but to effect desired change in every area of life. Includes a wide variety of affirmations.

Sayings of Paramahansa Yogananda

A collection of sayings and wise counsel that conveys Paramahansa Yogananda's candid and loving responses to those who came to him for guidance. Recorded by a number of his close disciples, the anecdotes in this book give the reader an opportunity to share in their personal encounters with the Master.

Songs of the Soul

Mystical poetry by Paramahansa Yogananda—an outpouring of his direct perceptions of God in the beauties of nature, in man, in everyday experiences, and in the spiritually awakened state of *samadhi* meditation.

The Law of Success

Explains dynamic principles for achieving one's goals in life, and outlines the universal laws that bring success and fulfillment—personal, professional, and spiritual.

Cosmic Chants: *Spiritualized Songs for Divine Communion*

Words and music to 60 songs of devotion, with an introduction explaining how spiritual chanting can lead to God-communion.

DVD Video

Awake: The Life of Yogananda

A film by CounterPoint Films

AUDIO RECORDINGS OF PARAMAHANSA YOGANANDA

- ***Beholding the One in All***
- ***Awake in the Cosmic Dream***
- ***Be a Smile Millionaire***
- ***The Great Light of God***
- ***To Make Heaven on Earth***
- ***One Life Versus Reincarnation***
- ***Removing All Sorrow and Suffering***
- ***In the Glory of the Spirit***
- ***Follow the Path of Christ, Krishna, and the Masters***
- ***Self-Realization: The Inner and the Outer Path***
- ***Songs of My Heart***

OTHER PUBLICATIONS FROM SELF-REALIZATION FELLOWSHIP

The Holy Science *by Swami Sri Yukteswar*

Only Love: Living the Spiritual Life in a Changing World *by Sri Daya Mata*

Finding the Joy Within You: Personal Counsel for God-Centered Living *by Sri Daya Mata*

Enter the Quiet Heart: Creating a Loving Relationship With God *by Sri Daya Mata*

God Alone: The Life and Letters of a Saint *by Sri Gyanamata*

"Mejda": The Family and the Early Life of Paramahansa Yogananda *by Sananda Lal Ghosh*

Self-Realization *(a magazine founded by Paramahansa Yogananda in 1925)*

Please visit srfbooks.org for a complete catalog describing all of the Self-Realization Fellowship publications and audio/video recordings.

SRF/YSS APP

A free resource for online meditations in multiple languages; guided meditations of different lengths; inspirational talks, video clips, and posts; the latest news from SRF; and for students of the *SRF Lessons,* digital versions of the *Lessons* and additional content—all to aid your spiritual journey.

Available on the App Store and Google Play.

GLOSSARY

affirmation. "An affirmation is the statement of a truth that you wish to realize and manifest in your life," Paramahansa Yogananda said. "Words are vibrations of thought. Thoughts, in turn, are vibrations of power and energy. Thought is the force that powers the complex cellular mechanism of the body, as well as the machinery of human destiny and the entire cosmos. Thoughts are responsible for all the chemical, nervous, and metabolic functions and psychological reactions of the body, just as the thoughts of the general citizenry, and of the political leaders especially, direct the activities of the national machinery.

"As the perfect thoughts of God have created the cosmos and keep it in balance and rhythm, so the right thoughts of His children, when expressed in rightly uttered words, or affirmations, set up corresponding rhythmic, etheric vibrations in the cosmos and in the individual who utters them. These creative vibrations, in turn, harmonize all circumstances and activate the forces necessary to bring into manifestation the desired result."

See *Scientific Healing Affirmations* by Paramahansa Yogananda as well as SRF Lesson 5 for more information about affirmations.

Arjuna. The exalted disciple to whom Bhagavan Krishna imparted the immortal message of the Bhagavad Gita *(q.v.)*; one of the five Pandava princes in the great Hindu epic, the *Mahabharata,* in which he was a key figure.

ashram. A spiritual hermitage; often a monastery.

astral body. Man's subtle body of light, *prana* or lifetrons; the second of three sheaths that successively encase the soul: the causal body *(q.v.),* the astral body, and the physical body. The powers of the astral body enliven the physical body, much as electricity illumines a bulb. The astral body has nineteen elements: intelligence, ego, feeling, mind (sense-consciousness); five instruments of knowledge (the sensory powers within the physical organs of sight, hearing, smell, taste, and touch); five instruments of action (the executive powers in the physical instruments of procreation, excretion, speech, locomotion, and the exercise of manual skill); and five instruments of life force that perform the functions of circulation, metabolization, assimilation, crystallization, and elimination.

astral light. The subtle light emanating from lifetrons (see *prana*); the structural essence of the astral world. Through the all-inclusive intuitive perception of the soul, devotees in concentrated states of meditation may perceive the astral light, particularly as the spiritual eye *(q.v.)*.

astral world. The subtle sphere of the Lord's creation, a universe of light and color composed of finer-than-atomic forces, i.e., vibrations of life energy or lifetrons (see *prana*). Every being, every object, every vibration on the material plane has an astral counterpart, for in the astral universe (heaven) is the blueprint of our material universe. At physical death, the soul of man, clothed in an astral body of light, ascends to one of the higher or lower astral planes, according to merit, to continue his spiritual evolution in the greater freedom of that subtle realm. There he remains for a karmically predetermined time until physical rebirth.

Aum (Om). The Sanskrit root word or seed-sound symbolizing that aspect of Godhead which creates and sustains all things; Cosmic Vibration. *Aum* of the Vedas became the sacred word *Hum* of the Tibetans; *Amin* of the Moslems; and *Amen* of the Egyptians, Greeks, Romans, Jews, and Christians. The world's great religions state that all created things originate in the cosmic vibratory energy of *Aum* or Amen, the Word or Holy Ghost. "In the beginning was the Word, and the Word was with God, and the Word was God....All things were made by him [the Word or *Aum*]; and without him was not any thing made that was made" (John 1:1,3).

Amen in Hebrew means *sure, faithful.* "These things saith the Amen, the faithful and true witness, the beginning of the creation of God" (Revelation 3:14). Even as sound is produced by the vibration of a running motor, so the omnipresent sound of *Aum* faithfully testifies to the running of the "Cosmic Motor," which upholds all life and every particle of creation through vibratory energy. In the *Self-Realization Fellowship Lessons (q.v.)*, Paramahansa Yogananda teaches techniques of meditation whose practice brings direct experience of God as *Aum* or Holy Ghost. That blissful communion with the invisible divine Power ("the Comforter, which is the Holy Ghost"—John 14:26) is the truly scientific basis of prayer.

avatar. Divine incarnation; from the Sanskrit *avatara,* with roots *ava,* "down," and *tri,* "to pass." One who attains union with Spirit and then returns to earth to help mankind is called an avatar.

avidya. Literally, "non-knowledge," ignorance; the manifestation in man of *maya,* the cosmic delusion *(q.v.)*. Essentially, *avidya* is man's ignorance of his divine nature and of the sole reality: Spirit.

Babaji. See *Mahavatar Babaji.*

Bhagavad Gita. "Song of the Lord." An ancient Indian scripture consisting of eighteen chapters from the sixth book *(Bhishma Parva)* of the *Mahabharata* epic. Presented in the form of a dialogue between the avatar *(q.v.)* Lord Krishna and his disciple Arjuna on the eve of the historic battle of Kurukshetra, the Gita is a profound treatise on the science of Yoga (union with God) and a timeless prescription for happiness and success in every-day living. The Gita is allegory as well as history, a spiritual dissertation on the inner battle between man's good and bad tendencies. Depending on the context, Krishna symbolizes the guru, the soul, or God; Arjuna represents the aspiring devotee. Of this universal scripture Mahatma Gandhi wrote: "Those who will meditate on the Gita will derive fresh joy and new meanings from it every day. There is not a single spiritual tangle which the Gita cannot unravel."

Unless otherwise indicated, the quotations from the Bhagavad Gita in this volume are from Paramahansa Yogananda's own translations, which he rendered from the Sanskrit sometimes literally and sometimes in paraphrase, depending on the context of his talk. Paramahansaji's comprehensive translation and commentary is entitled *God Talks With Arjuna: The Bhagavad Gita—Royal Science of God-Realization* (published by Self-Realization Fellowship).

Bhagavan Krishna. An avatar *(q.v.)* who lived in ancient India ages before the Christian era. One of the meanings given for the word *Krishna* in the Hindu scriptures is "Omniscient Spirit." Thus, *Krishna,* like *Christ,* is a spiritual title signifying the divine magnitude of the avatar—his oneness with God. The title *Bhagavan* means "Lord." At the time he gave the discourse recorded in the Bhagavad Gita, Lord Krishna was ruler of a kingdom in northern India. In his early life, Krishna lived as a cowherd who enchanted his companions with the music of his flute. In this role Krishna is often considered to represent allegorically the soul playing the flute of meditation to guide all misled thoughts back to the fold of omniscience.

Bhakti Yoga. The spiritual approach to God that stresses all-surrendering love as the principal means for communion and union with God. See *Yoga.*

Brahma-Vishnu-Shiva. Three aspects of God's immanence in creation. They represent that triune function of the Christ Intelligence *(Tat)* that guides Cosmic Nature's activities of creation, preservation, and dissolution. See *Trinity.*

Brahman (Brahma). Absolute Spirit.

breath. "The influx of innumerable cosmic currents into man by way of the breath induces restlessness in his mind," Paramahansa Yogananda wrote. "Thus the breath links him with the fleeting phenomenal worlds. To escape from the sorrows of transitoriness and to enter the blissful realm of Reality, the yogi learns to quiet the breath by scientific meditation."

caste. Caste in its original conception was not a hereditary status, but a classification based on man's natural capacities. In his evolution, man passes through four distinct grades, designated by ancient Hindu sages as *Sudra, Vaisya, Kshatriya,* and *Brahmin.* The *Sudra* is interested primarily in satisfying his bodily needs and desires; the work that best suits his state of development is bodily labor. The *Vaisya* is ambitious for worldly gain as well as for satisfaction of the senses; he has more creative ability than the *Sudra* and seeks occupation as a farmer, a businessman, an artist, or wherever his mental energy finds fulfillment. The *Kshatriya,* having through many lives fulfilled the desires of the *Sudra* and *Vaisya* states, begins to seek the meaning of life; he tries to overcome his bad habits, to control his senses, and to do what is right. *Kshatriyas* by occupation are noble rulers, statesmen, warriors. The *Brahmin* has overcome his lower nature, has a natural affinity for spiritual pursuits, and is God-knowing, able therefore to teach and help liberate others.

causal body. Essentially, man as a soul is a causal-bodied being. His causal body is an idea-matrix for the astral and physical bodies. The causal body is composed of 35 idea elements corresponding to the 19 elements of the astral body plus the 16 basic material elements of the physical body.

causal world. Behind the physical world of matter (atoms, protons, electrons), and the subtle astral world of luminous life energy (lifetrons), is the causal, or ideational, world of thought (thoughtrons). After man evolves sufficiently to transcend the physical and astral universes, he resides in the causal universe. In the consciousness of causal beings, the physical and astral universes are resolved to their thought essence. Whatever physical man can do in imagination, causal man can do in actuality—the only limitation being thought itself. Ultimately, man sheds the last soul covering—his causal body—to unite with omnipresent Spirit, beyond all vibratory realms.

chakras. In Yoga, the seven occult centers of life and consciousness in the spine and brain, which enliven the physical and astral bodies of man. These centers are referred to as *chakras* ("wheels") because the concentrated energy in each one is like a hub from which radiate rays of life-giving light and energy. In ascending order, these *chakras* are *muladhara* (the coccygeal, at the base of the spine); *svadhisthana* (the sacral, two inches above *muladhara*); *manipura* (the lumbar, opposite the navel); *anahata* (the dorsal, opposite the heart); *vishuddha* (the cervical, at the base of the neck); *ajna* (traditionally located between the eyebrows; in actuality, directly connected by polarity with the medulla; see also *medulla* and *spiritual eye*); and *sahasrara* (in the uppermost part of the cerebrum).

The seven centers are divinely planned exits or "trap doors" through which the soul has descended into the body and through which it must reascend by a process of meditation. By seven successive steps, the soul escapes into Cosmic Consciousness. In its conscious upward passage through the seven opened or "awakened" cerebrospinal centers, the soul travels the highway to the Infinite, the true path by which the soul must retrace its course to reunite with God.

Yoga treatises generally consider only the six lower centers as *chakras,* with *sahasrara* referred to separately as a seventh center. All seven centers, however, are often referred to as lotuses, whose petals open, or turn upward, in spiritual awakening as the life and consciousness travel up the spine.

chela. Hindi word for "disciple."

chitta. Intuitive feeling; the aggregate of consciousness, inherent in which is *ahamkara* (egoity), *buddhi* (intelligence), and *manas* (mind or sense consciousness).

Christ center. The *Kutastha* or *ajna chakra* at the point between the eyebrows, directly connected by polarity with the medulla *(q.v.);* center of will and concentration, and of Christ Consciousness *(q.v.);* seat of the spiritual eye *(q.v.).*

Christ Consciousness. "Christ" or "Christ Consciousness" is the projected consciousness of God immanent in all creation. In Christian scripture it is called the "only begotten son," the only pure reflection in creation of God the Father; in Hindu scripture it is called *Kutastha Chaitanya* or *Tat,* the cosmic intelligence of Spirit everywhere present in creation. It is the universal consciousness, oneness with God, manifested by Jesus, Krishna, and other avatars. Great saints and yogis know it as the state of *samadhi (q.v.)* meditation wherein their consciousness has become identified with the intelligence in every particle of creation; they feel the entire universe as their own body. See *Trinity.*

Concentration Technique. The Self-Realization Fellowship Technique of Concentration (also Hong-Sau Technique) taught in the *Self-Realization Fellowship Lessons.* This technique helps scientifically to withdraw the attention from all objects of distraction and to place it upon one thing at a time. Thus it is invaluable for meditation, concentration on God. The Hong-Sau Technique is an integral part of the science of *Kriya Yoga (q.v.).*

consciousness, states of. In mortal consciousness man experiences three states: waking consciousness, sleeping consciousness, and dreaming consciousness. But he does not experience his soul, superconsciousness, and he does not experience God. The Christ-man does. As mortal man is conscious throughout his body, so the Christ-man is conscious throughout the universe, which he feels as his body. Beyond the state of Christ consciousness is cosmic consciousness, the experience of oneness with God in His absolute consciousness beyond vibratory creation as well as with the Lord's omnipresence manifesting in the phenomenal worlds.

Cosmic Consciousness. The Absolute; Spirit beyond creation. Also the *samadhi*-meditation state of oneness with God both beyond and within vibratory creation. See *Trinity.*

cosmic delusion. See *maya.*

cosmic energy. See *prana.*

Cosmic Intelligent Vibration. See *Aum.*

Cosmic Sound. See *Aum.*

dharma. Eternal principles of righteousness that uphold all creation; man's inherent duty to live in harmony with these principles. See also *Sanatana Dharma.*

diksha. Spiritual initiation; from the Sanskrit verb-root *diksh,* to dedicate oneself. See also *disciple* and *Kriya Yoga.*

disciple. A spiritual aspirant who comes to a guru seeking introduction to God, and to this end establishes an eternal spiritual relationship with the guru. In Self-Realization Fellowship, the guru-disciple relationship is established by *diksha,* initiation, in *Kriya Yoga.* See also *guru* and *Kriya Yoga.*

Divine Mother. The aspect of God that is active in creation; the *shakti,* or power, of the Transcendent Creator. Other terms for this aspect of Divinity are Nature or Prakriti, *Aum,* Holy Ghost, Cosmic Intelligent Vibration. Also, the personal aspect of God as Mother, embodying the Lord's love and compassionate qualities.

The Hindu scriptures teach that God is both immanent and transcendent, personal and impersonal. He may be sought as the Absolute; as one of His manifest eternal qualities, such as love, wisdom, bliss, light; in the form of an *ishta* (deity); or in a concept such as Heavenly Father, Mother, Friend.

egoism. The ego-principle, *ahamkara* (lit., "I do"), is the root cause of dualism or the seeming separation between man and his Creator. *Ahamkara* brings human beings under the sway of *maya (q.v.),* by which the subject (ego) falsely appears as object; the creatures imagine themselves to be creators. By banishing ego-consciousness, man awakens to his divine identity, his oneness with the Sole Life: God.

elements (five). The Cosmic Vibration, or *Aum,* structures all physical creation, including man's physical body, through the manifestation of five *tattvas* (elements): earth, water, fire, air, and ether *(q.v.).* These are structural forces, intelligent and vibratory in nature. Without the earth element there would be no state of solid matter; without the water element, no liquid state; without the air element, no gaseous state; without the fire element, no heat; without the ether element, no background on which to produce the cosmic motion picture show. In the body, *prana* (cosmic vibratory energy) enters the medulla and is then divided into the five elemental currents by the action of the five lower *chakras (q.v.),* or centers: the coccygeal (earth), sacral (water), lumbar (fire), dorsal (air), and cervical (ether). The Sanskrit terminology for these elements is *prithivi, ap, tej, prana,* and *akasha.*

Encinitas, California. Encinitas, a seaside city in southern California, is the site of a Self-Realization Fellowship Ashram Center, Retreat, and

Hermitage, founded by Paramahansa Yogananda in 1937. The spacious grounds and Hermitage building, which is situated on a bluff overlooking the Pacific Ocean, was a gift to Paramahansaji from Rajarsi Janakananda (q.v.).

Energization Exercises. Man is surrounded by cosmic energy, much as a fish is surrounded by water. The Energization Exercises, originated by Paramahansa Yogananda and taught in the *Self-Realization Fellowship Lessons (q.v.),* enable man to recharge his body with this cosmic energy, or universal *prana.*

ether. Sanskrit *akasha.* Though not considered a factor in present scientific theory on the nature of the material universe, ether has for millenniums been so referred to by India's sages. Paramahansa Yogananda spoke of ether as the background on which God projects the cosmic motion picture of creation. Space gives dimension to objects; ether separates the images. This "background," a creative force that coordinates all spatial vibrations, is a necessary factor when considering the subtler forces—thought and life energy *(prana)*—and the nature of space and the origin of material forces and matter. See *elements.*

evil. The satanic force that obscures God's omnipresence in creation, manifesting as inharmonies in man and nature. Also, a broad term defining anything contrary to divine law (see *dharma*) that causes man to lose the consciousness of his essential unity with God, and that obstructs attainment of God-realization.

gunas. The three attributes of Nature: *tamas, rajas,* and *sattva*—obstruction, activity, and expansion; or, mass, energy, and intelligence. In man the three *gunas* express themselves as ignorance or inertia; activity or struggle; and wisdom.

guru. Spiritual teacher. Though the word *guru* is often misused to refer simply to any teacher or instructor, a true God-illumined guru is one who, in his attainment of self-mastery, has realized his identity with the omnipresent Spirit. Such a one is uniquely qualified to lead the seeker on his or her inward journey toward divine realization.

When a devotee is ready to seek God in earnest, the Lord sends him a guru. Through the wisdom, intelligence, Self realization, and teachings of such a master, God guides the disciple. By following the master's teachings and discipline, the disciple is able to fulfill his soul's desire for the manna of God-perception. A true guru, ordained by God to help sincere seekers in response to their deep soul craving, is not an ordinary teacher: he is a human vehicle whose body, speech, mind, and spirituality God uses as a channel to attract and guide lost souls back to their home of immortality. A guru is a living embodiment of scriptural truth. He is an agent of salvation appointed by God in response to a devotee's demand for release from the bondage of matter.

"To keep company with the Guru," wrote Swami Sri Yukteswar in *The Holy Science,* "is not only to be in his physical presence (as this is sometimes impossible), but mainly means to keep him in our hearts and to be one with him in principle and to attune ourselves with him." See *master.*

Gurudeva. "Divine teacher," a customary Sanskrit term of respect that is used in addressing and referring to one's spiritual preceptor; sometimes rendered in English as "Master."

Gurus of Self-Realization Fellowship. The Gurus of Self-Realization Fellowship (Yogoda Satsanga Society of India) are Jesus Christ, Bhagavan Krishna, and a line of exalted masters of contemporary times: Mahavatar Babaji, Lahiri Mahasaya, Swami Sri Yukteswar, and Paramahansa Yogananda. To show the harmony and essential unity of the teachings of Jesus Christ and the Yoga precepts of Bhagavan Krishna is an integral part of the SRF dispensation. All of these Gurus, by their sublime teachings and divine instrumentality, contribute to the fulfillment of the Self-Realization Fellowship mission of bringing to all mankind a practical spiritual science of God-realization.

Hatha Yoga. A system of techniques and physical postures *(asanas)* that promotes health and mental calm. See *Yoga.*

Holy Ghost. See *Aum* and *Trinity.*

intuition. The all-knowing faculty of the soul, which enables man to experience direct perception of truth without the intermediary of the senses.

ji. A suffix denoting respect, added to names and titles in India; as, Gandhiji, Paramahansaji, Guruji.

Jnana Yoga. The path to union with God through transmutation of the discriminative power of the intellect into the omniscient wisdom of the soul.

karma. Effects of past actions, from this or previous lifetimes; from the Sanskrit *kri,* to do. The equilibrating law of karma, as expounded in the Hindu scriptures, is that of action and reaction, cause and effect, sowing and reaping. In the course of natural righteousness, every human being by his thoughts and actions becomes the molder of his own destiny. Whatever energies he himself, wisely or unwisely, has set in motion must return to him as their starting point, like a circle inexorably completing itself. An understanding of karma as the law of justice serves to free the human mind from resentment against God and man. A person's karma follows him from incarnation to incarnation until fulfilled or spiritually transcended. (See *reincarnation.*)

The cumulative actions of human beings within communities, nations, or the world as a whole constitute mass karma, which produces local or far-ranging effects according to the degree and preponderance of good or evil. The thoughts and actions of every human being, therefore, contribute to the good or ill of this world and all peoples in it.

Karma Yoga. The path to God through nonattached action and service. By selfless service, by giving the fruits of one's actions to God, and by seeing God as the sole Doer, the devotee becomes free of the ego and experiences God. See *Yoga.*

Krishna. See *Bhagavan Krishna.*

Krishna Consciousness. Christ Consciousness; *Kutastha Chaitanya.* See *Christ Consciousness.*

Kriya Yoga. A sacred spiritual science, originating millenniums ago in India. It includes certain techniques of meditation whose devoted practice leads to realization of God. Paramahansa Yogananda has explained that the Sanskrit root of *kriya* is *kri,* to do, to act and react; the same root is found in the word *karma,* the natural principle of cause and effect. *Kriya Yoga* is thus "union *(yoga)* with the Infinite through a certain action or rite *(kriya).*" *Kriya Yoga,* a form of *Raja* ("royal" or "complete") *Yoga,* is extolled by Krishna in the Bhagavad Gita and by Patanjali in the *Yoga Sutras.* Revived in this age by Mahavatar Babaji *(q.v.), Kriya Yoga* is the *diksha* (spiritual initiation) bestowed by the Gurus of Self-Realization Fellowship. Since the *mahasamadhi (q.v.)* of Paramahansa Yogananda, *diksha* is conferred through his appointed spiritual representative, the president of Self-Realization Fellowship/Yogoda Satsanga Society of India (or through one appointed by the president). To qualify for *diksha* Self-Realization members must fulfill certain preliminary spiritual requirements. One who has received this *diksha* is a *Kriya Yogi* or *Kriyaban.* See also *guru* and *disciple.*

Lahiri Mahasaya. *Lahiri* was the family name of Shyama Charan Lahiri (1828–1895). *Mahasaya,* a Sanskrit religious title, means "large-minded." Lahiri Mahasaya was a disciple of Mahavatar Babaji, and the guru of Swami Sri Yukteswar (Paramahansa Yogananda's guru). A Christlike teacher with miraculous powers, he was also a family man with business responsibilities. His mission was to make known a yoga suitable for modern man, in which meditation is balanced by right performance of worldly duties. He has been called a *Yogavatar,* "Incarnation of Yoga." Lahiri Mahasaya was the disciple to whom Babaji revealed the ancient, almost lost science of *Kriya Yoga (q.v.),* instructing him in turn to initiate sincere seekers. Lahiri Mahasaya's life is described in *Autobiography of a Yogi.*

Laya Yoga. This yogic system teaches the absorption of mind in the perception of certain astral sounds, leading to union with God as the cosmic sound of *Aum.* See *Aum* and *Yoga.*

Lessons. See *Self-Realization Fellowship Lessons.*

life force. See *prana.*

lifetrons. See *prana.*

Lynn, James J. (St. Lynn). See *Rajarsi Janakananda.*

mahasamadhi. Sanskrit *maha,* "great," *samadhi.* The last meditation, or conscious communion with God, during which a perfected master merges himself in the cosmic *Aum* and casts off the physical body. A master invariably knows beforehand the time God has appointed for him to leave his bodily residence. See *samadhi.*

Mahavatar Babaji. The deathless *mahavatar* ("great *avatar*") who in 1861 gave *Kriya Yoga (q.v.)* initiation to Lahiri Mahasaya, and thereby restored to the world the ancient technique of salvation. Perennially youthful, he has lived for centuries in the Himalayas, bestowing a constant blessing on the world. His mission has been to assist prophets in carrying out their special dispensations. Many titles signifying his exalted spiritual stature have been given to him, but the *mahavatar* has generally adopted the simple name of Babaji, from the Sanskrit *baba,* "father," and the suffix *ji,* denoting respect. More information about his life and spiritual mission is given in *Autobiography of a Yogi.* See *avatar.*

Mantra Yoga. Divine communion attained through devotional, concentrated repetition of root-word sounds that have a spiritually beneficial vibratory potency. See *Yoga.*

master. One who has achieved self-mastery. Paramahansa Yogananda has pointed out that "the distinguishing qualifications of a master are not physical but spiritual....Proof that one is a master is supplied only by the ability to enter at will the breathless state *(sabikalpa samadhi)* and by the attainment of immutable bliss *(nirbikalpa samadhi).*" See *samadhi.*

Paramahansaji further states: "All scriptures proclaim that the Lord created man in His omnipotent image. Control over the universe appears to be supernatural, but in truth such power is inherent and natural in everyone who attains 'right remembrance' of his divine origin. Men of God-realization...are devoid of the ego-principle *(ahamkara)* and its uprisings of personal desires; the actions of true masters are in effortless conformity with *rita,* natural righteousness. In Emerson's words, all great ones become 'not virtuous, but Virtue; then is the end of the creation answered, and God is well pleased.'"

maya. The delusory power inherent in the structure of creation, by which the One appears as many. *Maya* is the principle of relativity, inversion, contrast, duality, oppositional states; the "Satan" (lit., in Hebrew, "the adversary") of the Old Testament prophets; and the "devil" whom Christ described picturesquely as a "murderer" and a "liar," because "there is no truth in him" (John 8:44).

Paramahansa Yogananda wrote:

"The Sanskrit word *maya* means 'the measurer'; it is the magical power in creation by which limitations and divisions are apparently present in the Immeasurable and Inseparable. *Maya* is Nature herself—the phenomenal worlds, ever in transitional flux as antithesis to Divine Immutability.

"In God's plan and play *(lila),* the sole function of Satan or *maya* is to attempt to divert man from Spirit to matter, from Reality to unreality. 'The devil sinneth from the beginning. For this purpose the Son of God was manifested, that he might destroy the works of the devil' (I John 3:8). That is, the manifestation of Christ Consciousness, within man's own being, effortlessly destroys the illusions or 'works of the devil.'

"*Maya* is the veil of transitoriness in Nature, the ceaseless becoming of creation; the veil that each man must lift in order to see behind it the Creator, the changeless Immutable, eternal Reality."

meditation. Concentration upon God. The term is used in a general sense to denote practice of any technique for interiorizing the attention and focusing it on some aspect of God. In the specific sense, meditation refers to the end result of successful practice of such techniques: direct experience of God through intuitive perception. It is the seventh step *(dhyana)* of the eightfold path of Yoga described by Patanjali *(q.v.),* achieved only after one has attained that fixed concentration within whereby he is completely undisturbed by sensory impressions from the outer world. In deepest meditation one experiences the eighth step of the Yoga path: *samadhi (q.v.),* communion, oneness with God. (See also *Yoga.*)

medulla. The principal point of entry of life force *(prana)* into the body; seat of the sixth cerebrospinal center, whose function is to receive and direct the incoming flow of cosmic energy. The life force is stored in the seventh center *(sahasrara)* in the topmost part of the brain. From that reservoir it is distributed throughout the body. The subtle center at the medulla is the main switch that controls the entrance, storage, and distribution of the life force.

Mt. Washington. Site of, and, by extension, a frequently used name for the Mother Center and international headquarters of Self-Realization Fellowship in Los Angeles. The 12 ½-acre estate was acquired in 1925 by Paramahansa Yogananda. He made it a training center for the Self-Realization monastics, and the administrative center for disseminating worldwide the ancient science of *Kriya Yoga.*

paramahansa. A spiritual title signifying a master *(q.v.).* It may be conferred only by a true guru on a qualified disciple. *Paramahansa* literally means "supreme swan." In the Hindu scriptures, the *hansa* or swan symbolizes spiritual discrimination. Swami Sri Yukteswar bestowed the title on his beloved disciple Yogananda in 1935.

paramguru. Literally, "the preceding guru"; the guru of one's guru. To Self-Realizationists (disciples of Paramahansa Yogananda), *paramguru* refers to Sri Yukteswar. To Paramahansaji, it meant Lahiri Mahasaya. Mahavatar Babaji is Paramahansaji's *param-paramguru.*

Patanjali. Ancient exponent of Yoga, whose *Yoga Sutras* outline the principles of the yogic path, dividing it into eight steps: (1) *yama,* moral conduct; (2) *niyama,* religious observances; (3) *asana,* right posture to still bodily restlessness; (4) *pranayama,* control of *prana,* subtle life currents; (5) *pratyahara,* interiorization; (6) *dharana,* concentration; (7) *dhyana,* meditation; and (8) *samadhi,* superconscious experience. See *Yoga.*

prana. Sparks of intelligent finer-than-atomic energy that constitute life, collectively referred to in Hindu scriptural treatises as *prana,* which Paramahansa Yogananda has translated as "lifetrons." In essence, condensed thoughts of God; substance of the astral world *(q.v.)* and life principle of the physical cosmos. In the physical world, there are two kinds of *prana:* (1) the cosmic vibratory energy that is omnipresent in the universe, structuring and sustaining all things; (2) the specific *prana* or energy that pervades and sustains each human body through five currents or functions. *Prana* current performs the function of crystallization; *Vyana* current, circulation; *Samana* current, assimilation; *Udana* current, metabolism; and *Apana* current, elimination.

pranam. A form of greeting in India. The hands are pressed, palms together, with the base of the hands at the heart and the fingertips touching the forehead. This gesture is actually a modification of the *pranam,* literally "complete salutation," from the Sanskrit root *nam,* "to salute or bow down," and the prefix *pra,* "completely." A *pranam* salutation is the general mode of greeting in India. Before renunciants and other persons held in high spiritual regard, it may be accompanied by the spoken word, *"Pranam."*

pranayama. Conscious control of *prana* (the creative vibration or energy that activates and sustains life in the body). The yoga science of *pranayama* is the direct way to consciously disconnect the mind from the life functions and sensory perceptions that tie man to body-consciousness. *Pranayama* thus frees man's consciousness to commune with God. All scientific techniques that bring about union of soul and Spirit may be classified as yoga, and *pranayama* is the greatest yogic method for attaining this divine union.

Raja Yoga. The "royal" or highest path to God-union. It teaches scientific meditation *(q.v.)* as the ultimate means for realizing God, and includes the highest essentials from all other forms of Yoga. The Self-Realization Fellowship *Raja Yoga* teachings outline a way of life leading to perfect unfoldment in body, mind, and soul, based on the foundation of *Kriya Yoga (q.v.)* meditation. See *Yoga.*

Ranchi school. Yogoda Satsanga Vidyalaya, founded by Paramahansa Yogananda in 1918 when the Maharaja of Kasimbazar gave his summer palace and twenty-five acres of land in Ranchi, Jharkhand, for use as a boys' school. The property was permanently acquired while Paramahansaji was in India in 1935–36. More than two thousand children now attend Yogoda schools at Ranchi, from nursery school through college. See *Yogoda Satsanga Society of India.*

reincarnation. The doctrine that human beings, compelled by the law of evolution, incarnate repeatedly in progressively higher lives—retarded by wrong actions and desires, and advanced by spiritual endeavors—until Self-realization and God-union are attained. Having thus transcended the limitations and imperfections of mortal consciousness, the soul is forever freed from compulsory reincarnation. "Him that overcometh will I make a pillar in the temple of my God, and he shall go no more out" (Revelation 3:12).

The concept of reincarnation is not exclusive to Eastern philosophy, but was held as a fundamental truth of life by many ancient civilizations. The early Christian Church accepted the principle of reincarnation, which was expounded by the Gnostics and by numerous Church fathers, including Clement of Alexandria, Origen, and St. Jerome. It was not until the Second Council of Constantinople in A.D. 553 that the doctrine was officially removed from church teachings. Today many Western thinkers are beginning to adopt the concept of the law of *karma (q.v.)* and reincarnation, seeing in it a grand and reassuring explanation of life's seeming inequities.

rishis. Seers, exalted beings who manifest divine wisdom; especially, the illumined sages of ancient India to whom the Vedas were intuitively revealed.

sadhana. Path of spiritual discipline. The specific instruction and meditation practices prescribed by the guru for his disciples, who by faithfully following them ultimately realize God.

samadhi. The highest step on the Eightfold Path of Yoga, as outlined by the sage Patanjali *(q.v.). Samadhi* is attained when the meditator, the process of meditation (by which the mind is withdrawn from the senses by interiorization), and the object of meditation (God) become One. Paramahansa Yogananda has explained that "in the initial states of God-communion *(sabikalpa samadhi)* the devotee's consciousness merges in the Cosmic Spirit; his life force is withdrawn from the body, which appears 'dead,' or motionless and rigid. The yogi is fully aware of his bodily condition of suspended animation. As he progresses to higher spiritual states *(nirbikalpa samadhi),* however, he communes with God without bodily fixation; and in his ordinary waking consciousness, even in the midst of exacting worldly duties." Both states are characterized by oneness with the ever new bliss of Spirit, but the *nirbikalpa* state is experienced by only the most highly advanced masters.

Sanatan Dharma. Literally, "eternal religion." The name given to the body of Vedic teachings that came to be called Hinduism after the Greeks designated the people on the banks of the river Indus as *Indoos,* or *Hindus.* See *dharma.*

Satan. Literally, in Hebrew, "the adversary." Satan is the conscious and independent universal force that keeps everything and everybody deluded with the unspiritual consciousness of finiteness and separateness from God. To accomplish this, Satan uses the weapons of *maya* (cosmic delusion) and *avidya* (individual delusion, ignorance). See *maya.*

Sat-Tat-Aum. *Sat,* Truth, the Absolute, Bliss; *Tat,* universal intelligence or consciousness; *Aum,* cosmic intelligent creative vibration, word-symbol for God. See *Aum* and *Trinity.*

Self. Capitalized to denote the *atman* or soul, the divine essence of man, as distinguished from the ordinary self, which is the human personality or ego. The Self is individualized Spirit, whose essential nature is ever-existing, ever-conscious, ever-new Bliss. The Self or soul is man's inner fountainhead of love, wisdom, peace, courage, compassion, and all other divine qualities.

Self-realization. Paramahansa Yogananda has defined Self-realization as follows: "Self-realization is the knowing—in body, mind, and soul—that we are one with the omnipresence of God; that we do not have to pray that it come to us, that we are not merely near it at all times, but that God's omnipresence is our omnipresence; that we are just as much a part of Him now as we ever will be. All we have to do is improve our knowing."

Self-Realization. An abbreviated way of referring to Self-Realization Fellowship, the society founded by Paramahansa Yogananda, often used by him in informal talks; e.g. "the Self-Realization teachings"; "the path of Self-Realization"; "Self-Realization headquarters in Los Angeles"; etc.

Self-Realization Fellowship. The society founded by Paramahansa Yogananda in the United States in 1920 (and as Yogoda Satsanga Society of India in 1917) for disseminating worldwide, for the aid and benefit of humanity, the spiritual principles and meditation techniques of *Kriya Yoga (q.v.).* The international headquarters, the Mother Center, is in Los Angeles, California. Paramahansa Yogananda has explained that the name Self-Realization Fellowship signifies: "Fellowship with God through Self-realization, and friendship with all truth-seeking souls." See also "Aims and Ideals of Self-Realization Fellowship," page 376.

Self-Realization Fellowship Lessons. The teachings of Paramahansa Yogananda, compiled into a comprehensive series of lessons for home study and made available to sincere truth-seekers all over the world. These lessons contain the yoga meditation techniques taught by Paramahansa Yogananda, including, for those who fulfill certain requirements, *Kriya Yoga (q.v.).* Information about the *Lessons* is available on request from Self-Realization Fellowship International Headquarters and at www.srflessons.org. See page 377. References to specific Lessons are included in this book for those readers who are also *Lessons* students.

Self-Realization magazine. A journal published by Self-Realization Fellowship, featuring the talks and writings of Paramahansa Yogananda; and containing other spiritual, practical, and informative articles of current interest and lasting value.

Shankara, Swami. Sometimes referred to as Adi ("the first") Shankaracharya (Shankara + *acharya,* "teacher"); India's most illustrious philosopher. His date is uncertain; many scholars assign him to the eighth or early ninth century. He expounded God not as a negative abstraction, but as positive, eternal, omnipresent, ever new Bliss. Shankara reorganized the ancient Swami Order, and founded four great *maths* (monastic centers of spiritual education), whose leaders in apostolic succession bear the title of Jagadguru Sri Shankaracharya. The meaning of *Jagadguru* is "world teacher."

siddha. Literally, "one who is successful." One who has attained Self-realization.

soul. Individualized Spirit. The soul or Self *(atman)* is the true and immortal nature of man, and of all living forms of life; it is cloaked only temporarily in the garments of causal, astral, and physical bodies. The nature of the soul is Spirit: ever-existing, ever-conscious, ever-new Bliss.

spiritual eye. The single eye of intuition and omnipresent perception at the Christ *(Kutastha)* center *(ajna chakra)* between the eyebrows. The deeply meditating devotee beholds the spiritual eye as a ring of golden light encircling a sphere of opalescent blue, and at the center, a pentagonal white star. Microcosmically, these forms and colors epitomize, respectively, the vibratory realm of creation (Cosmic Nature, Holy Ghost); the Son or intelligence of God in creation (Christ Consciousness); and the vibrationless Spirit beyond all creation (God the Father).

The spiritual eye is the entryway into the ultimate states of divine consciousness. In deep meditation, as the devotee's consciousness penetrates the spiritual eye, into the three realms epitomized therein, he experiences successively the following states: superconsciousness or the ever new joy of soul-realization, and oneness with God as *Aum (q.v.)* or Holy Ghost; Christ consciousness, oneness with the universal intelligence of God in all creation; and cosmic consciousness, unity with the omnipresence of God that is beyond as well as within vibratory manifestation. See also *consciousness, states of; superconsciousness; Christ Consciousness.*

Explaining a passage from Ezekiel (43:1–2), Paramahansa Yogananda has written: "Through the divine eye in the forehead, ('the east'), the yogi sails his consciousness into omnipresence, hearing the word or *Aum,* the divine sound of 'many waters': the vibrations of light that constitute the sole reality of creation." In Ezekiel's words: "Afterwards he brought me to the gate, even the gate that looketh towards the east; and behold, the glory of the God of Israel came from the way of the east; and His voice was like the noise of many waters; and the earth shined with His glory."

Jesus also spoke of the spiritual eye: "When thine eye is single, thy whole body also is full of light....Take heed therefore that the light which is in thee be not darkness" (Luke 11:34–35).

Sri. A title of respect. When used before the name of a religious person, it means "holy" or "revered."

Sri Yukteswar, Swami. Swami Sri Yukteswar Giri (1855–1936), India's *Jnanavatar,* "Incarnation of Wisdom"; guru of Paramahansa Yogananda, and *paramguru* of Self-Realization Fellowship *Kriyaban* members. Sri Yukteswarji was a disciple of Lahiri Mahasaya. At the behest of Lahiri Mahasaya's guru, Mahavatar Babaji, he wrote *The Holy Science,* a treatise on the underlying unity of Christian and Hindu scriptures, and trained Paramahansa Yogananda for his spiritual world-mission: the dissemination of *Kriya Yoga (q.v.).* Paramahansaji has lovingly described Sri Yukteswarji's life in *Autobiography of a Yogi.*

superconscious mind. The all-knowing power of the soul that perceives truth directly; intuition.

superconsciousness. The pure, intuitive, all-seeing, ever-blissful consciousness of the soul. Sometimes used generally to refer to all the various states of *samadhi (q.v.)* experienced in meditation, but specifically the first state of *samadhi,* wherein one transcends ego-consciousness and realizes his self as soul, made in the image of God. Thence follow the higher states of realization: Christ consciousness and cosmic consciousness *(q.v.).*

swami. A member of India's most ancient monastic order, reorganized in the eighth or early ninth century by Swami Shankara *(q.v.).* A swami takes formal vows of celibacy and renunciation of worldly ties and ambitions; he devotes himself to meditation and other spiritual practices, and to service to humanity. There are ten classificatory titles of the venerable Swami Order, as *Giri, Puri, Bharati, Tirtha, Saraswati,* and others. Swami Sri Yukteswar *(q.v.)* and Paramahansa Yogananda belonged to the *Giri* ("mountain") branch.

The Sanskrit word *swami* means "he who is one with the Self *(Swa).*"

Trinity. When Spirit manifests creation, It becomes the Trinity: Father, Son, Holy Ghost, or *Sat, Tat, Aum.* The Father *(Sat)* is God as the Creator existing beyond creation. The Son *(Tat)* is God's omnipresent intelligence existing in creation. The Holy Ghost *(Aum)* is the vibratory power of God that objectifies or becomes creation.

Many cycles of cosmic creation and dissolution have come and gone in Eternity (see *yuga*). At the time of cosmic dissolution, the Trinity and all other relativities of creation resolve into the Absolute Spirit.

Vedanta. Literally, "end of the Vedas"; the philosophy stemming from the *Upanishads,* or latter portion of the Vedas. Shankara (eighth or early ninth century) was the chief exponent of Vedanta, which declares that God is the only reality and that creation is essentially an illusion. As man is the only creature capable of conceiving of God, man himself must be divine, and his duty therefore is to realize his true nature.

Vedas. The four scriptural texts of the Hindus: Rig Veda, Sama Veda, Yajur Veda, and Atharva Veda. They are essentially a literature of chant, ritual, and recitation for vitalizing and spiritualizing all phases of man's life and activity. Among the immense texts of India, the Vedas (Sanskrit root *vid,* "to know") are the only writings to which no author is ascribed. The Rig Veda assigns a celestial origin to the hymns and tells us they have come down from "ancient times," reclothed in new language. Divinely revealed from age to age to the *rishis,* "seers," the four Vedas are said to possess *nityatva,* "timeless finality."

Yoga. From Sanskrit *yuj,* "union." Yoga means union of the individual soul with Spirit; also, the methods by which this goal is attained. Within the larger spectrum of Hindu philosophy, Yoga is one of six orthodox systems: *Vedanta, Mimamsa, Sankhya, Vaisesika, Nyaya,* and *Yoga.* There are also various types of yoga methods: *Hatha Yoga, Mantra Yoga, Laya Yoga, Karma Yoga, Jnana Yoga, Bhakti Yoga,* and *Raja Yoga. Raja Yoga,* the "royal" or complete yoga, is that which is taught by Self-Realization Fellowship, and which Bhagavan Krishna extols to his disciple Arjuna in the Bhagavad Gita: "The yogi is deemed greater than body-disciplining ascetics, greater even than the followers of the path of wisdom or of the path of action; be thou, O Arjuna, a yogi!" (Bhagavad Gita VI:46). The sage Patanjali, foremost exponent of Yoga, has outlined eight definite steps by which the *Raja Yogi* attains *samadhi,* or union with God. These are (1) *yama,* moral conduct; (2) *niyama,* religious observances; (3) *asana,* right posture to still bodily restlessness; (4) *pranayama,* control of *prana,* subtle life currents; (5) *pratyahara,* interiorization; (6) *dharana,* concentration, (7) *dhyana,* meditation; and (8) *samadhi,* superconscious experience.

yogi. One who practices yoga *(q.v.).* Anyone who practices a scientific technique for divine realization is a yogi. He may be either married or unmarried, either a man of worldly responsibilities or one of formal religious ties.

Yogoda Satsanga Society of India. The name by which Paramahansa Yogananda's society is known in India. The Society was founded by him in 1917. Its headquarters, Yogoda Satsanga Math, is situated on the banks of the Ganges at Dakshineswar, near Kolkata, with a branch *math* at Ranchi, Bihar. In addition to meditation centers and groups throughout India, Yogoda Satsanga Society has eighteen educational institutions, from primary through college level. *Yogoda,* a word coined by Paramahansa

Yogananda, is derived from *yoga,* "union, harmony, equilibrium"; and *da,* "that which imparts." *Satsanga* means "divine fellowship," or "fellowship with Truth." For the West, Paramahansaji translated the Indian name as "Self-Realization Fellowship" *(q.v.).*

yuga. A cycle or subperiod of creation, outlined in ancient Hindu texts. Sri Yukteswar *(q.v.)* describes in *The Holy Science* a 24,000-year Equinoctial Cycle and mankind's present place in it. This cycle occurs within the much longer universal cycle of the ancient texts, as calculated by the ancient *rishis* and noted in *Autobiography of a Yogi,* chapter 16: "The universal cycle of the scriptures is 4,300,560,000 years in extent, and measures out a 'Day of Creation.' This vast figure is based on the relationship between the length of the solar year and a multiple of pi (3.1416, the ratio of the circumference to the diameter of a circle).

"The life-span for a whole universe, according to the ancient seers, is 314,159,000,000,000 solar years, or 'One Age of Brahma.'"